GALLIPOLI

Tim Travers is Professor of History at the University of Calgary in Canada. His great uncle was killed in action at Gallipoli and the author has dedicated the last five years to finding out what really went wrong for the Allies in 1915. His other books include the widely praised *The Killing Ground* ('The most effective critic yet of Haig and his generals' *History*). He has also contributed to *The Oxford Illustrated History of the First World War* and *The Oxford History of the British Army*. He lives in Canada.

GALLIPOLI 1915

TIM TRAVERS

TEMPUS

Cover illustration: Turkish soldiers firing from Halil Bey Hill toward Gelik Lake, courtesy of the General Staff Archives, Ankara.

First published 2001
This edition first published 2004

Tempus Publishing Limited
The Mill, Brimscombe Port,
Stroud, Gloucestershire, GL5 2QG
www.tempus-publishing.com

British Library Cataloguing in Publication Data.
A catalogue record for this book is available from the British Library.

ISBN 0 7524 2972 8

Typesetting and origination by Tempus Publishing Limited
Printed in Great Britain by Midway Colour Print, Wiltshire.

CONTENTS

PROLOGUE

A Family's Sacrifice

Late in the afternoon, we finally found his grave. It was located in the Hill 10 cemetery at Gallipoli. Maj. Hugh Price Travers, the author's great uncle, was reported missing on 9 August 1915 at Suvla, and we had been searching for his grave for the better part of a day among all the beautifully kept cemeteries of Gallipoli. But how had he died? The war diary of his unit, the 8th Battalion, Duke of Wellington's (West Riding) Regiment, provided the only information. The battalion suffered 'heavy losses' on 9 August 1915 at Suvla, and a much stained war diary, written by Capt. V. Kidd, who by the time of writing on 17 August commanded the battalion in the absence of any more senior officers, offered the scanty details. At dusk on 8 August, the battalion moved up on the left of the West Yorkshire Regiment. At 4.00 a.m. on 9 August the Regiment advanced to attack the hills of Tekke Tepe, following along behind the East Yorkshire Pioneers. This was an attack that had been ordered late on 8 August by Sir Ian Hamilton, Commander-in-Chief, Mediterranean Expeditionary Force, who was desperate to attain the Tekke Tepe heights before the Turks arrived. At about 800 yards from the objective, the leading line of the East Yorkshire Pioneers appeared to retire, and 'so the order was given at once to advance to a small donga [a steep gully] and hold on there.' Then the operation began to go badly awry:

> By this time a lot of men from the leading Regt had rushed past saying that the Turks were advancing in force. The fire now became very hot and heavy casualties were rapidly being sustained. Lt-Col. Johnston had already been wounded before we advanced and at this moment Maj. Travers was seen to fall, the command then devolved upon me. The Turks were now beginning to turn my flanks and as I had only about 350 men

left and practically no officers and ammunition was running short, I decided to withdraw to a more suitable position.[1]

Hugh Price Travers was not seen again. And because the battalion withdrew, there was no chance then of recovering the body, or indeed of bringing him in if wounded, so he was reported missing. But his body must have been recovered later, for only then would a grave site have been assigned. All other missing or dead, whose bodies were never recovered, are now simply remembered by inscriptions on the monument at the Helles Memorial. This attack on the Tekke Tepe hills failed, and perhaps Hugh Price Travers never knew the importance and urgency of the attack. It is probable that he did know something of the operations of the 7th Battalion, Royal Munster Fusiliers, who also landed at Suvla and were attempting to fight their way along the Kiretch Tepe ridge on the left flank of Suvla Bay. This was because two of his cousins, brothers Lt Spenser Robert Valentine Travers and 2nd-Lt Arthur Stewart Travers, were serving with this Regiment.

On the same day as the attack on Tekke Tepe hills by the 8th Battalion, Duke of Wellington's Regiment, and the presumed death of Hugh Price Travers, the 7th Battalion, Royal Munster Fusiliers, also launched an attack at 9.30 a.m. toward Kidney Hill on the Kiretch Tepe ridge. The war diary of the Royal Munsters states that they and the Dorset Regiment got tangled up as they advanced, and the Munsters had to bear away sharply to the left. But as the Munsters advanced, they were covered by the fire of their machine-guns under the direction of Lt Spenser Travers. At about 12.30 p.m., the Munsters' advance was held up by Turkish fire and by the fact that the Dorset Regiment on their right 'did not advance.' This meant the right flank of the Munsters was well ahead of the Dorsets and thus exposed to heavy cross fire. But on the left flank, Maj. G. Drage of the Munsters and some of A Company managed to get within 500 yards of Kidney Hill, although they could not advance further. Despite an order at 1.30 p.m. to continue the attack, the war diary states: 'Owing to lack of cohesion both in the battalion and with other units, and to the general ignorance of the situation of the enemy and of what was required this was impossible to carry out.' Some time during Maj. Drage's advance, probably around midday, Lt Spenser Travers was hit and killed. According to Maj. Drage, two officers (one of whom must have been Travers), were shot 'either by snipers or men in shallow trenches'. The war diary also offers a short eulogy:

> Lieut. Travers was killed while directing M.G. covering fire. Brig-Gen. Nicol [30 Brigade commander] was present & said that he was particularly struck with the gallant conduct of Lieut. Travers.[2]

According to a War Office letter in early 1916, Lt S.R.V. Travers' body was recovered, and 'he was buried on 'A' Beach West. The grave is marked with a wooden cross.' Despite this information, he does not seem to have a grave site in a Gallipoli cemetery, but he is listed on the Helles Memorial. Private information also recounts that his brother, Arthur Stewart Travers, saw him killed, and while Arthur Travers survived the war, he died young and never recovered from the impact of this experience; in fact he was apparently 'sent' to hospital on 18 August 1915.[3] Lts Spenser and Arthur Travers no doubt recognized the potential significance of their advance along Kiretch Tepe ridge, but almost certainly did not realize that if this advance had been successful, then the Turkish forces could have been outflanked – in fact this would have been a more useful attack than the straightforward attempt to take the heights of Tekke Tepe.

Finally, one other officer at Suvla would have mourned the death of his uncle, Hugh Price Travers, and his cousin, Spenser Robert Valentine Travers, and this was Capt. Hugh Eaton Frederick Travers, of the 9th Battalion Lancashire Fusiliers. This officer was involved in the large-scale attack of 21 August at Suvla, in which his particular battalion aimed to take some advanced Turkish trenches and then the feature known as W Hills. Artillery preparation was poor, and the typed war diary only mentions that the battalion went over the top to be met by heavy rifle and shrapnel fire. Of seven officers who started the attack, only two remained, one of whom was badly wounded. Among those killed was Capt. Travers. He was originally reported as missing, but details are lacking because there is no original war diary for this date, the casualty appendices no longer exist and there is no mention of him in the War Office records. Due to confusion among the brigades attacking, the lack of artillery support, and strong Turkish resistance, the attack failed by late afternoon. Capt. Travers' body was never found, and once more his only remembrance is to be found on the Helles Memorial. One can only hope that he was not wounded and caught in the brush fires that started later in the day.[4]

When news reached the family in Ireland that three of these closely related officers were listed as missing or dead at Suvla, two on the same day, 9 August 1915, and the other on 21 August 1915, there was undoubtedly deep grief and mourning. But there was no questioning then of the nature of these particular casualties, for these officers were simply three among the thousands who had already died 'for freedom and honour', as the British World War I memorial plaque states.[5] Eighty-five years later, it is possible to raise questions, some of which were already noted in the war diaries of the units involved. In the attacks involving the deaths of these three officers, there did seem to be confusion and poor coordination of units, lack of accurate or supporting artillery and naval fire, lack of reconnaissance and maps, sometimes poor leadership, sometimes shortages of water and ammunition, and possibly low morale on occasion. But were these difficulties due to leadership problems in the staff or at the highest levels? Or were the problems connected to technologies that could not do the job? Maybe there were simply not enough men and munitions? Perhaps the problems were systemic? Or was the Mediterranean Expeditionary Force simply too inexperienced? And then there was the suggestion that Allied failure at Gallipoli was due to the Turks being too strong.

The rest of this book is dedicated to finding out what really went wrong for the Allies at Gallipoli in 1915, as well as what went right for the Turks. This will be a small mark of respect to the memory of Hugh Price, Spenser Robert Valentine and Hugh Eaton Frederick.

PREFACE

The Riddle of Gallipoli

Why another book on Gallipoli? There are three main reasons. Firstly, as the title of this introduction suggests, there has not been a totally satisfactory explanation of why the Allies did not succeed in the Gallipoli campaign, or alternatively why the Ottoman/Turkish forces prevailed at Canakkale, as the campaign is known today in Turkey. Therefore, this book sets out to attempt an explanation of this riddle.

Secondly, there has not been a serious effort before to use Ottoman/Turkish evidence and sources for the Gallipoli/Canakkale campaign. Apart from the Turkish official history, which has not often been consulted, there are also the main archives in Ankara, Turkey, at the General Staff headquarters. This is an untouched resource, with hundreds, if not thousands, of documents concerning the Ottoman/Turkish Fifth Army, which defended Gallipoli/Canakkale and the Straits against the Allied naval and land operations. This book is a modest attempt to use these Ottoman/Turkish sources for the first time in order to present a more balanced account of the 1915 campaign. It is also worth noting that Ottoman/Turkish officers and men did not keep private diaries, since this was not a cultural tradition in the Ottoman empire. Hence, the documents in Ankara are some of the few original resources for the Gallipoli/Canakkale campaign available to the researcher.[1]

In addition to these sources from the Ottoman/Turkish side, a new and valuable piece of evidence has emerged as a result of the release of German documents from East Germany. I am very grateful to my colleague Holger Herwig for discovering and translating this previously unknown material. This new document is an extensive 40 page manuscript letter, written from Gallipoli in June 1915 by

Capt. Carl Mühlmann, the future German historian of the campaign. In 1915 Mühlmann was a staff officer and aide to Gen. Liman von Sanders, commander of the Ottoman/Turkish 5th Army at Gallipoli, and thus Mühlmann was a first hand participant in many of the important events and decisions of the first two months of land operations. Many of the senior officers serving Fifth Army, including Liman von Sanders, were German, hence the value of German sources as well.[2]

From these new archival sources, a number of fresh arguments and theses are advanced in this book. These range from a different view of the Ottoman/Turkish ability to withstand a renewed naval attack, to Ottoman/Turkish expectations of Allied plans for their landings, to Ottoman/Turkish responses to these landings, to an Ottoman/Turkish crisis in May 1915, to a significant revisal of the timing of the Ottoman/Turkish response to the Allied August offensive at Suvla, to another look at whether the Allied evacuation in December 1915/January 1916 was anticipated by the defenders of Gallipoli. Mühlmann also offers a close-up view of Liman von Sanders' reaction to the Allied April landings, plus a surprising evaluation of the effects of Allied naval shelling, and an inside view of the Ottoman/Turkish crisis of May 1915.

Since the great majority of archival sources used in this book do stem from Allied archives, the emphasis remains on the Allied performance. Nevertheless, thirdly, this book attempts to present the Gallipoli campaign from as wide a perspective as possible. Quite understandably, most works on Gallipoli tend to be written from a British, Australian, New Zealand or French perspective, and these rely heavily on the archives of the relevant country involved. It is true that many authors do consider the actions of other nationalities, yet they rarely undertake an in-depth analysis. Hence, this book aims at an international evaluation of Gallipoli, rather than an approach from one point of view. As a result, extensive archival work was undertaken in Britain, France, Australia, New Zealand and Turkey, and it is hoped that this produces a more balanced discussion of the campaign.

Finally, as set forth in the Prologue, there is another, personal, reason for writing this book, and that concerns three of the members of the author's family who served at Gallipoli, and who were all killed at Suvla.

*

Any discussion of the Gallipoli campaign has to take into account the provenance of the sources available, especially three important British documents. These are: the Report of the Dardanelles Commission (First Report, 1917–1918; Final Report, 1919); the British official history of Gallipoli written by Brigadier-General Cecil Aspinall-Oglander (originally named Aspinall; the extra surname was added after the war); and the book published by Gen. Sir Ian Hamilton in 1920 in two volumes as *Gallipoli Diary*. The interpretations of the Gallipoli campaign developed by these documents have to be viewed critically since there is considerable evidence of collusion among witnesses to the Dardanelles Commission (reviewed in Chapter Eleven); the British official historian, Aspinall-Oglander, was also a key planner at GHQ during the Gallipoli campaign, leading to concern regarding bias in the official history; and, as commander-in-chief at Gallipoli, Sir Ian Hamilton clearly had good reason to present a favourable view of his role as overall commander (this is partially explored in Chapter Seven). With these caveats, it is possible to turn to a very brief historiography of the Gallipoli campaign.

So far, interpretations of the Gallipoli campaign have produced various reasons for Allied failure, or Ottoman/Turkish success, without coming to convincing conclusions. Initially, books such as John Masefield's *Gallipoli* (1916), Sir Ian Hamilton's *Gallipoli Diary* (1920), and Winston Churchill's *The World Crisis 1915* (1923) offered strong defences of the Allied campaign. Then the Australian official history, Charles Bean's *The Story of Anzac*, published in 1921 and 1924, and the British official history, Brigadier-General Cecil Aspinall-Oglander's *Military Operations: Gallipoli*, published in 1929 and 1932, both produced balanced accounts of the campaign, but with some criticisms of Gen. Sir Ian Hamilton, Commander-in-Chief of the Mediterranean

Expeditionary Force, as the Allied command was known. There was also criticism of selected Allied commanders, decisions, and troops. Moving forward, Alan Moorehead's popular *Gallipoli* (1956) reignited interest in the campaign, but it was Robert Rhodes James' outstanding book, *Gallipoli* (1965), which offered the best research and the deepest analysis of the Allied problems, and presented a criticism of Field Marshal Lord H.H. Kitchener, the British Secretary of State for War; of Winston Churchill, the First Lord of the Admiralty; of Sir Ian Hamilton; and of staff work in London and at Hamilton's General Headquarters (GHQ). Most recently, however, the pendulum has begun to swing the other way. Michael Hickey's *Gallipoli* (1995) often avoids criticism, and generally defends Hamilton, while Nigel Steel and Peter Hart's *Defeat at Gallipoli* (1994) blames Kitchener and the politicians in London and Paris for not providing enough troops and resources for the campaign to succeed. Finally, John Lee's portrait of Hamilton, *A Soldier's Life: General Sir Ian Hamilton 1853–1947* (2000), presents a balanced and reasonable defence of Hamilton's command.

Reviewing these analyses of the Gallipoli campaign, it is possible to see that a mixture of internal and external factors are invoked as explanations. In regard to internal factors, the chief reasons for Allied failure include the allegations that Hamilton was out of touch with the front line troops, was over-optimistic, and deferred too much to Kitchener over the vital supply of men and munitions. For reasons of military tradition, practice and etiquette, Hamilton also believed he could not intervene with his subordinates at critical moments. Other internal reasons for Allied failure include a lack of coordination, and sometimes understanding, between Army and Navy and between British and French forces, together with administrative, logistical and medical problems. Further internal reasons for Allied defeat point toward poor Allied leadership, such as Maj.-Gen. Aylmer Hunter-Weston, commanding 29 Division and VIII Corps at Helles; Maj.-Gen. Alexander Godley, commanding the Anzac Division and then the Anzac area; Lt-Gen. Sir Frederick Stopford, commanding IX Corps at Suvla; and Maj.-Gen. Frederick Hammersley, commanding 11 Division at Suvla.

Turning to external factors to explain Allied failure, attention has now especially focussed on Kitchener and the Cabinet in London for not preparing the enterprise properly, for not supporting the campaign with sufficient men and munitions once land operations commenced, and for underestimating the Ottoman/Turkish defenders. In fact, very recently, Edward Erickson's *Ordered to Die: A History of the Ottoman Army in World War I* (2000), sees the Ottoman/Turkish army as the major reason for Allied defeat, or conversely, for Ottoman/Turkish success at Gallipoli. Meanwhile, the Turkish official history condemns the Allies for not attacking with both army and navy at the same time, an Allied internal failure. The Turkish official history also stresses the value of German and Ottoman/Turkish leadership, particularly Mustafa Kemal, commanding 19 Division, and Liman von Sanders, the overall commander of Fifth Army on Gallipoli. This, plus the very strong nationalism and high morale of the Ottoman/Turkish army, were key factors, according to the Turkish official history, which resulted in Ottoman/Turkish victory at Gallipoli/Canakkale.[3]

The present book looks at several factors and, while intending to answer the basic questions of success and failure, does not aim to describe every detail of the Gallipoli campaign. Rather it focusses on areas where new information and interpretations are of value, while also trying to link events together and tell the story of the campaign. Some areas of the campaign are largely omitted, for example, logistics and administration, while the medical service is also sparingly discussed, partly because a useful book on that subject now exists.[4] Similarly, there is much on the Ottoman/Turkish side of affairs that is not attempted, either for lack of evidence or because of an inability to track down the relevant documents in the unindexed Turkish archives in Ankara.

In regard to nomenclature, it is important to note that the Gallipoli defenders should properly be called the Ottoman army, since the Ottoman empire still existed in 1915, and there were many ethnic nationalities inside the empire besides Turks. But popular usage means the English speaking world is so familiar with the words Turks, Turkish and Turkey in connection with Gallipoli, that these will be used in this study. Similarly, while from the Turkish point of view the campaign should properly be entitled the Canakkale campaign, because of its familiarity, Gallipoli (derived from the Turkish town on the peninsula called Gelibolu) will be used. On the other hand, since Istanbul has been the correct name of the Ottoman/Turkish capital since 1453, and since this name is familiar to readers, that appellation will be used rather than Constantinople, unless the latter appears in a quotation or original source.

*

This book could not have been written without the help of many individuals and institutions, and it is a genuine pleasure to recall all their kind efforts on behalf of the author.

In regard to Turkish archives, thanks are due to Dr Serge Bernier, Department of National Defence, Ottawa, who opened the door for my visit to Ankara. Then in Ankara, Corps General Yugnak, and Col. Gorur, were kind enough to grant me permission to work in the General Staff archives (the ATASE) in Ankara. A special tribute goes to Dr Birten Celik who gave up a month of her valuable time to translate documents from Ottoman Arabic and Turkish into English. Her contributions were absolutely essential, and cheerfully given, and I was fortunate to have the instruction and assistance of such a scholar. In Ankara, I was also grateful for the hospitality and help given by Dr Mete Tuncoku and Dr Secil Akgur. Many thanks also to the very helpful staff at the ATASE in Ankara, who worked hard to satisfy the multitude of document requests throughout the month of research. Following Ankara, it was necessary to visit the battlefield at Gallipoli, and here two companions made the trip a particular pleasure, the erudite, adaptable and cheerful Robert Lamond, and the author's wife, Heather, who always provided inspiration and support. Both valiantly endured the inspection of Anzac and Helles, and especially the lengthy searches through the beautifully kept cemeteries of Gallipoli, looking for family graves. In Turkey I was also considerably helped by a generous research grant from the University of Calgary.

In England, hospitality was kindly extended by Lt-Col. Hugh Travers, and Maj.-Gen. Ken and Maureen Shepheard, and also by Patricia and David Rogers and Jo and Charles Cumberlege. Librarians and archivists at the Public Record Office; the Liddell Hart Centre for Military Archives, King's College, London University; the Imperial War Museum; the National Army Museum; Churchill College, Cambridge; and the County Record Office, Newport, Isle of Wight; were all unfailingly helpful, and often made useful suggestions, thus saving the researcher much time and trouble. A special thanks to them all. I am also grateful for research undertaken in London by Martin Lubowski, who in the process became a personal friend.

In visiting Australia, I was aided by research grants from the University of Calgary and the Australian War Museum, Canberra. I am grateful to the archivists and librarians at the wonderfully well-organized Australian War Memorial. I also would like to thank the staff at the Mitchell Library, Sydney. Hospitality in Australia was extended by a wide range of generous individuals, including Jeffrey Grey and Peter Dennis, Michael Voelcker, Malcolm van Gelder, the Shergolds, Michael and Carla Hudson, and by several Wellington College alumni, especially Malcolm Little and the Dalys.

In New Zealand, I am grateful to the many helpful librarians and archivists in the following archives: the Auckland War Memorial Museum Library, Auckland; the Kippenberger Military Archive & Research Library Army Museum, Waiouru; the National Archives, Wellington; and the Turnbull Library, Wellington. Our time in New Zealand was made very pleasant by the hospitality of Peter and Judy Travers, Peter and Mary Morpeth, and Dick and Sue Ryan.

Finally, I wish to thank the staff of the military history archives at Vincennes, France, who efficiently arranged for all the documents to be ready for my arrival, and made research a much easier task. In Paris, it was a great pleasure to receive the friendship and hospitality of Paul René and Marie Jo Orban, and Hubert de Castelbajac.

Last but not least, office staff and colleagues in Calgary were always very helpful, none more so than the previously mentioned Holger Herwig. John and Naomi Lacey very kindly made available to me their fine collection of Gallipoli photographs. Nicholas Travers saved the author considerable time by doing a summary of key points in the Gallipoli volumes of the French official history. And on the home front, Heather was unfailingly supportive and enthusiastic about this lengthy research project, involving travel to several countries. More than this, Heather generously spent a tremendous amount of time in copy editing and correcting the manuscript. This book is thus as much hers as mine.

THE ORIGINS OF THE MILITARY CAMPAIGN AND THE NAVAL ATTACK AT GALLIPOLI

February – March

The Gallipoli campaign of 1915 began with an appeal from Russia for help. However, this was followed by disorganized planning in London. In February and March, Allied naval forces attempted to knock out Turkish artillery and forts at the Dardanelles Straits, while also sweeping up Turkish mines. It proved to be impossible to achieve this, and so on 18 March the frustrated Allied fleet made a final effort to break through the Straits. This, too, failed with the loss of three battleships sunk, leaving the Turkish defences still in good condition. So by 22 March the emphasis shifted to an Allied army landing. Strangely enough, Sir Ian Hamilton's decision to land the Army in the south of the Gallipoli peninsula rather than in the north at Bulair was a crucial factor in the British Navy's decision to give up the purely naval attack. In general, the Allied naval failure of February and March 1915 seems to have had deeper roots than simple technical inability.

*

The immediate origins of the Allied campaign began with an appeal by the Grand Duke Nicholas of Russia to Britain on 2 January 1915 for a demonstration to help against the Turks, who were attacking in the Caucasus. The significant word here is 'demonstration'; it was not a call for a large-scale attack. The next day, Kitchener and Churchill met to consider the situation, and later the same day, Kitchener wrote to Churchill saying that troops were not available, but that the only place where a demonstration might stop troops going east (presumably

Russia) was the Dardanelles. According to the First Sea Lord, Sir John ('Jacky') Fisher, this was the document that actually started the Dardanelles operation, plus Kitchener's advocacy of the plan in the War Council. The next day, Fisher sent Churchill a typically audacious but impractical plan for a large-scale joint army-navy operation against Turkey, involving Britain, Bulgaria, Greece, the Serbs and Russia. Fisher's mercurial personality soon led him to support another subsidiary plan a few days later, an attack on the Turkish port of Alexandretta, a favourite target of British strategists. The same day that Fisher's plan arrived, 3 January 1915, Churchill telegraphed to Vice-Admiral Sackville Carden, in charge of the British East Mediterranean fleet, asking his opinion on a naval operation against the Dardanelles. Probably both Kitchener's and Fisher's ideas were the immediate genesis of Churchill's action. But what is clear from the ferment of plans being discussed and advocated at the time – including the plan of Lt-Col. Maurice Hankey, Secretary to the War Council, to bomb crops in Germany, and Fisher's numerous plans for Zeebrugge, Borkum, Cuxhaven, or the Baltic generally – is that a group of intelligent and strong-minded individuals, principally Churchill, Kitchener, Fisher, Hankey and the Rt Hon. David Lloyd George, Chancellor of the Exchequer, were each putting forward their own ideas, without much coordination and without much professional advice. They were, in effect, amateur strategists and tacticians. It was likely that whoever could first put together a plan that was generally agreeable would carry the day.[1]

This was to be the case, as the naval attack really began with Churchill's previously mentioned telegram to Carden at Malta, asking whether the forcing of the Dardanelles Straits by ships alone was a practical operation. It is apparent in this telegram that Churchill was more concerned about mines than any other problem, since he included in the telegram a specific recommendation: 'It is assumed older Battleships fitted with mine bumpers would be used preceded by Colliers or other merchant craft as bumpers and sweepers.' Churchill concluded by stressing that the importance of the operation justified severe losses. Churchill's telegram obviously invited a favourable answer, and he was also dealing with an individual, Carden, who was seen in the Navy as slow, ineffective and on the shelf. So it was understandable that Carden bowed to the imperative telegram from Churchill, and agreed that although the Straits could not be rushed, yet 'a passage might be forced by extended operations with large number of ships.' This was quite a careful reply, and indeed a member of the Dardanelles Commission of 1916–1917 has written in green pencil the word 'Cautious' against Carden's answer. Some historians have also seen the use of Carden as chief architect of the Straits operation, rather than Rear-Admiral Arthur Limpus, who had been British navy chief at Istanbul, to be a significant mistake. But Limpus himself believed optimistically that once the Turkish Dardanelles forts had been demolished, the Turkish empire 'would cease to exist.' In any case, a few days later, on 11 January 1915, Carden's plan emerged, actually produced by Capt. Charles F. Sowerby and two staff officers, Commander the Hon. Alex Ramsay and Capt. W.W. Godfrey, Royal Marine Light Infantry, who apparently persuaded Carden that the plan could work.[2]

The Carden plan envisaged a methodical four stage naval attack on the Dardanelles. It all seemed very simple: clear out the outer forts, then destroy the forts up to Kephez Point, then the forts at the Narrows, and, finally, emerge into the Sea of Marmora. The idea behind the plan was to out-range the guns of the forts with long-range naval fire, and then when the forts' guns were silenced, or the gunners driven away, close in and destroy the forts, perhaps with naval landing parties. Preceding this, sweeping operations would take place, to enable safe passage of the fleet in the Straits. It is significant that Carden did not produce a joint Army-Navy plan because he was not asked to consider this, rather he was bidden only and specifically to consider a naval plan. Carden and his staff officers were undoubtedly encouraged by a naval intelligence document, which they referred to in their naval plan. This was the Admiralty's Intelligence booklet on Turkey's coastal defences, produced in 1908. The booklet stated that the poor tactical disposition of the Turkish batteries at the Straits prevented efficient use of the guns to 'oppose the rapid passage of ships of war.' The summary of the Turkish Dardanelles defences in the booklet also claimed: 'It may be generally considered that the defences are too dispersed, and not strong enough at the critical point.'[3]

As an example of naval optimism at the time, it is of interest that, in another unrelated plan produced in 1908 to support the Danes of Zealand against the Germans, it was assumed that British minesweepers would *not* actually have to face German land-based fire 'otherwise they [the Germans] would expose themselves to the full and uninterfered-with fire of our ships.'[4] Also, there was the general feeling that the Turks were an inferior opponent, or conversely, that the Allies were obviously a superior force. For example, Churchill himself was very confident that the Turkish forts could be dealt with by an Allied landing force 'after 2 or 3 days hard action.' Similarly, Churchill was reported by the Third Sea Lord, Admiral Frederick Tudor, as being confident of his 'ships alone' plan. Tudor recalled that he told Churchill, 'Well, you won't do it with ships alone.' Churchill replied, 'Oh yes, we will.' On the other hand, Commodore Roger Keyes, naval Chief of Staff at Gallipoli, reported a rather more speculative comment from Churchill in March 1915, that this was 'the biggest coup he [Churchill] has ever played for.' It is also the case that Kitchener, too, underrated the Turks, and expected that if the forts fell, then there would be a political revolution in Istanbul. He also believed that the slow and methodical overpowering of the forts 'will exert great moral effect on the Turk…' Even after 18 March and the failure of the naval operation, the War Office expected the Turks to 'throw up the sponge and… clear out of the Gallipoli Peninsula.'[5]

The naval attack was approved at the British War Council on 13 January 1915, and formally decided on 28 January 1915. Judging by preparations for the operation, the Navy was unsure of its capabilities for this role. On 9 February 1915, Vice-Admiral John M. de Robeck, then second in command of the naval attack, announced preparations for the assault on the Straits forts. De Robeck advocated the use of shrapnel, which required practice at fusing and fuse setting, 'as we have little or no experience with that type of projectile.' Floating mines would be dealt with by the use of seine nets ahead of ships when anchored. Torpedo nets would be used against locomotive torpedoes. Troops might have to land to deal with the forts after the guns had been silenced and their defenders driven off. Finally, paint should be removed from inside gun turrets because when hot, the burning paint 'appears to greatly inconvenience the turret guns' crews.' HMS *Vengeance* replied to this directive by saying that shrapnel was in very limited supply, so that common shell would have to be used against forts. Also, lime juice should be supplied for gun positions if the air became contaminated with carbon dioxide. HMS *Triumph* did not have shrapnel either, but Lyddite would be very good against the forts. A simple signalling system, using a clock code, would directly observe on a straight line from ship to fort. This was a reflection of the fact that the Navy had done little indirect fire or high-angle fire before the war.[6]

The naval bombardment commenced on 19 February but did not do much damage, as Carden discovered on 20 February, at least in regard to Fort 1. He informed the Admiralty of his trouble, but already on 16 February, and unknown to Carden, a small group, including Kitchener, Churchill, Lloyd George, the Right Honourable Herbert Asquith, Prime Minister, Sir Edward Grey, Foreign Secretary, and Fisher, but not Hankey, had decided to send the British 29 Division and Anzac forces in Egypt to the island of Lemnos to prepare for a landing. Even though Kitchener changed his mind about 29 Division three days later, this was really the specific origin of the military side of the Gallipoli campaign. At this point, on 16 February, Churchill told Rear-Admiral Rosslyn E. Wemyss, 1st Naval Squadron, that it had been decided that morning to force the Dardanelles, and Wemyss was sent to be governor of Lemnos in preparation. Kitchener informed Lt-Gen. Sir John Maxwell, Commander-in-Chief of forces in Egypt, of this decision, and told him to coordinate with Carden. According to Lloyd George, it was Kitchener who decided to increase the military side of the equation. For his part, Carden was undoubtedly startled to receive this informa-tion, but expected only 10,000 troops. With this small number he merely suggested occupying the southern Helles area on Gallipoli. Maxwell thought Carden's idea was 'helpless,' and told Kitchener that military authorities needed to take the initiative. Kitchener replied, trying to divide up the responsibilities of the Army and the Navy. The Navy would silence the guns and forts, while the Army would only land small parties under the support of naval guns 'to help in total demolition when ships get to close quarters.'[7]

Thus far, Kitchener had outlined limited aims for the Army, and until early March still relied strictly on the Navy. Maxwell concurred. On 26 February, he quoted Col. Maucorps, of the French Military Mission, who also cautioned that it would be 'extremely hazardous to land on the Gallipoli Peninsula as the peninsula is very strongly organised for defence.'[8] Carden must have certainly wondered what was going on, and in fact a key moment had now arrived. The campaign at this point could have, and should have, shifted to a joint Army–Navy operation. But Churchill's telegram of 24 February to Carden did not encourage this option. Churchill told Carden that the War Office did not consider the occupation of Helles on Gallipoli a necessary precondition for destroying the coastal permanent batteries, which was the primary object of the naval attack. The main army would remain at Lemnos until the 'Straits is in our hands…', still implying a 'ships alone' concept. Carden later said that he did not consider using the Army at this juncture because that 'was a military question.' Hankey argued that the real reason for the lack of an Army–Navy operation was because the Navy did not want the Army to interfere. This is reflected in Carden's message to de Robeck on 26 February, which stated that he considered army landing parties to be secondary to the fleet's forward movement. Perhaps all of this is the reason for a cryptic but important note in the diary of Lady Hamilton, wife of Gen. Sir Ian Hamilton, in October 1915, which reads that Churchill was very anxious in case it would come out publicly that Kitchener had wanted troops to go in before the fleet had eliminated surprise.[9] This implied that Churchill ignored the value of a joint Army–Navy plan, and disregarded the loss of surprise caused by his 'ships alone' plan.

So the situation was that there were really three plans emerging and going forward at the same time. These were: the 'ships alone' navy plan; the joint navy–army operations; and an evolving army-based plan. Kitchener, however, still thought in terms of landing parties rather than a full-scale operation because he was reluctant to part with sufficient troops for a full-scale army campaign. His decisions introduced further uncertainty into the muddled strategy at the Straits, but Kitchener was apparently impressed by the potential of the new and powerful *Queen*

Elizabeth, which was promised to Carden on 13 January, leading Carden to state that the ship would 'certainly shorten operations.'[10]

Meanwhile, at the Straits, Carden tried again with the fleet on 25 February against the outer forts. This was more successful, and Commander I. Worsley Gibson, on board *Albion*, watched their guns knock out Fort 4, but have more trouble with Fort 6 because it was protected by earth works rather than masonry: 'Still we blew the muzzle off one [gun] and saw another fall a bit sideways, then from the opposite shore a field battery opened fire on us...' This battery was hard to shut down: 'They stuck to it jolly well and not until we'd sent two windmills up into the air like a pack of cards, most humorous to watch, and planted several beauties right on top of them did they retire.' Then this battery started up again, 'so we gave them another dose of common, wish we had more shrapnel, that's what we want really for these fellows.' The next day, 26 February, *Albion* fired at a howitzer on a ridge, and 'let them have it, several very good salvos.' But in a portent of the future, Gibson also wrote that minesweepers came under fire from Fort 7, and had to retire. At the same time, parties of marines were landing at Seddulbahir and Kum Kale with success, meeting little resistance, and over the next few days, putting many guns out of action. Despite the incipient minesweeper problem, all seemed to be going well, as a junior officer on *Triumph* recalled:

> on the 27th February we bombarded the outer ports at Seddulbahr and Kam Kale [sic] we were surprised at the poor shooting they made, fully expecting a much hotter reception as we thought they were lying doggo waiting to give us a pasting when we got within a shorter range. However the next day we... closed the range and a close inspection showed that the defences were abandoned.[11]

Gibson's enthusiastic diary entries begin to change on 1 March. On this day, he noted that the gun layers were having trouble finding any prominent marks to lay on, and so *Albion* withdrew after half an hour. By now the ships were firing at the inner Straits batteries and forts, and these proved obdurate. Gibson remarked that:

there is a lack of organization. While some ships were keeping these [field gun] batteries amused, others should have pushed on and engaged Fort 8 and possibly Fort 7. These field gun batteries are very hard to damage, work as a rule close to a road, and constantly shift their position.

On 2 March, *Albion* fired at long range at Fort 8 at Dardanos, but did not achieve much. On 3 March, the Turks did not fire at all at the minesweepers, and Gibson became more cheerful. Carden, however, was only using three battleships out of eighteen on these two days, and continued to use only a small portion of his ships. This was partly because he was slow and lethargic in pushing operations along, and partly because he had become more pessimistic about the concealed batteries, which were now a key problem. In early March, Roger Keyes complained that Carden was 'very slow and I have often to say to myself… "Ye have need of patience" –.' But already at a conference on 2 March, Carden told Wemyss and Lt-Gen. Sir William Birdwood, future GOC Anzac, that the concealed guns and mobile batteries were making minesweeping impossible and that the inner forts could not be attacked before both mines and guns were dealt with. The solution was for troops to land and deal with the guns, so that the mines could then be cleared. The next day, 3 March, Carden informed de Robeck that he had developed a scheme for 'spotting ships inside [the Straits] *before* all the concealed guns are disposed of…' The scheme would require good wireless transmission for *Queen Elizabeth's* long range indirect fire, with spotting both by ship and air, which was de Robeck's basic idea. However, staff work was obviously poor, for on 5 March, *Albion* got notice to spot for the *Queen Elizabeth* at 8.45 a.m.: 'As we were 50 miles off, steam at 3 hours notice, and show began at 9 someone had blundered. Didn't get there till 3.30 p.m. when firing practically finished for day…' Nevertheless, *Queen Elizabeth* managed eight hits on Fort 13, and Gibson estimated the moral effect 'must be considerable.' The following day, 6 March, *Albion* continued spotting for *Queen Elizabeth* off Gaba Tepe, but artillery fire pushed the ships too far out, and the scheme was thus a 'dead failure.'[12]

Carden was now obviously thrashing about, looking for help. *Queen Elizabeth's* long range indirect fire was only a partial success, while the landing of Marines at Seddulbahir and Kum Kale on 4 March to deal with guns and forts now met with strong resistance, and the troops had to be re-embarked. However, later landing parties over a few days did destroy most of the guns at Seddulbahir, Kum Kale and Fort 4, while the two guns of Fort 1 had been destroyed by earlier shell fire. But what to do with the concealed guns which were preventing minesweeping? Carden still hoped to use air reconnaissance, which he told the Admiralty on 4 March was the only way to deal with the concealed guns. Unfortunately, this didn't work either, because seaplanes could not find gun locations unless they came in low, at which point they were hit by small arms fire, or the planes had engine trouble. In fact, Roger Keyes claimed the planes had only flown on four days. Yet another possibility was sweeping by night, but here the searchlights used by the Turks could not be knocked out, and so this too failed. At this point, the commander of the civilian-crewed minesweeping division lost his nerve, and had to be replaced. Gibson commented sympathetically: 'It must be very nerve wracking being up there sweeping at night expecting the batteries to open fire any minute.' Finally, Carden threw in the towel and wrote a pessimistic letter to Churchill on 10 March, emphasizing that he could not deal with the concealed fire of howitzers, whose plunging fire was 'very destructive' (during the shoot of 5 March, *Agammenon* lost the wardroom and the men's washrooms to gun fire), but without air reconnaissance the large number of mobile howitzers could not be dealt with, and so the mines could not be cleared. Moreover, there was not enough ammunition for the slow reduction of the forts. Churchill realized this was a crisis in the naval attack, and decided on a change in tactics. Carden's slow plan was abandoned and replaced by a vigorous attack. Carden was now to run risks, land to destroy guns, sweep 'as much as possible', and ships were to close to decisive range to hit the forts.[13]

Churchill's urgency has been explained on the grounds that he had received information that the forts were short of ammunition, and so a vigorous advance was likely to be successful. Another explanation behind Churchill's change of plan is that German submarines were shortly expected, and so quick action was required. A third explanation is that Churchill was aware of Carden's reputation for inaction.[14] It is interesting that Carden took some time to reply, in fact three days, at which time he agreed to vigorous action. It was during this three day period that Carden decided to go to Mudros, no doubt to confer with Wemyss, but at the same time he sent de Robeck to view the Bulair lines at the neck of the Gallipoli peninsula, thus leaving no one except the rather junior Roger Keyes in charge of minesweeping and naval action. Keyes argued with Carden, and persuaded him to order de Robeck to stay. Even so, the minesweepers had done nothing for five or six days, and de Robeck himself appeared slow to order full-scale minesweeping. Nevertheless, at the end of these three days, and under pressure from Churchill, Carden developed a new plan, if a last attempt at night sweeping failed. The night sweeping effort did fail, and so the new plan was for a bold battleship daylight attack on the forts, followed by attacks on mobile and fixed batteries, accompanied by minesweeping, and then a move into the Sea of Marmora supported by a large military force. Although Churchill stressed that there should not be a rush through, that was the initial impression gained by the Navy. According to Gibson, de Robeck said on 13 March that 'a heavy concerted bombardment and rush through the Narrows was to be considered.' Gibson felt that:

> Everyone or nearly so I believe knew really that it would be madness to try and rush them. The Narrows are sure to be mined… Personally I feel sure that it is pressure from our cursed politicians which is making him even consider such a thing – A large army 60 or 70 thousand is collecting for purpose of cooperation, the only way to tackle this job and why not wait for them.

The next day Gibson listened to:

> Captains Dent and Campbell [who] had a fierce scheme for us all attacking Narrows en masse. Most people in their hearts I'm certain think it's a huge mistake not to wait for soldiers and that cooperation of military is essential to success. VA [Carden] looked very worried, somehow he doesn't seem a strong enough man for the job.[15]

The mention of Captains Dent (*Irresistible*) and Campbell (*Prince George*) and their plan of attack introduces a useful post-war document written by Capt. Dent, and vetted by de Robeck. According to Dent, during this critical period before what turned out to be the final naval assault on 18 March, he suggested to de Robeck that two committees be formed, one to deal with the problem of the forts and one to deal with the problem of the mines. The forts committee comprised Capt. Dent, Capt. Campbell, and Commander the Hon. Ramsay. The mines committee was headed up by Capt. Heneage of the *Albion*. The forts committee came up with the basic plan that was eventually used on 18 March, and was essentially Capt. Dent's idea. This was to attack line abreast in two columns, with the heavier ships firing over the older ships in front. When the heavier battleships had temporarily silenced the guns of the forts, the older ships would be swept right up to the forts by fast sweepers, and at this range the older ships should be able to dismount the guns of the forts. Then the Narrows could be swept. The problem was the fast sweepers, which did not exist. So it was suggested that twelve French and British destroyers should be fitted with sweeps. But this idea was rejected by the French, whose admiral said that there were only a few destroyers capable of sweeping against the current, and these were 'indispensable for safety of my fleet so regret deeply I cannot spare them.' Capt. Charles Coode, commanding the British destroyers, also argued that his destroyers could not be used for sweeping. This rejection turned out to be extremely important, since minesweeping was actually the key to naval success. Carden had already 'urgently' asked for fleet sweepers on 14 March, at which time one third of his civilian sweepers were out of action. Some sweeps did arrive from Malta in the nick of time on 17 March, and two destroyers were fitted with these sweeps on 18 March. However, the eight destroyers of the British Beagle class did nothing on 18 March, the day of the naval attack, and the officers spent the day playing bridge. Meanwhile, too late, starting on 19 March, the Beagle-class destroyers began to be fitted with sweeps, and the smaller River-class destroyers, not powerful enough to sweep, were assigned to finding mines. De Robeck reported on 19 March: 'Experiments being carried out in fitting destroyers with sweeps in order to possess sweeping craft capable of working against current of Dardanelles.'[16]

The all-important minesweeper problem had not been properly addressed by Carden until too late, and Capt. Coode must also bear considerable blame for his rejection of the Beagle class destroyers as sweeps. But what about the significant mines committee headed up by Capt. Heneage? This committee, composed of Captains Dent and McClintock and Commander Ramsay, besides Heneage, did not meet before 18 March. Nevertheless, Heneage was once more put in charge of this committee, but only on 19 March, one day after the naval failure of 18 March. In fact, Carden already reported on 14 March that there were only two minesweepers fit to work, and so he was driven to using picket boats towing explosives to cut mine cables. These operated with seaplanes, which could theoretically spot mines to a depth of 18 feet.[17] The minesweeping aspect of Carden's original plan simply did not work, so Dent's naval attack was scheduled to start on 18 March. Just before this attack took place, Carden went sick. This was certainly through stress, but according to Roger Keyes, perhaps also through eating a 'beastly suet and treacle pudding, which, when he saw the menu, he sent for!'[18] De Robeck took command in place of Carden, and Gibson was happier with de Robeck: 'Captain [Heneage] thinks de Robeck will take no notice of Winston Churchill's wires to hurry up etc and says that he [de Robeck] is already not on speaking terms with Winston and doesn't care a d—- what they [the Admiralty] say. I was very pleased to hear this as I rather think Carden was not firm enough with them.' Gibson was also happy to hear that de Robeck had said there would be no 'wild cat rushing of Narrows… I am awfully glad', no ships to be risked in unswept areas, and more of the 'siege idea.'[19]

While all these tactics were being argued out in the Navy, what of the military operation, part of the haphazard two or three track strategy? In fact there was now a tug of war taking place. Churchill, Kitchener and the Navy wanted the Navy to succeed, with the assistance of the Army, while Birdwood and some in the Army were thinking of either combined operations or the Army succeeding with the help of the Navy. What had started out as a naval operation was thus gradually becoming a military operation, obscured by Kitchener's dithering over sending 29 Division to Gallipoli. At the beginning of March, Birdwood believed that a large military force was necessary, and his plan was to land near the Bulair lines. However, Kitchener refused, and only released 29 Division on 10 March, although he still hoped the Navy would do the job alone. Finally, Kitchener came around to considering a large Mediterranean Expeditionary Force (MEF), first choosing Birdwood to command, then Sir Leslie Rundle, and eventually, on 3 March, deciding on Gen. Sir Ian Hamilton as commander-in-chief. This was because he foresaw that a force of 120,000 was needed to take Istanbul, and felt that only Hamilton was senior enough to command French, British and Allied forces. Specifically, at the War Council on 10 March Kitchener wanted a force of 128,700 men, of which 47,600 would be Russians. However, the Russians and Greeks could not agree, and a simultaneous secret attempt to buy off the Turks failed. Despite ongoing naval operations, by 12 March, the British government believed the Navy was stuck, and Hamilton set forth on 13 March. Before Hamilton left, he told Hankey that he was in an embarrassing situation because Churchill wanted a 'big rush [through] Straits by a coup de main with such troops as are available in the Levant (30,000 Australians and 10,000 Naval Division). Lord K on the other hand wants him to go slow, to make the Navy continue pounding the Straits, and to wait for 29 Division.' So Churchill compromised and told Carden on 15 March that there would soon be 18,000 French and 16,000 British troops on Lemnos, with another 25,000 troops in Alexandria. Hence: 'Admiral Carden will therefore have [these troops] at his disposal on the spot...'[20]

Nevertheless, Churchill continued the Dardanelles action as a navy operation, with the Navy commanding the Army troops available, while Kitchener was now starting to think of combined operations. Carden must have been extremely puzzled by these options, which eventually envisaged the Navy organizing and leading a large-scale combined forces operation, after the Navy had entered the Sea of Marmora. The challenge was too much for Carden, so it was de Robeck who prepared for the major naval break-through attempt on 18 March, prior to any army operation. De Robeck's plan was now to use newer battleships in the first line of ships to outrange and silence the forts, then older battleships in the rear line would move to the front, anchor, and bombard the forts at close range. A third wave of battleships would then push forward to finish the job, followed by destroyers ranging further ahead through the Straits. At the same time, other ships on the flanks would temporarily silence the field artillery, all this to enable minesweeping in relative safety, followed finally by the fleet advancing through the Narrows, and then steadily into the Sea of Marmora. One who objected to his role in the plan was the French Vice-Admiral P-E. Guépratte, who was something of a fire eater. Guépratte did not want to anchor with his older ships, partly because they would be sitting ducks as targets, and partly because they would not be at decisive range. Instead, he wanted to close right in through a series of runs until the forts were engaged at very close quarters. De Robeck reportedly answered Guépratte: 'Yes! That's true! But what do you want! It's the eternal controversy between manoeuvre and fire! In these conditions, while recognising the strength of your argument, I will stand by my decision.' Guépratte wasn't finished, however, and he got three British naval captains, Davidson, Fyler, and McClintock, to intervene on his behalf. Guépratte got his way, and the French battleships were given permission to close in to short range. Guépratte decided to divide his command into two, one group on the Asian side, and one group on the Gallipoli side. Included in the group of ships for the Asian side was the doomed *Bouvet*. Ironically, the *Bouvet* was one ship Guépratte did not intend to use, due to her age and general state of decay. However, the captain of the *Bouvet*, Rageot de la Touche, pleaded with tears in his eyes to be part of the attack, and Guépratte fatally relented.[21]

The naval attack started at 8.45 a.m. on 18 March when the minesweepers reported all clear. But it was late in the morning when the first battleships opened fire on the forts, because the light was not good enough in the Straits for firing until then. An Associated Press reporter, George Schreiner, viewing from Chanak on the Asian side, reported the action. During most of the day, the Navy seemed to shell Chanak indiscriminately:

The heavy shells seemed to hit the town in pairs. Not merely fragments of the houses struck but whole floors sailed up high in the air. It began to literally rain roof tiles, bricks, rocks and timbers. Shells exploding in front of the old breakwater remains sent a vicious hail of steel fragments broadcast and the fumes of the explosions began to make breathing a difficult task.

Schreiner managed to find a safe spot outside the town, and observed the naval action:

For some time yet the Allies had things pretty much their own way. 'Queen Elizabeth' was sending her large 15½-inch shells into Fort Hamidieh at a truly terrifying rate… At 1.20 p.m. the Allies ceased to manoeuvre in the bay and for a short time took what is known as a battle position, lying still while firing. They had also ventured in close enough to get within range of the Turkish forts. The forts were replying in fine style, despite the fact that… it seemed impossible that men could live under conditions as existing in and about the forts.

But the Turkish shelling got more accurate, and then Schreiner watched the first Allied battleship to be hit, the *Bouvet,* go down:

a sheaf of fire seemed to start from some part of the vessel. A large, black column of smoke rose and for several seconds the ship took a heavy list. It soon righted itself, however… The next moment brought the beginning of a drama. Slowly the vessel settled astern, then listed to port. Already the aft deck was awash… The forward part of the ship, too, sagged a little. It rose again the next instant, the vessel righted a little… And then came the final plunge. The vessel for an instant showed her sharp prow clear against the sunlit water like a black triangle and then this too disappeared. The *Bouvet* had sunk. It was exactly 2 o'clock.[22]

The French account by Guépratte of the *Bouvet*'s end is curious. According to Guépratte, when de Robeck noticed the heavy Turkish fire from on shore, he sent in the next wave of ships, and Guépratte hoisted flag #4, the signal to the front line of six ships to rally. But *Bouvet* failed to acknowledge. She had ranged herself onto the Namazeid fort, and refused to move. Guépratte regarded this as similar to Nelson's refusal to break off his action at Copenhagen, and despite criticism from the officer in charge of the French frigates, approved de la Touche's attitude. Nevertheless, Guépratte fired a blank shot at the *Bouvet* to get de la Touche to move, but the latter shouted that he be allowed to fire his guns, after which he would retire. However, there were problems on the *Bouvet*, under fire from two forts, and in turret #1, after five or six shells had hit, the ventilation valve broke, and the crew fell insensible. Finally, the *Bouvet* moved astern into Eren Keui Bay, hit a mine, and sank in 45 seconds. As the ship went down, a survivor told Guépratte how de la Touche ordered him to jump, and then de la Touche went back to the bridge, to go down with his ship. Meanwhile Guépratte's own ship, the *Suffren*, was nearly sunk when a shell struck the magazine. But a young gunnery officer, François Lannuzel, flooded the magazine, and saved the ship. Guépratte also noted the problem of shells used by the French fleet, half of them being 'porcelain' shells, prone to prematures, and the other half the new steel cased shells. Consequently, Guépratte placed all the steel cased shells in the port side guns facing the forts on that flank, and the 'porcelain' shells on the harmless starboard side. So, Guépratte declared, 'we won't sneeze at the enemy with porcelain shells!'[23]

Gibson on *Albion* watched the events unfold. Theoretically, Gibson was in an excellent position to view the battle, since he was in the firetop. But 'We were nearly asphyxiated… besides not being able to see anything and cordite smoke sometimes obscured our view.' Gibson did not think that *Albion* knocked out the fort she was firing at, which in any case was the wrong fort, #17 instead of #13. Gibson also watched the *Bouvet* go down in what he thought was two or three minutes, and then watched helplessly as *Irresistible* also hit a mine, and drifted out of control. The shore batteries soon ranged on *Irresistible*: 'It was simply damnable to see her drifting helplessly along then with her men quietly standing about or throwing planks and anything that would float overboard and we couldn't locate the batteries tho' we fired at every place we thought they were or might be…' Under Roger Keyes' command, the battleship *Ocean* was sent to help *Irresistible*, but could not take her in tow because of shoaling water, at which point Keyes wanted to order *Ocean* to retire, but could not do so because *Ocean's* captain was senior to him! Hence, Keyes could only 'suggest' *Ocean* leave. The suggestion was not sufficient, for *Ocean* continued to circle *Irresistible* and then she also struck a mine, falling astern of *Albion*. *Albion's* captain refused to retire and leave these two ships, but the concealed guns were so well hidden that *Albion* could do little of value to assist them. Meanwhile, George Schreiner, watching from the shore, remarked that the Allied naval fire became 'erratic'. He saw *Irresistible* and *Ocean* in trouble, and *Queen Elizabeth* take hits from five shells. Finally, the unfortunate *Irresistible* was the prime target of guns from the European shore and Fort Dardanos. As evening fell: 'from the deck of the *Irresistible* rose the red flare of the exploding shell. A third shot. Again an explosion on deck.' By 7.30 p.m. *Irresistible* had sunk. Ironically, Turkish gunnery had saved the British from the task of sinking the stricken ship.[24]

De Robeck realized the forts were not destroyed, rather they had been silenced temporarily while the crews shifted debris out of the way. In addition, Turkish concealed artillery was generally not found or destroyed. And three capital ships had been mortally damaged by mines: *Bouvet* had gone down at 2.00 p.m., *Irresistible* was out of control and a write-off, as was *Ocean*. Other ships had been badly hit, particularly *Gaulois*, *Suffren* and *Inflexible*. Consequently, as soon as he was sure that the crew had been taken off *Irresistible*, de Robeck hoisted the 'General Recall'. That evening, de Robeck saw the day's action as a 'disaster', and assumed that the damage had been done by floating mines. This hypothesis was supported by Carden, who wrote to de Robeck after the attack: 'What terrible bad luck losing those ships by mines I can't understand it, except they are some which have got displaced by the creeping and sweeping and the current has dragged them, sinkers and all, down the Straits...'[25]

Strangely enough, the Turks themselves did not understand at first what had happened. On 24 March a cipher to the Ministry of War in Istanbul reported that three British battleships had been hit by Turkish batteries, and were forced to go to Malta for repairs. One hundred sailors on board *Queen Elizabeth* were casualties from Turkish artillery also. No

French ships were reported as sunk. A few days later, a German report of 4 April, using Turkish information, claimed that artillery shells had sunk *Bouvet* and badly damaged *Lord Nelson*. It was accepted that *Ocean* had been sunk by a mine, and the report also thought that both *Irresistible* and *Triumph* had been sunk. Gales prevented reconnaissance by air until 26 March, then it was reported that *Gaulois* was sunk and *Suffren* damaged. Obviously, the Turkish forces and their German allies did not know accurately what had happened, but realized that their artillery and mines had achieved their objectives, and anticipated severe problems for the Allies if they tried another naval attack. German and Turkish losses were small among their artillery crews: twenty-four killed, and seventy-nine wounded, while the main forts at Hamidiye and Guvenlik only lost 1 gun; and 1 gun and two barrels; respectively.[26]

Two other pieces of information are of considerable importance. Firstly, the mines that sank the three Allied ships were laid on the night of 7/8 March in the Eren Keui Bay area, but in contrast to the twenty usually reported by historians, in fact twenty-six Carbon mines were laid parallel to the shore. A Turkish report also notes that seventeen Carbon and Russian mines had been laid *across* the Straits in the Eren Keui Bay area in four separate groups. It is possible that some of the damage was done by these latter mines.[27] Secondly, Churchill, and some historians since, have asserted that a second immediate attempt at forcing the Straits by de Robeck and the Allied fleet would have succeeded because the forts were out of heavy ammunition. It appears, however, that Churchill's information on a shortage of Turkish ammunition was incorrect, and it is clear the Turkish forts and artillery had plenty of ammunition left. The British naval historian, Sir Julian Corbett, reported there were an average of 70 rounds per Turkish heavy gun left for the next attack, 130 rounds per 6in howitzer, and 150 per gun for the mine defence guns. Corbett did not know how many rounds the other howitzers and field guns had left. However, Turkish evidence suggests that there was plenty available. For example, in the Eren Keui region, the Turkish 8th Regiment heavy howitzers had 3,634 shells left on the evening of 18 March, the 4th heavy gun Regiment had 992 shells left of 1100, the Kepezdeki batteries had 492 shells left of 2672, and the Muinizafar battery had 691 shells remaining. Then at the Narrows, one battery used 374 shells on 18 March, and had 756 shells remaining, the naval gun battery in the Kephez region used 260 shells but still retained 658, the three mortar batteries had 924 shells in hand, and the mountain gun battery at Sili used 64 shells but still counted 720 in reserve.[28]

Bearing in mind that these guns really only had to keep the minesweepers at bay, in order to halt the progress of the fleet, which was only just starting to enter the more heavily mined area, then de Robeck's eventual decision to hand over operations to the Army, was an excellent one. But de Robeck did not immediately think so. Although he was evidently depressed on the evening of 18 March, and even expected to be relieved of his command, de Robeck's view was not entirely negative. He wrote Wemyss after the action on 18 March, obviously seeking advice: 'Will you come to Tenedos and see me tomorrow. We have had disastrous day owing either to floating mines or torpedos from shore fired at long range.' But de Robeck added that 'we had much the best of the forts.' On 19 March, de Robeck was cheered up by Wemyss, and was particularly persuaded by Godfrey and Roger Keyes, who convinced him to continue the battle. Consequently on 19 March, de Robeck was able to telegraph Hamilton that:

> We are all getting ready for another 'go' and not in the least beaten or down-hearted. The big forts were silenced for a long time, and everything was going well, until *Bouvet* struck a mine. It is hard to say what amount of damage we did I don't know, there were many big explosions in the forts!

It seems that de Robeck was replying to Hamilton's message of the same day, from *Franconia*, from which Hamilton had viewed the battle of 18 March. Hamilton telegraphed that he had seen the Navy's 'brave fellows', and expected that, 'All will go well in the long run where everyone is animated with such a fine spirit.'[29]

Hamilton telegraphed Kitchener, saying that he was impressed by de Robeck, who would exhaust every effort before calling for military assistance. But despite Hamilton's cheerful words, he had apparently already decided, as had Birdwood, that the Navy had failed. So, on 19 March,

Hamilton wired Kitchener that since the Navy had failed, he thought the campaign needed 'a deliberate and progressive military operation carried out in force in order to make good the passage of the Navy'. Kitchener wired back the same day that the Dardanelles must be forced: 'military operations must be carried through.' Kitchener meant that the campaign must be carried through regardless, but while he continued to focus on a major operation against Istanbul, talking vaguely of concentrating 120,000 troops around Istanbul, Hamilton was now aiming at clearing the Gallipoli peninsula itself. Hamilton was evidently anxious to use the Army, perhaps too anxious, and Kitchener's telegram appeared to give him the go-ahead. Hamilton's proposal was not as much for a joint army-navy operation as for an army campaign, although with the final objective of getting the Navy through the Straits. One cannot help thinking that Hamilton now wanted his day in the sun, and the chance to try his luck with a military operation. So this was the point at which the campaign shifted from navy to army under the force of circumstances, although it was not clear whether it was to be a joint operation, or primarily an army campaign. In fact, there was a good deal of confusion over what the Navy was going to do, and what the Army was going to do.[30]

According to Roger Keyes, both de Robeck and Wemyss changed their minds on 19 March and decided on joint operations – a carefully planned combined army landing and naval attack. But did de Robeck give up on the purely naval effort? According to Churchill, de Robeck did indeed change his mind and give up on the naval option, partly because of the forts and mines and partly because of the arrival of the Army. Churchill was actually wrong about the forts, since de Robeck thought that was one area where the ships had achieved their objectives, but de Robeck did worry about the mines. Even so, immediately after 18 March, it seems clear that de Robeck wished to continue naval operations, and preparations regarding minesweeping proceeded. It is important to note here that it is only with hindsight that historians know the naval attack had come to an end. At the time, the Navy simply planned to continue their attack, albeit with the help of the Army. However, gales for several days from 19 to 24 March prevented immediate naval action.

At the same time, de Robeck was becoming more and more pessimistic about the Navy's chances of a successful attack on the Narrows. In a meeting of naval captains on 19 March, it is striking how many ships had seen mines in supposedly swept areas on 18 March, as well as newly spotted lines of mines. At this meeting, Capt. Dent also said that the Eren Keui Bay area had been swept on the night of 17/18 March, though 'sweeping at night… is not accurate.' It is also notable that on 21 March the replaced Carden already expected that de Robeck would have met with Hamilton and organized a military operation, and Carden anticipated the Army sending as many as 150,000 or 200,000 troops.[31]

Hence, de Robeck began to think of an army–navy assault, with the Navy trying again for the Narrows after the Army was ashore. Yet, since the Army needed the Navy both for landing troops and for fire support, this option would eventually peter out. According to Capt. (later Lt-Col.) Cecil Aspinall, GHQ, 'Some sailors didn't like this, hence suggestions for renewing the naval attack.' In fact, the Navy still would have launched another attack, despite the needs of the Army, if the Army had chosen to land at Bulair. This was, in fact, Kitchener's original objective in his instructions to Hamilton before the latter left London on 12 March. But when Hamilton decided on landing the Army in the southern Helles area, with the Navy assisting on both sides of the peninsula, this changed naval minds, and finally committed the Navy to a supporting role.[32] Yet why did the question of Bulair cause de Robeck to change his mind, and abandon the naval option?

In a 1917 letter, Roger Keyes sets out the reason why Bulair was crucial to a renewed naval attack. According to Keyes, it was on the evening of 22 March that de Robeck learnt Hamilton proposed to land his army, when the 29 Division arrived,

> at the heel of the peninsula instead of Bulair or Enos, the position which we had every reason to suppose they would select. Birdwood had telegraphed to this effect from Egypt about 12th March. Had Sir Ian adhered to the Egypt plan it would have been absolutely essential to get a fleet into the Marmora to cover his eastern flank. At that time Sir Ian hoped to be able to land in early April, and as we could not be ready with

our new and very necessary sweeping force before the 2nd or 3rd April, the Admiral was of course right to see the Army safely on shore first. The three weeks delay, quite unforeseen on the 22nd March, was fatal...[33]

Keyes meant that an army landing at Bulair would have compelled the Navy to get through the Straits and into the Sea of Marmora via a renewed naval attack, in order to protect the eastern, Sea of Marmora side of the Army landing. Since a Bulair landing was rejected, the decision was changed to the Navy seeing the Army ashore before mounting any further naval attack. This decision was taken on board *Queen Elizabeth* on 22 March at 10.00 a.m., with Hamilton, Maj.-Gen. Walter Braithwaite, GHQ, Birdwood, de Robeck and Roger Keyes attending. According to Keyes,

> When Sir Ian said he was prepared to land on the toe of the Peninsula, the Admiral made up his mind to put the Army on shore before delivering another Naval attack. This was after he heard from Sir Ian that he hoped to be ready to land on the 14th April, and I had given my opinion that our new sweeping force and net-laying vessels could not be ready more than about 10 days before that date.

In other words, the Army would be ready at about the same time as the Navy. So de Robeck's choice was apparently between risking another hazardous naval attack, with less ammunition, fewer capital ships, still suspect sweeping operations and once more the unsolved problem of Turkish mines, forts and guns; or a well-planned operation, which would land the Army, and keep naval communications open at the Straits for a possible future naval attack. The only argument at the meeting was whether the Army should land now, as Birdwood wanted, or wait for 29 Division and plan an organized landing, as Kitchener, and thus Hamilton, wanted. Of course, Kitchener's view was likely to prevail.[34]

The decision to postpone another naval 'ships alone' attack was probably an easy one for de Robeck to make. It was harder to persuade Churchill, who advanced several arguments in favour of continuing. One in particular was prescient. He asked de Robeck on 28 March what would happen if the Army was checked? De Robeck had no real answer to this, except to say that an intact navy could still try to force the Straits if required. But de Robeck noted the danger of the Straits closing up behind the fleet if they did get through to the Sea of Marmora, so he advised Churchill that it was better to prepare for a decisive joint effort about mid-April, 'rather than risk a great deal for what may possibly be only a partial solution.' It would only be a delay of about fourteen days before the Army opened the Straits. De Robeck added that it was not a practical operation to land a force just to destroy the guns, because of considerable Turkish opposition, and Ian Hamilton had agreed with this. And there was no point in occupying Bulair because the Turks would not abandon the peninsula. But de Robeck did expect that as soon as the Army was established ashore, with the Army's main objective being the Kilid Bahr plateau, then the combined army-navy attack on the Narrows would be able to start, with the Army and Navy side by side. Indeed, de Robeck's plans after the Army landing of 25 April called for bombarding the forts and sweeping the Kephez mine field by the third day, i.e. 27 April. For de Robeck and the Navy, therefore, 25 April was still going to be a joint operation, with the original naval objective still realizable in the near future. But since the Navy could not deal with the Turkish mines and forts, then the Army was needed to open the Straits. For the Army, however, the naval objective was initially subordinated to making sure the Army was properly ashore. As it turned out, of course, this joint scheme did not work, and it was de Robeck who eventually cabled Churchill on 11 May, saying that the Army had failed, and asking whether the Navy should try again to force the Straits. It was not until 13 May, after a strongly worded note from First Sea Lord Admiral Sir Henry Jackson on 11 May, arguing against further naval attacks, together with pressure from Fisher, Asquith, Hankey and others, 'to bring Churchill to his bearings', that Churchill theoretically gave up on the idea of an independent naval attack.[35]

However, after the meeting of 22 March, Hamilton wired de Robeck that the War Office still cherished hopes of a naval breakthrough, and suggested to de Robeck that 'I think wisest procedure will be [for the Navy] to push on systematically though not recklessly in attack on Forts.'

If the Navy succeeded, Hamilton wanted de Robeck to leave him enough light cruisers for his own military operations. If the Navy did not succeed, then they understood each other, i.e. the Navy would simply help the Army. Hamilton was being generous to de Robeck, because he did not really expect the Navy to succeed, and already on 23 March, Aspinall produced the outline of what was basically to be the plan for the landing of 25 April, focussing on Helles, Morto Bay, and the area north of Gaba Tepe. On the same day 23, March, Hamilton wired Kitchener that he now needed the whole army force to deal with the 40,000 Turks on Gallipoli. Meanwhile, on Hamilton's General Staff, the cipher officer, Capt. Orlo Williams, remarked in his diary that the Army had little faith in the Navy, who could not touch the enemy howitzers, and would not be able deal with the new Turkish lines of defence and mines.[36]

As it turned out, the Allied naval attack was over after 18 March, though the Navy did not think so until May. What had gone wrong? On 19 March Hankey wrote a memo to Asquith, imploring him 'to appoint naval and military technical committee to plan out military attack on Dardanelles so as to avoid repetition of naval fiasco, which is largely due to inadequate staff preparation.' Hankey was quite right – the planning and staff work for the naval attack had been amateur and ineffective in London and at the Dardanelles. In the absence of proper planning a number of prominent politicians, together with Churchill and Kitchener, simply indulged in a Darwinian struggle for control of operations. Imaginative and grandiose ideas by a confident and optimistic ruling class, with an eye to their own reputations, were no substitute for careful planning. Even after the naval setback on 18 March and before the landing of 25 April, Hankey's diary reveals a bewildering variety of ideas, made more dangerous by the lack of a War Council meeting between 19 March and 14 May. Hankey himself wanted to switch objectives from the Dardanelles and attack Haifa and Beirut instead. Then on 6 April a meeting of Kitchener, Hankey and Churchill took place to discuss the Dardanelles operation and Hamilton's plans. One wonders who was actually in charge. No doubt this system, or rather, non-system, reflected the radical change from the simpler colonial warfare of the past to the professional needs of modern warfare.[37]

Even at the time, participants in the campaign worried about this simpler tradition. For example, on 30 March 1915, Wemyss argued that 'Amateur strategists and amateur warriors is what we are suffering from…' Wemyss was referring to London, but closer to home, a major cause of the naval failure lay with Carden himself, who proved very slow in implementing his own plans, and equally slow to recognize and solve the key difficulty of minesweeping. Carden was simply a poor commander, but he was senior to Limpus, Wemyss and de Robeck, and in the Navy, seniority meant everything. Another problem, according to the future Admiral Godfrey, present as Lt J.H. Godfrey, the navigating officer on *Euryalus*, was the low quality of de Robeck's staff. Godfrey felt they were light weights, chosen for their social skills rather than technical proficiency. Hence, the technical side of gunnery and communications was poor, especially because the problem of indirect naval fire was very difficult to solve. At a deeper level, the rivalry between army and navy also made for inefficiency. The competition between navy and army led the Navy to try their own operations in February and March without interference from the Army. Hence the Admiralty on 28 March simply stated that it had hoped not to involve the Army, but now the Army was necessary. In general, according to Godfrey, cooperation between the War Office and the Admiralty was limited: 'There was the land war and the sea war and that was that.' One example of this is the scribbled note by Hamilton, referring to his original purely verbal instructions from Kitchener: 'Wire K 'I would be glad if you would say to First Lord [Churchill] would like fleet'.' Godfrey also believed that conflicting relations at the top filtered down to the two organizations: 'During 1914–1916 relations at the top were strained and the subordinates followed suit. Mixing was not exactly frowned on but it was not encouraged…' More specifically, at the Dardanelles, 'close co-operation on the [naval] Commander – GSO (1) level was discouraged. The principals were too intent on getting their own way and didn't want staff officers interfering with their plans.' Of course, naval officers and men were keen to do their best, and did so bravely, yet the system tended to undermine their efforts.[38]

Finally, why continue the Allied campaign after the naval setback on 18 March? According to Hankey, the key reasons were the agreement to help Russia, and the need to maintain British prestige. Another reason was the optimism of important individuals, for example Churchill, Kitchener, and Hamilton himself, who underrated the Turks, overrated themselves, and relied on the fire power of the Navy. Underlying everything was the momentum of an operation, which grew more complex and more compelling all the time, especially after the mid-February government decision to provide troops, and Kitchener's telegram of 20 February to Maxwell in Cairo, that he was sending 10,000 troops to Lemnos, and warning Maxwell to prepare to send 30,000 Australian and New Zealand troops (Anzacs) to Lemnos also. The critical problem with Kitchener's idea was that he did not think the Navy would fail, and based his plans on that assumption. So he thought the troops would only be there to hold positions and forts already gained by the Navy, or would later form part of a large force to take Istanbul after the naval break through. When this didn't happen, Kitchener was left with issuing the unhelpful order that the operation must be carried through. Perhaps, as an unsigned note in Aspinall's papers claims, Kitchener was starting to become senile in 1915 (he was 65), and thus making poor decisions. In contrast, Birdwood and Hamilton thought in army terms of capturing either the Asian or Gallipoli side of the Straits in a major operation, and so getting the Navy through. Meanwhile, Churchill wanted a 'ships alone' victory, and when that did not happen, a joint army–navy operation, thereby still giving the Navy a second chance. Whatever the reasons for the growing number of Allied troops in the Straits area, their unorganized accumulation was the beginning of the chain of events that led to the Allied landing of 25 April on Gallipoli.[39]

Meanwhile, what were Liman von Sanders and the Turkish Fifth Army doing to anticipate an Allied landing?

TURKISH EXPECTATIONS OF THE ALLIED LANDINGS

Liman von Sanders, the German officer commanding Turkish Fifth Army, which defended Gallipoli and the Straits against the Allied landings of 25 April, generally anticipated the Allied landing sites quite accurately. However, one other area, Bulair/Saros, at the neck of the Gallipoli peninsula, particularly attracted his attention. This turned out not to be an Allied landing site, but the capture and interrogation of a British naval officer just before the Allied landings helped focus Liman von Sanders' attention on Bulair/Saros from 25 to 28 April.

★

Following the end of Allied naval attempts to force the Straits on 18 March, Turkish attention turned naturally to defence against the possibility of Allied landings on either side of the Straits. On 24 March 1915 Liman von Sanders, a German cavalry officer, Inspector of the Turkish Army, commander of the pre-war German military mission to update the Turkish army and commander of Turkish forces in the Caucasus in 1914, was chosen to command Fifth Army, defending Gallipoli and the Asian shore area. Already in January 1915, von Sanders had outlined his ideas for a defensive system. His first point was that the present defensive structure, set up by Enver Pasa, Supreme Military Commander in Istanbul, scattered the Turkish divisions too widely. This was feasible against small landings, but, 'Against landings of large troop formations, our divisions must be much more concentrated in order to be able to attack the enemy in strength during or after landing.'' This was easily remedied, but here, though, was the central problem, where would the Allies land?

Liman von Sanders suggested three possible landing sites, all based on the assumption that the Allies would land so as to attack Turkish batteries and fortifications from the rear. Starting firstly with the Asian shore, he predicted a landing at either Besike Bay or Kum Kale (where the French landing did actually take place), in order to attack the strong Turkish batteries and fortifications along the Straits' shore from the rear. Liman von Sanders argued for a defensive counterattack as the enemy troops moved inland from Kum Kale and crossed the Mendere River. Also, 3 and 11 Turkish Divisions were to be combined in a corps stationed at Erenkeui, where they could go in any direction, according to the Allied landing site. Officers were to be stationed where they could judge whether the landings were a feint or a serious operation. Mines were to be laid at Kum Kale, which was to be defended by one battalion. Bridges over the Mendere River were to be prepared for demolition. (As it turned out, the French did not reach the Mendere River, partly because their landing was a feint. On the other hand, the Turkish 3 Division did little, and actually used the Mendere River as a means of protecting themselves!) Secondly, Liman von Sanders turned his attention to what he called the European shore. Here, he predicted landings at either Seddulbahir (Helles) or Gaba Tepe, or both simultaneously, 'in order to advance against the batteries from the rear.' The 9 Division was to be moved closer to the middle of the sector, and 19 Division was to be stationed at Maidos. In this sector, Liman von Sanders was prescient, because Helles was the site of the main Allied landing, while Gaba Tepe was just south of the intended Anzac landing site of Brighton Beach. Finally, thirdly, Liman von Sanders identified the Saros/Bulair area. He suggested two aims of a potential Allied landing in this area. One was the rather difficult Allied task of covering the ground necessary to cross the isthmus and disable the Turkish batteries on the Sea of Marmora side. The other was to totally cut off Turkish troops on the peninsula by simply capturing the narrow neck of the isthmus. Without actually saying so, Liman von Sanders revealed his particular bias toward the Saros/Bulair area by assigning three divisions to guard it, 4 and 5 Turkish Divisions, which could be amalgamated, and 7 Division.[2]

This emphasis on the Bulair/Saros area is at variance with Liman von Sanders' later memoirs, where he claimed that he saw the Asiatic area as the greatest danger, then Seddulbahir, then Gaba Tepe, and last, Bulair/Saros. But he was quite correct in his memoirs when he identified intelligence reports and rumours out of Turkish embassies or consulates in such places as Athens, Sofia and Bucharest, which gave information on British and French forces preparing to land.[3] Turkish archives actually reveal a bewildering variety of alleged Allied plans. For example, on 22 March it was reported from sources in Italy that a combined Russian, French, British plan was underway. Russians would land on the Black Sea coast, and the French would land an African division at Saros. The British army from Egypt would land near Izmir. The Allied navy would also attack. The aim was the capture of Istanbul. On the same day, the Turkish military attaché in Rome focussed on French intervention. This report said that about 40,000 French would land, including colonial troops from Mauritania and Senegal. The commander was to be General d'Amade. Indian troops and Australians would also arrive from Egypt. Altogether, the force amounted to some 80,000 troops, which the military attaché thought exaggerated. (He was not so far out, since about 75,000 Allied troops did take part in the April landings. And he was correct about d'Amade and the French colonial troops.)[4]

With these various Turkish reports, and many others, it is not surprising that Liman von Sanders was unsure about Allied intentions. Yet, curiously, although his predictions as to where the Allies would land had all been based on the idea that the Allies were aiming to capture or demolish Turkish batteries and forts from the rear, Liman von Sanders was remarkably accurate in forecasting Allied plans, which actually had other reasons behind their choice of landing sites. There was one exception, however, to Liman von Sanders' accurate predictions, which he tried to play down in later years, and this was the Saros/Bulair area. One probable reason for this emphasis in Liman von Sanders' mind, was a remarkable incident that took place on 17 April, just eight days before the 25 April Allied landings. On this day, the British submarine E 15, commanded by

Capt. T.S. Brodie, tried to run the Straits to get into the Sea of Marmora. The submarine first hit one of the Turkish nets, and then was caught in a strong eddy off Kephez Point, and ran aground on a sandbank. As luck would have it, this was just by the Turkish Dardanos battery, which lost no time in shelling the submarine. One shell hit the conning tower and cut the unfortunate Brodie in half, plus six other crew were killed during the shelling, and the submarine filled with thick smoke. The rest of the crew surrendered, and were taken into captivity, including a certain Lt Palmer. This individual, who was an officer in the Royal Naval Volunteer Reserve, had been the British vice consul at Chanak. After hostilities broke out, Palmer apparently arrived in Athens in early March 1915 to report on the location of Turkish guns in the Straits. Palmer then joined the staff of de Robeck at Gallipoli as an Intelligence Officer. Wishing to see active service, Palmer volunteered to serve on E 15 as an Intelligence officer. After Palmer's capture, he was interrogated by Col. Djevad Bey, commanding the Straits Forts. Djevad Bey then sent a lengthy cipher to the Supreme Command in Istanbul on 20 April, with the results of Palmer's interrogation.[5]

Since this cipher message containing Palmer's interrogation is of critical significance, as it occurred just five days before the Allied landings of 25 April, it is given in full:

> Palmer, who was the Consul at Chanak, was captured and made a prisoner of war. He was accused of being a spy for the Allied powers. Also a certificate was found in the submarine showing that Palmer was a reserve officer. But we did not tell him that we had found this certificate. Palmer was told that he was accused of being a spy, and that is why he might be executed. Because no soldier wants to give information openly, Palmer wanted to talk privately. So I promised him that he would be regarded as a prisoner of war. Then, he agreed to give us information. I asked him about the Allied attack that was planned. He said that a British attack would be made against the Dardanelles with a force of 100,000 men, landing under the command of Gen. Hamilton. According to Palmer's statement, the Allies planned to land at Gaba Tepe. But as soon as they found out that the Turks had learnt of this attack, they changed their plans concerning Gaba

Tepe and Seddulbahir [Helles]. Also they did not think that their landing at Seddulbahir would be successful. Consequently, they decided to land in the Gulf of Saros, and in the region of the northern part of the Peninsula. Previously, they had planned to attack Gaba Tepe, Seddulbahir and even Besike. To support their attacks in these regions, they needed the support of their navy. In fact, they planned to make these attacks last Monday [presumably 12 April: the original date for the landings was 14 April], but they have now given up this plan. He does not have any information about the new attack plan. This information has been given by the ex-consul on the condition that his life be spared under this agreement. Please do not give the origins of this information, in order to ensure his safety. I have sent the prisoner of war [Palmer], and his goods that have been taken from the submarine, with this cipher. I beg you to accept him as a prisoner of war.

20 April 1915, the Commander of the Forts, Col. Djevad.[6]

The next day, the Supreme Command in Istanbul, obviously interested in what might be a real Intelligence coup, wanted Palmer to identify the threatened northern area. Djevad Bey replied: 'The name of the region which is around the Gulf of Saros as mentioned by the ex-consul that I wrote in the cipher, is the region between Imbros and Karacali on the northern coast of the Gulf [of Saros]. 21 April 1915.'[7]

It would seem that Palmer had to think quickly on his feet during this interrogation. On the one hand, he certainly did not want to be shot, but on the other hand, he did not want to give away the real Allied landing sites, which he certainly knew, having been an Intelligence officer on de Robeck's staff. So he adopted the risky strategy of giving the actual Allied landing sites, but then suggesting these had been cancelled due to a security leak. In their place, Palmer directed Turkish attention north to Saros/Bulair as the new Allied landing area. In his further explanation of what the northern region consisted of, Palmer gave a vague answer, although it did include the Anzac landing zone. As for the 100,000 Allied troops that would land, Palmer probably did not know the exact Allied figure, otherwise the logical solution would have been to minimize the number of Allied troops, in order to cause Turkish over-confidence. On the other hand, Palmer may just have been unable to think quickly enough on the question of numbers, or he did not think the question of numbers was significant. (Ironically, the actual number of Allied soldiers involved in the landings was in fact discovered by Fifth Army through a Turkish wireless intercept on 25 April.) Nevertheless, the timing of Palmer's capture and interrogation was extremely critical – just five days before the Allied landings on 25 April, although he did not give away this information. Now the question was: would the Supreme Command, and especially Liman von Sanders, be taken in by the Bulair/Saros disinformation from Palmer?[8]

Documents in the Turkish archives do not definitely answer this question, but one message on 22 April, and correspondence between Fifth Army and Supreme Command on 20 April, show that the information was at least disseminated. Other messages suggest a considerable focus on the Saros/Bulair region. For example, Fifth Army reported on 25 April that Allied ships were in Saros, and that help was needed. The next day, 26 April, Fifth Army urgently requested more ammunition for the Saros area. On the other hand, while the Turkish Official History mentions Palmer, it does so without emphasis, and does not claim an Intelligence coup. It is also the case that Liman von Sanders does not mention Palmer in his memoirs. Yet a significant first hand observer of Liman von Sanders at his GHQ on 25 April and following days, Capt. Carl Mühlmann, describes in detail how Liman von Sanders focussed on the Saros/Bulair region to an unusual degree over the next four days.[9]

Mühlmann awoke early on Sunday 25 April, to the sound of gunfire. He was at Liman von Sanders' GHQ at the town of Gelibolu, when a staff officer rushed in with news of landings at Seddulbahir and Ari Burnu (Anzac), as well as of a transport flotilla in the Gulf of Saros. (This was part of an Allied feint by Hamilton at Bulair/Saros.) Liman von Sanders immediately alerted 4 Division to march to Bulair. Mühlmann takes up the story:

> Unfortunately, L[iman] was somewhat nervous and instead of centralizing all telephone connections and remaining at the choke point – GHQ – he swung up on his horse and, accompanied by the two of us [Mühlmann

and another staff officer] rode up to the heights near Bulair. Unfortunately, this meant that all reports were delayed 1–2 hours and the entire traffic between us and GHQ was made much more difficult…

Admittedly Bulair was the nearest danger zone to the German GHQ at the town of Gelibolu, but Liman von Sanders could also have headed toward Ari Burnu, or to Maidos, as a more central location to the known landings of Ari Burnu and Seddulbahir. In fact, while Liman von Sanders' party was at Bulair, news of the Kum Kale French landing came in. Esat Pasa, GOC Turkish III Corps asked permission to move his HQ to Maidos, and this was granted. Yet Liman von Sanders continued to focus on Bulair.[10]

Mühlmann relates that the small party reached the heights above Bulair in time to see a heavy naval bombardment of the fort there. Mühlmann already noted the limited effect of naval fire – the shell craters were immense, but did no damage unless there was a direct hit, although 'the psychological effect is tremendous.' Perhaps this influenced Liman von Sanders, because when evening came on 25 April, instead of returning to his GHQ at Gelibolu, Mühlmann commented: 'to our great surprise, he [Liman] decided to spend the night out here; we could not find out why because we had no telephone line to GHQ.' Mühlmann was sent on a mission the next day, 26 April, to Maidos with orders to concentrate 5 Division closer to Bulair, while 7 Division was sent to Seddulbahir. However, Liman von Sanders again planned to spend the entire day of 26 April on the heights above Bulair. (Meanwhile, Mühlmann was now down at Maidos, where an Allied submarine, evidently the Australian submarine AE2, fired nine torpedoes at a troop transport and missed, probably because the torpedoes failed to explode. Then AE2 surfaced and hailed a sail boat to ask directions, 'really an incredible piece of cheek!' noted Mühlmann. The AE2 sailed into the Sea of Marmora and, according to Mühlmann, did not sink any transports before being forced to the surface and scuttled. A Turkish message notes that the AE2 was followed by the German Capt. Merten, and fired on.) After the submarine episode, Mühlmann returned to Liman von Sanders at Bulair, and was ordered to remain there to observe, while

Liman von Sanders went, on 27 April, to check on the situation at Maidos and Ari Burnu.[11]

Mühlmann thought his sojourn at Bulair was over on 27 April, when the fleet disappeared from the Gulf of Saros. Liman von Sanders met Mühlmann at GHQ at Gelibolu and informed him that all was well at Ari Burnu, and that the French were hurled into the sea at Kum Kale, which was, of course, the planned French re-embarkation from Kum Kale. Liman von Sanders had also witnessed the shelling across the peninsula by the *Queen Elizabeth* of a Turkish transport, usually seen by historians as a significant blow, but Mühlmann remarked 'Thank God, it was not loaded, and sank within one minute.' Apparently Liman von Sanders returned from Maidos to his GHQ at Gelibolu by sea on 27 April, aboard the *Barbarossa*, at which a submarine fired two torpedoes and missed. This was probably the British submarine E14, and a success-ful torpedo attack would certainly have changed the campaign had Liman von Sanders gone down with this ship. The next day, 28 April, news came into von Sanders' GHQ that the enemy was being reinforced at both Ari Burnu and Seddulbahir, and so, at this time, 7 Division and most of 5 Division were recalled from Bulair to move south via Maidos. This decision is at variance with Liman von Sanders' memoirs, where he claimed to have recognized Bulair/Saros as a feint by 26 April.[12]

However, neither Liman von Sanders nor Mühlmann were finished with Bulair. While on his way to a different task on 28 April, Mühlmann,

> became despondent when, looking beyond the heights [at Bulair] I saw the transport fleet back in the Gulf of Saros. It was clear to all of us that we were only dealing with a bluff, otherwise they would have landed several days ago – in addition, the ships rode too high in the water to be fully loaded. Of course, L[iman's] specific concern about protecting his rear at Bulair was to be expected, and therewith came the danger that I was to be left there again.

Mühlmann's fear was only too accurate, since Liman von Sanders came up, and informed Mühlmann that he would move his HQ to Maidos, but Mühlmann was to be stationed at Bulair as Liman von Sanders'

plenipotentiary and general staff officer. I [Mühlmann] made a deeply disappointed face and explained my wish to him [to get closer to the actual
war theatre]. At first, he [Liman von Sanders] did not wish to consider it,
because after seeing the enemy fleet, new fears had swelled up in him. But,
finally, he gave in…[13]

Thus, it is clear that Liman von Sanders remained heavily preoccupied
with the Bulair/Saros area over the period of four days between 25 and
28 April, and was still inclined to worry about this area as late as 28 April,
when major Allied operations were obviously focussed at Anzac and
Helles. Of course, Liman von Sanders was right to consider Saros/Bulair
as a danger area, and in addition there was the Allied naval feint at
Saros/Bulair, but Liman von Sanders also appeared to show an unreason-
able interest in this area.[14] It is entirely possible that the capture and interrogation of Lt Palmer just before 25 April, with his disinformation about
the Allies choosing Saros/Bulair as their main landing area, helped to
confirm Liman von Sanders' preoccupation with this zone. The documents do not specifically reveal this, but Liman von Sanders' focus on
Saros/Bulair, and his hesitation in sending the Bulair divisions south, certainly gave the Allied landings on 25 April a breathing space they might
not otherwise have expected.

THE ALLIED LANDINGS AT HELLES AND KUM KALE

25 April 1915

Planning for the Allied landings of 25 April was complicated by a lack of under-standing between army and navy. In the Helles area, five landing sites were selected: S, V, W, X and Y. The British troops assigned to these beaches from 29 Division and the Royal Naval Division, were as follows: S Beach: three compa-nies of the 2nd Battalion South Wales Borderers, and a detachment of Royal Engineers. V Beach: the 1st Battalion Royal Dublin Fusiliers; the 1st Battalion Royal Munster Fusiliers; part of the 2nd Battalion Hampshire Regiment; part of the Anson Battalion of the Royal Naval Division; and a company of Royal Engineers. W Beach: 1st Battalion Lancashire Fusiliers, followed by the 4th Battalion Worcestershire Regiment. X Beach: the 2nd Battalion Royal Fusiliers, followed by the 1st Battalion Royal Inniskilling Fusiliers and the 1st Battalion Border Regiment. Y Beach: the 1st Battalion Kings Own Scottish Borderers and the Plymouth Battalion Royal Marines of the Royal Naval Division. At Kum Kale, the French 6th Colonial Regiment of 1 French Division landed. Generally speaking, where the Navy succeeded in its tasks, so also did the particular landing. The temporary landing of the French at Kum Kale caught the Turkish defenders unprepared, but elsewhere the defensive strength of modern Turkish weapons and trenches caused heavy Allied losses, especially at V and W beaches.

★

As far back as 18 March, Hamilton told Kitchener that if the Army had to take Gallipoli by force, then 'we shall have to proceed bit by bit.' Hamilton also considered that, 'It is the first step of landing under fire which is the most anxious as well as the most important in this operation.'[1] The fact was that an amphibious landing was going to be a very complex and difficult mission, and it was not clear how it was going to be achieved. So much so that Hunter-Weston, commanding 29 Division, the key element of the landing at Helles, wondered beforehand whether the operation should be cancelled, and wrote to his wife on 7 April 1915 that 'the odds against us are very heavy. However, nothing is impossible...'[2] In addition, Birdwood, who had been involved in the operation longer than Hamilton, blamed the Navy very much for taking away surprise, which gave the Turks time to produce 'a network of wire and entrenchments...' Birdwood particularly feared Turkish artillery fire at the landings, and believed that a landing on the Asian side would have the greatest chance of success. But, if this was not possible, Birdwood felt, like Hamilton, that once his troops had got a footing ashore, 'all will be well.' Faced with some pessimism among his senior commanders, Hamilton rather naturally complained to Kitchener of three or four senior officers seeing too many difficulties, although Braithwaite, his chief of staff, was supportive. It is certainly understandable that Hamilton wanted optimism and a cheerful outlook, rather than defeatism, among the commanders who would actually carry out the landings.[3]

In fact, this pessimism is a little strange, and may perhaps represent a safety outlet by Birdwood and Hunter-Weston, who, if there was a disaster, could point to their earlier warnings. And despite Hamilton's defence of Braithwaite to Kitchener, Braithwaite was also a little apprehensive about the landing himself, since he felt that there was no surprise left, and if the weather turned foul in the middle of the landing, there would certainly be trouble.[4]

One other problem was confusion between army and navy – the Army thought the Navy was there in April to soften up the defences, and help them land, while the Navy focussed on preparing for a combined army/navy attack on the Narrows. This probably accounts for the modest effort the Navy made between late March and the landings in April in attacking Turkish positions, together with the long delay in working out efficient sweeping operations. In this regard, Lt Blackie wrote of the rather casual operations of his battleship, the *Triumph,* in April:

> For our part we patrolled the coast from Cape Helles to Suvla Bay occa-
> sionally putting a salvo into any place where we saw the Turk making fresh
> trenches. Some amusing incidents occurred. I remember the *Scorpion*
> destroyer signalling to her opposite number on patrol: 'Have just fired 6
> rounds at a camel but the beggar is still grazing peacefully.'

Then on 5 April, Gibson, on the *Albion,* remarked that the Captain of the *Albion* was now the new commander of sweepers. This was positive because 'up to date sweepers have been shockingly run and achieved very little.' On 7 April, he wrote rather surprisingly that the Army was all for helping the Navy, and 'not for making it a military operation. So it's cheering.' Later, on 25 April, startled by the problems of the landings, Gibson commented: 'All through we've been kept terribly ignorant of the military situation.' On the same lines, signs of strife between army and navy began to appear. For example, Wemyss wrote angrily to de Robeck, around 25 April: 'I think that the GHQ are the most inconsid-erate people I have ever come across… they look upon the Navy as their sort of slavey.' A few days later, Wemyss complained about both the French and the Anzacs, and scolded Col. Elliott, a Staff officer on the Lines of Communication, who either could not, or would not, build piers: 'Is there nobody who can give him an order!'[5]

Whatever the difference of viewpoint between navy and army, the key question in late March and early April, was where to land the Army. Liman von Sanders had already made some clever appreciations of the possibilities. Now Hamilton had to make the actual decision. Some unsigned and undated notes in the Keyes papers appear to be Hamilton's original plans laid out for Keyes and de Robeck at the critical meeting of 22 March. These called for landings at Helles and Morto Bay (the future S Beach), with Achi Baba as the first objective, then the Kilid Bahr plateau as the ultimate objective. At the same time 'a feint will be made near Kaba Tepe which will probably develop into a landing and the securing of a covering position on foothills of Sari Bair…' Finally, a demonstration would be made at Bulair/Saros. Of interest here is the fact that the Anzac landing was not yet fully established, except as a feint, and there is no mention of Asia. But at the beginning of April, Birdwood counselled an Asian side landing, fearing Turkish gunfire from the Asian side onto Morto Bay and Helles generally. Hamilton replied, telling him that the Turks could not reach Morto Bay, the nearest beach to the Asian side, because they needed a 9.2 inch or better gun to make the distance (Hamilton was later proved wrong here – Asian guns did reach Morto Bay). Next, Hamilton pointed out that Kitchener's instructions forbade the Asiatic side. Then, Hamilton rejected the Bulair/Saros area because the landing could be attacked from several directions, as would also be the case at Besike Bay, south of Tenedos. Finally, Hamilton stressed what was obviously the most important point for him, which related to the original idea of the landing. The Army must work with the fleet 'thereby and thereby alone, am I fully acting on the spirit of my Instructions. I have not come here with any other purpose whatsoever but to help get the Fleet through the Dardanelles.' Later, Hunter-Weston produced a mild criticism of Hamilton when he said that Hamilton had been over influenced by the power of naval guns to help cover the landings. Hamilton replied that he was justified in this; for example, on 28 April he saw a whole company of Turks wiped out by a shell from the *Queen Elizabeth*. But after this, the Turks carefully avoided naval shelling by moving at night, or using cover in the day. In any case, what is clear is that plans for the choice of landing at Helles were based almost entirely on the need for naval support. So the Army was landing purely to help the Navy, but in order to do so, the Navy was crucial in helping the Army to land. Ends and means were getting a little confused.[6]

Further plans were suggested by Aspinall on 23 March. He rejected the Asian side, not only because of Kitchener's views, but because it would leave an exposed flank, the country was difficult, and in particular, the chief Turkish defence of the Narrows was on the European side. Bulair/Saros was heavily defended, the front was narrow, the Navy could not help much, and it was far from Kilid Bahr, the ultimate objective. On the other hand, Cape Helles and Morto Bay would be best supported by navy guns, and Achi Baba was not as strong an obstacle to Kilid Bahr as

Bulair. Another landing north of Gaba Tepe would provide a simultaneous attack on Kilid Bahr, and prevent reserves from reaching Helles.
Because surprise was no longer possible, an important factor would be to
mislead the enemy with a feint at Bulair/Saros. Up to this point, there
was no plan for the French.[7]

Surprise had been given up, not only because of the naval assault, but
because the Royal Naval Division and the 29 Division had not been
shipped in an organized manner for combat, and so had to shift to
Alexandria to repack. Hamilton and his staff also left for Egypt in late
March to organize the landing, and did not arrive back in Mudros until
10 April. More details were worked out at this time, including Hamilton's
basic strategy to upset the equilibrium of the Turks by rapid deployment
of his forces over a wide area, plus feints all along the coast. The Anzacs
would land at Gaba Tepe, but the main landing was to be at Seddulbahir,
Cape Helles and Morto Bay. The Naval Division would feint at Bulair.
Hamilton's idea of dislocating the Turks over a large area was a good one,
and this concept was what produced the large number of landing sites, S
at Morto Bay, V, W and X at Helles, with Y a late Hamilton addition to
create even more dislocation for the Turks. Then there was the Anzac
landing north of Gaba Tepe with a joint plan to cut off Turkish reserves
going south, as well as the goal of reaching Mal Tepe. There were also two
important feints at Kum Kale on the Asian side, and at Bulair/Saros. Here
it is interesting that the basic landing areas, apart from the French feint at
Kum Kale, came from the 22 March meeting and Aspinall's 23 March
plan, to which Hamilton had simply added his disequilibrium concept,
resulting in the larger number of beaches and feints. An enigmatic note
from Aspinall also noted that there were not enough boats for larger
landings at Krithia (Y Beach) and Morto Bay (S Beach), hence these
covering forces would be smaller landings.[8]

Hamilton's message of 15 April to Kitchener revealed his worry over
new trenches and entanglements created by the Turks. But on 23 April,
Hamilton revealed his basic attitude to the operation, which was that
the landing itself was the decisive act.[9] This attitude resulted in an
important under-emphasis on what was to happen *after* the landing. Of
course, Hunter-Weston had grandiose plans for a four phase advance to

beyond Achi Baba on the first day, but in a letter to his wife on 27 April, he also stressed the landing itself, because he had reckoned there was a 4 to 1 chance against the landing succeeding: 'We have managed it, we have achieved the impossible! Wonderful gallantry on the part of Regimental officers and men has done it.' Hunter-Weston thought that with the landing achieved, half the difficulties were over, and then with Achi Baba taken, three quarters of the difficulties would be over.[10] Hence, part of the problem over the next few days was that the incredible effort and resulting casualties put into the landing itself undermined future operations.

One important question to be considered was whether the landings should be undertaken in the dark or at dawn. Hamilton actually favoured a night landing, but Hunter-Weston argued for a dawn landing, fearing that darkness would lead to confusion via unknown beaches and strong currents. Hunter-Weston got his way, and it is hard to argue with his reasoning.[11] In this, as in several other decisions, Hamilton deferred to the general who would actually carry out the landings. Another point was what the troops were to do immediately after the landings were completed. Aspinall was one of the chief planners at GHQ, and he placed Brigadier-General Hare, GOC of 86 Brigade, 29 Division, in charge of the covering force at Helles from Y Beach to S Beach. But at a meeting on 21 April, Hunter-Weston told Hare he was only in charge of V, W and X Beaches, and then only to make good the line from Y Beach to Seddulbahir. At that point Hunter-Weston would take charge of the whole 29 Division, and advance on Achi Baba. In other words, Hunter-Weston wanted to be in charge of the triumphant advance to Achi Baba, while it is notable that Y and S Beaches were devalued to being only anchors for the other beaches to advance. Part of the later difficulties with Y Beach no doubt also occurred because this beach was Hamilton's idea, and did not please Hunter-Weston. For Hunter-Weston and 29 Division staff, Y Beach was too far away from the other landings to be useful. Thus Hunter-Weston had his own ideas, and did not welcome suggestions or alterations. The GSO 3 of 29 Division remarked in his diary for 24 April: 'Gen. Hunter-Weston again, in his highly strung way, going through the arrangements for the landing, the naval artillery support of the ships and his over sanguine four phases of the advance to beyond Achi Baba on the very first day. We none of us said what we thought.'[12] Evidently Hunter-Weston did not expect free discussion, and was becoming more optimistic as the actual landing approached, a psychological phenomena which was not peculiar to him alone, but tended to influence Western Front generals just before offensives started.

Looking at the actual landings, it will be convenient to start with S Beach, in Morto Bay, the furthest east of the landings. This beach, together with Y, was supposed to be a flanking beach for the main operations at V, W and X. Strangely enough, given the relative ease with which the landings actually occurred at S, there was particular apprehension beforehand about the problems of this beach. Rear-Admiral Wemyss, in charge of naval cooperation at Helles, considered S Beach a more doubtful landing than any other, and so sent a message (2043) to Capt. Alexander Davidson, commanding *Cornwallis*, the ship that was to conduct the S Beach landing, at 9.16 p.m. on 24 April. The message read: 'When you take trawlers up to Morto Bay, instead of returning immediately, you are to remain to support them until the troops are landed then returning to your anchorage. Destroyers will also be there. Report if you thoroughly understand.' Davidson reported back obediently: 'Thoroughly understood.' However, it seems that Davidson took the implied anxiety about S Beach only too thoroughly to heart. The landing was to be a small one due to the shortage of boats, and not because the beach was unsuitable – Morto Bay was in fact a wider and more suitable beach than the next-door V Beach.[13] In any case, only two companies of the South Wales Borderers, and a detachment of engineers, were assigned to the S Beach landing, which was on the far side of Morto Bay. Their task was to land close to a battery located there and ensure that the battery did not fire on the flanks of the main landings at Helles as they advanced. But as it turned out, the Turkish opposition consisted of only one platoon, and the landing was successful, due to surprise and the tactic of outflanking the Turkish opposition. Davidson also personally landed at S Beach, a most unusual step, and he also landed marines and sailors from *Cornwallis*, a completely unauthorized action. Davidson said that he landed to 'personally assume naval direction', and because he feared that the boats would not arrive. Davidson did this because he had made prior arrangements with the South Wales Borderers to support their landing with some of his crew, since the landing force was so small. Davidson also argued that he kept *Cornwallis* longer at S Beach than necessary because he 'felt bound in humanity to bring off the wounded', because he feared fouling the transports, and because of the need to fire at Turkish resistance at S Beach.[14]

The S beach landing was a success, with a total of 63 casualties to the South Wales Borderers, marines and sailors. Davidson's actions at S Beach might partly be explained by the duties of attendant ships, which, among other things, were to oversee beach parties, and to evacuate the wounded.[15] Still, Davidson's actions were not only strange but were damaging to the situation at V Beach next door. This was because Davidson's orders were that as soon as the S Beach landing was completed, *Cornwallis,*

> was to [immediately] proceed to V when [where] she was attendant and charged with the duty of regulating the landing. Admiral Wemyss' signal 2043 in no way qualified this… several tows went in [to V Beach] to suffer severe loss – which should have been diverted or held up – Fleet sweepers full of men hung about waiting for orders – in fact the landing at V Beach was not regulated!

Keyes reported that 'V Beach was left for some hours with *Albion* only in attendance – But for the arrival of the *Queen Elizabeth* the Military might well have had good reason to complain at the failure of the Navy to carry out the covering and landing operations as arranged.'[16] Keyes had good reason to criticize Davidson and *Cornwallis*, but although Davidson could have mitigated the problems at V Beach, there were other difficulties, including naval errors, that made V Beach a very dangerous place for those trying to land there.

V beach was a natural amphitheatre. There was a broad and gentle sandy beach, but this was surrounded by high ground behind the beach, and by headlands to the left and right. Viewed from the sea, the old fortress of Seddulbahir, with massive walls, also dominated the beach from its location on the eastern side. Under Liman von Sanders, the Turks had prepared trenches and wire, and put in place four machine-guns and four 37mm pom poms. It was in fact a very strong Turkish defensive position, and Allied success depended on the naval bombardment to destroy these defences before the men landed. But here there was considerable confusion. On 12 April, de Robeck issued a memo to Ian Hamilton, informing him that the covering ships would 'anchor to enable ranges to be obtained (by firing ranging shots at likely targets) and thus ensure rapidity in shifting fire to a new object.' Thus it was important to anchor for the ships' fire to be accurate. The first targets would be enemy artillery, and then, secondly, enemy troops in the open or in trenches, although 'the shelling of enemy's trenches, except to cover an infantry attack or for other specific object, is, as a rule, a waste of ammunition.' Despite de Robeck's caution, the Army did rely heavily on the Navy, for example, Godley, commanding the Anzac Division, wrote that the heavy naval bombardment would 'clear away all the obstacles etc., on the beach, and so batter the enemy's defences as to make it comparatively easy for the troops to land.'[17]

It was on 21 April that a critical meeting of naval captains took place on board *Euryalus*, with Wemyss in the chair. At this meeting, the original idea of anchoring offshore and bombarding the beaches and approaches was changed to bombarding the coast ridges during the landings, although the beaches would still be shelled *before* the landings. However, Capt. Lockyer of the *Implacable*, declared that he would also shell the beaches on the way in to land the troops. Roger Keyes opposed Lockyer's idea and replied vehemently that 'You will never be able to pick up the range quick enough', referring to the lack of an effective change of range gunnery system, meaning that ships' guns could not easily assimilate moving range changes and bearings. As a result, no definite decision was reached over close-in fire support for the landings, and the initiative was left up to individual captains, with the orders for 23 April simply stating: 'Ships will cover the landing and support its advance.' According to Lt-Col. W.G. Braithwaite, GSO 1, Anzac Division, this open-ended decision annoyed the Army, since 'the Army naturally wants everything cut and dried, [but] the Navy appears averse to this.'

Nevertheless, the Navy did also decide that in order to allow the captains to make their own decisions, the directive that battleships and destroyers should anchor offshore was cancelled. But, according to Capt. Lockyer, commanding *Implacable*, the 'Chief of Staff's [Keyes] remark carried a great influence', meaning that naval captains would now be reluctant to shift from their anchored positions, and move in to closely support the landings with shelling. This reluctance to approach the shore was to be the case for the two landings that initially suffered the greatest infantry losses, V and W, while close-in naval support helped the Army very considerably at S, X and Anzac. Moreover, Keyes seems to have over-looked the fact that while it was difficult to adjust firing ranges as the ships approached the shore, once anchored close to shore, the problem presumably disappeared, unless enemy artillery fire drove the ships further offshore.[18]

At V Beach, the plan was to first land the great majority of the Dublin Fusiliers from tows. Then, 30 minutes later, the Munster Fusiliers, plus the remaining Dublins, and half of the 2nd Hampshire Regiment, were to land from a converted collier named the *River Clyde*. The concept was a good one, the *River Clyde* was thought of partly as a naval Wooden Horse, to protect the troops from fire as they closed in to the beach, partly as a means of overcoming the shortage of small craft, and partly to be used later as a depot. The *River Clyde* would be driven into shore until she grounded, but since this would still be too far from shore for the troops to land, an attached steam hopper, and three wooden lighters were to act as bridges to the beach. Unfortunately, the plan miscarried. As Wemyss explained later, when the *River Clyde* touched bottom, the steam hopper, instead of going ahead as planned,

> hung up alongside. It was only a long time afterwards that it was ascertained that her engines had been stopped before the *River Clyde* touched and that she consequently was pulled up at the same time, kept back by the towing line which did not slacken. When at last this was cleared and the hopper free, the latter was struck by a gust of wind as she forged ahead, and swinging away failed to place herself between the ship and the shore.

According to the historian Eric Bush, the engines of the hopper were actually reversed by the Greek crew. In addition, the wooden lighters, towed alongside the hopper, also did not move forward as required. This small mistake regarding the steam hopper was actually very costly for the troops inside the *River Clyde*, since they now did not have a bridge to the beach. Commander Edward Unwin and Able Seaman Williams jumped into the water and heroically formed a bridge by linking two of the lighters to a spit of rocks jutting out from the right side of the beach, but even so this was a death trap for the troops leaving the *River Clyde*. As Capt. Guy Geddes of the Royal Munster Fusiliers reported: 'there was a small rocky spit jutting out into the sea which was absolutely taped down by the Turks and few, if any, survived who attempted to land there.' Others who jumped into the sea and attempted to swim ashore were weighed down with a full pack, 250 rounds of ammunition, and rations for three days, and many drowned. No doubt if the steam hopper and attendant lighters had been placed according to plan, this would have provided a quicker and easier route to the beach, and would have saved lives, although casualties would probably still have been heavy.[19]

Capt. Geddes' account relates that the men of the Dublins who came in on tows, rather than in the *River Clyde*, 'were literally slaughtered like rats in a trap' as the Turks opened a 'terrific rifle and machine-gun fire.' As for his own company, leaving from the port side of the ship, Geddes heard later that the first 48 men who followed him all fell wounded or killed. Those who did reach the beach were saved by one curious factor – there was a sandy bank or ledge running across the beach, some three to five feet tall, behind which all the survivors sheltered. Without this, all those except for the troops who landed on the far right-hand side of the beach underneath the fort would have become casualties. Even on the right-hand side, it seems that the actions of one man, Sergeant Ryan, who continuously kept the right flank under reconnaissance, prevented the Turks from enfilading the line from the right of the fort. In this situation, the only thing that could have helped was accurate naval fire. But this did not happen for a number of reasons. First, the covering ship, *Albion*, was anchored some 1,400 yards out, too far away to do any useful shooting without observation, while secondly, *Cornwallis* did not arrive at V Beach from S Beach until 11.45 a.m., and only then took over as 'attendant ship', due to Capt. Davidson's unusual behaviour. Even when *Cornwallis* did arrive, Davidson reported that although his ship plastered the slopes between Seddulbahir and the light house (on the left headland), this did not produce 'any tangible result.' This was because, like *Albion*, *Cornwallis* was also too far out to fire accurately. A somewhat intemperate letter after the war from Commander Unwin claimed that if *Cornwallis* had come round to V Beach immediately and sailed right in, this would have saved hundreds of lives. Instead, wrote Unwin, Davidson chose to go for a 'joy ride' at S Beach, where 25 Turks opposed his landing, and so 'he ought to have been court martialled.' In fairness to Davidson, he did not know of the problems at V Beach until he arrived there, but his actions were still unfortunate.[20]

It seems, therefore, that the attending and covering ships were too far out to do any useful observation of targets at V Beach. This critical problem really stemmed back to Roger Keyes' pronouncement at the Admiral's meeting of 21 April. Without surprise, or good observation, either from an observer on shore, or from close in ships, naval fire was never going to be decisive, and yet accurate naval fire was essential. Theoretically, naval fire could have been observed from the *River Clyde*, but communications were not set up to do this, and according to signals information, there was only visual communication from shore to ship at V Beach, and no information could be got out of the *River Clyde*. Visual communication was also obscured by smoke and mist. However, naval fire was not totally useless. Two of the Turkish pom poms were knocked out early, and the other two were hit by the end of the day. *Albion* also 'fired at intervals at places where maxims might be concealed…', and despite the vagueness of this, it was later claimed, managed to knock out a machine-gun in Seddulbahir fort at 2.00 p.m. Later, at 6.30 p.m., *Albion* was ordered to close in to support an attack, and did so, and probably knocked out another machine-gun. But why not do this earlier? Capt. Geddes summed up the lack of success of the naval fire in his account of the action, by writing simply: 'The guns of *Albion* did no material good.' The other ship involved was *Queen Elizabeth*, which arrived at V Beach around 8.30 a.m. Here, according to Aspinall, an unfortunate message was received at that hour reading: 'Do not shell the forts and village of Seddulbahir. Our troops are there.' *Queen Elizabeth* then asked: 'Where do you want us to fire?' The answer was 'At large white building on West of Beach V towards Hill 138.' This was the lighthouse on the left headland, and no doubt assisted the troops, but not as much as firing at the round tower at Seddulbahir would have done, because the tower, according to Aspinall, contained machine-guns. Aspinall may have been wrong about the tower, but the village was the source of much enemy fire.[21]

Queen Elizabeth's fire was not without effect, however, as she later plastered the village and fort in the early afternoon of 25 April, and did compel four sections of Turks to retire, although this was not enough to allow an Allied advance. A final factor, which prevented naval fire from being effective at V Beach, was reported by Gibson on board *Albion*. In his diary, Gibson noted that as the first tows of the Dublins approached the shore at V Beach at about 6.20 a.m., RA 1 (Wemyss) made the signal: "Cease Fire'. I don't know why, but so far as I can remember we were stopped firing while troops were landing, a great mistake, we ought to have gone on firing over their heads. The risk was not great.' Gibson also commented critically 'The landing arrangements seem to me to have been very badly thought out and to make no allowance for any enemy being there to oppose…'[22]

Another major problem, due to communication difficulties and military etiquette, prevented intervention at V Beach to improve matters. According to an irate Roger Keyes, RA1 (Wemyss) and Hunter-Weston (in charge of the landings at Helles) 'were in complete ignorance of what was going on anywhere except at W and possibly X Beach.' This may not be entirely accurate, since Hunter-Weston did realize that V was not succeeding. The wording of his diary, however, suggests that he thought the problems at V were temporary, and so he did not appear concerned. Hence, Hunter-Weston noted that S, W and X were all right, but 'V is hung up still.' However, Roger Keyes went on to argue that 'Nothing would induce Hamilton or de Robeck to interfere with Wemyss or Hunter-Weston…', so 'we sat off V all day, I nearly went crazy.' This non-interference policy by commanders in chief was a strong rule among Staff College trained officers, but equally among senior officers such as

Hamilton. The rule made sense in that interference by superiors with those carrying out orders would soon create chaos, plus resentment and resignations. On the other hand, at crisis points, such as V Beach on 25 April, intervention was certainly necessary. In fact, Hamilton did intervene to some extent when, at 11.30 a.m. and at 12.41 p.m., he ordered that troops bound for V Beach be diverted to W Beach. At the same time, communications were unreliable, since wireless transmission was not working at V Beach because of the severe conditions. Also, as the Signals War Diary noted:

> *Queen Elizabeth* [from which Hamilton commanded] not in WT touch as a rule with shore stations as she worked on 'S' wave. Delay therefore in getting shore messages through, due to (a) coding and (b) retransmission. Found impossible to work simultaneously on 'S' and 'S or Q' waves. Aeroplane WT unreliable. Signals from shore stations good, but very little sent through to *Queen Elizabeth*.[23]

At this point, Wemyss and Hunter-Weston were on board *Euryalus*, which was the attendant ship at W Beach. This meant that *Euryalus* could not leave W, and so both senior commanders were effectively locked in to one location at W, and unable to properly appreciate the problems at V or, as will be seen later, the opportunities at Y. To add to their problems, Wemyss' staff was too small for effective command, while Hunter-Weston and his chief of staff, Brigadier-General H.E. Street, were on the bridge of *Euryalus*, where every five minutes the 9.2 inch gun went off, making chaos of their papers![24]

Meanwhile, the frustration of the moment led Hunter-Weston into a typically 'Romantic War' gesture in trying to land personally to lead the V Beach troops. He was dissuaded, and it was pointed out to him that Seddulbahir could be more or less ignored, because troops on the flanks from S and W could enfilade the defenders of V Beach. This in fact began to happen from around 3.00 p.m., supported by accurate shooting from *Swiftsure* on Hill 138 in the centre of Helles. Meanwhile, at V Beach, the remaining troops from the ship were only able to disembark at night at about 8.30 p.m., this time with little trouble. The survivors lay down to spend a wet and unpleasant night. The next day, 26 April, a courageous series of attacks cleared the fort and village, and by 4.00 p.m., the Turks were reported to be in full retreat. In fact, although accounts of V Beach always stress the problems of the Allied landing, the Turks were not without their difficulties too. Capt. Merten, a German naval officer, sent a message on 25 April saying that he could not understand the situation at Helles. Another Turkish message of 25 April regretted that the Helles landings were out of the range of their artillery. Despite the valiant memoirs of Turkish Col. (then Maj.) Mahmut (commanding the 3rd Battalion of the 26th Regiment), which give the impression that the situation was relatively under control, captured papers suggest that Mahmut was confused. He did not discover the location of the landings for some time, and sent understandably strong appeals for help to 25th Regiment, which promised to arrive at 2.45 p.m. and promised arrival again at 4.15 p.m. on 25 April, before finally arriving at 1.00 a.m. on 26 April. One of Mahmut's platoon commanders, Abdul Rahman sent a pitiful response to Mahmut's orders to launch a charge at Seddulbahir. Rahman reported he only had 25 men, and instead appealed for help:

> Send the doctors to carry off my wounded, alas! alas! My Captain for God's sake send me reinforcements because hundreds of soldiers are landing. Hurry up, what on earth will happen, my Captain. From Abdul Rahman.[25]

Nevertheless, Col. Mahmut's memoirs do provide some insights into the Turkish attitude towards the initial overwhelming odds of the landings. Mahmut recalled that as the Turkish wounded came in, they obediently repeated what they had been trained to say: 'I have been wounded and cannot continue my duty, I have given my ammunition to my comrades in the section, here is my rifle, who should I hand it over to?' Mahmut also noted that the shore at V Beach 'became full of enemy corpses, like a shoal of fish. At Seddulbahir pier five boat loads of men were completely sunk.' However, Mahmut reported that at 3.00 p.m. on 25 April, Sergeant Yaha, defending the fort and flank at V Beach was forced to retreat, while Mahmut's battalion suffered over fifty per cent casualties. Mahmut goes on to record an apparent break-down of Turkish morale the next day, 26 April. At 1.30 p.m. that day, the remaining Turkish troops at V, outflanked by the S Beach landing, retreated up the Kirte and Kanlidere stream beds, leaving about seventy wounded behind, who were weeping and complaining. But no-one, except a stretcher bearer and a trumpeter, followed Mahmut to the second line of defence because of heavy Allied naval shelling. Although these two men shouted 'The second line of defence is here. The major is here, come on', none did so. Eventually, Mahmut's men retreated to within about one and a half kilometres from Krithia around 5.30 p.m. on 26 April. Casualties were 5 officers and 570 men. Then on 27 April there was relative calm for Mahmut's command, which lasted until the Allied offensive of 28 April.[26]

The landing at V Beach showed that without surprise, unless naval fire could overcome the heavy Turkish defensive advantage of trenches, wire, rifles and machine-guns, the attacker would suffer very considerably. This is what inevitably happened at V Beach, and the same situation essentially occurred at W Beach. Here, the landing by a covering force of the 1st Battalion Lancashire Fusiliers went ashore in eight tows, with four rowing boats per tow. The defending Turks had been reinforced by Maj. Mahmut, while W beach was surrounded by high ground, and formed a perfect trap for the landing parties. Capt. C.A. Milward, GSO 3 of 29 Division, on board *Euryalus*, described the conditions of W Beach as:

> a short stretch of sandy beach about 200 yards long and 10 yards wide, cliffs on each side, those on the left climbable, those on the right precipitous with a track accessible beneath them. The beach itself was covered with wire down to the water's edge and beneath it.

Inevitably, as the boats came within about 50 yards of this beach, Turkish fire began to devastate the Fusiliers. Milward heard the sound of rifle fire and then machine-gun fire, and wrote, strangely: 'Such a thing as the possibility of a landing effected against heavy machine-gun fire never entered one's head.' Why Milward should be surprised by this is not clear.[27]

Milward was disconcerted to notice a row of dead men on the beach, and boats empty of men coming back, each rowed by a sole wounded survivor, 'feebly swinging his oar.' Then a few Lancashire Fusiliers began to climb over the wire, but only two got across. Tows now began to land boats under the cover of the cliffs on both sides as protection. On the left in particular a group began to climb the cliff. At this point the Turks sent in a counterattack, but the Fusilier advance, led by the Brigade Major of 86th Brigade, Maj. Thomas Frankland, who seized a man's rifle and bowled over two of the leading Turks, continued over the edge of the cliff. Then the Turks again had a good field of fire, but Milward pointed out the offending Turkish trench to naval officers on board *Euryalus*, and some 9.2 inch shells cleared the trench out. This enabled the Lancashire Fusiliers to advance. It seems that naval fire was decisive here in enabling the landing to succeed, and the reason was that observation from *Euryalus* was obviously good enough to see the trenches on top of the cliff, which enabled accurate fire to be obtained. In support of this, a rating on board *Euryalus* wrote that while the Fusiliers were charging ahead, the ships (including destroyers) were 'raking the ground with shells and the Turks were also killed by their hundreds as they retreated.' However, a night time Turkish counterattack at W almost succeeded, so much so that the boats were called up by naval Commander Marriott to re-embark the Fusiliers. According to Capt. Milward, 'A good many men drifted back towards the beach, many bullets were flying about, and for a time there was a good deal of confusion in the dark.' All work parties on the beach were told to get their rifles and move to the trenches. Milward commented: 'But the sea stopped any long retirement and luckily there were no boats.' It was in response to this action that Turkish messages at this time considered the fight at W was already won. For example, one message announced that units of 26th Regiment had forced the Allies back to the beach with a bayonet charge; and another simply stated that the Allies who had landed at W were repelled. On the other hand, the second Turkish message was accurate in evaluating the number of new troops from the Essex, Worcester, Hampshire and Royal Scots battalions that were put ashore at W.[28]

W Beach appears to have succeeded due to the dash and bravery of the Lancashire Fusiliers, to the subsequent accurate shelling of *Euryalus* and other ships (particularly noted by the Turks), and to the fact that the cove at W was sheltered from Turkish covering fire from Hill 138. The next beach to the west was X Beach. Here, the landing of the 2nd Battalion Royal Fusiliers was accomplished with little difficulty because the one Turkish platoon that patrolled the area did not anticipate a landing at X Beach. In addition, *Implacable* under Capt. Lockyer, came in closer than *Euryalus* at W, and covered the landing with 'every available gun and except for distant rifle fire there was no opposition…' Nevertheless, there were strong Turkish attacks during the day, and in the evening, according to Hyde Harrison of the 1st Battalion Border Regiment, in the second wave of landings at X this Regiment nearly withdrew because they were 50 to 100 yards in front of the cliffs, and felt they were too extended. But when the Turks attacked at 11.00 p.m., they were able to close the gap between them and the Royal Inniskilling Fusiliers, and repel the attack. As well, Capt. Lockyer, when aroused at midnight due to the Turkish attack, reportedly exclaimed "What! The blighters attacking my beach? – give them hell', and dashes up to the bridge'. So the big shells from *Implacable* helped to smother the Turkish attempt to drive the Allied defenders of X into the sea.[29]

If X was an Allied success, Y Beach was a different story. It has already been noted that Hunter-Weston in his plans tended to devalue Y and S Beaches in favour of the main landings at V, W and X, and their subsequent projected advance to Achi Baba. Hamilton simply intended Y Beach to threaten the retreat of the Turks and prevent Turkish reinforcements from arriving. Hence there was no Turkish trench to take at Y, nor any particular objective, but just open ground. It is also remarkable that the Navy previously received orders to be extra careful with Y Beach. Trawlers, plus the destroyers *Amethyst* and *Sapphire*, would prepare to disembark the landing, yet 'Everything is to be ready for re-embarkation until orders are received from *Queen Elizabeth* 'that this battalion being established the boats can be withdrawn from the beach."[30] This was a sensible precaution, but reflected the late addition of Y Beach to the landings, and the peripheral function of the beach in the plans of Hunter-Weston.

The Y Beach landing went in successfully at 5.00 a.m., and the King's Own Scottish Borderers (KOSB) were on the cliff top by 5.15 a.m., with the Marines following soon after. Two and a half battalions of infantry landed easily at Y, some 2,000 men, but as there was no particular objective, the men wandered around, and no entrenching was done at that time. Patrols were sent out, and according to the KOSB officer, Stirling Cookson, C Company of the KOSBs entered Krithia. Essentially the troops did little during the day, until they were shelled by the Turks from the direction of Krithia at about 4.00 p.m. with shrapnel, and then attacked with infantry at 5.00 p.m. There was also an argument as to who was the senior officer present, Lt-Col. Koe of the KOSBs or Lt-Col. Matthews of the Royal Marines. This should obviously have been decided beforehand. As it turned out, Koe apparently landed with a temperature of 103 degrees, then was badly wounded, taken down to the beach, and later died of his wounds. Matthews twice tried to get in touch with the troops at X Beach, but failed, no doubt because of the distance between the two beaches, and the very steep gully in between. Then after one more venture inland, he decided to entrench around the head of the gully that led up from the beach, probably because there was water available there, and this location was where the troops defended against an all night attack from the Turks. Early the next morning, 26 April, around dawn, Matthews realized he was in trouble, since parties of men without ammunition were filtering down to the beach, as well as others taking the wounded down to the boats. In subsequent testimony, Matthews stated that he believed his depleted force could not withstand another enemy attack without reinforcements, and in particular, there was no ammunition left, so he acquiesced in the withdrawal to the beach and re-embarkation. Other sources believe that the Senior Naval Officer (SNO) present, Roger Keyes' brother, Adrian Keyes, ordered the withdrawal. Referring to the 600 wounded at Y, but perhaps with wider implications, Roger Keyes, wrote that 'Adrian did much towards extracting them and *ran* it...' On the other hand, Stirling Cookson stated that Matthews re-embarked his force because, with the rest of 29 Division held up, the timetable of the landing could not be maintained; because there were no picks and shovels; and because it was only a question of time before the force at Y was pushed into the sea. These appear to be after the fact arguments, and it seems more likely that Matthews lost control of the situation, and was forced to acquiesce in an already established withdrawal as the men began to trickle down to the beach without orders to do so.Yet, throughout 25 April the two and a half battalions at Y had been stronger than all the Turks at Helles and Seddulbahir.[31]

It is noteworthy that the log of *Sapphire*, one of two attending ships at Y Beach, records that she landed 20,000 rounds of .303 Mark VI ammunition at 5.00 a.m. on 26 April at Y Beach. Therefore, ammunition should not have been a problem for Matthews at that time. Reading between the lines, it seems that a breakdown in morale occurred at Y Beach after a sleepless night of heavy fighting. In the early morning of 26 April, *Sapphire*, and another attending ship, *Amethyst*, reported firing heavily on Turkish attacks at 5.00 a.m. and 6.00 a.m., but these salvos unfortunately hit their own troops, as it was difficult for the Navy to fire accurately at the flat land on top of the cliffs. But with clear daylight emerging, the Turks withdrew to avoid naval shelling. Even so, straggling was obviously occurring at Y, as was to be the case at Anzac Cove during the late afternoon and evening of 25 April, and also occurred at W Beach during the evening of 25 April. It is not surprising that straggling took place on some beaches because these were unfamiliar and intensely stressful situations. In addition, at Y Beach, communications were poor with 29 Division, and the sense of strain is evident in the several messages sent to 29 Division HQ by Matthews. It is normally assumed that Y Beach was ignored at 29 Division HQ, but in fact because Y Beach was considered less important than V, W and X, 29 Division HQ did not feel they could afford reinforcements for Y, and so answered Y Beach messages by essentially saying 'Don't shout – mind your own business, etc.' The other controversy surrounding Y Beach was Hamilton's effort to get Hunter-Weston and 29 Division staff to pay attention to this initial success. Thus, at 9.21 a.m. on 25 April, Hamilton asked 29 Division whether they would like to get men ashore on Y Beach if 10 trawlers were available. There was no answer, so Hamilton repeated the question and required an answer. At 10.45 a.m., 29 Division replied, on the advice of Wemyss, saying that putting men on Y Beach would delay disembarkation of troops elsewhere, so this was inadvisable.Yet only 15 minutes later, *Albion* reported that no more troops could be landed at V Beach anyway.

29 Division HQ was obviously at fault here, and once more was overly focussed on the main three beaches, and devalued Y Beach.[32]

There has been general condemnation of Hamilton for not ordering Hunter-Weston and 29 Division to land more troops on Y Beach. But it was not just that Hamilton did not want to interfere with Hunter-Weston, since GHQ did actually intervene on different occasions on 25 April, for example by diverting reserve troops from V to W at midday. In reality, the situation at V was not clear to Hamilton until *after* the reply from Hunter-Weston, while Hamilton did not want to intervene with the actual landings themselves. After all, GHQ's intervention could indeed have delayed disembarkation elsewhere, as far as GHQ knew on the early morning of 25 April. Later, Hunter-Weston did not mention Y Beach in his diary for 25 April, and focussed entirely on V and W, and Hill 138, also paying little attention elsewhere. His gaze was fixed firmly on the toe of the peninsula. In this context, Hunter-Weston was absolutely consistent with Western Front generals who tended to focus on where the opposition was strongest rather than where the enemy was weakest, and at this stage of the war, usually reinforced failure. One final note on Y is that Hunter-Weston, subsequently conscious of his mistake at Y, concealed the evidence from Hamilton until July 1915, by which time he had retired from the field of battle.[33]

One other landing in the south has often been overlooked, and this was the French landing at Kum Kale on the Asian shore. Despite criticism from Robert Rhodes James, this was one of the most successful landings on 25 April, albeit in strange circumstances. Originally the French were not to be involved in a landing, but it was deemed wasteful to have the French stand idly by, so a temporary landing was devised for Kum Kale, with the primary intention of specifically preventing the Turks from bombarding the S Beach transports. However, Franco-British relations were always a little awkward. Early in the naval stage of operations, the French army commander, Gen. Albert d'Amade, reported on 8 March that he and Carden were obviously using different codes, and couldn't contact each other. Then, on 15 March, when d'Amade arrived at Lemnos with half of his force, he had no idea of his objectives, dates, areas of operation, or whether he should disembark or not. Again, on 30 March, d'Amade cabled his Cabinet that Admiral Roneck [sic! – de Robeck] wanted to continue the naval attack, while Hamilton was entirely under the orders and influence of Lord Kitchener. Even on 22 April, things were still confused, because d'Amade didn't know whether to concentrate his forces at Tenedos or Mudros for the landing at Kum Kale. Finally, shortly after 25 April, d'Amade drafted a pointed telegram, asking Hamilton what his own role was to be – was he to command his own troops or not?[34]

The French landing of the 6th Colonial Regiment and an artillery battery at Kum Kale on 25 April started with a naval bombardment from *Henri IV*, *Prince George* and the Russian *Askold* at 5.30 a.m. However, the landing, commanded by Col. Ruef, was delayed because a strong four knot current meant that more powerful transports were required. This took time, and the first boats approached a broken wharf where it was difficult to disembark. The landing finally took place at around 9.30 a.m. There may have been some reluctance to land because of shelling that destroyed one Company, but strong leadership by Capitaine Brison (wounded) and Lt Bonavita (killed) produced the capture of the fort and village of Kum Kale by 11.15 a.m. on 25 April. Considerable assistance was provided by *Henri IV*, which came to within 25 metres of the shore and knocked out two machine-guns and their crews in a prominent windmill. At midday the second transports arrived, and all were finally ashore by 5.00 p.m. The artillery then played a large role in halting seven violent Turkish counterattacks at night. But the next morning, 26 April, a strange scene took place. The cemetery at Kum Kale was occupied by the Turks around 7.00 a.m., and it was here that some 50 to 60 Turks came forward holding white flags and handkerchiefs. These Turks threw down their arms and surrendered, but others waved white flags while still keeping their arms, and Turkish officers shouted 'Cease Fire'. Meanwhile, Turkish and French soldiers became mixed up, and so Capitaine Roeckel went forward to parlay with the senior Turkish officer at the cemetery. However, Roeckel was surrounded and never reappeared. Then the French resumed artillery and infantry fire, but this was difficult because French and Turks were mixed up together. In the confusion a number of Turks had been able to talk their way into French lines, and into houses occupied by the French, as well as capture two machine-guns. By midday the French managed to regain the lost houses and ground, although an attempt to recapture the machine-guns failed with large losses.[35]

The French remained puzzled and angry by this Turkish mixture of surrender and defiance, but concluded that the first deserters had been genuine in their desire to surrender, being Greeks and Armenians, while the later groups had indeed intended to trick the French soldiers. As a result the Turkish commander of the second group and eight of his men were shot as war criminals. On the Turkish side, there was initial confidence in dealing with the French at Kum Kale, because four battalions were in the area, but by 26 April, the Turkish commander reported that the French Algerian soldiers had done well, and reinforcements were needed quickly. Later evaluation of the Turkish reaction singled out the commander of Turkish XV Corps (Gen. Weber Pasa) at Kum Kale for not being prepared, and for poor tactics, communications and leadership. He was also hampered by the relatively flat landscape that assisted Allied naval fire, by the impact of the French artillery, and by the initial panic of the Turkish defenders. Regardless, Turkish resistance stiffened, and was able to halt the French on 26 April. Nevertheless, the French did capture 500 prisoners during the whole operation, while suffering 250 casualties and causing severe losses to the Turks. Still it was clear that the French could not advance further without large reinforcements, so a conference on board *Queen Elizabeth* at midday on 26 April between d'Amade and Hamilton resulted in the decision to re-embark the French.[36]

At this point the story becomes murky. In a post war letter, Hamilton quoted from his 'diary' of 26 April:

> After he [d'Amade] had gone the Admiral [de Robeck] and Braithwaite – both attacked me and urged their view that the French should hold on another 24 hours at least – even if for no longer. The Admiral has always been keen on Kum Kale and I quite understand that naval aspect of the case. But it is all I can do, as far as things have gone, to hold my own on the Peninsula and I dare not get entangled in big Asiatic operations before I

have made good Achi Baba, especially in face of Kitchener's instructions (both stringent and specific) to the contrary.

However, Hamilton then reversed his decision, thinking that the French 'might have been better to have stayed another 24 hours', and so at 5.30 p.m. on 26 April, he asked the French to hold on at Kum Kale. Braithwaite and de Robeck were probably still thinking of the naval breakthrough, since the Navy would have been considerably helped in this endeavour if the Allies held the Asiatic side of the Straits as well as the Gallipoli side. On the other hand, Braithwaite gives a different slant to the story by arguing that d'Amade was desperate to get the French forces off Kum Kale, and Hamilton gave a reluctant consent to this. Braithwaite also reports that Hamilton changed his mind and tried to stop the French re-embarkation with a telegram. But the French replied that it was too late, although Braithwaite added: 'I don't think it was really, but that's another story.'[37]

On the French side, evidence for Hamilton's change of mind does not exist. Orders for re-embarkation reached Col. Ruef at 5.00 p.m. on 26 April. Ships were alerted by 3.00 p.m., and arrived at Kum Kale at 5.30 p.m. The actual re-embarkation was organized at 7.00 p.m., started at 11.00 p.m., and continued through the night. Hunter-Weston reported that the French transports were in sight at 4.00 p.m. on 26 April, presumably on their way to re-embark the French forces, and Hunter-Weston made arrangements for the French to land at V Beach the same day. By 7.00 p.m., he realized the French could not achieve this on 26 April, so he understood they would arrive on 27 April. Meanwhile, at Kum Kale, the re-embarkation proceeded smoothly despite rather severe casualties caused by a Turkish battery located at In Tepe. In defence, *Savoie* came in close and scored hits on the Turkish troops. The French subsequently did land on 27 April on the right of the Allied line at Helles.[38]

The landings of 25 April were a mixture of Allied success and failure. The landings that were relatively successful – S, X, Y and Kum Kale – were also the landings that were of lesser importance in comparison to V and W, where the heaviest casualties occurred. S, X, and Kum Kale appeared to succeed through a mixture of surprise, lack of strong opposition, and close naval support. Where the Navy ignored orders and came in close to the beaches, landings went well. At W, after initial heavy losses, naval fire then played a key role. Only at V did the Navy fail to achieve much, either with accurate naval fire from close in, or with proper arrangements for the steam hopper, and primarily for these reasons, V did not succeed until 26 April. Y Beach was the 'odd man out', and this beach simply worked because of complete surprise and absence of opposition. Yet even here, one can surmise that had the lay of the land been more favourable to naval fire, this beach would not have evacuated on 26 April. Other explanations for problems encountered at the beaches can be summed up by referring to simple inexperience and technical inability, for example, the relative immobility of senior commanders on board attendant ships. In addition, a series of senior commanders, de Robeck, Hamilton, Hunter-Weston and Wemyss, were prevented by military etiquette and their military sensibilities from playing more flexible and dynamic roles. Some of these same problems were to influence the other major Allied landing on 25 April, at Z Beach, later called Anzac Cove. Meanwhile, the Turkish defenders, although heavily outnumbered, made full use of the defensive strength of machine-guns, rifles and trenches and were critically successful in preventing significant Allied advances inland on 25 April. For different reasons, Turkish forces were also able to check the inland advance of the Anzacs at Z Beach on 25 April.

THE ANZAC LANDING

25 April 1915

The Anzac landing planned for Z Beach on 25 April anticipated coming ashore at first light in the Brighton Beach area. However, the Navy landed the troops too far north, at what came to be known as Anzac Cove. This, together with the normal confusion of war, Turkish snipers, and the slow landing of some Anzac troops, especially artillery, caused Allied problems. Turkish artillery fire and Anzac difficulties inland then led to Anzacs straggling down to the beach, and a contro-versial decision by some Anzac commanders late on 25 April to evacuate the Anzac troops. This could not be carried out by the Navy, so the troops were urged to dig in and hang on. Allied naval fire the next day, 26 April, helped the Anzac beach head to establish itself. On the Turkish side, there was more difficulty than previously recognized, although Mustafa Kemal proved to be a decisive com-mander. Ultimately, the Turkish defenders could not drive the Anzacs into the sea during late April and May, and an Allied decision was made to maintain the Anzac beach head.

*

Plans for the landing at Z Beach have a curiously vague quality. It was understood that the Helles landings were a greater risk than Z Beach, and so the more experienced 29 Division was used at Helles. But hopes were high for the Anzacs at Z Beach (comprising 1 Australian Division and the Anzac Division). The objective for the main force was to reach far inland to the moderate heights 'in the vicinity of Mal Tepe.'

The overall concept here was reasonable, which was to disrupt the Turkish defence, cut north–south communications, and halt enemy forces retreating from Helles, or enemy reserves moving south toward Helles. Finally, the ultimate objective was for the Anzacs to subsequently move south and invest the Kilid Bahr range. The covering force, as suggested by Aspinall on 23 March, and fully laid out on 13 April, was to land somewhere between Gaba Tepe and Fisherman's Hut, and establish itself on the high ground of map squares 224, 237 and 238. This was a large area from Gaba Tepe and the second ridge all the way to the Sari Bair heights, including Koja Cimen Tepe. Rather hopefully, the GSO 1 for the Anzac Division, Lt-Col. W.G. Braithwaite, described this semi-circular system of hills as useful ground for the covering force. Because of fear of Turkish artillery from Gaba Tepe, by 18 April the objective of the covering force was even more ambitious: to obtain the high ground all the way from the ground above Gaba Tepe to Gun Ridge and the Sari Bair heights. On 21 April, W.G. Braithwaite wrote in his diary that his division was to land at Gaba Tepe, meaning probably that general area. Because there were understood to be no Turkish defences north of the wire and guns at Gaba Tepe, there was no need for a bombardment, and hence no need to land in daylight to give the Navy observation for firing support. Thus, the landing was to take advantage of darkness and land at first light, with surprise as the key element. Surprise was also likely because the Turks would not expect a landing in such difficult country. Overall this plan was extraordinarily optimistic, but if total surprise was obtained, there was a chance of Allied success.[1]

Understanding of this Allied plan was sometimes vague. For example, Lt Colvin Algie, of the New Zealand Hauraki Battalion, noted in his diary that the objective explained to them on 21 April was a ridge two miles inland, to cut off the retreat of the Turks from Helles. This seems to be a mixture of the plan for the covering force and the main Mal Tepe objective. As well, there was a difference of opinion between GHQ and the commander of the Anzac force, Lt-Gen. Sir William Birdwood, about the direction of the Anzac advance. It appears that GHQ was afraid Birdwood would try to move the landing northwards, away from the main objective to the south, the Kilid Bahr plateau. Probably for this reason GHQ did not give Birdwood a look at a paper of Aspinall's at GHQ which evaluated the objectives of the landing, but which minimized the difficulty of the Sari Bair heights to the north of the Anzac landing. Hamilton was hard put to explain this omission to the Dardanelles Commission, saying that only he and the CGS, Braithwaite, had seen Aspinall's paper, and that he now placed it in front of the Commission merely as a 'curiosity.' On the other hand, Hamilton was quite right, Birdwood did indeed plan to move the landing north, near Fisherman's Hut, if enemy fire on his ships lying off the beach became too heavy, and his plan for the first objective of the landing was also definitely north facing, including a north flank in the Fisherman's Hut area.[2]

Birdwood was also one of those senior commanders who were pessimistic about the chances of the Gallipoli landings as a whole. He did not expect the landings to get a footing at Helles, while at Z Beach he felt the plan was a gamble. Birdwood feared enemy wire and trenches, and especially Turkish artillery, directed by planes. In fact, Birdwood's original idea had been simply to hold Gaba Tepe with naval fire and small detachments of troops, while the main landing went in on the Asian side to dominate the Turkish artillery at Chanak and Nagara from there. But since this was not going to be the plan, Birdwood remained pessimistic. He also wanted the landing to arrive in the dark, to heighten surprise, but realized this could not be done if the country was too difficult. Another method of ensuring success was the Allied plan for a false landing at Bulair, although Birdwood correctly feared there was not enough emphasis at GHQ on this deception. Finally, with some justification, Birdwood worried about supplies, especially water, and here he blamed GHQ for ignoring his staff. According to Birdwood, when his staff went to GHQ, they 'generally came back saying they did not seem to be wanted which seems to me a mistake.' But, like Hamilton, Birdwood felt that once his force had a good footing, then 'all will be well.' Nevertheless, Birdwood seems to have been mesmerized by the threat of enemy artillery, and perhaps he had a point because Turkish sources indicate there were six Turkish artillery pieces at Gaba Tepe, and four on Gun Ridge, with a large number of pieces in reserve, waiting for ammunition. According to Dawnay, Birdwood retained his original pessimism through the first few days of the landing at Anzac, and this frame of mind might have undermined to some extent the future Anzac counter-attack of 27 April.[3]

Birdwood was not the only pessimistic officer before the landing. In fact it is both understandable and surprising that so many should have voiced trepidation about the chances of the landing. For example, on 15 April, Brigadier-General Cunliffe-Owen, the Anzac artillery commander, understood that the Turks had a large number of guns in position and were heavily entrenched, so the landing force would make heavy work of their task. Similarly, Maj.-Gen. Godley thought that if the landing came off, 'it will be one of the greatest feats of arms that have ever been done...'[4] It seems that reports of enemy wire and artillery caused foreboding among many officers. Brigadier James McCay, commanding 2nd Infantry Brigade, on 21 April was reportedly very pessimistic, and this may have played a part in his temporary break down on the beach on 25 April. The commander of 3rd Infantry Brigade, Brigadier Sinclair MacLagan, addressed his men before the landing and warned of shelling and casualties, but exhorted his troops to hang onto whatever land was gained, 'even to the last man.'[5]

Meanwhile, Birdwood was still settling the date of the landing, but was surprised to learn on 21 April that the landing had been postponed by 24 hours to 23 April: 'we only heard this by chance!' A recent book suggests that this postponement, and a second one to 25 April, may have worked against the surprise that was the key element in the landing, since the period of darkness after moonset was reduced to one hour, between 3.00 a.m. and 4.00 a.m., rather than the hour and a half of 23 April. But the Anzac War Diary states that the Turks may have detected the ships as early as 2.00 a.m. on 25 April, while Turkish sources suggest that the 27th Regiment of 9 Division was alerted at 2.30 a.m., and rifle fire was opened on the Anzacs at 3.00 a.m. on 25 April. Hence, the postponement does not seem to have made much difference.[6]

Before looking at operations, it is useful to review the controversy over the actual Anzac landing site, which continues to this day. After 25 April, everyone from Birdwood down agreed that the Navy had placed the Anzac troops around one mile, or one and a half miles, too far north, since the intended landing site was Brighton Beach, while the actual landing took place around Anzac Cove (see map). One or two officers, such as the Anzac GSO 1, Braithwaite, believed the landing was up to two miles north of the proper spot. Maj.-Gen. Godley believed that the landing was one and a half miles too far north. Maj.-Gen. Bridges considered the landing was one and three quarter miles too far north. Others such as Lt Algie thought it was only just north of the correct place. In fact, it was by no means clear how far north of Gaba Tepe the intended landing site was to be. The sketch map attached to Force Order #1 of 13 April, shows the landing spot as only just south of Hell Spit Point, on the southern edge of what was to become Anzac Cove. Birdwood himself wrote later that he intended to land on a broad front one mile north of Gaba Tepe. But he also told the Navy that if it was shelled the landing could take place around the point to the north, i.e. Anzac Cove, where the actual landing did occur. The Navy, on the other hand, seemed to think that the landing was to be closer to Gaba Tepe. Thus, Rear-Admiral Thursby, in charge of the naval side of the landing, seemed to suggest a site just north of Gaba Tepe on 17 April, but in his instructions he ordered that the right hand boats should land one mile north of Gaba Tepe, and the other boats, 800 and 1600 yards respectively, north of the right hand boats. Later, Thursby argued that the landing did actually occur within a few hundred yards of the assigned position. But Commander Charles Dix, in charge of the covering force landing, recalls that he was ordered to land with the right hand boat only 500 yards north of Gaba Tepe, and the left hand boat just south of Hell Spit Point.[7]

All of this suggests that the choice of landing place was actually quite flexible, especially as far as Birdwood was concerned. One other important factor is that the Admiralty map did not apparently go as far north as Anzac, and was inaccurate. De Robeck told Churchill this on 4 May:

> Admiralty map does not extend sufficiently far North to include this position [Anzac] also land features on map are inaccurate. Military squared map is being used... It was assumed Military positions would be obtained from War Office; I am of necessity not in touch with Army HQ and positions I send will not always be quite up to date.

Although written a few days after the landing, this problem could well have had an impact on the Navy finding the correct landing site.[8] Much has been written on the reasons for the Navy landing the troops further north than intended, and most recently it has been argued that the actual landing spot was probably only 500 yards north of what was intended. In reality, the difficulty of locating the correct headland in the dark as a guiding point, the different changes of course made by the various midshipmen and naval commanders as the tows went in, partly because of apprehension concerning the enemy artillery and infantry on Gaba Tepe, and the problem of faulty Admiralty maps, are all quite sufficient to explain the northward shift of the landing. Subsequently, Birdwood and others all stressed that the change of landing site was fortunate, since the actual landing area was unsuspected by the Turks, and the steep cliffs protected the troops. As Birdwood wrote, without the protection of the steep cliffs at Anzac 'we should probably have had to vacate…', because of heavy enemy shell fire. Birdwood seems to have always been preoccupied with the defences of Gaba Tepe, while the protection of the cliffs above Anzac Cove was a double edged sword, since the covering force was confused by landing in the wrong place, and it did not take long for the Turks to react to the actual landing, regardless of location.[9]

Turning to the landing itself, a previously unpublished manuscript gives a rather typical story for those Australian infantry who landed that day. Corporal William Guy, 11th Battalion, 3rd Brigade, 1 Australian Division, landed north of Ari Burnu, and found himself facing the steep cliffs of North Beach. Guy was part of the covering force, and must have landed between 4.30 and 5.30 a.m. Writing a few days later, Guy wrote: 'Have come through ten days terrible fighting without hurt… Have lost nearly all my friends killed or wounded – feel a lonely man.' In another letter, Guy recalled that before the landing he went on board *London* on 24 April, and found the sailors to be very friendly. So much so that they renamed Port and Starboard as A and C after the two Australian companies on board. Then he climbed into the tows, but the 'watchful enemy was waiting for us, and before the pinnaces had cast us off, a shower of bullets from rifles and machine-guns rained in and around the boats.' Many were wounded or killed before the boats landed, but then the survivors scrambled ashore where Guy jettisoned his heavy greatcoat and pack. Then up the first slope he went, leading to what came to be known as Plugge's Plateau. Two thirds of the way up, the Turks retired, and according to Guy, he and his company reached the third ridge. This seems to be a mistake, since Guy probably only reached the subsequently named 400 Plateau. Here Guy's company met the main enemy force. 'Everyone was separated from his comrades and his Company, but we took orders from the nearest officer. Digging in was not an easy matter for we were in a veritable hell of Lead and Shrapnel, and this continued almost unceasingly for over three days.' Guy got mixed up with the Australian 10th Battalion, and saw men dropping all round him. On the third night, the Turkish fire slackened slightly, so 'I crawled down the valley to obtain water. Before I returned the shelling had recommenced and the valley was lit up by bursting shrapnel. I got back unhurt, though how, I do not know.' A bullet did strike his rifle on the third day, and on the fourth, his group was relieved. Guy then located his own company, which had lost some fifty per cent of its strength. According to Guy, his Brigadier (Sinclair MacLagan), an old Imperial soldier, said to our Colonel 'I will not say they are better than the British "Tommy", but a finer body of men have never landed on any shore.'[10]

Guy's story is absolutely typical of the conditions experienced by the Anzacs as they landed. Confusion at the landing spot, a rush up the nearest slope, heavy Turkish rifle and shrapnel fire, separation from comrades and units in the scrub and steep valleys, chaos inland, small ad hoc groups defending against Turkish counterattacks, some small groups far inland, others withdrawing, and heavy casualties. Probably the most disconcerting feature of the landing was not only the wrong landing place, but that the battalions did not come ashore in the order planned, hence the fog of war started to multiply errors. The explanation for the confusion that occurs most often in personal accounts is that the wily Turk lured the troops inland, and then turned on the advancing Anzacs. Other reports speak of astonishment at the intensity of Turkish fire, and at the number of wounded, while some accounts discuss the decline of morale during the late afternoon of 25 April. Thus Lt-Col. Fenwick, the Anzac Division medical officer, wrote of the chaos on the beach as the wounded accumulated, as many as 400 men lying on the beach: 'It seemed impossible for men to live under the hail of bullets. Capt. Craig dressed over 100 cases under fire… I certainly was very much astonished that I was alive.' Fenwick estimated that about 1,600 wounded men were evacuated. Capt. Rhodes, ADC to Godley, remarked that the dead and wounded on 25 April nearly made him sick, but he soon became callous. The New Zealand situation was made more difficult by fact that Brigadier-General F.E. Johnston, an Anzac brigade commander, was temporarily 'indisposed.' It was generally believed that Johnston was something of an alcoholic. No doubt because of the uncertain nature of Johnston's recovery, a replacement was not appointed until several hours later, at 12.30 p.m. on 25 April. Meanwhile, on the Australian side, some battalion commanders found the stress too much and did not properly command – this was the case with the 5th, 6th and 9th Battalions. For example, Lt-Col. C. Rosenthal, commanding 3rd Australian Artillery Brigade, met the commander of the 9th Battalion, who said his battalion was practically wiped out – Rosenthal described him as being in a terrible state. Lt-Col. W.G. Malone, commanding the New Zealand Wellington Battalion, who did not land until 4.30 p.m. on 25 April, also noticed problems among the commanders. The chief officers were fine, wrote Malone, but the executive officers 'have no idea of order, method, etc. They… hang up everything on the ground. The whole army does.' And according to Maj. C.H. Brand, Brigade Major in 3rd Brigade,

> no Bn commander in [3rd] Brigade except for old Weir got into… real touch with their troops – Weir was the one they expected least of. Brand was out there doing what the Bn commanders should have done.[11]

On the other hand, just as many officers performed bravely and efficiently, for example, among several candidates, Maj. H.G. Bennett, 6th Battalion; Lt A.P. Derham, 5th Battalion; Lt H.T. Elder, signals officer, 5th Battalion; Maj. A.G. Salisbury, commanding 9th Battalion on 400 Plateau; Maj. S.P. Weir, commanding 10th Battalion; and of course, Maj.-Gen. W.T. Bridges, commanding 1 Australian Division. The difficulties of the landing are well captured by the interviews that Charles Bean conducted with surviving officers during and after the landing. From these it is possible to see that a major problem was the southward shift of the focus of the landing. This occurred because Sinclair MacLagan, commanding 3rd Brigade, conscious of enemy forces that had previously been identified in the Gaba Tepe area, and realizing that the landing was too far north, believed that the right flank of the landing was not properly protected. He therefore proceeded to change the focus of the landing around 9.00 a.m., and told Brigadier McCay to take his 2nd Brigade to the right. Bean reported the conversation, not all of which he put into the Australian official history. MacLagan said to McCay,

> I want you to take your whole Bde. to my right. McCay said: I was ordered to take it to my left. It is a bit stiff to disobey orders first thing. MacLagan said: I assure you my right will be turned. McCay said: I had better go forward and have a look. MacLagan said: There is not time. McCay said: Will you assure me that the left will be allright and the right will be turned if I do not do this? MacLagan said: I assure you it is so. McCay said: I accept the assurance and issued his orders.

Later on, McCay also obtained Bridges' last reserve battalion to go in on the right, because of a gap. The net result was that the right flank was strong, while the centre and left flanks suffered many problems. Ultimately, there were simply not enough organized troops to advance and hold the line everywhere in such difficult country, while communications were haphazard at best, and the confusion was very severe.[12]

One other factor that helped the right flank was the resourcefulness of the captain of the *Bacchante*. Navy fire was initially not particularly useful in supporting the troops because of the confusion ashore, the broken nature of the ground, the thick scrub, lack of observation, and the fact that most covering ships did not come in close. But an eye witness noted 'the *Bacchante* did a wonderfully fine thing, she stood right in till her bows were practically on the rocks, it was fairly rough, about 600 yards on the beach side of Gaba Tepe and stayed there till dark firing broadsides. If it had not been for her, I do not think we could have accomplished the landing.' This observer went on to note that

'The *Bacchante* and *Triumph* were also the only ships that appeared to take any interest in altering their fire according to observations from the shore.' Hence, a junior officer of *Triumph* remarked that 'by means of heliograph signals we were able to direct a steady fire on the Turkish positions.' As for *Bacchante*, Charles Bean also noted her vital defensive role in firing on the Gaba Tepe guns, and the *Bacchante* log shows that she closed in to three cables from the shore at 7.15 a.m., and at 10.00 a.m. fired on the battery north of Gaba Tepe 'as necessary to keep it from firing at boats.' However, despite *Bacchante*, this battery caused trouble all day, and it was not until 6.00 p.m. that it was put out of action with the help of one piece of field artillery. On the other hand, certain ships were not so useful. It appears that *Ribble*, landing troops near Fisherman's Hut, would not use the after 12-pounder, because 'there were strict orders not to use those guns.' Possibly this was for fear of firing on their own men.[13]

Meanwhile, partly because of the emphasis on the right flank, the centre of the line was weak, especially at locations known as Russell's Top, the Nek and Baby 700. Here the Turkish 57th Regiment of 19 Division mounted a strong counterattack during the late afternoon, and drove the Anzacs off Baby 700 and the Nek, and threatened Russell's Top. In his original official history draft of this area of fighting, Aspinall recorded that the Anzacs had reached 'breaking point' and this allowed the Turkish counterattack to partially succeed. However, Brigadier-General J.E. Edmonds, the overall director of the British Official History of World War I, did not like the 'breaking point' phrase, and ordered Aspinall to omit it. This caused Aspinall to write privately:

> If this is omitted there is nothing of the truth left. Actually the [whole – crossed out] left flank at Russell's Top was now held by only a corporal & 2 men [of the Anzacs], the rest having 'chucked it'. Luckily there were no Turks, or disaster would have come quickly. I have already omitted the fact that the left was bare in deference to Australian susceptibilities.

Aspinall's information is a little hard to follow in Bean's history, but perhaps Bean's reference to Corporal Howe of the 11th Battalion and a

New Zealand corporal as the last two left on Baby 700 is the incident Aspinall had in mind. Aspinall also believed that a well-coordinated attack could have driven back the Turks, against which Edmonds argued that only a body of fresh troops could have succeeded. Aspinall's reply was that fresh troops were frequently appearing, but were 'continually becoming disintegrated on arrival owing to lack of discipline.' Bean's response to this would have been what he wrote in regard to the need for fresh troops on the left flank: 'From 12.30 to about 4 p.m. not an infantryman arrived on the beach.'[14]

Aspinall's comments seem a little harsh, given the circumstances. Perhaps he was a little biased because as GSO 3 at GHQ, he, among others, was responsible for planning the landings at Gallipoli. In this respect he insisted that the task of the Anzac landing was 'not an impossibility.' In support of Aspinall, two external factors should have helped the landing – surprise and naval supporting fire. There was a certain element of surprise, due to the unsuitable and therefore unexpected landing area of Anzac Cove. But naval fire proved disappointing on 25 April, apart from *Bacchante* and *Triumph*. Two key problems were observation (to locate targets and avoid firing on friendly troops) and spotting (relaying back to naval layers the fall of shell) in such difficult country. Hence, naval accuracy was always difficult. Once observers were ashore, the situation improved, but enemy artillery was still hard to locate, enemy troops were well hidden in the thick scrub, and there were some situations in which friendly troops were too close to the Turks. Hence, on 25 April a message at 12.20 p.m. from *Queen* reported that map reference 224K was too close to friendly troops to be shelled. *Queen* was thus not able to help, but suggested that the mountain battery should assist, and that field artillery would be landed soon. Understandably in a moving battle, the communication system was improvized. So, at 1.15 p.m., a forward observation officer asked 3rd Australian Brigade whether the Navy should fire into map square 237ZL (Sari Bair range) at 1,000 yards. Five minutes later, at 1.15 p.m., 3rd Brigade replied 'yes', and requested Maj. Mackworth, Signals Officer for 1 Australian Division, to send this message to *Queen* at once. In fact, *Queen*'s guns were heavily requested, for example at 3.10 p.m., an enemy battery at

238M5 (Sari Bair range) was located, and fire was required. Not surprisingly, given the nature of the country, this battery was hard to knock out, and at 6.20 p.m., naval fire was still urgently requested on the same battery at 238M. Then, with Anzac troops wavering under enemy shrapnel, around 6.00 p.m., there were several urgent demands for naval fire. There were also some success stories, for example when Maj. Bennett reported Turkish guns on Gun Ridge opposite them, and about two hours later, the Navy got onto them.[15]

At dawn the next morning, 26 April, *Queen* and *Queen Elizabeth* were in action before 6.30 a.m. By 9.25 a.m., *Queen* was congratulated for her fire on 224D (Gun Ridge), 'which is doing great execution.' But at 10.18 a.m., and indicative of the problems of observation, 2nd Australian Brigade complained that the Navy was shelling their trenches. Then, at 11.35 a.m., *Queen* reported that she was about to shell 225T (the Mal Tepe area), with 12 inch, but wanted shore observers to direct fire. The observer, W5, noted that *Queen*'s fire 'appears correct', but later sent the message that *Queen* should fire 'Close to summit of knoll south west of the 2 huts in saddle.' Evidently, maps could not be relied upon. Then there were communication difficulties. For example, at 2.30 p.m., *Queen Elizabeth* signalled to her observer, W4, 'help me by spotting.' A laconic note on the pad simply stated 'Done.' An hour later, *Queen Elizabeth* signalled that her fire was again directed at 224D, and this time the scribbled note on the pad was 'Spotted for *Queen Elizabeth*. Observation officer said all shots were correct.' But clearly there were problems, since two minutes later, at 3.37 p.m., *Queen Elizabeth* repeated to W4: 'Help me by spotting my fire.' As before, the single word 'Done' was scribbled on the pad. Yet, the problem was obviously not solved, since at 4.10 p.m., *Queen Elizabeth* asked W4 to 'Pass further corrections visually', i.e. by helio. Despite the relative crudity of this system, it generally seemed to work, for at 4.26 p.m., the 8th Battalion sent a message that naval guns were doing great execution among Turkish troops. *Queen Elizabeth* also innovated on 26 April by zeroing in on the bursts of friendly mountain gun fire, which had better observation.[16]

Overall, the Navy clearly had a difficult time at Anzac in supplying supporting fire because the fire had to be straight on, which made both range and direction difficult to get right. This was because spotting and observation was best done at right angles. Helles did not have this problem because flanking observation was possible there. As previously noted, the rugged country at Anzac was also much more difficult to observe and spot in than the relatively flat Helles. Thus, the New Zealand War Diary suggests somewhat unfairly 'We had obtained no gun support from the Navy, whilst enemy had made free use of artillery.'[17] However, naval shelling would not have been so crucial a factor at Anzac if field artillery, in addition to mountain batteries, had been brought into action on 25 April. Here there was a controversy.

In regard to Allied mountain batteries, these small 13 pounders were scheduled to be the first ashore. They were judged well suited to the terrain, but were of limited value because of their low calibre. It seems that the 26th Mountain Battery came ashore at 10.30 a.m., and went into action at 11.55 a.m. Then at 2.25 p.m., the battery retired to the beach, partly because of heavy casualties, and partly 'to cover retiring infantry.' Meanwhile, the 21st Kohat Battery was due ashore at 8.30 a.m., but there were no lighters or horse boats until 3.00 p.m., and no tugs until 5.30 p.m. In a hand written note, referring to his official history, Aspinall argued that this second mountain battery 'remained on board ship, or on lighters which awaited a tug boat in vain; I am unable to say which. I thought the latter was true and said so in my first draft; but it was queried, so I omitted the reference.' The lack of tug boats appears to be the reason for the non-arrival of this battery until around 6.00 p.m., together with 56 mules and ammunition.[18]

The mountain batteries were valuable, yet field artillery was really essential to support the Anzac landing. But here controversy continues. Early on 25 April, 1 Australian Division artillery staff came ashore to scout for gun positions. By 11.30 a.m., two positions were found on the right, but only one gun was available, which came into action, as noted above, at 6.00 p.m. It seems, however, that someone was not anxious for the field artillery to land. According to Lt-Col. Rosenthal, who landed at 1.00 p.m., Col. J.J.T. Hobbs, artillery commander of 1 Australian Division, said no guns were to be landed during the day, and doubted there were suitable gun locations. Rosenthal wrote that Hobbs hadn't been over the ground, while he himself had found places for a battery on the right flank. Maj.-Gen. Bridges agreed to one battery, then two guns, and then cancelled the order. Another source related that Bridges, 'considering country unsuitable, forbade landing of Australian Field Guns.' Yet another source cites Bridges as saying that no guns were to be landed on 25 April. The signal log of *Queen* shows that Godley wanted a howitzer battery ashore quickly at 1.45 p.m., but at 1.54 p.m., Birdwood wired that there were no horse boats available to disembark the howitzers. At 2.15 p.m., 1 Australian Division called for two field guns, plus two teams of horses. At around 3.25 p.m., three guns came ashore, but very soon after, at 3.45 p.m., after he came ashore, Birdwood signalled his naval counterpart, Rear-Admiral Thursby, to stop sending field artillery ashore. Three guns did come ashore, but were later sent back on the order of Bridges, again apparently because the country was bad and positions could not easily be found for them, but in reality because of the deteriorating situation of the Anzacs. Then finally at 6.30 p.m., Col. Hobbs found positions for four guns and sent an urgent request to the Navy, who 'promised to send guns ashore Sunday evening [25 April] as they were then urgently wanted to open fire at dawn on Monday but none came until noon Monday.'[19]

As the situation ashore deteriorated in the late afternoon of 25 April, Bridges ordered the re-embarkation of the field artillery, and this took place at 7.30 p.m. The New Zealand Brigade Major, Maj. A.C. Temperley, found this an inexplicable order. This was especially the case because two hours later, at 9.30 p.m., came orders to land two batteries at 2.00 a.m. the next day, 26 April. In fact, even on 26 April the landing of guns was peculiar. One gun of 4th Battery and one gun of 1st Battery landed early and went into action on the morning of 26 April. Around noon, four guns of 7th Battery also arrived and went into action. But two guns of 3rd Battery and four guns of 8th Battery came ashore in error and were sent back again, as was the one gun of 4th battery and one gun of 1st Battery which had already landed. The ordeal of 8th Battery was especially strange – at 2.00 a.m. on 26 April the guns arrived at the beach but were reloaded back onto floats and towed away. Then at 7.00 a.m. the floats were once more towed ashore.

Positions for the 8th Battery guns were reconnoitred all day, and by 6.30 p.m. on 26 April positions had been found. The guns were ready to move into action when the order came to take the guns back to the beach and once more re-embark them. As the War Diary states 'This was a big undertaking as the floats had grounded with the receding tide.' At 8.30 p.m., the 8th battery guns therefore were towed to the transports, and for the next few days sailed around as part of the feints at Bulair.[20]

Something had gone very wrong with the artillery staff work, no doubt made worse by conflict between Bridges and the artillery commanders. Fortunately, the lack of guns was not so acute on 26 April, because the Navy launched a furious bombardment soon after dawn. But why were field guns not landed at Anzac and put into action on 25 April, apart from a single gun? This was particularly pressing since the troops complained especially of Turkish shrapnel, which the Navy could not properly reply to. For example, George Tuck, a New Zealand soldier, describes the shrapnel landing in groups of four, branches and leaves leaping into the air, with soldiers hugging the earth, but even so 'men were dropping all around.' The shrapnel drove Tuck back to the beach, passing as he did so hundreds of 'exhausted and wounded men…'. Tuck took a machine-gun and some ammunition and climbed back up, close to collapse, but he found that his battalion and company were broken up and scattered. Meanwhile the wounded were asking if they were to be left to be shot to pieces, with one wounded man quietly saying 'Oh, My God! My God! [it] was simply terrible.' According to another New Zealand account, on 25 April the Turks swept 'the hill with shrapnel and they must have done some great damage – accuracy of bursts. Our warships replied but did not appear to be able to find the battery giving the trouble…'. Temperley believed that the men were demoralized not so much by Turkish shelling, but because there was no reply from Allied artillery. It seems that Turkish shrapnel and the lack of Allied artillery reply was the major reason for the disintegration that took place at Anzac late on 25 April.[21]

So, again, why, except for one gun, did Allied field artillery fail to land and reply to Turkish shrapnel? It appears that Bridges (and to some extent Hobbs) were the individuals responsible for recalling the guns and not allowing guns to land at Anzac. The reasons for this are harder to pin down. At the time, Birdwood argued that the guns did not land because just as they were heading for the beach, enemy artillery opened up and forced the transports out to sea. On the other hand, Aspinall believed that Bridges had not landed the guns because with the position ashore being precarious, he did not want to risk losing the guns. Aspinall was later forced to amend this argument in the official history by Australian protests, but he did still make Bridges accountable for the decision not to land guns. As for Australian explanations, Lt-Col. C.B. Brudenell-White, GSO 1 of 1 Australian Division, asserted in 1923 that Bridges was a gunner, who had seen the Anzac landing place, and could not conceive of moving the guns into position 'with manpower only. I confess that it looked pretty impossible to do anything with them.' Later, in 1927, Brudenell-White said the guns had not landed because Artillery staff could find no place for them. Then in 1928, Brudenell-White amended this explanation by advancing three reasons for Bridges' decision. Firstly, as before, Bridges thought of moving guns with horses or mules, and did not imagine doing the job with manpower. Secondly, Bridges did not think the Anzacs held a connected front, so this was too vague a situation for artillery to be properly employed. And thirdly, Bridges thought the Anzacs had failed. One other point is worth noting. In Aspinall's 23 March 1915 original Appreciation of landing plans, he had written: 'The Australian Division, with mountain guns, but in the first instance without other artillery, to land at daybreak…'. It seems possible that this original plan for the Anzac landing without artillery also carried some weight in de-emphasizing the landing of field artillery.[22]

Judging by the timing of Bridges' decisions about landing and removing guns, it does seem that Bridges was primarily apprehensive about losing the guns, and therefore opposed their landing. Besides the very important lack of artillery ashore, there was another key difficulty for the Anzacs on 25 April, and this was the slow landing of troops by the Navy. Lt-Col. Malone remarked that Birdwood and Godley were disappointed because only half of the New Zealand Brigade had landed, and noted laconically in his diary that the Navy had 'knocked off disembarkation.'

According to Lt-Col. W.G. Braithwaite, there was a complete halt in the landing of troops during the afternoon of 25 April from 12.30 to 4.00 p.m. The explanation was that the early rapid disembarkation of troops threw the timetable out, but the Navy still adhered to the original timetable. Some ships remained at Lemnos, and other ships carrying the New Zealand 'A' Echelon and other echelons 'were not hurried on.' In general, New Zealand HQ complained that naval arrangements for landing troops toward the close of day and during the night 'appeared defective – launches and lighters scarce and work slow.' Another New Zealand explanation was that the landing had stopped for several hours because it was thought the troops might have to re-embark. Later, in 1927, W.G. Braithwaite still complained that there was a gap of three hours on 25 April when troops were not landed, and this was because the Navy was ahead of their schedule. Similarly, in regard to the Australians, the late afternoon delay in landing the 4th Brigade was critical. At 5.40 p.m., an HQ message to *Queen* asked urgently for the disembarkation of the 4th Brigade. This was repeated at 7.05 p.m. from 3rd Brigade. One officer believed that the delay in landing 4th Brigade, plus the commencement of evacuating large numbers of wounded around 5.30 p.m., may have resulted in the loss of the summit of the second ridge, Baby 700. As for the Navy, their explanation was that enemy artillery, as well as fire from Turkish ships in the Narrows, drove the transports out to sea, and this was the reason for the delay. Birdwood also thought this the correct explanation. Regardless, it appears that the Navy should have accelerated the rate of landing, despite the attention of enemy artillery.[23]

The most controversial aspect of the Z Beach/Anzac landing is undoubtedly the loss of morale in the late afternoon of 25 April, resulting in men straggling down to the beach, or finding shelter in gullies and valleys. This situation led to suggestions of re-embarkation of the Anzac force. There is not much doubt that straggling took place on a large scale, although lengthy post-war arguments over this between Bean and Aspinall covered many nuances of the word 'straggling', and resulted in Aspinall considerably altering the first volume of his official history.[24] This is not to deny the courage of the great majority of Anzac troops ashore on 25 April. However, the situation was extreme – untried and disorganized troops under intense shelling and sniper fire, usually in small isolated groups, lost and unsure of their location or where neighbouring Anzac forces were, with no response from friendly artillery, and often with their own officers wounded, killed or absent. All of this understandably led to some break down in morale. Birdwood himself noted there were stragglers in all the Nullahs (gullies) on 25 April, usually in groups of 20 saying they were the last survivors. Anzac HQ also received a message at 5.20 p.m. on 25 April: 'Regret say considerable number unwounded men leaving firing line.' Many officers in post-war correspondence confirmed the straggling situation, for example Maj. J. Gellibrand, Col. N.R. Howse V.C., and Temperley, the last of whom described gullies full of unwounded men and hundreds of Australians coming to the beach with the story 'the Australians have orders to "concentrate on the beach".' Temperley wrote that 'It exceeded anything in my previous or subsequent experience.'[25]

However, it is important to remember something, which is never pointed out, namely, that the Anzac landing was not alone in its straggling problems. As noted above, there were numerous stragglers at Y Beach that actually did result in evacuation of that beach. W Beach had its stragglers, too, and Bean, when defending the Anzac record, reported that he had met a Major of 29 Division, who 'had been impressed by the amount of straggling in his division at the southern Landing [Helles]...'. So Anzac fits a pattern, and given the problems unique to Anzac, it is not surprising that certain signs of strain began to emerge as early as midday on 25 April. A message at 12.50 p.m. to GHQ reported that the left centre on the 400 Plateau could not stand against enemy fire unless supported by artillery. At 3.11 p.m., Maj. T.A. Blamey, GSO 3 of the Anzac Corps declared that the men could not hold on, the situation was very dangerous and men were giving way. Blamey was ordered to come back and lead the 4th Battalion up onto Bolton's Ridge. At 5.20 p.m. came the message that men were leaving the firing line. Not surprisingly, 20 minutes later, at 5.40 p.m., the 4th Brigade was urgently required to disembark. Then, in the early evening, Godley requested that Birdwood come ashore at once. According to Birdwood's diary, it was about 8.00 p.m. when Bridges and Godley stated that it was necessary to re-embark.

They said the men would be unable to stand the strain of another day, there were 500 dead, and 2,500 wounded. Birdwood himself felt that the terrible shrapnel fire at Anzac was similar to that observed at Spion Kop during the Boer War, when Birdwood was present, and that hill top was subjected to such shrapnel shelling that it was abandoned by British troops. Consequently, at 8.45 p.m. Birdwood sent a long wire to Hamilton's GHQ on board the *Queen Elizabeth*, saying that the position was not very good, the shelling was severe, and the country was very difficult to operate in.[26]

Soon after Birdwood's wire was sent, there came another message at 9.20 p.m., from 'an officer on shore' to *Queen*, saying 'All available boats are required on shore.' This message did not come from Birdwood, who was not ashore then, but possibly was sent by Capt. V. Vyvyan, the naval beach master. The journalist Ellis Ashmead-Bartlett also claimed that Capt. Grant of the *Canopus* was ordered to take off the Australians. Thursby, the naval officer in charge of the Anzac landing, did not take action at that point, but 10 minutes later, at about 9.30 p.m., Birdwood went ashore. At 10.00 p.m., there was a conference of Anzac commanding officers, including Bridges, Godley, Brigadier-General H.B. Walker, commanding 1st Infantry Brigade, Brudenell-White, Sinclair MacLagan and McCay. At 11.00 p.m., there was another conference at 1 New Zealand Brigade HQ, including Birdwood, Bridges, Godley and Walker. It was at this conference that Godley and Bridges urged evacuation. They would not wait for Hamilton's agreement before carrying out this plan, but wanted immediate evacuation, if practical, while sending a message to Hamilton informing him of their decision. Because of this, the *Lutzow* sent boats ashore at 11.00 p.m. as a precaution, in order to re-embark the troops if necessary. Ashmead-Bartlett, on board the *London* that night, reported that 'we went round to every transport telling them to get ready to send in their boats to take the Expedition off…' However, Birdwood continued to believe that all was not lost, and sent a message at 11.35 p.m. to units that the troops must hold on, entrench and fight with all their might. Then around this time a controversial message, in Godley's handwriting, but addressed to no one, and signed 'Birdwood', was written. The message was taken by Capt. Vyvyan to Thursby on *Queen*, where it was probably, but not certainly, intended to be signalled on to Hamilton on board *Queen Elizabeth*. The message was that Birdwood's two Anzac divisional generals urged evacuation, on the basis that there were no more reserves, the men were dribbling down to the beach, and there was likely to be a fiasco the next morning. If evacuation was decided on, then it must be at once. There were actually three different viewpoints around 11.00 p.m.: Birdwood, who wanted to hang on; Bridges, Godley and other senior officers who wanted to re-embark; and Thursby, who did not consider that evacuation was feasible, but thinking the Birdwood/Godley message was for him, sent a warning signal to transports to be ready to send boats into the beach. Hence, at 12.05 a.m., just after midnight, Thursby sent a message to de Robeck, saying that he was coming to see him, no doubt to urgently discuss the whole situation. In fact, Thursby then did issue an order, timed at 12.20 a.m.: 'Lower all boats and stand by to send them in to beach.' But at this crucial point the *Queen Elizabeth* appeared, with Hamilton on board, and the Birdwood/Godley message was therefore by chance delivered to Hamilton.[27]

It is significant that when a draft of Aspinall's chapter regarding these important events, including the Birdwood/Godley message, was circulated in Australia, there were some interesting changes made to the history. Among the words and phrases omitted in Aspinall's published volume was Aspinall's suggested phrase that the officers ashore wanted 'immediate' evacuation. Also omitted was Aspinall's sentence that if Hamilton decided the Anzacs should hold on, it was thought at the time this might lead to the 'complete sacrifice of the Australian and New Zealand Corps.' Another word that was omitted was Aspinall's evaluation of the Birdwood/Godley message as 'ominous'. Aspinall's original draft also placed greater emphasis on Thursby, who finally took the decision that the force could not be re-embarked, while the original chapter explained more fully how the Birdwood/Godley message got to Hamilton.[28] Aspinall's original draft therefore tended to stress the dangers of the situation. But on board the *Queen Elizabeth*, the Birdwood/Godley message understandably caused shock. The message came first to Aspinall and Dawnay on the bridge. Then, as the dramatic story goes, Hamilton was roused from his bed by his CGS, Braithwaite, who told him he must make the life and death decision about the re-embarkation of the Anzacs. Yet, according to other sources, it was the presence of Brigadier-General R.A. Carruthers of the Anzac Corps staff, and Cunliffe-Owen, with their story of the desperate situation ashore at Anzac, who made as much or more impact than the notorious Birdwood/Godley message. Orlo Williams, the cipher officer, empha-sized Carruthers' role, and according to Roger Keyes, who was present, the two Australian Brigadiers 'did not seem to think the men could stick it much longer…' Following this, and subsequent to Hamilton's reading of the Birdwood/Godley message, a discussion took place between Hamilton, Thursby and the CGS, Braithwaite, and the decision was a communal one: 'they must stick it, the embarkation would be more costly than the wait for two or three days until the pressure was relieved by the Southern force coming up –'. Another key factor in the discus-sion was that many boats and lighters had been destroyed or damaged and so re-embarkation would be very difficult. In a rather self congratu-latory mode, Keyes recalled 'I was most awfully strong on telling them to stay. They had made a most gallant landing…' At this juncture a mes-sage came in reporting the success of the Australian submarine AE2. For Keyes, who took the message, it was a fine case of 'Joss' – good luck – 'as they say in China', which tipped the balance in favour of the Anzacs staying. Following this, writes Keyes, 'Sir Ian and of course my Admiral [de Robeck] and Admiral Thursby backed this up.' However, other sources indicate that it was Thursby's declaration that re-embarkation was difficult or impossible which really settled the matter. Hamilton thereupon drafted his equally famous message to Birdwood, stressing the points discussed and urging the Anzacs to 'dig, dig, dig, until you are safe.'[29]

However, one aspect of this story tends to undermine the dramatic nature of Hamilton's decision, which he himself wondered about after the war. If Thursby had already decided that evacuation was impossible, Hamilton asked Aspinall, why didn't Thursby tell Hamilton this before? Why wait for the discussion and news of the AE2? Aspinall himself con-tinued to be puzzled by this. But the decision was taken, and the men ashore spent a desperate night. Yet there were a few contrary voices, one being the New Zealander, Lt-Col. Malone, who reported that although there was some question of re-embarkation, 'Personally I could see nothing to require it.' Perhaps Malone was fresher than most, since he had not landed until 4.30 p.m. on 25 April.[30] Nevertheless, because the Anzacs did hold on, and remained there until the final evacuation, there was some post-war manoeuvring by senior officers who wanted to distance themselves from the allegation that they had wanted to re-embark the Anzacs on 25 April. An interesting series of letters ensued between Aspinall and Bean as official historians, and the key Anzac figures. The publication of Hamilton's book *Gallipoli Diary* in 1920 also publicly revealed the Birdwood/Godley message for the first time. This elicited a lengthy letter from Birdwood to Bean, in which the former related that Walker had been most pessimistic on 25 April, thought his flanks were in the air, and Turks all around him. Later that night, Birdwood said that Godley, Bridges and a deputation came to see him, arguing that the men were hard pressed and fatigued, there were fears of a debacle in the morning, and men were 'dribbling back in large numbers through the dense bush on to the shore.' So there was a demand for immediate evacuation and for Birdwood to make arrangements to do so with Thursby before consulting Hamilton and de Robeck. Bridges took Birdwood aside and urged the evacuation, but Birdwood allegedly said he would 'rather wait and die there on the spot in the morning than re-embark.' Still, Birdwood decided that Hamilton should know the situation, hence the message, in case Hamilton chose to concentrate both the forces of Helles and Anzac at either spot.[31]

This was Birdwood's basic thesis regarding the origins of the Birdwood/Godley message. But it did not get by Aspinall as official historian without a fight. Birdwood opened his defence with a letter to Aspinall in August 1926. Here he repeated his assertions that Bridges and Godley were emphatic about evacuation because the next morning would bring about a complete debacle, since men with shattered nerves were heading to the beach. This did not appeal to Godley, who in a verbal communication to Aspinall, said that 'Birdwood is a ——— ' and attempted to deflect blame from himself by saying that Bean thought

Bridges was the one to urge evacuation. This was indeed Bean's opinion, but Bean also thought Godley was mistaken when the latter considered his troops 'completely demoralised', because Godley only came into contact with stragglers and shaken men. Meanwhile, Birdwood reiterated that Godley was the one who was most definite about evacuation, and wanted to start evacuation preparations before telling Hamilton. After a series of heated letters between Aspinall, Godley and Birdwood, it does transpire that Birdwood wanted to stay rather than evacuate, a position that received corroboration from Col. Joly de Lotbinière, chief Anzac engineer, who was also present on the beach, while Godley and Bridges clearly did want to evacuate. And Birdwood's argument that he only sent the message because he wanted Hamilton to decide between Helles and Anzac is not mentioned in the Birdwood/Godley message, and is unlikely to be true.[32]

Aspinall was conscious of the reputations involved and the contradictory nature of the evidence. So in the official history he protected Bridges and Godley on the question of immediate evacuation, and he protected Birdwood by being careful to say that it was up to Hamilton to decide whether evacuation should occur or not. This implied that the Birdwood/Godley message was always intended for Hamilton. Birdwood was grateful for the changes, and Godley was happy to be able to get words like 'despondency' and 'disaster' removed from Aspinall's forthcoming text. Bean was also circumspect in his text, and defended Bridges and Birdwood, while making Godley's comment about demoralization an anonymous remark.[33]

If there were obvious Allied problems at Anzac, what of the Turkish side of the story? According to the Turkish Official History, noises off Ari Burnu alerted troops of the 2nd Battalion, 27th Regiment of 9 Division as early as 2.30 a.m. on 25 April. Lt-Col. Yarbay Sefik, commanding 27th Regiment, offered to commence operations against the landing early on, at 5.45 a.m. But this offer was not possible due to the wide distribution of the 27th Regiment troops, and because of confusion caused by reports of other landings. Meanwhile, naval fire and the Anzacs' initial rush drove the men of the Turkish 2nd Battalion, 27th Regiment, inland. Then, Col. Mustafa Kemal, commanding 19 Division, located near Boghali, heard the firing at Ari Burnu, and was informed at 6.30 a.m. by Col. Halil Sami Bey (GOC 9 Division) that the enemy had succeeded in climbing the heights of Ari Burnu. Kemal ordered two thirds of his division (57 and 77 Regiments) to march toward the fighting, and especially his reliable 57th Regiment, which was already on parade for training purposes. At the same time, Kemal initially held back the 72nd Regiment, which was an Arab regiment that he believed to be less trustworthy.[34]

Essentially, 57th Regiment of 19 Division attacked the northern flank of the Anzac landing, while 27th Regiment of 9 Division attacked the southern centre and right flank of the landing. Despite the natural focus of English language historians on the difficulties of the Anzac landing, there were numerous problems with the Turkish defence. Maj. Zeki Bey, commanding the 1st Battalion of the 57th Regiment of 19 Division, notes that the 2nd Battalion of the 57th Regiment simply disappeared in the fighting around Fisherman's Hut, possibly due to panic by the battalion commander. The Turkish official history relates that naval fire, casualties, and loss of communications, caused the 2nd Battalion to retreat towards Chunuk Bair. Also in the area of the Sphinx, the Turkish official history states that there were only eight to ten Turks left to defend the area, and these retreated to Russell's Top. The 3rd Battalion of 57th Regiment, attacking at dusk, reported they only had eighty to ninety men left to guard Russell's Top. It also appears that although 57th Regiment got smartly onto the scene, Kemal's 77th Regiment was slow to arrive, partly because of the distance it had to travel, and partly because Kemal received a false message that the Allies had also landed at Kum Tepe (halfway between Gaba Tepe and Helles). Kemal thus temporarily diverted this regiment south, until he found the report was false. Consequently, 77th Regiment did not commence operations until quite late on 25 April, perhaps around dusk. Meanwhile, due to the false information about Kum Tepe, Kemal wasted some hours in the middle of the day going south to see if this information was correct. He did not learn that it was false until about 1.00 p.m., when, by chance, he came across III Corps HQ at Mal Tepe. This excursion south could have been a fatal error, and Kemal did leave 19 Division without its commander for some critical hours.[35]

That evening, when 77th Regiment did finally come into the line, because the regiment was Arab and contained elderly soldiers, it caused severe problems by firing wildly, even before it reached the line. Consequently, 27th Regiment thought 57th Regiment was firing at it, and shouted throughout the night to what they thought was their neighbouring regiment to stop firing – similarly 57th Regiment cried out to 27th Regiment to stop firing! Neither appeared to know that 77th Regiment was actually located between them, while the Arabs of the 77th Regiment could not understand the language of the other two Regiments. To compound these problems, after some naval shelling, or according to Zeki Bey, as a result of Australian machine-gun fire, the 77th Regiment then fled and hid in the bushes, dragging back 27th Regiment with it. The Turkish official history blames the commanding officer of 27th Regiment for this. Consequently, the Lone Pine area was left open and vulnerable for some time, and this also caused a crisis in 19 Division. Later, 77th Regiment was sent to the south of the line at Gaba Tepe because it was a quiet part of the line where the regiment was less likely to cause trouble. On the other hand, the suspect 72nd Regiment became steadier, and one battalion came up to the Chunuk Bair area as a reserve in the late afternoon or early evening of 25 April, around 4.30 p.m. According to the Turkish official history, this was too late to prepare for an attack, but two battalions of this regiment did stop the Turkish retirement from Lone Pine the next day. Given less than satisfactory regiments, and the confusion of the day, Kemal did well with his 19 Division. His actions with 57th Regiment were quick, decisive and admirable, but he was understandably slow with his poorer Arab regiments. Kemal's post facto account is not always consistent with other accounts, and this may partly be due to translation errors. For example, according to Zeki Bey, Kemal did not put the mountain battery into action on Hill 241 (Suyatagi) as Kemal states, but quite a lot further south, just north of Scrubby Knoll. This might indicate that Kemal did not get as far north toward Chunuk Bair as quickly as he says. Also, when Kemal remarks that he put the 77th Regiment of 19 Division into action on the *left* of the 27th Regiment, of course he meant on the *right* of 27th Regiment, between the 27th and 57th Regiments.[36] Thus, overall, the task of the defending Turks was a lot more difficult than the attackers, or subsequent historians, imagined.

★

To summarize the reasons for Anzac problems on 25 April, these are actually rather numerous: loss of surprise; an incorrect landing place; the last-minute shift to a right flank orientation after the landing by Sinclair MacLagan; confusion in the difficult scrub country resulting in lack of cohesion, communication, discipline and direction; mediocre leadership in certain areas by some battalion commanders; failure to land field artillery, leaving Anzac troops under demoralizing and continuous shrapnel fire; a stern baptism of fire for mostly untried troops; relative failure of naval supporting fire; the lengthy four-hour halt in landing troops in the afternoon of 25 April; a reasonably quick Turkish response; and very effective Turkish shrapnel and sniper fire. Of all these reasons, the last seems the most significant. It is hardly surprising that Godley, Bridges and others contemplated evacuation, and really the wonder is that the Anzac troops did as well as they did.

The next few days tried the Anzacs severely, but they continued to hang on to the Anzac enclave. Groups started to sort themselves out, but still suffered from extreme exhaustion, and lack of water and supplies. Proper reorganization did not take place until the gradual arrival of four battalions of the Royal Naval Division on 28 and 29 April, which allowed Anzac troops to withdraw and rejoin their proper units. However, Birdwood was less than complimentary about the Naval Division troops, calling them 'children under untrained officers and I feel sorry for them.' Birdwood's anxiety was partly justified during a Turkish attack, when the Naval Brigade had a scare, shot their commanding officer, and fired wildly. Meanwhile, a Turkish counterattack on 27 April was stopped on Battleship Hill primarily by naval fire, and elsewhere by artillery, rifle and machine-gun fire. But an aggressive report on the same day from the Turkish Fifth Army, gives no hint of Turkish difficulties: 'From this morning onwards the 19th Division with reinforcements began to attack the enemy in the area of Ariburnu and Kabatepe. Despite the dense Allied fire, the attack went forward successfully. The attack is continued violently.' According to Kemal's own version, the attack was successful in the area of Lone Pine and Johnston's Jolly, where the Anzacs 'left their rifles and, almost as a body, came out in front of their trenches, and waving hats, white handkerchiefs and flags sought to give themselves up. These scenes were watched by myself and my whole staff with the naked eye from Kemalyeri [Scrubby Knoll].' Although there were still groups of stragglers about, there is no Anzac record of this incident.[37] Kemal was not yet done, and despite the fact that his 5 and 19 Divisions were mixed up on 30 April, tried for another mass attack with 24 battalions, this time at 4.00 a.m. on 1 May, still dark enough to avoid naval fire. By his own description, Kemal's troops only had mountain batteries for artillery support, and thus relied almost entirely on the bayonet. The attack appears to have been poorly organized, with little coordination, and the net result was failure with very heavy casualties. In these attacks, Kemal and the Turks showed courage but very little finesse.[38]

On the Anzac side, there were differences of opinion about tactics and strategy. Defending against Turkish pressure earlier on 26 and 27 April, Australian and New Zealand commanders in the Baby 700 area came into conflict. A series of messages from the 1st Battalion Wellington Rifles on 27 April reveals the problem. At 5.15 p.m., Maj. Young of this battalion sent a message: 'A colonel of the Australians has ordered my front platoons to charge on they are in rather a bad way but I have thought it wiser to hang on here.' Lt-Col. Malone, replied, also at 5.15 p.m.: 'Hang on. Do not take orders from Australian Colonel unless you agree with his proposition. Dig in.' At 5.50 p.m., a New Zealand officer reported that men were coming in saying that an Australian Colonel (now identified as Lt-Col. G.F. Braund, commanding Australian 2nd Battalion) had sent them in with no water, and ammunition had run out, so they were retiring. At 6.00 p.m., Malone communicated directly with Braund, telling him to hang on to the position he had retired to, and to dig in. Rather pointedly, Malone asked: 'Have the NZ Coys retired too, or have you left them with gap in line?' Finally, at 7.00 p.m., Maj. Young reported that his front line was wiped out by being ordered to charge by an Australian Colonel, despite his orders to entrench where they were.[39]

In his private diary, Malone was a good deal more critical of Braund. Already on 26 April, Malone was protesting that his men were being pushed forward into a chaotic situation. Malone met Braund in the region of Walker's Ridge and Russell's Top. According to Malone, Braund 'knew nothing. Had no defensive position, no plan, nothing but a murderous notion that the only thing to do was to plunge troops out of the neck of the ridge into the jungle beyond.' Malone told his battalion officers, including Maj. Young, to dig in, but Braund 'as Senior Officer [claimed] their obedience to his orders, and so on they went and got slaughtered. Lt [E.R.] Wilson and his two machine-guns were treated in the same way.' According to Malone, when he refused further reinforcements for Braund, the latter said he would have to retire to his first position. Malone told him he should not have left it, and asked Braund why he was behaving in this manner. Braund reportedly replied that 'he feared if he didn't go on his men would run away. I [Malone] said that was no reason to sacrifice aimlessly *my* men.' Malone wrote that he had driven some Australians forward 'pelting the leading ones, on the track, when they stopped, with stones, and putting my toe into the rear ones.' Malone continued to complain on 27 April about the 'frightful murderous slaughter bungled by Col Braund…', and insisted that the Australians be withdrawn from the area. The Australians fired all through the night on 27 April, and when Braund came to ask for ammunition, Malone refused. At 6.00 a.m. on 28 April, the Australians were relieved. Malone wrote:

> It was an enormous relief to see the last of them. I believe they are spasmodically brave and probably the best of them had been killed or wounded. They have been, I think, badly handled and trained. Officers in most cases no good. I am thinking of asking for a Court Martial on Col. Braund. It makes me mad when I think of my grand men being sacrificed by his incapacity and folly.[40]

Malone admitted that Braund was brave, and in the end he did not ask for a court martial. However, Malone's diary reveals that he objected mainly to the loss of his men, and secondly, to disorganization. In his opinion, the deaths were needless. Malone preferred order and structure on the battlefield, so that it was better to hold a defensive position in an orderly manner, even if it meant giving up ground to the attacking Turks. Also, like the British, Malone objected to the casual ways of the Australians, writing that they swarmed about his lines 'like flies. I keep getting them sent out. They are like masterless men going their own ways.' On the other hand, Braund accepted the chaotic battlefield, wanted to gain ground, perhaps feared that withdrawal meant loss of morale, and was willing to sacrifice men in bayonet charges or in holding the front line. For example, it is notable that Malone objected to what he considered was the improper use of his machine-guns when Braund ordered Lt Wilson and two machine-guns forward to deal with the Turkish attack on 27 April. If they had been properly handled, Malone probably would not have objected. So, Malone wrote: 'It was skirmishing with machine-guns. Quite wrong. My officers knew better, but Col. Braund took the attitude "I am your senior officer… and I order you to do what I tell you."' On the other hand, Braund's use of the New Zealand machine-guns drove the Turks off on the morning of 27 April, although the Australian charge in the afternoon of 27 April, including the machine-guns, resulted in the loss of New Zealander Lt Wilson, two sergeants as casualties, and one machine-gun. The other machine-gun continued to be worked through the night. The tactical views of Malone and Braund both had merits and faults. Yet it is hard to be as critical of Braund as Malone was, since Braund did beat off the Turkish attack, and hold on to key positions at Russell's Top and Walker's Ridge. Perhaps, in the chaotic situation of 27 April, Braund's actions had the greater merit, while Malone's emphasis on order and discipline was less useful then than it was later.[41]

Not all New Zealand commanders were as professional as Malone. The Auckland Battalion's Col. A. Plugge appears to have been unpopular and inefficient. Thus Lt Levenson-Gower West remarked on 28 April that Plugge appeared in the front line on the left flank in the evening, and complained about the siting of their trenches: 'He had never been near us all day and had never expressed any desire to have trenches in a particular spot…'. Fortunately, Birdwood had approved the trench line, so Plugge was rebuffed. Then on 30 April, after Plugge cancelled a raid on a Turkish outpost, West wrote: 'Everybody nowadays is angry and discontented with the Colonel. Even Price [the Adjutant, Maj. Price] looks hopeless and tired.' The next day, back on the beach, there was 'No Colonel [and] no orders…'. Plugge then appeared and authorized tea and a swim for the troops, but a little later a staff officer, Col. E.W.C. Chaytor, told them they were in a most dangerous spot, and moved the troops around the corner and under a ridge.[42] New Zealand staff work also seemed to be a problem with the offensive action attempted on 2 May. Birdwood planned a major attack aimed at Baby 700 and on the right, to move the line forward from the 400 Plateau. The right wing of the attack could not be done because 1 Australian Division was still reorganizing, but Godley, from his headquarters, ordered the attack on Baby 700 via Monash Valley by a combined Anzac force to go ahead. The two Australian battalions attacked on time, but the Otago Battalion was late getting to the jump off spot. So the New Zealanders attacked at 8.30 p.m., about an hour after the Australian battalions had moved forward. After an artillery and naval bombardment, the disjointed offensive failed. The New Zealand war diary simply recorded: 'The two attacks should have been simultaneous, and might then have been successful. By 8.30 p.m. the enemy had recovered from effects of bombardment.' Malone was not so sure. He recorded that the naval bombardment either fell 1,000 yards short or long of the Turkish trenches. And why attack where the Turks had been attacked for days? Malone thought the attack should have gone in on the left flank.[43]

There is no doubt that the cooperation of naval fire, artillery and infantry took a lot of sorting out at Anzac. The diaries of artillery units are understandably full of adjustments to cooperation, and there were many complaints about short firing, which the artillery units generally denied. On 30 April there took place a conference of Forward Observation Officers (FOOs) and Signal Message Officers in direct contact with ships, and this service then improved markedly. But it was difficult for the artillery to find good positions, observation was necessarily poor, the trenches of Anzacs and Turks were too close together for safe firing, the howitzers were short of ammunition, planes were not available for artillery shoots, telephone wires kept getting cut, and

Turkish gun positions were hard to spot and in some places such as the Olive Grove, impossible to destroy. From the perspective of the infantry, Malone noted that it was difficult to get the artillery to respond to targets. Hence on 5 May, when the Turks dug new trenches on the left flank, Malone could not get the mountain artillery to respond: 'It seems strange that there is such difficulty about it. My Brigadier [F.E. Johnston] won't let me go to Divisional HQ about it, and is busy himself with other things I suppose.' Ultimately, *Majestic* got onto the Turkish trenches and obliterated them. Malone felt there was a wasted opportunity here to exploit this situation, which was allowed to pass because Hamilton had called for the New Zealanders to move to Helles to take part in an offensive there.[44]

It is not surprising that Hamilton, needing troops at Helles, which he regarded as the main battle area, and noting the disadvantages of the cramped and over-looked Anzac area, suggested to Birdwood on 8 May that Anzac be evacuated. Hamilton had visited Anzac to check on progress there on 3 May, although couching his decision to investigate in a strangely diffident manner to Roger Keyes. According to Keyes, Hamilton:

> came up to me and whispered 'don't you think we might go and have a look at it' – rather like a naughty school boy… It really was very important that we should see the position.

The visit stimulated Hamilton's idea to leave Anzac, but Birdwood was not pleased, and persuaded Hamilton on 10 May that it was not a good plan. This was probably correct, since the later break out plan from the Anzac front in early August did promise success. Meanwhile, Malone criticized the 'plunging policy' or 'rushing tactics' of early May, with heavy Allied losses, and argued that now it was trench war, as in Flanders, 'sap, sap, dig, dig…'. Malone felt that:

> We and the other troops [at Helles] have suffered tremendous losses because our directors failed to quickly appreciate that this is a day of digging and machine-guns, and that prepared positions cannot be rushed.

But this was a slow game, so Malone already suggested in his diary on 14 May the future August plan for a left hook at Anzac. Malone told Gen. Paris' staff of the Royal Naval Division of this idea, and on 13 May Birdwood wrote Hamilton with a similar plan.[45]

Meanwhile, despite heavy attacks and counterattacks on both sides at Anzac, the situation basically did not change in May. Better Turkish tactics might have made a difference, and the New Zealand war diary frequently commented on strange Turkish tactics. On 17 May, it was reported that the Turks shelled the beaches and lighters, yet when troops landed, there was practically no shelling: 'I cannot understand the work of their observers.' More critically, the heavy Turkish attacks in the early hours of 19 May were countered by Anzac artillery and machine-gun fire, yet the diary noted: 'It is difficult to understand their [Turkish] tactics in assaulting us in the piecemeal and disjointed fashion.' It would appear from a Turkish message of 13 May that Mustafa Kemal and his 19 Division were more interested in forcing the Anzacs back at any cost than in the careful organization of attacks. Thus the Turkish offensive of 19 May simply featured mass attacks, which were readily stopped with heavy Turkish losses, perhaps with as many as 10,000 casualties. Kemal asked for casualty figures from all units of his 19 Division on 21 May, and a ceasefire to bury the dead was proposed. Both Allied and Turkish sources say that it was the Australians who first proposed the ceasefire on 20 May, via the Red Cross who came out of the lines at German Officers Trench. On the other hand, Turkish 7 Division sent out stretcher bearers on 19 May, who were captured by the Anzacs but then sent back. After some arguments against the 20 May plan by Enver Pasa, the Turkish Minister of War, who did not want the Turks to lose face by being the first to ask for a halt to the fighting, the ceasefire was agreed, and took place on 24 May. Other ceasefires were later proposed in June and July to bury the dead, but it was Hamilton on 9 July who turned down the last ceasefire offer.[46]

During May, on the Allied side, the New Zealand war diary was particularly critical of the Navy. Hence, on 26 May, when reinforcements for the New Zealand Brigade and 4th Australian Brigade arrived at 5 p.m., these were heavily shelled while their boat lay at anchor 200 yards from shore. The war diary commented: 'It was a lamentable piece of work on the part of the Staffs of GHQ and the Navy.' The Navy was also blamed earlier, on 5 May, for the long delay in moving the New Zealand Brigade to Helles. The New Zealand writer of the war diary was also sceptical of the accuracy of naval fire. So when Turks were reported massing in Kucuk Anafarta at 4.30 p.m. on 18 May, the Navy claimed to have put two shells in among them. The diary laconically noted: 'It is doubtful.' However, the sinking of *Triumph* by a German submarine on 25 May elicited a strangely emotional response in the war diary, which reported that:

> with one long drawn out moan, she turned completely over on her right side very slowly but without a check, and gradually her funnels touched the water, and then over she went on her side, and turned turtle. The most ghastly sight on God's earth, and to think that the 20,000 of us men who saw this going on from the shore were powerless to turn a finger to help. My God, it made one's blood boil.

The commentary continued: 'If only the men in the trenches had seen it, I think they would all have dashed forward and bayonetted everything that came in their way.'[47]

From the perspective of a previously unpublished account by one junior officer, Lt Robert Blackie, on board *Triumph*, there was a more prosaic reaction. It seems that *Triumph* relied on her anti-torpedo nets for protection, but when a periscope was reported in the morning, most scoffed, saying 'Take more water with it', and thought it was a shark or some other fish. Around 12.20 midday, the scare started properly, and Blackie began shutting off cooling plants and watertight doors. When the torpedo hit, Blackie thought at first it was an enemy shell, but as the ship listed to starboard, it was evident this was a torpedo. Blackie asked Commander Egerton if it was alright to abandon ship, and on getting the affirmative, prepared to dive off the port anchor. Blackie saw the captain on the port side of the bridge calmly blowing up his Gieve floatable waistcoat, with eyeglass in eye. The captain survived. Meanwhile, Blackie dove off the high side of the ship: 'I seemed to be an age in the air before

I struck the water, fortunately I made a fair dive, but stung my forehead a bit on striking and had a slight headache after. I took off my trews and shoes and clad in vest and cap swam clear of her.' Blackie then swam to the destroyer *Chelmer*, and grabbed a boat fall, but:

> just then she went astern and the wash from the propellor sent two men on to me who grabbed me. I found this too much to support so getting one of them, a big marine, to lay hold of the fall I let go and grabbed the forward fall and only had myself to keep up. However, she soon stopped going astern and I was hauled up on deck and right glad to get there.

Blackie watched *Triumph* which 'turned bottom up in about ten minutes, and after stopping in this position for a few minutes more, went down by the head. A cry of 'Goodbye Triumph' went up from everyone as she took the plunge.' The Turks then started shelling *Chelmer*, which made for Kephalo and then Mudros. There Blackie was outfitted with new clothes, 'and having had my sovereign case around my neck I was able to buy a bottle of whiskey with the contents.'[48]

Two days later, *Majestic* was torpedoed by the same submarine, and the remaining battleships were withdrawn to harbour. As a wounded Australian told Blackie, after watching *Triumph* go down, 'There's no back door there my boys.' Henceforth, naval fire would be supplied by destroyers and, later, by monitors. In fact, this proved to be adequate. Anzac had been a bold Allied gamble, but by May it had failed in its purpose, and June and July brought no basic change, except for growing sickness lists. However, in August the Anzac battle would be renewed, while down at Helles the Allies commenced their assaults on the Achi Baba heights.

THE FIGHTING AT HELLES AND THE MAY TURKISH CRISIS

April – July

After the British landings at Helles, and the French re-embarkation from Kum Kale to reinforce the right wing at Helles, the Allies prepared to launch a series of offensives aimed at capturing the high point of Achi Baba. These offensives were labelled First Krithia (28 April); Second Krithia (6–8 May); and Third Krithia (4 June). There was also a major Allied offensive on 12 and 13 July.

Allied casualties were very heavy in these offensives, yet the Turks suffered their own problems during their costly night attacks of 1–2 and 3–4 May. These led to a crisis of confidence in the southern Turkish/German command system, and very nearly produced a Turkish retreat behind Achi Baba. The arrival of German submarines later in May drove off the Allied battleships and helped to stabilize the Turkish line.

★

Following the intense fighting and bloodshed of the 25 April landing, the next day, 26 April, Anzac stabilized, V Beach consolidated, Y Beach evacuated, and a rough Allied line was formed across the southern tip of Helles. The French came back from Kum Kale, and landed overnight on the extreme right of the line at Helles. As far as the defence was concerned, the Turks were in considerable disarray, retreating two miles or more, as far as Achi Baba, and so the night of 26/27 April passed reasonably quietly. On 27 April, the British and French continued to reorganize, and various units reported little activity. The 1st Battalion, Lancashire

Fusiliers, remarked that at 8.00 a.m. on 27 April, the 'Turks withdrew – All quiet and patrols in front for 1 mile.' The 2nd Battalion, Royal Dublin Fusiliers, simply commented that 'nothing happened all day…'. The 1st Battalion, Royal Munster Fusiliers, reported on 26 April at 4.00 p.m.: 'Turks in full retreat for 2 miles…'. In perfect hindsight, it appears so much attention was paid to the landing itself that golden opportunities were lost to the Allies on 27 April. Of course, reorganization was very necessary: the heavy casualties certainly needed attention, stores and guns had to be landed, the French integrated at Helles, and offensive plans formulated. But on this day the Allies could have advanced a good deal further at Helles than was later achieved, because Liman von Sanders and the Turks were a little slow to react to the landing.[1]

The Allied system seemed inflexible and cumbersome, but the problem really lay with Hunter-Weston, who told Hamilton that he could not attack on 27 April because the men were exhausted, casualties were high, and ammunition was short. All this was only too true, yet another day might only lead to greater exhaustion, and more casualties, although stores, food and water, reserves, artillery and ammunition would land. Judging by Hunter-Weston's letters on 27 April, he was too much influenced by the achievement of the actual landing, against his previous pessimism, to think differently. In various letters, he emphasized the miracle of the landing rather than what could be immediately achieved: 'my men have effected the impossible…', he wrote, and again 'we have managed it, we have achieved the impossible!'. Hunter-Weston reckoned that the landing was a four to one chance against, and that half his difficulties were over. With Achi Baba taken, he felt that three quarters of the problem would be over. Ominously, he added that this would take some time.[2]

So 27 April passed quietly enough, though there were some cautious advances, while the process of landing stores, men, guns and horses continued. This was no easy task, as Maj. D.E. Forman, Royal Horse Artillery, described. His B Battery of 15 Brigade, 29 Division, was originally supposed to land at V Beach, but problems there made this impossible. Therefore, the battery began to land at W Beach at midday on 27 April, the first battery of the brigade. Only 56 horses of the original 161 could be landed, due to lack of horse boats. The task took nine hours, and twelve horse teams were needed to drag the guns off the beach. Yet, already the next day, 28 April, at 8.00 a.m., Forman and his battery were in action to support what came to be known as the First Battle of Krithia.[3]

In hindsight, this offensive, planned by Hunter-Weston, became typical of the whole Gallipoli campaign, in that it asked too much of the troops – it was too ambitious against a strengthening defence. The aim was to reach a line that could then be used as a launching pad against Achi Baba. One brigade was to advance on the extreme left, and two other brigades in the centre would advance until reaching the road north of Krithia, and would then wheel to the right. The French were to act as a pivot on the right, and advance along the coast, although on 27 April the French commander, d'Amade, was confused about his responsibilities.[4] There was no time for conferences, and in Maj. Forman's case, he could only deploy three guns and 200 rounds. On the other hand, the Turkish guns were bursting their shrapnel too high, and were incapable of counter-battery action. But the Allied barrage was meagre, and the attacking line thin and very weary as the offensive started at 8.00 a.m.. On the left, good initial progress was made by 87 Brigade, despite the surprising discovery of the existence of Gully Ravine, but at about midday the brigade came up against Turkish defences. Later in the day this brigade was saved from a Turkish counterattack by the guns of *Queen Elizabeth*. In the centre, 88 Brigade lost coordination, and dissolved into unrelated actions, besides meeting stiff Turkish resistance. The war diary of 86 Brigade, in reserve, reveals the fog of war. According to this diary, 86 Brigade moved up to support the attack and made good progress toward Krithia. But the war diary claims 86 Brigade could not attack properly because a staff officer of 88 Brigade deflected some Munsters and Dublins to the right, 'saying it was a matter of life and death to his Brigade.' Also the French on the right retreated, as did 88 Brigade. Some men also retired further than they should have 'due to a C.O. making no effort to communicate with Brigade headquarters.' Eventually, tired, disorganized, and lacking sufficient weight, the offensive halted by the late afternoon. Allegedly, some men did reach Krithia village before retiring and digging in.[5]

On 30 April, Hamilton wrote to Lady Hamilton complaining of 'the various alarmist and despondent tendencies of some of my commanders. They are more alarming than the enemy…' Hamilton was thinking mainly of the French, whose green troops were easily rattled, especially at night. But on the other side of the hill, the Turkish picture was not as happy as the Allies might have imagined. On 28 and 29 April Turkish Fifth Army appealed for more officers, because of casualties, and for more artillery shells, which were running dangerously short. Maj. Mahmut, commanding 3rd Battalion, 26 Regiment, recalled that a panic withdrawal had started among his troops, at which point the Colonel of the 26th Regiment ordered a retreat to Soanlidere, a defensive line well behind Achi Baba. Mahmut refused, and, just in time, nine companies of Turkish reserves arrived. Four hours later, 19th Regiment of 7 Division also arrived. So a Turkish disaster was narrowly averted. The story is now taken up by Capt. Carl Mühlmann, ADC to Liman von Sanders, whose lengthy first hand account of the next few days at the beginning of May is absolutely critical in showing the problems the Turkish command faced. English language historians have usually looked at this period from the Allied point of view, and stressed Allied problems, and so Mühlmann's account provides a badly needed counterpoise. On 28 April, Mühlmann witnessed many wounded Turks streaming up from Helles toward the Turkish hospital at Maidos unaided, since there was absolutely no Turkish medical service at all. On the night of 28 April, after the Allied attack had been repulsed, Mühlmann described the scene:

> In a semi-circle around the sharply defined Seddulbahir peninsula lay the ships, all brightly lit. On our side, the burning village of Krithia offered dim illumination. Several enemy bivouac fires lit up the distant horizon; our poor troops sat huddled together and freezing in ravines; we dared not light fires.

It was also necessary for Mühlmann to try and reorganize the Turkish troops at Helles, who had arrived from all directions, usually without baggage, knowing nothing of the terrain, and all mixed up. At the same time, the Allied fleet around Helles sent a hail of shells against all targets, big and small, accurately guided by balloon or plane. As Mühlmann noted: 'The fleet's fire is impressively accurate,' so much so that travel by daylight was almost impossible:

> At one time losses were incredibly high – before the troops learned to use even the smallest terrain defile and to move in only the smallest groups… some battalions lost up to thirty per cent of their strength before they had marched to the front lines.[6]

Nevertheless, despite the problems, Enver Pasa and Field Marshal von der Goltz, the aged German military advisor at Istanbul, urged attacks at Helles to drive the Allies into the sea. Von der Goltz in particular criticized Fifth Army for not doing enough, and demanded that the Allies be driven off the peninsula within two days, because a long campaign would lead to disaster and the capture of Istanbul. In fact Liman von Sanders was already preparing a two-division attack at Helles, for the night of 1/2 May. Attacking at night was essential because of the Allied naval guns, which could decimate an offensive, but naturally a night offensive was a very difficult undertaking. Besides, even night was a limited defence, since the fleet possessed search lights, and previously reconnoitred targets could be destroyed. Thus Mühlmann reported:

> Around 11 p.m. [on 1 May], a colossal bombardment from the heavy guns landed on the quarters in which our staff resided… The Turks manning a battery near us ran off; our horses became extremely nervous; the telephone staff disappeared; even on the [general] staff we saw many shirkers. We could hear the whistling and cracking of shells very close to us… we were showered with stones and dirt.[7]

At first, as the Turkish night attack started at 10.00 p.m. on 1 May, Mühlmann received some news of its success. But by 3.30 a.m. on 2 May the night had become totally silent, and so at dawn Mühlmann rode off to get news, being particularly anxious since he was the chief planner of the offensive. The attack had been partially successful, especially against the French, but with the dawn of 2 May came the destructive ships' fire which slammed into the Turkish lines retreating on the Hissarlik slopes on the eastern edge of Helles. Mühlmann watched as:

> the troops suffered great numbers of casualties – not only while retreating due to the ships' fire on three sides, but also during the day due to enfilading fire. *Agamemnon* – which is my mortal enemy and for which I wish a quick end at the hands of a German U Boat – took our left wing… under heavy shrapnel fire all day long…

Mühlmann particularly criticized the Straits batteries for not supporting the Turkish attack, since these batteries would not have resumed supporting the offensive, except for a direct order to do so from Liman von Sanders. Next, the proposed Turkish attack for the following night of 2/3 May was prevented from occurring by an earlier Allied attack. This was actually fortunate for the Turks because two new batteries, essential for the resumption of the Turkish offensive, had not arrived, and did not do so until 3.30 a.m. Around 2.00 a.m., the Allied attacks were halted, and Mühlmann considered reviving the Turkish attack, but this was postponed due to the late arrival of the batteries, and the coming dawn.[8]

The next day, 3 May, Mühlmann went to work preparing orders for a resumption of the Turkish attack for that night, 3/4 May. These orders were delayed by malfunctioning telephone lines, so the Turkish divisions received their orders late. As night fell, Mühlmann was alarmed by a huge naval searchlight which 'lit up the entire area bright as day; nothing could move unobserved in this powerful circle of light.' But by 10.00 p.m. the search lights went out, and this time a three division Turkish attack was planned, 9 Division in the west of Helles, 7 Division in the centre, and 15 Division in the east, against the French. However, this offensive, particularly against Hissarlik, came unstuck. Mühlmann wrote:

> It is incredible what levels of talent the senior Turkish officers can attain when it comes to disappearing. The scenes that we witnessed were not encouraging. Instead of advancing silently in previously agreed-upon directions, the skirmish line ran up and down in all directions, yelling like

Jews in a synagogue; the officers also failed in this regard. Divisional and regimental commanders were nowhere to be seen…

Bullets whistled around Mühlmann and the Turkish staff, but they could see nothing of what was happening. Mühlmann volunteered to ride up to the front at dawn to find out the situation. His first contact was with some Turkish soldiers,

who informed me excitedly that they had captured an English machine-gun company; with a certain degree of surprise, but also anger, I recognized the so-called Englishmen as the 6 German machine-gun companies that the *Breslau* had given us… they had been seized, beaten, and above all not allowed to move up to the front… And now, at this decisive moment, when the Turks had so few machine-guns and when 6 well-led machine-guns could have achieved so much, I found them captured.

This is probably the incident reported in a Turkish message, in which Turkish soldiers killed three German sailors by accident.[9]

However, worse was to follow for Mühlmann. Running ahead to find out the exact situation, he described a wild scene:

And what sights did I see!! A horrible confusion! Thick lines of skirmishers were streaming backwards; on the other side, new skirmish lines were again assaulting the slope; all with wild shouts of Allah. I searched for officers, and with my few words of Turkish, I drove the men forward. Where I was, they followed me to the front, but when I went to a different sector of the Turkish lines, they followed me there… They all screamed at me excitedly; one showed me his wounds; another wanted to charge forward, the next backward; still another told me a long tale of the previous day's fighting. It got even lighter; I saw the masts of *Agamemnon* rising above Morto Bay; any second the devastating shrapnel fire would commence…

Mühlmann tried to restore order, and eventually got the men to form a defensive line, anchored by the now released German machine-gun companies. Leaving them, Mühlmann returned to his headquarters, passing on the way the two newly arrived artillery batteries. On asking the batteries why they did not support the attack better, the reply annoyed Mühlmann – that this would have exposed them to flanking fire from the ships. In general it was clear that leadership of the Turkish troops had been lost, and there was nothing to be done but dig in and hold the line at all costs.[10]

Why had the Turkish offensive of 3/4 May failed? Mühlmann considered that the first and most important factor was the Allied fleet, which checked the Turkish attacks from all three sides. Next, the offensive had been rushed. Infantry had been brought up from all directions, without provisions, baggage, or knowledge of the ground. This also related to the third factor, lack of training of men and officers, especially for night attacks. For example, senior commanders stayed behind in rear echelons, out of touch with the battle. Finally, 9 Division on the right or western wing, let the Turks down:

> Both nights… regiments of 7 Division had penetrated down to the landing sites of Seddulbahir, had bombarded the landing piers: but, despite all orders to attack, 9 Division made only weak attempts to advance. Thus, the enemy facing 9 Division… could deploy his forces against the right flank of the forward positioned 7 Division and thus force it to retreat.

This is an interesting comment, because historians assume that the attack of 3/4 May was made only against the French line. In fact, the Turkish offensive was intended to be against the whole Helles sector. Mühlmann commented: 'Is that not a shame? So much blood was needlessly spilt as a result. For the losses sustained by 7 Division, which had to withdraw in daylight under a murderous fire from three sides, were naturally very, very high.' It seems that 15 Division was protected by the rough country at Hissarlik on the eastern flank, while 7 Division, in the centre, suffered particularly from the French 75s, a quick-firing artillery piece.[11]

Mention of the French draws attention to the sliding morale of these troops during the Turkish attacks of 1/2 May and 3/4 May. During the night of 1/2 May, the Senegalese broke and ran, and the French line was reinforced with the Anson Battalion of the Royal Naval Division

(RND), as well as some Worcesters. However, at dawn on 2 May d'Amade demanded a counterattack by the entire French line. In Gallic style, he ordered 'En avant partout. Faites sonner aux clarions la sonnerie. En avant.' The French did advance later that morning, and recovered some ground in the Kereves Dere region. Meanwhile, at 8.20 a.m., Hunter-Weston wanted the Anson Battalion and the Worcesters back. But at 2.45 p.m. on 2 May the commander of 1 French Division, Gen. Masnou, wrote that the coming night was the moment of danger and it was necessary to keep the British troops to help French morale. Still, at 8.58 p.m. on the evening of 2 May, Hunter-Weston repeated his request for the return of the Anson Battalion, or they would have no food or ammunition left. Hunter-Weston also told d'Amade, quite correctly as it turned out, that the Turks were not attacking with any determination. For his part, d'Amade was genuinely afraid that French morale would break in some units, and Hunter-Weston sent in his last reserves to help at 11.30 p.m. on 2 May. But ten minutes later, d'Amade requested a further two Indian Battalions at once, or his right would be in serious trouble. He wrote that the French were involved in several bayonet fights, and there were no reserves. The French line survived the night, and at 9.45 p.m. on 3 May Hunter-Weston once more tried to get the Anson Battalion back. But the Turks repeated their offensive that night, and d'Amade at 5.25 a.m. on 4 May now wanted an attack by the whole 29 Division to relieve the situation. This was probably stimulated by news that the Senegalese had left their lines early that morning. Two hours later, d'Amade requested another battalion to support his left flank. A few minutes later, Hamilton told d'Amade that the latter's telegram, saying the British were falling back, was 'entirely erroneous.' Hunter-Weston said all was well, but half a battalion would be sent over. Yet at midday on 4 May, although the Turkish attack was over, Lt-Col. Nogues, commanding the Metropolitan Brigade, told Gen. Masnou that the Anson Battalion refused to leave, saying that if they did, it would be a disaster. Then at 4.00 p.m., still on 4 May, the Zouaves fell back and fled, but this time the French themselves restored the line with a bayonet charge by the 6th Colonial Battalion and two companies of the French Foreign Legion.[12]

It is not surprising that Orlo Williams noted on 4 May that the morale of the French officers and men had 'gone', while Milward simply wrote that Hunter-Weston was cheerful and firm with the French. In fairness, the most severe attacks had been against the French, and on 1/2 May they suffered 2,000 casualties compared to 700 for the British. By 11 May, French casualties amounted to 246 officers and 12,364 men. Clearly, the French were playing their part, and Hamilton agreed to lend the French the 2nd Naval Brigade to help stabilize their line. Then, on 21 May, Gen. Gouraud, who replaced d'Amade on 15 May, ordered that the Senegalese Colonial troops be mixed in with the Metropolitan (mainland French) battalions, to further maintain morale. This order recalls the 'amalgames' of the French Revolution, whereby inexperienced troops were mixed in with veteran units to stabilize the former.[13]

As far as the Turks were concerned, despite the relative failure and chaotic nature of the Turkish attacks in early May, Mühlmann soon realized that the Turkish troops were actually of very good quality. Even on the morning of 4 May, when confusion reigned in the Turkish lines, Mühlmann felt that a few energetic officers could have created order and mounted a strong attack: 'I heard pleas from all side: "But where are we to go? No one told us. We have no officers." And so they ran off in all directions. It was truly decimating.' A little later in May, discovering that the Turkish defence lines were in a mess in the Kereves Dere (French) sector, with no latrines and very shallow trenches, Mühlmann knelt down with the troops amid flying bullets and persuaded them to improve their trenches: 'As I left, they began to dig. Really, truly contented and willing soldier material.'[14]

So, the Turkish soldiers were excellent, but what of their commanders? Here, there occurred a crisis in the German/Turkish command system, exacerbated by the Allied Helles attacks of 6–8 May. English language historians frequently stress the exhaustion and poor condition of the Allies at Helles, without proper consideration of the state of the Turkish army. First of all, the Turkish Fifth Army had suffered considerable casualties, some 15,000 since operations began. Then the attacks, designed to push the Allies into the sea, were clearly not working, and were often rushed. Reserves were quickly used up, and units were thoroughly mixed up and disorganized. So, on 4 May, an urgent and private message went from Kiazim Bey (chief of staff to Liman von Sanders), to Enver Pasa. Kiazim had been a room mate of Enver Pasa at the military academy, and so felt safe in expressing the inner thoughts of Liman von Sanders, even though these would be unwelcome to Enver Pasa. The message essentially spelled out the problems of Fifth Army and asked for permission to go on the defensive. Predictably, Enver Pasa was very annoyed, and demanded further offensive action. A series of messages passed back and forth between Enver Pasa and Kiazim Bey, representing Fifth Army, and on 9 May Enver Pasa came to Gallipoli to see for himself. However, with the end of the Allied offensives at Helles from 6–8 May, the situation stabilized, and the conflict between Enver Pasa and Fifth Army calmed down.[15]

In addition, another conflict developed among German and Turkish commanders at Helles in early May. Col. Halil Bey, commanding Turkish 7 Division, reported to Mühlmann on 6 May that soldiers were exhausted in the extreme, there were incredible losses, there were no officers, individual battalions were led by officer cadets, companies led by sergeants and all units mixed up together. Naval fire made the troops' situation ever worse, officer losses were colossal and naval fire also prevented movement by day to reorganize the mixed up units. Hearing these reports, the Southern Group GHQ, led by Gen. Weber Pasa, with Maj. von Thauvenay as chief of staff, became more and more pessimistic. For example, on 4 May Mühlmann fought with von Thauvenay over the disposition of eight battalions of reserves that were coming up, and the question was whether they should be thrown in to the confusion to support the right wing, or whether the Turkish troops should retreat to the second line of defence. Thauvenay wanted the retreat, Mühlmann and Weber wanted to throw in the eight battalions, and hold the front line. Eventually Weber and Mühlmann prevailed, and now a few days later, during the Allied attacks of 6–8 May, Thauvenay again wanted to retreat. According to Mühlmann:

> Gradually, Thauvenay influenced Weber with his pessimistic views, with the result that [Weber] the next day [8 May] telephoned [Admiral Guido

von] Usedom [commander of the Straits] to say that the situation had become critical, and that a withdrawal had to be discussed… Could we not withdraw as far as Soanlidere?[16]

Soanlidere was actually a line of defence some three miles *behind* Achi Baba, and naturally von Usedom was alarmed. He replied that this would mean the surrender of the most important Turkish batteries, and indeed the surrender of the Straits to the enemy fleet. Mühlmann was also deeply alarmed by the suggestion and wondered why 'all the front areas purchased with so much blood were to be surrendered; the most important terrain given to the enemy without a fight… where every yard surrendered was a loss for our troops and a gain for the enemy?' Mühlmann told Weber and Thauvenay that they ought not to withdraw one step, and then reluctantly went behind the backs of Weber and Thauvenay to inform Liman von Sanders what was happening, 'a very distasteful task for me – that an energetic intervention by the Army's leader was utterly necessary.' Stern orders by Liman von Sanders and the gradual cessation of Allied artillery gradually brought all thoughts of withdrawal to an end. However, von Thauvenay was relieved of his command by Liman von Sanders, Mühlmann noting that 'the manner in which Thauvenay was dismissed was really terribly curt and damaged Germany's reputation. But, in many areas L[iman] simply cannot be advised.'[17]

Thus did the twin crises in the German/Turkish high command in early May eventually get resolved, the one concerning the necessity of Fifth Army going on the defensive, and the other, the growing pessimism in the Southern Group command. The Allied command did not really grasp the severity of Turkish problems at Helles in early May, and the possibilities this opened up had Hamilton fully realized what was going on. Subsequent historians have also under-estimated the Turkish crises of early May. During this period, Mühlmann described the depressing situation of the Turkish defences in the Helles eastern sector:

A horrible field of corpses contaminated the air… partly already in an advanced state of decomposition. The defensive works were miserable, without any system and utterly inadequate. The communication trenches were filled with corpses, so that I, and all reinforcements, had to go to the front over open terrain.

At night, Allied flares and rockets lit up the night, and Mühlmann commented that it 'was lucky for the Turks that the enemy could thus illuminate only small stretches of land at a time, and that ravine cover was available for most of the troops. Otherwise, they could have bombarded us throughout the night.' 9 May was uneventful, and the Allied artillery and ships' fire largely died down with the conclusion of the Allied offensive. Then, on the night of 12/13 May *Goliath* was torpedoed, and as a result the fleet blacked out and largely ceased to use their searchlights – a very big advantage for the Turks. The arrival of German submarines in late May also proved an important factor, since they drove the Allied battleships into port, having sunk *Triumph* on 25 May and *Majestic* on 27 May. Moreover, the quiet days after the Allied offensive of 6–8 May and before the next Allied offensive of 4 June (Third Krithia), allowed the Turks time to perfect their defensive positions. All of this solidified the Turkish hold on Helles, and made future Allied offensives unlikely to succeed.[18]

The Turkish crises of early May actually made the Allied offensive of 6–8 May at Helles (Second Krithia) rather significant, because it was probably the last real chance to break through at Helles. Robert Rhodes James' comment that First Krithia (28 April) spelled the collapse of Hamilton's strategy, seems incorrect in light of Mühlmann's discussion.[19] Hunter-Weston's plans for the attack of 6 May were rather complicated, involving a three stage attack aimed at capturing Achi Baba. 125 Brigade of the now arriving 42 Division would attack on the left, a composite 88 Brigade in the centre, then a Naval Brigade, and the French on the right. Although Hamilton tried to get Hunter-Weston to attack just before dawn to use darkness to shield the troops, the latter refused, saying that too many company officers had been lost, who would have provided leadership for a night assault. D'Amade agreed, and Hamilton, conscious of their Western Front experience, which he lacked, decided to 'not force their hands.' Hunter-Weston acknowledged that Hamilton 'has left things here very greatly to me.' It is worth noting, though, that a night attack was not necessarily a panacea for success. Thus, John Goate, a soldier with the 5th Royal Scots near the French lines, wrote on 6 May:

> Advanced to a night attack at 8 p.m. A rotten job – barbed wire and shrapnel. Got into the Worcester lines and then among the Sikhs and Gurkhas. A wretched, cold night and had to lie out in the open. A weird night altogether. Don't want another like it.

The 1st Battalion Royal Munster Fusiliers also advanced 500 yards in this same night attack, but at 4.00 a.m. it was seen that they had reached an untenable position, and they were forced to retire.[20]

Prior to this abortive night adventure, the day-time offensive of 6 May commenced at 11.00 a.m., and was preceded by an Allied artillery preparation. This only lasted half an hour, and has often been derided, but Col. Hans Kannengiesser, commanding the Turkish XVI Corps, described it in truly superlative terms:

> A frightful thunderstorm which broke with elemental force and with never ceasing thunder and lightning against the forces concentrated on that small portion of the Peninsula… Even later, in August 1917, in the battles of Flanders [Passchendaele], I did not have the same overwhelming impression of concentrated shelling as during this period.

Despite this, the barrage could not pick up the Turkish machine-gunners in the centre, while the French on the right, although usually criticized for starting late, mostly did start promptly at 11.00 a.m. However, the 4th Zouave Battalion did not start until 11.30 a.m. because of a translation error, and halted at 5.30 p.m. due to fatigue and loss of morale. At 8.30 p.m. the French line retreated, although the Zouaves refused to leave their trenches, and Lt-Col. Nogues called for the French 75s to restore the situation. On the extreme left flank, a similar timing error afflicted the 125 Brigade of 42 East Lancashire Territorial Division, which also did not advance until 11.30 a.m., and halted after reaching the first objective, a ridge 400 yards ahead. Overall, the offensive had advanced about 400 or 500 yards, but any break through was stopped by Turkish machine-guns, often from skirmishers lying ahead of their regular trenches, and by shrapnel fire. [21]

Col. Wolley Dod, GS 29 Division, with the advantage of hindsight, called the Second Battle of Krithia 'a mad adventure without the necessary artillery support.' In particular, after the failure of 6 May, he felt 'it was useless to persevere without some considerable alteration of plan.' For example, the Territorial troops on the left, 125 Brigade, were knocked out by their efforts, and Wolley Dod 'had some difference of opinion with Hunter-Weston about employing them again.' However, Hunter-Weston persevered with similar attacks on 7 and 8 May, with diminishing supplies of men and artillery shells. On 8 May, in the late afternoon, Hamilton, desperate after realizing the failure of three days of fighting, reverted to an antique concept of warfare. The whole line was to fix bayonets, slope arms, and move forward en masse at precisely 5.30 p.m. Hamilton also quaintly wished for bands to play, or a display of colours, or at least a strong show of bayonets, in order to encourage the French, who were to similarly attack on the right flank. In this strange offensive, New Zealanders and Australians distinguished themselves with courageous assaults up Krithia Spur. The Australian 2nd Brigade advance was memorably described by Bean:

> as the cry ran up the trench – 'On Australians! Come on Australians!' –
> men scrambled from every part over its dry parapet. At the top, many
> stood for an instant… gripping their rifles and glaring at the dry heath and
> distant hills… Then they flung themselves forward into the storm.

The bare plain and Turkish machine-gunners halted even this strong effort, and at dark, there remained only the task of finding and caring for the dead and wounded. In the 2nd Australian Brigade, 1,056 of 2,900 were casualties, and in the New Zealand Brigade, 771 of 2,676 were casualties. [22]

At this juncture it should have been obvious that a new approach was required by the Allies. Aspinall confessed that he was 'with Sir Ian Hamilton when the third attack [of Second Krithia] was launched, and he [Aspinall]… was dumbfounded.' After the failed offensive, Milward thought that 'It is really a badly planned and ill conceived expedition.' Sholto Newman, 2nd Naval Brigade, considered the problem was lack of experience and training. In regard to the French, often condemned by British officers and by historians, there were only nine officers left in the Metropolitan Brigade, and twenty-five in the Colonial Brigade. At the bottom of the Kereves Dere ravine was a terrible mixture of 600 to 700 French troops: company, battalion, regiment, all signified nothing, the brigade was really just debris, and just about all officers there were killed or wounded. Only Lt-Col. Niéger was safe, although his regiment consisted of just two companies.[23] What was to be done? Hunter-Weston, Hamilton and others at GHQ resorted to the 'more and more' thesis: if an attack failed, then the answer was surely more men, guns and ammunition. On 10 May Hamilton also considered a tactical concept from the Western Front, brought to him by Birdwood – the 'bite and hold' idea – bite off a tactical point, which the Turks would feel compelled to counterattack and regain, and then kill large numbers of Turks as this was attempted. But this was a slow process, and not going to result in the capture of Achi Baba. The critical commander at the centre of affairs, Hunter-Weston, believed that battering away at Achi Baba was fruitless, and on 15 May suggested a new landing at Enos (a port on the western coast of Thrace), with six of Kitchener's new divisions. This was at least original, but meanwhile Hunter-Weston failed to re-think his image of warfare at Helles.[24]

There was a certain mental and physical detachment from reality in Hunter-Weston's attitude. Referring to the Territorial 125 Brigade, Hunter-Weston noted on 6 May that 'it was blooded today. It did fairly well, and will do better still as it gets more experience.' In the same letter to his wife, Hunter-Weston's detachment allowed him to write that the rattle of musketry 'lulls me to sleep.' Then on 6 May, Hunter-Weston spelled out the need for this detachment to Col. Clive Wigram, Private Secretary to the King: 'Now is the time for detachment, for a healthy body and a calm and confident mind…' Similarly, a certain detachment from reality permitted Hunter-Weston to argue that he had been able 'to dominate the situation', despite the failure of Second Krithia. Along with this detachment went self satisfaction. Hunter-Weston assured his wife that Hamilton thought him a great commander, worth a brigade of troops, which Hunter-Weston carefully spelled out as being equivalent to 4,000 men. (Hamilton did indeed think Hunter-Weston had 'truly great qualities as a Commander', although he was also grasping, tiresome and talkative.) Apart from detachment and self-praise, in his letters and diary Hunter-Weston also reveals an underlying romanticized view of war. After the 25 April landing at Helles, Hunter-Weston emphasized the gallantry of the men at W beach as a 'most marvellous feat', disregarding the problems that made this necessary. On 15 May, after listing the severe casualties suffered by 29 Division, Hunter-Weston' reaction was to see them as 'Glorious fellows.' On 11 June, Hunter-Weston wanted more men, guns and ammunition, in order to achieve a 'glorious victory.' This followed an offensive that was poorly planned and delivered, but still 'glorious in execution.' Curiously enough, the loss of Allied ships did not worry him, the sinking of *Majestic* was 'A marvellous sight…', while the sinking of a French transport liner was equally 'a wonderful sight…'[25]

Later on, when Hunter-Weston became a Corps commander on the Western Front, descriptions of him reveal an officer of intelligence, but lacking mental balance, given to extravagant and flamboyant gestures, and far too interested in irrelevant detail, a romantic out of place in an industrial war. One observer claimed that Hunter-Weston had the brain of an inexperienced boy who was much given to heroics and self-importance. He was in fact a mountebank.[26] For his part, Hamilton had a penchant for bayonet charges, and a deep aversion to 'ghastly trench warfare'. But Hamilton's own view of war met the new reality at Gallipoli, and in June, although he was considering a new Anzac offensive, he believed tactics at Helles to be a straightforward 'gain ground and suffer loss' concept. As he told Kitchener: 'There is no strategy, no tactics; all that is wanted is a high courage, a quick eye for probable points of attack or defence, and clear determination not to let loss of life stand in the way of gaining a few yards of ground.' A few days later, Hamilton wrote in similar vein to Churchill: 'But for this trench warfare no great technical knowledge is required. A high moral standard and a healthy stomach – these are the best.' However, Hamilton did achieve a mental breakthrough at the beginning of July. Birdwood had written to Hamilton on 1 July, recounting the costly Turkish attack at the end of June:

> If only Enver would continue to get impatient like this and urge attacks, we should very soon be through here, for I do not think they could stand very many more of them, though they undoubtedly… fight like tigers if you come up against their trenches.

As a direct result of this message, Hamilton wrote to Kitchener the next day:

> The old battle tactics have clean vanished. I have only quite lately realised the new conditions. Whether your entrenchments are on the top of a hill or at the bottom of a valley matters precious little… The only thing is by cunning or surprise, or skill, or tremendous expenditure of high explosives, or great expenditure of good troops, to win some small tactical position which the enemy may be bound… to attack. Then you can begin to kill them pretty fast. To attack all along the line is perfect nonsense – madness!

Similarly, Hamilton wrote to Asquith, arguing that gaining four lines of Turkish trenches was less important than depleting Turkish numbers by resisting Turkish counterattacks. Hamilton had obviously abandoned the gain ground idea, and reverted to his earlier 'bite and hold' concept, directly stimulated by examples at Anzac. This was actually an evolution to what may be called 'rational' thinking by Hamilton, while for Hunter-Weston there was always an underlying vision of battlefield romanticism and gallant sacrifice. When Hunter-Weston went home in July, possibly suffering from enteric or sun stroke, Godley wrote, as critically as was possible at that time:

> with all his faults Hunter-Weston was a gallant soul… At the same time, one is rather thankful to think he will not be (as he calls it) 'blooding' Freddy Stopford's [IX Corps] reinforcements against Achi Baba.[27]

However, Hamilton's switch to a 'bite and hold' concept at the end of June was in the future when the next major attempt to gain Achi Baba was launched on 4 June as the Third Battle of Krithia. The Allies at Helles now consisted of two French divisions on the extreme right, then the RND, then 42 Territorial Division, then 88 Brigade of 29 Division on the left, and the 14th Sikhs at Gully Ravine on the extreme left. Meanwhile, the 52 Lowland Territorial Division had not yet arrived, but Hunter-Weston decided not to wait for them. Details for the 4 June attack were more carefully worked out than before, with an attacking wave to be followed by a consolidation wave, and a strong artillery barrage. There were even some armoured cars to be used along the Krithia road. Originally, Hunter-Weston wanted a 6.00 p.m. attack, since this would allow time for Allied consolidation but not time for a Turkish counterattack. He also wanted a false attack for a 10-minute period before the real assault. The ships' fire should stop five minutes before zero hour, and the artillery barrage should shift forward two minutes before the attack started, so that the infantry would not hesitate to rush forward. French artillery would also support the British attack. At GHQ, Braithwaite complained that Hunter-Weston's promised timetable for the attack had not arrived and asked the very good question: why should the artillery stop firing two minutes before the infantry attack? This was the very time that the infantry most needed the guns. (As a curiosity, Hunter-Weston repeated the same mistake later at the Somme, ordering both the heavy artillery to lift, and a mine blown, at 10 minutes before zero hour on 1 July 1916.)[28]

Braithwaite's idea was excellent, and was mirrored by French ideas which called for the artillery barrage to lift only at the last moment. Probably this was not feasible in the early days of 1915, when accurate artillery barrages were difficult to achieve. Hence, the Allied artillery switched to the rear before the Allied infantry arrived, which Turkish reports timed at 10 minutes after the artillery lifted. Hunter-Weston's timetable for attack was also altered from evening to 12 noon, but still with a 10-minute false assault at 11.20 a.m. There was much complaint about Hunter-Weston's vagueness, for example, Col. J.T.R. Wilson, 88 Brigade, said that:

none of Hunter-Weston's orders were ever intelligible, and always had to be changed or modified or ignored. He could never give a definite objective for an attack, but would end up every order with:'Go as far as you can and then entrench.' June 4 was a cold blooded massacre…[29]

However, it was not clear at the time that there would be a failure on 4 June, indeed Milward described the barrage favourably: 'Never had I seen such a bombardment.' On the right, the French attack failed early on, riddled by machine-guns hidden in the folded ground. A post battle French report claimed that because the Turkish and French trenches were often so close together, 80m in some places, the French barrage could not hit the front Turkish trenches. In contrast, the Turkish and British trenches in the Naval Division and 42 Division areas were usually 200m apart, and the ground to be attacked was more favourable than the French region, being a slow rise toward Krithia. On the other hand, another French report stated that one company of 175 Regiment refused to leave their trenches, while the Turkish hold on the strong Haricot Redoubt made an integrated French attack impossible.[30] French difficulties were noted by the RND, which asked for support from French 2 Division, but only got 400 Zouaves into their already crowded trenches. According to Maj.-Gen. Paris, commander of the RND, French 2 Division did not advance when asked to do so, at 3.00 p.m., at 4.00 p.m., and at 5.30 p.m. However, Turkish reports said that the French 175 Regiment did capture 200 metres of trench, while French units initially attacked the Haricot Redoubt, and captured a trench, but were later forced out. Many French troops were lost. It seems the French did have a more difficult task, and did more than the RND allowed, while suffering from inaccurate artillery support. Hamilton and GHQ always seemed to minimize the much more difficult geography of the French sector, where the deep Kereves Dere river valley proved a very awkward obstacle. In general, during this attack the Naval Brigade lost heavily, especially the Collingwood Battalion, and total losses in the 2nd Naval Brigade were some 1,000 out of 1,700, and most of their officers. On the other hand, their opponents, 12 Turkish Division, also suffered badly, becoming tired, running out of reserves and having to call for help at 1. 45 p.m. on 4 June.[31]

Judging by Turkish reports, the most successful of the British attacks on 4 June was 42 Division against the Turkish 9 Division, especially because the right side of 9 Division was destroyed by the Allied artillery barrage. This attack by 42 Division, especially the Manchesters, got to the third line of Turkish trenches, advanced 500 metres, and took control of 1 kilometre of Turkish trenches. This was about 2.50 p.m. Turkish 9 Division was ordered to fire from behind walls, trenches, shell holes, and fight to the last. If necessary 9 Division field artillery was to keep firing to the end and then be disabled. But, as was also the case on the Western Front in 1915, an attack could break in to a defensive line, but to break out was almost impossible. There was a similar situation at Third Krithia. Turkish reserves came up, and the isolated 42 Division could do no more. On the left, there was success by 88 Brigade, whose KOSBs particularly suffered from German machine-guns taken off *Breslau*. But the Worcesters advanced well into the Turkish lines before meeting fresh Turkish reserves. On the extreme left the Sikhs on both sides of Gully Ravine were sadly depleted by machine-gun fire. Hunter-Weston still had several battalions of reserves, as did the French, but as was also the case on the Western Front, failure stimulated more than success, and so he tried to overcome failure in the French/Naval Division area rather than exploit success.[32]

Kannengiesser afterwards wrote that another attack the next day would have done the trick: 'As often previously, the English again failed to draw the utmost results from their success.' On the other hand, behind Achi Baba lay the whole massif of Kilid Bahr, while Maj.-Gen. B. de Lisle (the new commander of 29 Division), wrote: 'I doubt if anyone at GHQ or VIII Corps realised the state of despondency after the 4th June attack.' The heavy casualties among the attackers (4,500 British, 2,000 French), the need to reorganize and tend to dead and wounded, the lack of artillery ammunition, the impending arrival of 52 Lowland Division on 6 June, ignorance of Turkish problems, and a strong sense that a fresh front was now required, prevented immediate follow-up assaults.[33] Hunter-Weston blamed wire, machine-gun fire, and the French for the failure, also the RND for not holding onto their captured trenches because of lack of training, plus the loss of officers. However, artillery commanders tended to blame tactical failures, for example, not capturing the Turkish J10 trench on the left centre, where there was some short shooting, and failing to notice Boomerang Redoubt in Gully Ravine. Orlo Williams, reflecting GHQ thinking, blamed the French, and, with Dawnay, wanted a new front opened. Even Hamilton contemplated a fresh front, though he was still focussed on Achi Baba, and complained that ground could only be gained by 'ghastly sacrifice.' But all argued that more men and munitions were now required, and by 8 June Kitchener agreed to send three fresh divisions of the New Army to Gallipoli.[34]

Meanwhile, at Helles, trench warfare set in, punctuated by small-scale attacks and sapping. Ironically, both the most successful and the most disastrous effort, was made by 52 Division, the RND and the French on 12/13 July, really deserving to be called Fourth Krithia. Ironic, because, despite this offensive being a poorly mounted effort by Maj.-Gen. G. Egerton, GOC 52 Division, and Hunter-Weston, nevertheless the attack caught the Turks in a changeover, while the 4th KOSBs of 52 Division, untutored in trench warfare, pressed ahead regardless and nearly caused a genuine rupture in the Turkish lines. The primary concept of the attack was to distract the Turks, and maintain pressure at Helles, while the August Anzac/Suvla offensive was being organized. The actual structure of the attack was for two brigades of 52 Division to advance, separated in time by nine hours, to enable the artillery to focus its support for each attack. According to Egerton, there was little discussion of the plan, which Egerton later called 'positively wicked', since Hunter-Weston 'merely enunciated it.' But Col. McNeile of the 4th KOSBs apparently had a heated discussion with Hunter-Weston before the attack, in which McNeile was later killed, over the objectives for the assault. This final objective was actually the third line of Turkish trenches, which did not exist except as a shallow scrape. Another officer, R.R. Thompson, stated that Hunter-Weston's VIII Corps staff knew beforehand that the third line of Turkish trenches did not exist, but did not tell 52 Division's H.Q.[35]

On 12 July, the offensive commenced with an excellent artillery barrage, mainly French 75s, firing High Explosive. According to Maj. Forman 'they simply poured [the shells] on to the hostile trenches… Our infantry had an easy task that day.' This judgement was initially correct, since 155 Brigade, launched at 7.35 a.m., made good progress until they reached the Turkish trenches. Then, the lack of a proper objective caused confusion, so that the 4th KOSBs disappeared off into the distance, and only a few survivors were seen again. 156 Brigade then received orders to move up in support around midday. Lt Wills, of the 7th Cameronians, reports in his diary that he came across a Turkish sap trench that ran directly toward the Turkish lines and was swept by Turkish fire:

> it was literally filled from end to end with Scottish dead and dying, lying longwise, cross-wise, body heaped on body, so that there was not at any point of its length a vacant space of ground on which one might set foot. There was nothing for it but to crawl on hands and knees over the heaps of dead for some 150 yards. Occasionally, I would pass a man in which there still remained a spark of life, who would move feebly or groan in pain, but the vast majority would never move again.

The captured Turkish trench was in similar condition, wrote Wills:

> carpeted with the dead bodies of Turks horribly mangled and dismembered by our shell fire. The men who were endeavouring to get this shambles into order seemed almost exhausted and had hardly the strength necessary for this work.

Here it seems that the Allied artillery had done its job, but also there was tremendous waste of life among attackers, for example the 4th KOSBs lost 18 officers and 535 other ranks. Following on from this result, it can be argued that Helles generally did not suffer from shortage of men as much as from poor tactics and staff work, which led to enormous casualties. Regardless, carrying on the assault, late in the afternoon 157 Brigade attacked, and gained their supposed objective, the small scrape third Turkish trench. There, the situation was as bad as in the Cameronian trenches. 2nd-Lt D.E. Brand, 5th Highland Light Infantry (HLI), went up to support the 7th HLI, and found them exhausted by the struggle:

> Their officers sat at either end [of the trench] doing nothing, N.C.O.'s use-
> less, there was a sapper officer but he said he would do nothing without
> [sand] bags and kept on saying this all through the night. After about three
> hours I found a sub. [lieutenant] and told him what to do, an hour or so
> later I found he had dug a little bit of trench for himself on the lines sug-
> gested, and that was all, never looked near his men. Such gross incompe-
> tence I would never have believed possible…

In this case, it seems that officers and men had been strained beyond
endurance by the devastation and intensity of modern warfare.[36]

The next day, 13 July, Hunter-Weston, alarmed by a reported panic,
decided to reinforce failure, and ordered his reserve, three battalions of
the RND, to move forward in support of 155 Brigade. Confusion was
intense among the survivors of 52 Division, and it is well understandable
that a temporary panic set in. According to one officer's memory: 'our
men were simply led away by a Major of the Battalion line on our right,
who came shouting through our lines that we were to retire as the
French were about to bombard.' This officer commented that the men
were badly served by Brigade and Division staff that day. The position
was restored within the hour, although Ashmead-Bartlett, the journalist,
wrote darkly of muddle and near mutiny:

> There was practically a mutiny out there, and a great number of the
> Brigadier-Generals openly refused to take any further orders from Gen.
> Hunter-Weston, who was responsible for the muddle… They all said that
> at the time he had been affected by the sun a little, and was incapable of
> giving orders.

Also there were many wounded men left out in No Man's Land, with no
local armistices to bring them in: 'There was a lack of all human feeling
toward those lying out there.' After 12/13 July Ashmead-Bartlett claimed
that everyone was talking and criticizing freely. It seems that he was particularly referring to the supporting attack by the RND battalions, at
4.30 p.m. on 13 July. They found great confusion and congestion in the
captured trenches, with 52 Division very mixed up and disorganized.

Maj.-Gen. Paris reported that it was impossible to get a clear idea of the situation. Worse,

> conditions in the captured trenches beggars description. A large number of dead bodies in and out of the trenches – some must have been there since 4 June – rendering the whole area most nauseating. Large numbers of men became physically exhausted from vomiting and unable to eat. The medical officers reported a most serious state of affairs.

In this situation, Lt-Col. Wilson, commanding Hawke and Drake Battalions, decided not to continue the attack, given the state of the trenches, the fierce Turkish artillery, and large numbers of Turkish reserves. Paris commented: 'I considered he acted very properly.' Brig.-Gen. C. Trotman, (GOC 3rd Royal Marine Brigade, RND) also described 'the rotting bodies in heaps everywhere, vomiting and sickness very bad.' Another battalion, the Portsmouth, withdrew on 14 July, citing the 'indescribable' trenches, 'dead and wounded being impossible to clear away.'[37]

Hunter-Weston, annoyed at the confusion and panic among some 52 Division troops, decided to relieve Egerton of his command of this division on 13 July and sent him to a ship for a one night rest. It was a surprising move, and unauthorized by Hamilton, but probably a good one because Egerton *was* extremely tired, and badly in need of rest. However, Hunter-Weston himself was to follow a rather similar route some days later, when he was sent home on 23 July, allegedly suffering from sunstroke or enteric. *Allegedly*, since Hamilton informed Aspinall later that Lady Hunter-Weston was certainly told that her husband was being sent home, i.e. relieved of his duties. If so, this was a useful move, since his generalship was very questionable, and continued to be so later on the Western Front. Perhaps the sunstroke or enteric gave GHQ a good excuse to remove Hunter-Weston.[38]

Earlier, the French Colonial troops, often blamed for causing retreats, and sometimes ignored in British accounts, maintained contact with the British attack on 12/13 July and on 13 July captured a Turkish trench, as described in a post-action French report. According to this report, at 4.45 p.m. on 13 July, despite violent Turkish fire, troops of the 2nd Battalion of the 6th Colonial Regiment willingly jumped off, and captured a Turkish trench. Lt Feziers of 8 Company was the first in, but was immediately wounded and fell. The Senegalese who followed him avenged him. The Turks were led by a young blond enemy officer, who must have been German, although he wore a turban. A violent bayonet fight took place, and a machine-gun opened up on them. However, Lt Alary of 5 Company and his men built a wall of sandbags and consolidated the trench. French reserves followed up, but dead and wounded congested the trench and it was decided not to renew the attack. At 5.45 p.m., part of the trench had to be given up, but the rest of the Turkish trench was reinforced and dug in by 9.00 p.m. Casualties were heavy, and the men were very weary because of being in the front trenches from 2 to 11 July, and again for 12 and 13 July. Yet morale was satisfactory. Still, despite this success, the next day, the auspicious 14 July, the French were reported by Milward to be very angry 'at this mad Dardanelles enterprise…'. An ironic French report on the operations of 12 and 13 July declared that they had been told the Turks were short of ammunition and that when the attack was renewed on the second day, the Turks would be at their mercy. 'Permit us to doubt this! The Turks fired night and day without ceasing.' The report concluded that the Turks were as strong as ever, in fact stronger, although some Greeks did desert.[39]

On the other side of the hill, the Turks regained their composure. The attack had been very hard to halt, and the last reserves had been used up. Echoing Kannengiesser's earlier comment, Liman von Sanders, referring to 12/13 July, wrote: 'It was very fortunate for us that the British attacks never lasted more than one day, and were punctuated by pauses of several days. Otherwise it would have been impossible to replenish our artillery ammunition.' Liman von Sanders was not strictly accurate, since the 12/13 July Allied offensive obviously lasted more than one day, but it was probably beyond the abilities of the Allies to sustain a lengthy offensive on Gallipoli, unlike the Western Front, with its much greater resources. Mühlmann also pointed out the almost invincible Turkish defensive capabilities: four new Turkish divisions arrived in June from V and XIX Corps, there was a much better supply of artillery ammunition, a new higher technical proficiency in the Turkish artillery emerged, a German engineer company had just arrived, as well as a company of flame throwers. At the same time, Mühlmann noted, the Allies still had a narrow base at Helles, making it difficult to manoeuvre, their observation position was obviously poor compared to the Turks, and their continuing attacks on Eltichu Tepe (Achi Baba) was causing them heavy losses.[40]

Clearly, the Allies faced a very difficult situation. At GHQ, insiders began to question the ability of their commander, Hamilton. Already, in May, Lt-Col. Pollen, Hamilton's military secretary, had told Orlo Williams, the cipher officer at GHQ, that Hamilton was 'too afraid of K[itchener], and never would run his own show in his own way, a thing he [Pollen] was always trying to buck him up to do.' Williams commented:

> I fear the General [Hamilton] is run by the CGS [Braithwaite], who may
> be a good soldier, but is a stupid man, with no ideas… [and] fond of his
> own way. CGS relies almost wholly on Aspinall and Dawnay…

Orlo Williams and others all agreed that the real brain at GHQ was Dawnay. In early June, Williams reiterated his criticism of Hamilton: 'Really Sir Ian does not impress me. He can't say a thing direct, nor bring himself to stand up to K[itchener].' A few days later, Williams quoted Dawnay's view that Hamilton was really a journalist in command. Then in late July, Williams wrote in his diary a harsher critique of Hamilton:

> I find that he [Hamilton] really does nothing at all, has a shallow, at times
> obstinate mind, no grasp of detail. His first dispatch, so praised in London,
> was almost wholly written by his staff. This plan of the second big push [at
> Anzac and Suvla], not only was not thought out by the General, but was
> Dawnay's idea, which, supported by Dawnay's arguments, induced him to
> give up his own idea of still plugging away at Achi Baba, simply, as Dawnay
> says, that the D.M. [*Daily Mail*] might come out with the poster ACHI
> BABA. He doesn't for a moment realise how serious and extraordinary
> the situation is here. If this next attack fails, it means, in all probability,
> thorough and complete failure. This campaign is practically run by
> Dawnay and Aspinall, one a dug out Captain and the other a Captain in

the Munster Fusiliers… It is also run by Hunter-Weston and Skeen, Birdy's [Birdwood's] GSO 1.[41]

Orlo Williams and Dawnay were a little unfair here, because Hamilton was already thinking of the Anzac break out by the middle of June, but their comments reflect the critical feeling at GHQ. Meanwhile, attacks at Helles were continued partly to keep up morale, and partly to divert Turkish attention away from future operations at Anzac.[42] Quite apart from stresses within GHQ, and doubts about Hamilton's command qualities, it was evident to most that a stalemate had been reached at Helles at least by June. But what was to be done? As was also becoming abundantly clear on the Western Front, the defensive potential of trenches, wire, artillery and machine-guns heavily favoured the defence, and would have offset even a two to one superiority in Allied numbers at Gallipoli. And yet, the Allies generally did not have a two to one superiority, while Turkish reserves were readily available.[43] So, what were the options? At the time, there were at least seven alternatives, some of which overlapped:

One: gain ground in the old style, and continue to batter away at Achi Baba. This was really abandoned as a serious enterprise after Third Krithia.

Two: destroy Turkish morale, while maintaining Allied morale. Thus, writing to Churchill at the end of June, Hamilton considered the Turks to be demoralized, or at least their morale was beginning to crack. At the end of September, Hamilton was still hopeful: 'The Turks are morally on their last legs.' Even if the Turks did not crack, Hamilton learnt from de Lisle the need for small aggressive operations to 'keep up the pecker of the troops. He [de Lisle] tells me that in the divisions in France where such enterprises are encouraged the enemy is completely cowed and held under.'[44]

Three: apply technology, especially naval fire, but also artillery, monitors, mining, submarines, etc. Applying artillery was understood by many such as Brigadier-General Reed, chief of staff to Stopford at Suvla, to be the particular lesson of the Western Front. At the same time, naval fire had been expected to be the trump card at Helles.

Four: request more and more men and munitions. This was a 'rational' concept implying that eventually enough men and munitions would succeed.

Five: use attrition favourably through the 'bite and hold' concept, by inviting Turkish attacks. This was occurring, but was not likely to be decisive.

Six: try to overcome tactical failure at Helles with strategic surprise elsewhere. This entailed a new offensive and a new landing, as alluded to in Hamilton's letter to Birdwood, and Orlo Williams' discussion in GHQ.

Seven: withdraw from Gallipoli. This last option was not considered until August in Gallipoli.

GHQ's decision was to try surprise again at Anzac and Suvla, plus more men, and to some extent, more munitions. The plan for Anzac was exciting and daring, but would it avoid the problems that engulfed the Krithia battles? And how quickly would the Turks react to a new offensive?

THE ANZAC BREAKOUT

August

To break the stalemate at Helles, Hamilton and GHQ planned a major break out and left hook from the northern flank of the Anzac position. This would take place during the night of 6/7 August and would aim to capture the Sari Bair heights. Maj.-Gen. Sir Alexander Godley was placed in overall charge of the Anzac break out offensive. The plan involved two main columns and two covering forces. The main Left Assault Column was composed of the 29th Indian Brigade and the 4th Australian Brigade, and a left covering force preceding this main column comprised half of 40th Brigade from 13 Division. The main Right Assault Column consisted of the New Zealand Infantry Brigade, with its preceding covering force composed of the New Zealand Mounted Rifle Brigade and the Otago Mounted Rifles.

The specific aim of the main Left Assault Column was to make its way up the Aghyl Dere gully to the top of Koja Cimen Tepe and Hill Q. The goal of the main Right Assault Column was to capture the summit of Chunuk Bair, with part of the column moving up through the Chailak Dere gully to the Rhododendron Ridge, where it would be joined by the other part of the column, which would advance via the Sazli Dere gully. Then the reunited column would assault the summit of Chunuk Bair. To assist the Anzac break out, diversionary attacks were planned at Helles and at Lone Pine, in the south of the Anzac position. A further plan involved Australian attacks at the Nek (celebrated in the film Gallipoli*) and surrounding area on 7 August, in conjunction with anticipated success at Chunuk Bair.*

The Turks were at first confused and in a state of disorganization as the Anzac offensive unfolded. This was partly because of uncertainty over command boundaries. But on 8 August Mustafa Kemal was appointed as commander of the whole

area, and brought some order to the situation. Also on 8 August, the New Zealand
Wellington Battalion under Lt-Col. Malone captured Chunuk Bair, and at dawn
on 9 August a small force of Gurkhas, Warwickshires and South Lancashires
reached Hill Q, only to retreat in controversial circumstances shortly afterwards. On
Chunuk Bair, a dawn attack on 10 August by Mustafa Kemal and a large Turkish
force drove the Allied defenders off the summit.

★

A number of Allied officers were already thinking of an Anzac break
out early in the campaign. One was Lt-Col. Malone, as outlined in
his diary entry of 14 May 1915. Another was Rear-Admiral Thursby, who
on 3 May 1915 sent a note to Birdwood, arguing for holding a line from
Gaba Tepe to Mal Tepe, thus cutting off Turkish troops from the south,
and establishing a northern flank on Hill 971 (Koja Cimen Tepe), supported by naval fire up the valleys. The line could be established with the
addition of only a small extra force from Helles: 'Here we lie on the flank
of their communications which a small addition to our force would
enable us to cut.' On the other hand, in the south, Thursby argued that
Allied attacks just drove the enemy back onto their strong position at
Kilid Bahr and did not interfere with their communications. This suggestion by Thursby made plenty of sense, especially the comment that
the Helles attacks were playing into Turkish strength. Thursby's idea was
probably the stimulus for Birdwood's letter of 13 May to Hamilton, suggesting a north flanking move and the capture of the highest Sari Bair
peak, Koja Cimen Tepe.[1]

Cautious New Zealand scouting in May revealed safe routes up
toward the Sari Bair heights via the steep gullies of Sazli Dere, Chailak
Dere and Aghyl Dere. These routes were partially threatened by a foolish
move to capture a new Turkish outpost, number 3, which overlooked
Sazli Dere and Chailak Dere. One New Zealand soldier blamed this on
his brigadier, who looked at things from a safe distance through his field
glasses and desired the outpost to be held 'at all costs.' The outpost was
untenable because it was overlooked from three sides, and the attempt to
capture it was '...all caused by a foolish error of judgement in putting a

weak outpost, entirely unsupported, a long distance from our main position. We feel we have lost a lot of our best men all for nothing.'[2] This outpost incident may have stimulated the fears of Mustafa Kemal, who suspected a possible Allied advance up the Sazli Dere valley toward the Sari Bair heights. But his Corps commander, Esat Pasa, believed that only raiding parties could cross such treacherous ground, and refused to accept Kemal's predictions. According to Mustafa Kemal, he and Esat Pasa and staff officers viewed the Sazli Dere area (between Rhododendron Ridge and Battleship Hill, known as Seaweed Valley) in late July. Esat Pasa asked Kemal where the Allied attack would come from, and Kemal gestured from Anzac Cove to Koja Cimen Tepe. Esat Pasa patted Kemal's shoulder:

'Don't you worry, he can't do it', he said. Seeing that it was impossible for me to put over my point of view I felt it unnecessary to prolong the argument any further. I confined myself to saying, 'God willing, sir, things will turn out as you expect'.[3]

Meanwhile, Allied preparations went forward for some kind of offensive on the Anzac flank. Lt-Col. Skeen, GSO 1 on Birdwood's staff, put together a bold left hook plan to capture Koja Cimen Tepe with a night march, using one new division and a brigade. This memorandum was presented to Hamilton on 30 May, but Hamilton had already been thinking of future action at Anzac, writing to Birdwood on 18 May that:

More and more it seems to me that when we have once got Achi Baba, we may not find it advisable to press on from the south. Then, if my half formed ideas mature... the main push and decisive movement will be made from the base you are so gallantly holding.

Hamilton even speculated that Sari Bair might be the fulcrum that could end up defeating Germany. But Hamilton remained focussed on Achi Baba, while at GHQ, Dawnay, perhaps the most original thinker on the staff, also wanted a new front, and suggested landing 60,000 men at Anzac. Hamilton came round to the Anzac idea by 6 June: 'Even Sir Ian was contemplating this if more troops sent…'. Then, in early June, GHQ were informed that Kitchener would in fact be sending three divisions of the New Army to Gallipoli. Hence, in mid-June, Hamilton wrote to Birdwood:

> I am gradually forming the conclusion in my mind that ANZAC is even more important – and immediately important – than it had appeared in my original concept… I will not put more on paper; it is too dangerous. But we must have a talk soon.

Various ideas therefore circulated at GHQ in May and June. Hamilton was gradually converted to the Anzac idea, although still clinging to hopes of capturing Achi Baba. Braithwaite also remained keen on Achi Baba, wanting to land a force near Helles and turn the Achi Baba defences, and so was not converted to the Anzac idea until early July. On the other hand, Capt. Wyndham Deedes, a staff officer at GHQ, wanted to use the three new divisions for an attack on the Asian side, leading to the capture of Chanak before winter. Finally, Kitchener, issuing instructions to Stopford and Ellison, in an interview on 11 July, urged one massive attack in the Anzac area towards Maidos. From all of these ideas evolved the Skeen plan, incorporating the three new divisions, which was presented to GHQ on 1 July. Dawnay and Aspinall then worked out the details of an ambitious scheme to capture all three of the high points of the Sari Bair range, but awaiting the arrival of the new divisions, postponed the attack until August.[4]

The Anzac breakout concept had a real chance of success, although it is interesting to note that Dawnay, who according to Orlo Williams was the real architect of the Anzac scheme, had considerable doubts before the Anzac attack. So, on 21 July 1915, Orlo Williams reported Dawnay as being 'not very optimistic even about the result of success in our next big push. Seems to think that the best we could hope for would be to get a strong position across the peninsula and build a safe base at Suvla Bay.'[5] Hamilton was open to new ideas, even if he took some time to persuade, and the Anzac plan was obviously a winner, if it could be properly carried out. Basically, the new Allied offensive consisted of:

– Continuing attacks in June and July at Helles to keep Turkish eyes focussed there, with objectless attacks at Anzac in June and July to avoid suspicion, plus use of disinformation to make the Turks focus on Bulair, which always attracted Liman von Sanders' interest.

– Secret landing of 13 Division and 29 Indian Brigade at Anzac on 4–6 August.

– Diversionary attacks at Helles on 6–7 August.

– Diversionary attack at Lone Pine in the south Anzac area on 6 August.

– The main Anzac offensive, consisting of a night advance on 6/7 August toward Sari Bair, with two main columns, assisted by two covering columns. The task of the main Left Assault Column, commanded by Maj.-Gen. H.V. Cox, was to take a long left hook up the Aghyl Dere valley, and then split into two, one half crossing to the Abdul Rahman Bair height and capturing Koja Cimen Tepe from the north, and the other half turning to the right to capture Hill Q. The task of the main Right Assault Column, commanded by Brigadier-General F.E. Johnston, was to capture Chunuk Bair, by using the Chailak Dere and Sazli Dere valleys, then establish a strong position on Chunuk Bair, and finally turn around and attack the Turks on Battleship Hill from the rear. Both main columns were to be ready to assault the high ground of Koja Cimen Tepe, Hill Q and Chunuk Bair at dawn on 7 August.

– Supporting attacks on Turkish trenches at the head of Monash Valley on 7 August, including an assault at a location called the Nek. These attacks were to be in conjunction with the Battleship Hill assault.

– The landing of two British divisions, 11th and 10th, at Suvla, on the evening of 6 August and at dawn on 7 August respectively. Suvla to be occupied as a port.

Clearly, this was all very ambitious, but looked feasible to the main planners, Aspinall and Dawnay.

Discussion of the whole Anzac offensive begins by looking first at the Lone Pine diversion at Anzac. This was launched on the far right wing of Anzac, with the idea of diverting attention away from the left hook aimed at the Sari Bair range. This diversion initially caused arguments over the start time, which was finally pushed back to 5.30 p.m. on 6 August to coincide more closely with the main night advance. The Australian attack was both hindered and helped by the situation on the Turkish side. Maj. Zeki Bey, commanding the 1st Battalion of the 57th Regiment in the Lone Pine area, was finally relieved after forty-five days in the line, on the very day of the attack, 6 August. Zeki Bey's battalion was replaced by an Arab battalion of the 72nd Regiment. This battalion was less capable than Zeki Bey's battalion of Turks, but it was fresh and rested. As well, when the attack commenced, Zeki Bey's battalion was still in the vicinity, and could, therefore, provide a readily available reserve, which also knew the trench system well. Fortune therefore happened to favour the Turkish side.

From the Allied point of view, the attacking force of the 1st Australian Brigade had the advantage of surprise, plus the use of tunnels which had been dug toward the Lone Pine trenches. However, the artillery support could not provide counter-battery fire to save the first two lines of the Australian attack, which, according to a New Zealand forward artillery observer, Maj. Curry, were heavily cut up by Turkish shrapnel. According to Maj.-Gen. N.M. Smyth, commanding the 1st Australian Brigade, wire cutting was also a problem, which is surprising given that Curry's battery on Walker's Ridge was just 600 yards from the Lone Pine trenches, while the wire was only 60 yards in front of Curry's observation post, and could be easily observed except for some dead ground. Maj. Curry followed the Australian attackers into the captured Turkish trenches, and reported that some Australian wounded and Turkish dead 'lay 4 deep and we had to walk on top of them. It took several days to clear the trenches and our dead on top of the ground had to be left there.' Nevertheless, the Turkish front trenches at Lone Pine were taken by the bold Australian rush, despite the problem of unsuspected timber coverings over these trenches. In this remarkable action, seven Victoria Crosses were won, and the 1st Australian Brigade suffered some 1,700 casualties out of 2,900.[6]

Curry described the horrors of the attack: 'There were all sorts of wounds, one fellow was shot in the neck and with protruding eyes was gasping for breath…'. In addition, one of Curry's telephonists suffered from shell shock and had to retire. The stench, flies, heat, and lack of water undermined health in the captured trenches, as did the food: 'Hard biscuits, bacon and jam were the fare, and this had to be eaten in the midst of 700 dead Turks and a lot of our own dead.' Soon Curry found he could only keep down condensed milk, water and a spoonful of jelly, and was eventually forced to go sick.[7]

On the Turkish side, Mustafa Kemal argued that the reason for the Australian victory at Lone Pine was that the defenders left only observers in the front line trenches when the Allied artillery opened, so these trenches were therefore nearly empty. Also, because the distance the Australians had to cover was so small, they got in quickly. On the other hand, Zeki Bey later told Charles Bean his story of the Turkish defence. Reading between the lines, it seems that Turkish leadership was at fault. The commanding officers of the Turkish battalions at Lone Pine, and the commanding officer of the 47th Regiment at Lone Pine, Tewfik Bey, who was 'very much upset', were all some distance behind the trenches, and obviously out of touch with the struggle and with their troops. Later, Tewfik Bey, conscious of his failures, and of sending a message that the Lone Pine trenches had been recaptured when this was not the case, personally led a counterattack and was killed. There was evidently Turkish shock and panic at Lone Pine, and one Turkish battalion commander that Zeki Bey met kept on repeating, 'We're lost, we're lost!' Eventually, the Turks managed to stabilize the line with troops of 5 Division, but Turkish counterattacks did not succeed. Zeki Bey described one such attack on the morning of 8 August. First, Zeki Bey asked for a counterattack over the top. But his soldiers said: 'There are all those men lying on the top who tried to make an attack over the top there. They were caught by fire the moment they got over. You can't go there.' Zeki Bey then tried an attack from the left side, preceded by bomb throwing. But a shell hit the lieutenant leading the attack 'and the others were immediately swept down by a machine-gun… Eight or nine – all but one of the party – fell back dead and wounded. We then understood that all measures were hopeless.' Therefore, all Turkish counterattacks were cancelled. This was a wise decision, but not an easy choice since Turkish tactics always called for counterattacks to recapture lost ground.[8]

Another equally famous part of the Anzac action, this time at dawn on 7 August, was the attempt to take the Turkish trenches at the Nek, followed by an advance onto Baby 700. Because of its notoriety, this attack, and others at the same time, will be analysed in some detail. The attack was supposed to be launched in conjunction with the main Right Assault Column attacking downhill from Chunuk Bair toward Battleship Hill. As it turned out, Chunuk Bair was not taken by dawn on 7 August, but the Nek assault went ahead anyway, now simply as a feint to assist the Chunuk Bair offensive. It is often forgotten that the Nek attack was part of a number of other similar attacks on Turkish positions at the Chessboard, Dead Man's Ridge and German Officers' Trench. These also therefore became feints to assist the Chunuk Bair attack. Lt-Col. Brudenell-White (GSO 1, 1st Australian Division) admitted later that these attacks were not seen as so important as the Lone Pine attack, and so arrangements at Division and Brigade were not so good. The arrangements really called for something else succeeding elsewhere, and much better staff work. It is also usually forgotten that the attack of the Australian Light Horse against the Nek was not the only assault that was repeated fruitlessly, since Brig.-Gen. J.K. Forsyth, organizing the German Officers' Trench assault, was also forced by his Divisional HQ to order a second and then a third attack. Fortunately, the third attack on German Officers' Trench, unlike that at the Nek, was questioned by an officer on the spot, in this case, Maj. D.J. Glasfurd (GSO 2, 1st Australian Division). The first attack by the 6th Battalion of 1 Australian Division on German Officers' Trench had failed due to lack of coordination with other attacks, plus enemy shelling, the explosion of Anzac mines which did no harm and a frontal assault against well manned and alert Turkish trenches, held by the Turkish 72nd Regiment. When news of this failure reached Walker and Brudenell-White via Forsyth they ordered the attack renewed. It failed for much the same reasons. Walker, usually seen as the best of the Allied commanders at Gallipoli, personally ordered Forsyth to make a third attempt. Glasfurd passed on his doubts that a third attempt would succeed, and Birdwood decided to cancel the attack.[9]

It is interesting to note the post-war explanations for repeating the German Officers' Trench assault. Brudenell White later admitted his culpability: 'Walker and I blundered in telling Forsyth to do it again but his reports gave a definite impression of lack of resolution.' White argued that the second effort at least was necessary because of training lessons: 'In war as every soldier knows resolution is almost invincible and the lack of it the cause of most failures. From his youth up therefore, the officer has instilled in him that he must not flinch or hesitate at loss.' So Brudenell-White persuaded himself that the second effort was necessary, based on his evaluation of Forsyth's attitude. But Brudenell-White did admit that the problem at German Officers' Trench was that neither brigadiers nor staff officers really understood the situation. Probably, Brudenell-White and Walker would still have ordered the second attack, and possibly the third, since failure was not easily accepted, and these were now expendable feints, required to help the desperate Chunk Bair offensive succeed.[10]

Just to the north of German Officers' Trench, and the other feint operations on 7 August, there took place the attack at the Nek, which has gained much attention through the Australian film *Gallipoli*. At dawn on 7 August the 3rd Australian Light Horse Brigade was to assault across the narrow ground known as the Nek and capture the Turkish trenches defending the area. If successful, the attack would move upwards onto Baby 700 and Battleship Hill. The plan was straightforward, an attack across a narrow but open space (an area of about three tennis courts) to the Turkish trenches, supported by artillery and naval fire. The artillery and naval bombardment was actually crucial to the success of the attack. But according to all accounts, the Allied bombardment ceased seven minutes before zero hour for the attack, leaving the Australian attackers to go over the top without supporting fire, and this was the critical factor that led to the decimation of the Australian Light Horse. The explanation always given for this seven-minute gap is that watches were not synchronized. This explanation will be addressed below, but the very fact that the time gap existed shows again that staff work was poorer than at Lone Pine.

Looking first at the artillery, three Australian batteries, plus one battery of the 69th Howitzer Brigade, and half a battery of the 39th Howitzer Brigade were involved, as well as naval fire support from the cruiser *Endymion*, and the destroyers *Chelmer* and *Colne*, plus a naval monitor. It seems that the barrage times in the artillery orders were changed twice, but the final instructions were for the batteries to fire slowly on the Nek from 10.30 p.m. on 6 August until 4.00 a.m. on 7 August, and then a quick rate of fire from 4.00 a.m. to 4.30 a.m., and at 4.30 a.m. switch to firing on Battleship Hill. The navy also was given orders to fire at a quick rate at the Neck [sic] from 4.00 a.m. to 4.30 a.m. The ship's log of *Endymion* states that she fired from 4.00 a.m. to 4.30 a.m. at the Nek, and switched to Battleship Hill at 4.40 a.m. *Colne* simply states that she started firing at 4.00 a.m., but not when she finished firing. Similarly, *Chelmer*'s log states that she started firing at 4.00 a.m. 'at intervals on Neck [sic] on left flank', but did not mention when her firing ceased.[11]

An inkling of the artillery/naval fire problem emerges when it is realized that fire was supposed to switch from the Nek to other targets, such as Quinn's and the Chessboard, at exactly 4.30 a.m. Neither artillery nor naval fire can easily switch at exactly that split moment to a new target, and so it is not surprising to find that Clyde McGilp, 1st New Zealand Field Artillery, reflecting the official New Zealand timetable for all the batteries involved, planned to switch fire away from the Nek at 4.27 a.m., and start on their new targets. Hence, the artillery support was *always* going to stop at least three minutes early at the Nek. Similarly, the Navy was always consistent in not being able to fire accurately in support of troops who were close to the enemy, and it seems certain that the Navy also allowed some time to elapse between their cease of fire and the infantry attack, in order to avoid hitting their own troops.[12] Further support for this reason for ceasing fire early comes from Bean himself, who wrote in 1923 that the artillery/naval fire stopped three minutes early at the Nek. Bean explained that the journalist, Schuler, told him this, and that some artillery officers said 'that they were ordered to fire much too close to their attacking troops on the Nek, and that they were not going to take any risk but would take good care that there was no chance of a mistake and hitting their own men.'[13] Hence, it can be argued that the problem was not so much the poor synchronization of watches, as the decision by artillery and naval fire to cease fire at least three minutes early in order to avoid hitting their own men, as well as the pre-arranged switch to other targets. This still leaves another four minutes to account for. The origin of the synchronization story is two letters from Lt-Col. Brazier (CO 10th Light Horse Regiment) to Bean after the war. Brazier did not actually state that watches were not synchronized, instead he simply assumed that the gap of seven minutes meant that watches had not been synchronized. Moreover, the New Zealand artillery, in charge of the artillery support on 7 August, had orders on 5 August to check their watches at least once daily during operations, because it was well understood that artillery-infantry cooperation required a careful timetable. Added controversy comes from Col. J.J.T. Hobbs, CO 1st Australian Division Artillery, who blamed his opposing number, Lt-Col. G.N. Johnston, commanding the New Zealand artillery, to whom all batteries involved at the Nek were handed over at 9.00 p.m. on 6 August. Hobbs wrote in his diary that he had a heart to heart talk with his commanding officer over the artillery problems at the Nek, and he blamed Johnston for the mistakes, since he had handed over the Australian batteries to the New Zealanders before the attack began. Then, on 28 August, there was an enquiry into the role of the artillery at the Nek, and Hobbs reported that Johnston charged the Australian batteries with neglect, but Hobbs easily defended himself because his batteries had been handed over at 9.00 p.m. on 6 August to Johnston, but added, very strangely, that the Australian Field Artillery 'were never informed of the attack…'. Similarly, according to Brazier, the officer commanding the Western Australian field artillery was not informed of the Nek attack either, and watched the Light Horse go over feeling that they could have helped. Unfortunately, and perhaps deliberately, the New Zealand Artillery Brigade war diary only opens at 5.00 a.m. on 7 August, thus omitting mention of the Nek attack.[14]

However, the war diary of 69th Brigade field artillery exists, and this simply states that there was an intense bombardment of Baby 700 and Battleship Hill from 4.00 to 4.30 a.m. on 7 August. There is no mention of the Nek, but a note for 7 August suggests another possible reason for problems with the artillery bombardment:

> During bombardment our forward trenches in which the four O.S.s [observation stations] are situated heavily shelled by enemy, great difficulty in keeping telephone communication, and two of O.S.s blown in.

Curiously, *none* of the war diaries, either artillery or infantry, mention the silent seven minutes before the Light Horse attack. Instead, all war diaries blame the costly Australian failure on the fact that Turkish machine-guns were not silenced. The 3rd Australian Light Horse Brigade blamed heavy machine-gun fire and bombs, and the 10th Light Horse war diary stated:

> The artillery were to smash enemy's machine-guns and trenches preparatory to our assault. This was not done. The Destroyer [sic] opened fire in the direction of the Nek at 4.00 a.m. and continued to 4.30 a.m. [no gap of seven minutes here], with apparently little effective result. Bombardment ceased at 4.30 a.m. and almost immediately and before the first line of ours had left our trenches, enemy rifle and machine-gun fire opened on our parapets…

The 8th Light Horse simply noted that at 4.30 a.m. the attack commenced, but, 'Owing to a deadly machine-gun fire, the attack failed to get home.' Finally, the war diary of the General Staff, Anzac Corps, reported that the artillery bombardment had no effect on the heavy machine-gun fire, although 'A few men got into the Turkish trenches but were unable to hold their own…'. The Anzac Corps war diary noted the same, that the 8th Light Horse was checked by machine-guns, which the bombardment 'does not seem to have affected at all,' although a few men got into the trenches. Nor were matters any better at the neighbouring Chessboard, where the Royal Welch Fusiliers were attached to the 3rd Light Horse Brigade but these 'were also mown down and unable to scale cliffs or make good – reinforced later with two companies of Cheshires but no impression could be made at either place (or at Quinn's or Pope's…)'.[15]

To summarize, the problem at the Nek was not so much the silent seven minutes, but the fact that the naval and artillery bombardment did not destroy the Turkish machine-guns, nor do much damage to the front Turkish trench. Besides this controversy, Lt-Col. Brazier's letters to Bean uncorked another problem. This had to do with the waste of lives due to sending two further lines into the attack after the first line had been decimated, and then sending part of yet another line. These further lines were all destroyed, as was the first. In 1931 Brazier argued that Brig.-Gen. F.G. Hughes, GOC 3rd Light Horse Brigade, nominally in charge of the attack, and Col. J.M. Antill, his Brigade Major, were both incompetent. Brazier commanded the 10th Light Horse, which was to be in the third line of attack. Brazier had seen the first two lines wiped out under extremely heavy fire, and did not notice any flags to indicate that any Australians had got into the Turkish trenches. Brazier wrote:

> I reported to Col Antill… who was alone in the HQ dug-out with his back to the wall. He said there was a flag in the Turks' trenches and ordered me to push on. I replied there was no flag then in the enemy's trenches, and that it was murder to push on. He simply roared 'Push on.' Returning to my position… I said 'I am sorry boys the order is to go.' Ten seconds later the men near me had nearly all been killed or wounded and were falling back into the trench.

Brazier reported back again to Antill, who again refused to listen to Brazier and once more ordered the troops to push on. Brazier then received messages from officers at both flanks asking for orders, and so Brazier decided to go to Hughes. Hughes listened to Brazier and suggested if the attack on the Nek was impossible from that location, to try Bully Beef Sap. This was an Anzac trench some way back down Monash Valley, and would simply have exposed the attackers to fire for a much longer period. Brazier claimed that the suggestion to try Bully Beef Sap was the 'last straw in incompetence.' Brazier also stated that Antill stayed in his dugout until an hour after the attack was over.[16]

Antill defended himself after the war by writing to Bean that Col. Skeen and others at Divisional HQ had seriously underestimated the

Turkish opposition. There was heavy fire for half an hour from the Turkish trenches before the attack, and so Antill had sent two urgent phone messages to Divisional HQ, who, however, said the attack must go ahead. Antill also later claimed there had been no Australian flag seen in the Turkish trenches. In addition, Brigadier-General Hughes was present, and did not stop the attack either. Antill concluded by blaming Divisional HQ for all the problems at the Nek. Brigadier-General Hughes also spent time defending himself to Bean, and claimed that staff officers got orders to stop the third line going over, but the regimental commander had left his post, and so the runner had no-one to give his message to. Hence, some of the third line went over, but none of the fourth line. Bean rejected these defences, and wrote to Edmonds that:

> Antill's comments are worthless: he says he never heard of a flag appearing in the Turkish trenches – actually he was the first man who, three or four days later, gave me an account of the incident! His statements are dangerously inaccurate in every respect in which I can readily check them; many of his facts seem to have been invented in the intervening years. The comments of Gen. Hughes, also, are incorrect. There is no question whatever that the third line and part of the fourth went out.[17]

Perhaps Antill was not so far wrong when he blamed Divisional HQ for the problems. Staff work in coordinating the attack at the Nek was poor, although obviously Antill himself, and Hughes, were out of touch with the situation, and failed to do their jobs. It may also be that some Australian Light Horse did get into the Turkish trenches. If Atatürk's 'Memoirs' do refer to the Nek attack, as seems likely, he states that the assault on 7 August started at 4.00 a.m. with artillery fire, that the infantry went over at 4.45 a.m., and that some Australians got into the trenches on the right and centre of the Turkish line.[18]

Turning next to the diversionary attacks at Helles, these did not succeed in their object. The Helles attacks of 6 and 7 August called for 88 Brigade of 29 Division to attack the spur north of Krithia nullah on the afternoon of 6 August, while 127 Brigade of 42 Division was to attack the spur south of Krithia nullah on the morning of 7 August. The attack of 6 August was a fiasco, despite careful planning and artillery preparation. It was just not possible to cross open ground in front of machine-guns and artillery. Lt-Col. Bolton, CO of the 4th Worcesters, reported afterwards that the artillery preparation had done no damage to the wire, and as for the Turkish trenches, when the Allied artillery commenced the Turks left the trenches for a gully, only to return when the artillery fire was over. 88 Brigade HQ knew in 30 minutes that the attack was a failure, but 29 Division HQ would not believe the reports, while Corps HQ staff noticed 88 Brigade men with discs flashing in the sun in the Turkish trenches, and ordered 86 Brigade reserves up to support. Unfortunately, the discs, placed there to guide friendly fire, were on the backs of dead men. Nevertheless, Col. Wolley Dod, GOC 86 Brigade, was told to make good the trenches 88 Brigade had taken. Wolley Dod reported to de Lisle, commanding 29 Division, that 88 Brigade only held one untenable area, and that it was impossible to continue in these trenches. De Lisle claimed he had better information than this, but Wolley Dod managed to keep postponing 86 Brigade's supporting assault several times until de Lisle eventually cancelled the order.[19]

At a lower level, one officer in 86 Brigade, Lt-Col. Geddes, CO 1st Munster Fusiliers, had the courage to refuse to attack in these hopeless conditions. According to Geddes (known as 'Tuli' to his friend Aspinall), he discussed the futility of the forthcoming attack with the CO of the 1st Dublin Fusiliers, whose battalion was part of the proposed operation, and told him that the supporting attack would share the same fate 88 Brigade had suffered. Geddes recalled that the CO of the 1st Dublin Fusiliers agreed with him, but would not cancel the attack. Geddes accused the Dublins' CO of not having the guts of a louse, and in the late evening told 86 Brigade of the hopeless situation. Despite Wolley Dod's assertion, mentioned above, that he tried to halt the attack, 86 Brigade HQ actually did reorder the assault. Once more Geddes advised against the attack, and the proposed assault was finally cancelled at 3.30 a.m. on 7 August. Not many officers would have refused a direct order, but Geddes' argument was that an attack required proper artillery registration, followed by a proper bombardment. Geddes stated later this was a tactical argument: he was not afraid of his own battalion and that of the Dublin Fusiliers being wiped out, but of a Turkish counterattack that would move through the decimated troops and onto the beach. Regardless, Geddes was removed from his command to a ship the next day. However, Geddes' removal was temporary and, as a capable officer, he soon resumed command of his battalion. Meanwhile, the attack of 127 Brigade of 42 Division on the morning of 7 August was only a little more successful than 88 Brigade's the day before, since a section of the area known as the Vineyard was captured and held.[20]

The Helles diversion did not work, despite the heavy casualties of 3,500 men. Instead, Turkish reserves from Helles were ordered north, where the Turks realized the main offensive was taking place. Turning, then, to the main offensive by the Allied columns at Anzac over the night of 6/7 August, it is of interest that the Turks had already been expecting a new landing and a new offensive by July, although the disinformation campaign by Hamilton's GHQ was having a good effect by focussing attention on the Bulair/Saros region. In mid- to late July, at least three separate Turkish Intelligence reports pointed to Bulair/Saros as the new landing spot, while a landing on the Asian shore was also seen as a possibility. However, Liman von Sanders himself showed a canny instinct in late July by playing down the Bulair/Saros region. In a previously unpublished Fifth Army message of 19 July, Liman von Sanders wrote:

> The necessary orders for the Gulf of Saros have been issued. But at the moment I doubt a landing there, because for this the enemy will need heavy equipment, such as landing piers and magazines and much more. He [the Allies] often spreads information by all sorts of means designed to mislead us. More probable to me at the moment is the area of Gaba Tepe, because he [the Allies] can there use existing facilities, and simultaneously threaten both groups [i.e. both north and south] – while his front-line troops tie us down at Ari Burnu [Anzac] and Sed el Bahr [Helles] by way of an attack. It is striking that daily he [the Allies] withdraws and embarks some forces – about sixty to seventy men – from the north group. He probably wants to deceive us, in which case he [the Allies] is up to something.

Despite Allied deceptions, therefore, Liman von Sanders managed to remain focussed on roughly the correct location, and sent Col. Hans Kannengiesser to reinforce the area with 9 Division. Liman von Sanders was also being harassed by the Operations Department in Istanbul, who wanted Fifth Army to defend the coasts of Gallipoli rather than wait for the Allies to try a new landing and then defeat them. Meanwhile, the III Corps commander, Esat Pasa, expected an attack somewhere between Gaba Tepe and Helles, while Mustafa Kemal still reportedly focussed on Koja Cimen Tepe and Chunuk Bair.[21]

As for the Allies, their plan was innovative, but it was hindered by several important factors – the extremely rough and largely unknown nature of the ground; the poor quality of several key commanders; the eventual loss of control of the offensive by Godley; a plan that was much too ambitious; and the rapidly increasing impact of dysentery and disease on the key Anzac assault forces, which severely undermined their fighting ability and endurance. Thus Percy Doherty, 8th Canterbury Mounted Rifles, remarked in his diary that there were very few troops in his battalion because of sickness, the 8th Squadron had 59 men instead of 150, and the rest of the battalion was similar. In his memoir of the attack, Leonard Leary of the Wellington Mounted Rifles noted that half the men should have been in hospital. Men would go down to the sick parade on the beach with faltering steps and staring eyes. A few hours later they would return in the same uncertain condition. Unless men were almost dead they were not evacuated, and according to Leary, men 'were sometimes found dead on the latrines in the morning.' Along the same lines, Lt-Col. Malone wrote in his diary that he had little faith in his brigadier, F.E. Johnston, who was completely subservient to Divisional HQ, and who readily volunteered the Wellington Battalion for the offensive without knowing the serious physical state of his brigade. Johnston's choice was all the stranger for being against the advice of Birdwood, who said the New Zealanders had been knocked about too much. But Johnston insisted. Malone wrote: 'He is too airy for me and does not know the weakness of his Brigade.' Malone correctly pointed out that the other two battalions were rested, while the Wellington Battalion was not, and also contained a large percentage of new men.

Malone emphasized that his battalion did *not* volunteer for the new offensive. Much the same occurred with the choice of the 4th Australian Brigade for the Koja Cimen Tepe attack, the least healthy of all the Australian brigades. Birdwood must take ultimate responsibility for these choices.[22]

Malone was also not convinced by the actual plan, correctly fearing confusion in the dark:

> The Brigadier will not get down to bed rock. He seems to think that night attack and the taking of entrenched positions without artillery preparation is like 'kissing one's hand'. Yesterday he burst forth: 'If there's any hitch I shall go right up and take the place myself'. All, as it were, in a minute and on his own! He is an extraordinary man… If it were not so serious it would be laughable.

Malone warned: 'No airy plunging and disregard of the rules and chances.' Yet, *ad hoc* plunging is what Malone got, and the offensive cost him his life, while Johnston, far from adopting a heroic role, made some poor decisions and either, allegedly, lapsed into an alcoholic state or, according to Maj. A.C. Temperley, into a confused mental state: 'he sat for hours in absolute silence, he was frequently barely coherent and his judgement and mind were obviously clouded.' Johnston proved therefore to be an absolutely terrible choice for a key commander in this offensive.[23] However, all this was in the future when at sunset on 6 August the left and right covering columns set out to clear the lower slopes for the two main Assault Columns to follow.

The covering columns made full use of surprise, and achieved their goals of capturing Turkish strong points on the foothills of Sari Bair by around the middle of the night. In the right covering force, Percy Doherty recalled that the password that night was 'Godley' and the countersign, 'Success'. The Brigade call was 'Waitangi'. Among the captures of this group was a Turkish officer's tent, which Doherty noted contained powders, puffs, face ointments and nail trimmers – a regular 'city fop.' More to the point, the right covering force captured Outpost #3 and then Destroyer Hill. Tpr Law, of the 4th Waikato New Zealand

Regiment remembers that at Outpost #3, when they charged the post the Turks fled, except for two who were bayonetted, carrying 'dynamo [sic = dynamite] ready to blow up the Hill.' The covering force reached the Table Top area by 11.00 p.m., where Pte Harry Ernest Browne of the Wellington Mountain Rifles claimed he took 150 Turkish prisoners. Most of these were sturdy individuals, but one small frightened man called out repeatedly 'Tesleem' – 'surrender'. Bauchop's Hill was also captured by the New Zealanders. [24]

Next came the main Right Assault Column, which split into two. The left half reached Table Top around 1.00 a.m., where some Turks that had been missed earlier were happy to surrender. According to Lt-Col. Gibson, the Turks actually helped his Otago company up and kissed them. Fifty Turks were taken prisoner here. Up to Rhododendron Ridge went the group, where the Turks were 'absolutely demoralised and fleeing in all directions. We did not have a shot fired at us.' But Gibson only had fifteen men with him, and they were ordered to dig in. The Turks rallied and covered Rhododendron Ridge with fire, preventing the full battalion from joining this group. However, the right hand half of the main Right Assault Column reached Rhododendron Ridge early on 7 August, where Johnston called a halt. The reason for this delay was to wait for the Canterbury Battalion which had got lost. Strangely enough, the Canterbury Battalion's commander, Lt-Col. J.G. Hughes, when the battalion lost direction, simply ordered it to march back to the beach. When Godley discovered this, he angrily ordered Hughes back up to Rhododendron Ridge. [25]

Although Johnston had used up precious time by simply waiting, at 7.00 a.m. on 7 August he set forth with two battalions toward Chunuk Bair, leaving one battalion behind. But just at this crucial moment, Col. Hans Kannengiesser appeared on the slopes of Chunuk Bair, ironically brought to the area by the Australian Lone Pine diversionary attack, and managed to bring the Right Assault Column of Anzacs to a halt in an area called the Apex. Temperley advised this halt, and Johnston informed Godley of this decision at 8.00 a.m., producing various reasons for not attacking again until night time. Temperley and Johnston argued that without supporting machine-gun and artillery fire, their main Right

Assault Column could not reach the crest. Hence one proposal was to attack at night. On the other hand, Lt-Col. R.Young, commanding the Auckland Battalion, thought the Right Assault Column could take the crest if given time to rest, prepare an attack and get the machine-guns forward. But Godley instructed Johnston to 'Attack at once'. Therefore, some two and a half hours later, at 10.30 a.m. on 7 August, part of the Auckland Battalion and some of the Gurkhas who had come over from the Left Assault Column, began their attack. But the Turks, by now reinforced, focussed on the Apex gap, and the Auckland Battalion lost 200 to 300 men in just 10 minutes. Johnston was 'overcome by the thought that he had sent us against such odds against our and his own judgement.' Another attempt was made by the Canterbury Battalion under Lt-Col. Hughes, who had now arrived. But Hughes foolishly formed his battalion up in full view of the Turks in dense ranks, and his battalion was also decimated, leaving only thirty-seven men. Hughes broke down, with 'tears pouring down his cheeks.' Another source, Lt H. Stewart, a company commander in the Canterbury Battalion, recalled that Hughes telephoned down to W.G. Braithwaite at New Zealand HQ, saying that 'the hill lines are all unfamiliar…', and 'I'm Jacky [Hughes] the most miserable man on earth…' Godley accepted the need for reinforcements, and ordered an attack for dawn the next morning, 8 August, with the support of 13 Division as a reserve force.[26]

Evidently, two different concepts of the main Right Assault Column attack were in operation – Godley and HQ's idea of surprise and a rapid ascent to Chunuk Bair – and the Temperley/Johnston/Young idea of a night or set piece attack. Temperley, who claims he really ran the show, considered that Godley and the Corps staff were 'ridiculously optimistic'. He believed there were Turks well entrenched on Chunuk Bair and it was thus foolhardy to attack without proper artillery and machine-gun support. The disastrous efforts at 10.30 a.m. and following on 7 August seemed to confirm Temperley's fears. On the other hand, Aspinall considered that the Turks were not on Chunuk Bair in any strength until 9.00 a.m. on 7 August, and 'that it was the [Temperley/Johnston] "prophecy of disaster" which boiled the show!' Although Johnston's caution and halt early on 7 August have been much criticized, there were defenders of his order. Firstly, by his own account, it was Temperley who suggested the halt to Johnston, and Temperley who advised him to oppose Godley's attack order. Secondly, according to Lt-Col. Young, commanding the Auckland Battalion, there were good reasons to halt. The troops were physically exhausted, and were afraid of going off into the blue without proper preparation. In addition, thirdly, many men did not actually realize the urgency to reach Chunuk Bair. Lt H. Stewart wrote later:

> Had all ranks realised that it was essential to get at Chunuk Bair, I have no doubt at all that it would have been done that morning. The fire was nothing like heavy enough to stop us.

Stewart though does end by noting: 'I am afraid the Brigadier [Johnston] was far from free of blame.' Fourthly, Temperley blames Godley for his poor handling of the whole situation, and certainly Godley was far away at Outpost #2, and completely out of personal touch with conditions. Somehow, there had developed two different conceptions of how to proceed, but which was correct?[27]

For example, was Aspinall correct that Chunuk Bair was poorly defended until 9.00 a.m. on 7 August? Judging by the telegrams between Fifth Army and the Supreme Command in Istanbul, Fifth Army did not pay as much attention to Chunuk Bair as it did to Suvla and Helles. However, Kannengiesser's memoirs show that by 8.00 a.m. on 7 August, he had a platoon of twenty men, plus two companies of the 72nd Regiment, in a defensive line on Chunuk Bair. It also seems that the 1st Battalion of 14th Regiment was on Chunuk Bair before 9.00 a.m. on 7 August, according to Mustafa Kemal's reprint of a report he received from Lt Hayri Effendi. The 25th and 64th Regiments were also on their way, and were probably close to Chunuk Bair and Koja Cimen Tepe by 10.00 a.m. on 7 August. All that can be said now is that Kannengiesser had a reasonably formidable line of defence on Chunuk Bair by 8.00 a.m. on 7 August, probably 250 men, and with the 1st Battalion of the 14th Regiment perhaps another 500 men. And hour by hour the defence certainly got stronger. On the other hand, had the

Johnston/Temperley column pressed forward at dawn on 7 August without waiting for the Canterbury Battalion, they probably could have taken Chunuk Bair. As Lt-Col. Bishop claimed later, his Otagos stayed just below the Chunuk Bair summit for four hours, presumably from dawn to 10.30 a.m. on 7 August, and were not fired upon. One battalion could have made good the summit, but by the time the Otago Battalion was collected and organized, it was too late to attack that day.[28]

Meanwhile, to the north, the main Left Assault Column headed for Koja Cimen Tepe and Hill Q, but became entangled in the steep valleys and hills of the area (and also had much further to go). Brigadier-General J. Monash, commanding 4th Australian Brigade, apparently lost his head in the confusion, and halted the column at first light on 7 August. Admittedly the men going up Aghyl Dere toward the Abdul Rahman spur were very tired, due to poor health, lack of sleep and the much longer, more difficult route. All were thirsty and exhausted and the track was narrow and full of slippery boulders, allowing only single file passage. Turkish snipers were also a deadly impediment to movement. To counteract the snipers, the Gurkhas were called upon. Taking out their kukris, the Gurkhas disappeared into the bushes, and each would 'soon emerge to wipe his knife on the bushes and again disappear after another thus soon clearing out these pests of snipers.'[29] But, apart from the 29th Indian Brigade which pressed on, especially the 1/6th Gurkhas under Maj. C. Allanson, which landed up only 1,000 yards under Hill Q early on 7 August, the rest of the column spent the day resting, reorganizing, and calling up reserves.

Yet all was not lost for the Allies, since the Turks were in considerable disarray on Chunuk Bair and units were very mixed up across Sari Bair generally. Units from three separate Turkish divisions had been sent to Chunuk Bair, and they were in a crowded and confused state. In particular, there was no single commander in charge of Turkish troops at Chunuk Bair. There appear to have been at least five different sequential Turkish commanders from 7 to 8 August, and the situation was made worse because it was not clear where the dividing line for command lay between Kemal's 19 Division, itself deployed south of Chunuk Bair but in command of the 10th Regiment there, and the other troops at Chunuk Bair, all under the command of the Northern Group. Confusion reigned, so, for example, Ali Riza Pasa, commanding 8 Division at Chunuk Bair, started to panic, and did not know what to do. In order to clear up the confusion, Liman von Sanders conferred command of the whole Sari Bair/Suvla area to Mustafa Kemal at 9.45 p.m. on 8 August. Reportedly, Liman von Sanders asked Kemal whether this would be too many troops, evidently meaning not that there were too many troops in the area but that there were too many troops for one commander, namely Kemal, to control. Kemal took the question the wrong way, and answered that the troops under his control would not be too many but too few to stem the Allied offensive.[30]

But this is to get ahead of the story. At very first light, actually 4.15 a.m., on 8 August, following an accurate half-hour of naval and artillery bombardment, which the Turks themselves admitted was very heavy and which scattered the defenders, the main Right Assault Column, now comprising Malone's Wellington Battalion together with the 7th Battalion Gloucesters and 8th Battalion Welch Pioneers, advanced to take the crest of Chunuk Bair by 4.40 a.m. But as soon as the troops began to dig, the Turks responded and opened fire from both left and right. According to one source, this was the signal for the British units to move behind the Wellington Battalion, and reportedly these units did not dig trenches but lay behind steep parts of the crest and stood up to fire when the Turks attacked. This source, Maj. Bill Cunningham of the Wellington Battalion, also recorded that several times there was near panic when two or three of the lightly wounded Gloucesters and Welch threw 'their equipment to the winds…[and bolted] headlong…' from the front trenches. Cunningham's letter appears unjust, since the Gloucesters lost every officer and 350 men, while the Welch Pioneers lost seventeen officers and 400 men. Also, according to the war diary of the Welch Pioneers, this unit was heavily shelled by 'fire from the rear.' By the end of the day, when the Wellington Battalion was relieved, some 750 Wellington men had gone up to Chunuk Bair, but only three officers and sixty men came down.[31]

Later, a controversy arose over whether Malone made a crucial error in digging in on the reverse crest below the summit, rather than on the forward crest on the Turkish side of the summit. Naturally, the latter would be of greater value, as the troops in the trench could then look down and fire on any Turkish counterattack. Previously, an unpleasant rivalry had developed between Malone and Temperley, and it was Temperley who survived the battle and criticized Malone for his Chunuk Bair dispositions. Malone earlier called Temperley 'a poisonous sneak', while Temperley described Malone as 'stubborn' and possessing a 'narrow mind'. Temperley reported that Malone dug in on the reverse crest, 'some 50 to 100 feet beneath, surrendering everything to the Turk.' This was due to the 'obstinacy of the man', since Malone did not listen to advice to dig in on the forward slope. As the Brigade Major, Temperley could influence the war diaries, and possibly for this reason the New Zealand Mounted Brigade war diary alluded to 'the extremely bad siting of the trenches…' at Chunuk Bair, being some 15 yards below the crest, allowing the Turks to roll bombs down and gather for attacks. Others felt the same; for example, Lt-Col. Bishop wrote: 'It was unfortunate that our trench line was sited below the crest, and in my opinion a great mistake.' However, Bishop was writing in the 1920s, when the Temperley line of criticism was accepted. It seems that Malone did actually make every effort to dig trenches both on the forward and reverse crests, but the Wellington Battalion were unable to dig in on the actual top of the ridge because of stones and hard clay, and after about half an hour, the Wellington Battalion came under heavy fire from Hill Q, and then from Battleship Hill. Finally, attacks by the Turks killed or made prisoner of everyone in the forward defences, and drove the wounded and survivors over the crest and back into the reverse crest trenches.[32]

The New Zealanders held on, and that night, the Wellington Mounted Rifles (WMR) and the Otago Battalion came forward to relieve the Wellington infantry battalion. Before this occurred, the very capable Malone was killed around 5.00 p.m. by Allied naval shelling while in his HQ trench. Meanwhile, the relieving troops came up over ground filled with dead and wounded. Harry Browne of the WMR recalled that about 8.00 p.m. his unit charged upward toward Chunuk

Bair, and as they ran might accidentally kick a wounded man. They would apologize, and the man would say: 'It's all right mate, I know you did not mean to.' On the WMR right was the Gloucester Battalion, though allegedly their wild yells and lack of discipline tended to give their position away. Another participant from the Otagos wrote that they charged upward at 8.30 p.m., but soon many came streaming back wounded, while some of the South Wales Borderers allegedly found shelter among the wounded. The ordeal of these men is difficult to imagine, but the diary of Tpr Law gives an idea of the situation. Moving up to replace the Wellington Battalion, Law started his journey the night before, early on 8 August. He ran 'over the side of a hill with bullets raining around us like hail from machine-guns.' Law found a hollow to shelter in, but 'Men were killed and wounded all around me. Legs, arm and other portions being blown off...' Law waited there for over seven hours, without moving, and then from this

> Valley of Death (6 or 700 dead and wounded here) on into the mouth of
> Hell, charged up the side of Chunuk Bair... our men fell like apples in a
> gale, the Turks rushed us with bombs only to be mowed down by us. One
> came up with white flag and party [of] bomb throwers behind him. They
> all fell...

Early on 9 August, at 4.30 a.m., several men around Law were hit by shells from an Allied warship, including one man who had several wounds. Law found him 'quite cheerful. I bound him up in six places, he thanked me but died about two hours after.' Law carried some other wounded down to a dressing station, and simply went to sleep in a dugout at about 5.00 a.m. Woken by a bombardment, he had breakfast, and then rejoined his regiment.[33]

Pte Harry Browne also recounted the story of the same Turkish counterattack against Chunuk Bair at dawn on 9 August. Not only were they attacked by the Turks, but shelling from an Allied destroyer landed amongst the men. One naval shell blew a man 30 feet into the air, limbs outstretched, 'his whole body in silhouette against the sky.' Another shell, and the charred trunk of a body fell near Browne. The Turks attacked with hand grenades, and one of the men, an ex-sergeant who had just come up as a reinforcement the day before, cried out 'Come on boys, retire.' Browne and a fellow soldier threatened to kill him. Then another shell, and a few more WMR were wounded. A counterattack by Sergeant Perrett and a handful of men failed, and the rush down carried the ex-sergeant and several others back from the trench. Then there were only four men left to defend what had become the front trench on Chunuk Bair. A 75 French gun from Walker's Ridge and an Allied battery from Anafarta dropped fire onto them. Phoning out and waving flags to stop the friendly fire only produced more shelling. In front of the four men was a communication trench leading to the main front trench – but those were both quiet, because they were piled with the dead of the WMR. Then Allied shelling became more accurate and got onto the Turks, and the Turkish attack halted. A few more Anzac men came up, and raised the number of defenders to eight or ten. Browne and three others went up the communication trench, and started shooting to the right, although standing on their own dead, 'but they wouldn't mind and we were too exhausted to lift them out.' Shortly after this, in a neighbouring trench came a feeble voice calling 'New Zealand', and the stump of an arm now and then waved. But the four listeners could give or get no help for him. After this episode, Browne's diary ends.[34]

While the New Zealand and British units held on grimly at Chunuk Bair, the 4th Australian Brigade of the Left Assault Column was still in so much confusion, with reserves lost in the maze of gullies, that little could be done about Koja Cimen Tepe. The column had been met by heavy machine-gun fire on Abdul Rahman spur, and could not advance. But at Hill Q, Allanson and his Gurkhas, plus some of the 8th Warwickshire Battalion, made a dash for Hill Q at dawn on 9 August. A tremendous Allied bombardment prepared the way for them, and then a fierce struggle took place for the crest, which turned out to be the saddle between Hill Q and Chunuk Bair. Allanson recalled: 'At the top we met the Turks; Le Marchand was down, a bayonet through the heart. I got one through the leg, and then for about what appeared to be 10 minutes, we fought hand to hand, we bit and fisted, and used rifles and pistols as clubs; and then the Turks turned and fled...' It seems likely the Turks were outnumbered, since the Gurkhas and two companies of the South Lancashire Regiment got to the saddle, while Allanson himself said that 450 of his men got to the top. Of this group, Allanson and the Gurkhas went over the saddle and onto the forward slope, where, according to Allanson, a celebrated incident took place. Some six or eight big shells exploded, causing panic among the Gurkhas, and the small group fled back. It is curious that of 450 men, less than fifteen or so went over the crest, but the Turks saw what was happening, came up quickly, and drove Allanson and the other troops back from Hill Q. Allanson blamed the Navy for the shells which destroyed the Hill Q assault. But this is unlikely, given Allanson's position over the crest, allowing a view of the Straits. However, the ship's log of *Bacchante*, supporting the operation, shows that she opened fire at 5.20 a.m. on 9 August on Hill Q with 6 inch shells and the 12 inch shells of a monitor might also have been responsible. But what historians have overlooked is that the pre-arranged artillery timetable called for Anzac howitzers to search the forward crest at 5.15 a.m. on 9 August, obviously to defend Hill Q against Turkish counterat-tacks, and for the Navy to switch to flank fire at this time. Since Allanson and his Gurkhas were hit on the forward crest at about 5.35 a.m., the responsibility for this unfortunate 'friendly fire' incident obviously lies with poor staff work, while the 'very excitable' but brave and energetic Allanson unintentionally put his Gurkhas at risk after 5.15 a.m. Clearly, Allanson did not know what the Allied fire plan was.[35]

Strangely, Allanson's story of naval shelling was later undercut by his own letters to Aspinall in 1930. In these Allanson says that he did not stay on the summit (or saddle) of Hill Q on 9 August, not because of naval shelling or other friendly fire, but because of the extreme exposure of the summit, where a few shells would dislodge them. He does not actually refer to any naval shelling. Allanson's 'naval shells' theory was also indi-rectly challenged by Lt Savory, an officer of the 14th Sikhs, who remained on Hill Q after Allanson was wounded and forced to retire. Savory recalled: 'There was no question of our seeing the Narrows… owing to the bursting of shells… Unfortunately, I was compelled to order a return owing to an enormous number of Turkish reinforcements appearing in sight.' So Savory believed it was *not* naval or howitzer shells but the large number of Turkish reinforcements which caused the with-drawal.[36] Even so, Allanson and Savory might yet have survived on Hill Q if they had been supported by a reserve column led by Brigadier-General A.H. Baldwin, commanding 38th Brigade of 13 Division. This column was supposed to come in on Allanson's right, and attack at the same time as Allanson. This plan should have been worked out between Godley and Baldwin at a conference on 8 August. But, at the last minute, Godley did not appear for the conference, and according to Temperley neither did any Division or Corps staff officer. Why did Godley fail to appear for this critical meeting, or indeed why did Godley fail to come up closer to the battle and personally direct operations? Godley's excuses have a hollow ring, and reflect what may be called 'HQitis' – the tendency to stick to HQ and command from the end of a telephone. Godley claimed he had started up a gully 'when I was recalled to speak to Gen. Cox [GOC 29th Indian Brigade] on the telephone. Rightly or wrongly, I turned back, became engaged in a long conversation with Cox, and found other things to engage my attention.' These other things were 'telephone reports and conversations, signal messages, reports of liaison officers, getting out of orders, sending up reinforcements, &c., &c., and the general control of the long [telephone] line… and it was not so easy for us to leave our Headquarters as it might seem.'[37]

Godley failed as a commander at this point, and his future career reveals that he was not a great success on the Western Front either. Godley's absence meant that the decision regarding Baldwin's route up toward Hill Q was settled by Johnston, who was sinking into incoherence at this point. Temperley suggested Baldwin's column move north along Rhododendron Ridge, gather under Chunuk Bair, and then move on to Hill Q. But Johnston struggled to 'run the show' himself, and said that the best route was up the Chailak Dere, across to the Aghyl Dere, and then up to Hill Q via a small building known as the Farm. Baldwin's Brigade spent the whole day trying to reach the Farm, through gullies jammed with wounded and dead men and animals. It seems the wounded being moved down against the upward flow of Baldwin's men was a critical factor in delaying the column. One participant in the march, Capt. Hicks, 10th Battalion, Hampshire Regiment, remembered the 'hot dusty swollen brown stinking corpses lying about everywhere.' In the area of the Farm, heavy machine-gun fire halted the advance, caused very heavy casualties, and prevented any attack in conjunction with Allanson. The column lay down, and when ordered to move, Hicks and his men could do little because of heat and exhaustion. But he did notice two New Zealanders bringing in four snipers they had just captured. The snipers were being led off to be shot: 'The Turks caught us by the hand and begged for mercy. But we weren't feeling very merciful to snipers just then.' According to Capt. Hicks, his company was then sent up from the Farm onto Rhododendron Spur under heavy shrapnel fire, but were told there 'we were not wanted. I received a very cold welcome from Gen. Johnston, and had to take my half company down the Chailak Dere and round up the Aghyl Dere again.' At the same time, according to Temperley, morale in Baldwin's column generally became poor, and some 300 men from the column tried to surrender to the Turks. Temperley stopped this by turning a machine-gun onto them. No doubt morale was low because Baldwin's column was punished heavily in the Farm area that day, although the war diary of the 6th Battalion Royal Irish Rifles, part of Baldwin's column, merely recorded on 9 August that they were told to take the left ridge of Sari Bair (either the left flank of Chunuk Bair, or Hill Q), but stopped 250 yards from the summit, and entrenched, while suffering just one man killed, and a few wounded. Later on, when the Turks attacked with a massive assault at dawn the next day, 10 August, all along the Sari Bair crest, the 6th Battalion Royal Irish Rifles stayed for an hour and a half, and then were given orders to retire: 'by whom it has not been possible to ascertain.' Hicks remembered that the gullies were 'full of men running for all they were worth'. Two courageous officers stood in the gully and stopped the rout. Evidently, the men had reached the end of their tether.[38]

Turning then to look at events from the Turkish point of view, there was initially much confusion. This was particularly the case on 8 August, when Fifth Army admitted the Allies had captured 100 metres near the Chunuk Bair summit, and were defending strongly. This gave the Allies a powerful advantage, Fifth Army reported, although it was also argued the Allies were not properly using this achievement to their benefit. Next, on the morning of 9 August, Fifth Army was confused about the intentions of the Anzac troops and what was called the new front at Chunuk Bair. The Turks were obviously puzzled as to whether the Anzac area was the prime battle front or not. One strange Turkish suggestion was that the Australians and a British division were going to exchange troops. However, men from five Turkish divisions were being collected for Turkish counterattacks, 7 and 12 Divisions from the north, and 5, 8 and 9 Divisions from the south and elsewhere. Munitions were badly needed, and hand bombs were urgently requested.[39]

On 9 August, Mustafa Kemal launched some Turkish attacks, especially at Hill 60 and Damakjelik Bair, with the previously mentioned 7 Division from the Bulair/Saros area. The idea behind this attack was to get the Allies to divert troops from the Sari Bair offensive, but this did not happen. Finally, in desperation, Mustafa Kemal assembled a number of battalions from all directions, but mainly from 8 Division, for a dawn attack on 10 August along the Sari Bair crest, especially aimed at Chunuk Bair. There remains some confusion as to which regiments and battalions were involved, but this attack certainly included 23rd and 24th Regiments from 8 Division. The Fifth Army Journal for 8 August mentions one battalion from 33 Regiment of 4 Division being called in, which, under Hulusi Bey, actually defended against the 4th Australian Brigade at Abdul Rahman spur that day, and the 22nd Regiment of 8 Division, which was sent the same day to Chunuk Bair under Col. Hakki.[40] Then a Turkish message on 9 August to 8 and 9 Divisions called for hot food to be delivered to the two regiments that would be used against Chunuk Bair the next day. Another reliable source indicates that 26th Regiment of 13 Division was also involved. If three Turkish regiments were involved, as many as five to six thousand men were involved in Mustafa Kemal's Chunuk Bair offensive.

So there was undoubtedly a mixture of troops from different regiments under Mustafa Kemal, and perhaps for that reason there was no finesse about his 10 August attack on Chunuk Bair. There was simply a dense mass of men in the grey dawn attacking the 6th North Lancashire Regiment and, just below the crest, the exhausted 5th Wiltshire Regiment. These two regiments had replaced the New Zealanders, and probably comprised about 1,000 rifles. At very first light, encouraged by Mustafa Kemal's leadership, the mass bayonet-style attack went in and overwhelmed the North Lancashire Regiment. The Wiltshires also tumbled back, and the Turks poured down the slopes, taking the Pinnacle, but were actually turned back on the Turkish left by New Zealand machine-guns at the Apex. Veering to the right, the Turks then overwhelmed Baldwin and the defenders in the Farm area. Capt. Hicks, somewhere between the Farm and Hill Q, was suddenly roused from sleep by men of the North Lancashire Regiment running into his position, shouting 'retire, the Turks are on you.' Hicks and others stopped the panic, and even tried a counterattack toward the crest between Hill Q and Chunuk Bair: 'we crept up to 40 yards from the crest and then started to run… I went on: the men cheered but hung back.' Hicks found himself with only two men in a trench, and was ordered to retire down the main gully. He did so, but,

> in the nullah at the bad corners people there, as always, said 'run': so the nullah was full of men running to the rear for all they were worth. We rallied the Hants and [Royal Irish] Rifles in a cross nullah. Staff Captain Street centre of rallying.

Another counterattack was attempted, but Hicks was then hit and limped along, admitting honestly 'I had only one desire and that was to get safe away.' Baldwin's force was largely destroyed, and Baldwin himself was killed. Although the Farm was recaptured in a counterattack, it had to be abandoned later that night.[41]

Mustafa Kemal's dawn assault had succeeded, and the fight for the Sari Bair heights was over. A Turkish sketch map of 10 August shows the attack succeeding everywhere except on the Turkish left, where the 11th Regiment was turned back by the New Zealand machine-guns. Kemal matter of factly told the Istanbul Supreme Command on 10 August:

> Today, the Allies' force on the front of 8 Division at 4.30 a.m. was expelled. They were forced to retreat from Chunuk Bair. We even took back the

front of the higher ground of Sahintepe [Rhododendron Ridge].We have no information about our losses and the captured guns and equipment. As soon as we learn this we will report. Chunuk Bair and its area is under heavy bombardment by the Allies from both sea and land.

Later, Fifth Army casualties were listed as 4,119 by 9 August, and then, with incomplete numbers, as 4,373 by 11 August. If accurate, this means that Turkish casualties were comparatively light for the 10 August attack, perhaps about 250, no doubt as a result of the surprise and swiftness of the attack. Another source gives 3,680 Turkish casualties for the whole period 7 August to 13 August. Later, on 10 August, Liman von Sanders was not so calm as Kemal, and sent the following telegram:

> As I informed you, the Allied forces were completely expelled from the right wing of Anafartaler [Suvla] and Kocacimen [Sari Bair]. To do so I had to use all the troops I could get from all units. With the favour of God, I hope to finally defeat all our enemies. I don't know precisely whether they will receive reinforcements or not. But we have to have reserve divisions. Please, send new and fit divisions. This will be necessary.[42]

The extent of the Turkish attack on 10 August indicates that it was actually necessary for the Allies to capture all three of the high points of Sari Bair for the whole operation to succeed. The capture of a single height, for example, Chunuk Bair, was probably not sustainable, both logistically and tactically, as events proved. Could the capture of the whole Sari Bair heights have been achieved? Certainly the odds would have been much better if Godley and his staff had exercised greater control over the battle, and had ventured out of their distant HQ.[43] The odds would also have improved if more competent leaders than Godley, Johnston, Hughes, Monash and others had been selected, and if some others, such as Lt-Col. Malone and Maj. P.J. Overton, leader of the Left Column, had not been killed. In addition, the Allied troops needed to be much healthier and stronger, and at night time, the routes needed better guides and far easier going. So there was a chance of success, especially because the Turks were surprised, and there was a two day window of opportunity at

Sari Bair. Yet the odds were still against success, partly because the Turks were able to quite quickly call on large numbers of reserves, partly because there were some very capable Turkish/German commanders available, and partly because the many aspects of the Allied operation all had to go smoothly and be properly coordinated for overall victory, including artillery and naval fire, and infantry co-operation. Ultimately, it can be argued that the whole operation, despite its initial achievements at Hill Q and Chunuk Bair, was too ambitious, and probably beyond the capabilities of the senior officers, staff, Allied technology, and the troops involved. Senior Allied commanders were often not up to the test of the intensity of modern warfare, while Liman von Sanders, Kannengiesser, and Mustafa Kemal simply moved at a higher tempo.

One other aspect of the plan would certainly have helped, although it is important to note that it was not critical to the success of the Anzac offensive, and this was the neighbouring Suvla operation.

OPERATIONS AT SUVLA AND THE TURKISH REACTION

The Suvla part of the August offensive called for the capture of Suvla Bay as a port, just to the north of the Anzac break out. Subsequently, a controversy arose over whether Hamilton and GHQ intended Suvla to be a much more aggressive operation than simply capturing Suvla Bay as a port. The officer in charge of the Suvla operation, Lt-Gen. Sir Frederick Stopford, commanding IX Corps, denied the offensive potential of Suvla, and was content to advance very cautiously, especially on 8 August. By 9 August Turkish reserves were sufficient to halt the British offensive at Suvla. Further operations never advanced the Allied beach head at Suvla more than one mile inland.

Stopford's IX Corps contained 11 Division, GOC Maj.-Gen. F. Hammersley (32, 33 and 34 Brigades), which landed at Suvla on the evening of 6 August, and 10 Division, GOC Lt-Gen. Sir Bryan Mahon (29, 30 and 31 Brigades), which landed at Suvla early on 7 August. Other units included in IX Corps were 13 Division, largely used at Anzac, and in reserve the Territorial Divisions, 53, GOC Maj.-Gen. J.E. Lindley (158, 159 and 160 Brigades), which landed on 9 August, and 54, GOC Maj.-Gen. F.S. Inglefield (161, 162 and 163 Brigades), which landed on 10 August. Still later arrived the 2nd Mounted Division, which landed on 20 August, while the depleted Royal Naval Division continued on as part of IX Corps.

Landing problems at Suvla plagued 11 and 10 Division and created much confusion. Among the problems were lack of orders, poor maps, ineffective leadership, inadequate staff work, and, especially, water shortages. Lack of water in the intense heat of August was a critical problem, and the reasons for its absence require evalu-

ation. Similar difficulties faced 53 and 54 Divisions. On the other hand, heavily outnumbered, the Turkish defenders fought a masterly defensive battle, and Liman von Sanders reacted very quickly and delivered 7 and 12 Turkish Divisions to the Suvla area by the night of 7 August/8, earlier than historians have realized. By late August, the British attacks at Suvla petered out, including the mysterious 'disappearance' of the 1/5 Norfolk Battalion on 12 August. Allied offensives on 15 and 21 August at Suvla did not succeed, although Hill 60 was partially taken in heavy fighting. Then stalemate set in.

★

According to Edgar Anstey, ADC at GHQ, the idea of a Suvla operation emerged independently at GHQ and at Anzac HQ between 24 June and 1 July. On the other hand, Dawnay claimed that the idea of Suvla first saw the light of day at GHQ. Wherever it came from, the original concept was that W Hills, an area of high ground behind Suvla Bay, from which enemy artillery could damage troops and trenches on the Sari Bair ridge, might be taken from the sea rather than from land by the Anzacs. This meant that Suvla was originally intended to help the Anzac offensive directly. Birdwood then turned this concept into a plan on 1 July and suggested landing one division at Suvla instead of Anzac, because of congestion at Anzac, and giving the division an offensive role.

Thus the early plans for Suvla were aggressive but still vague, and it seems that GHQ and the Navy were at cross purposes initially. For Hamilton at GHQ, building on Birdwood's suggestion, the concept was for the Navy to land 10,000 troops between Suvla Bay and Fisherman's Hut, so that these troops would act in concert with the Anzac offensive, launching simultaneous attacks. In contrast, for the Navy, de Robeck saw what he called the 'Sulva' Bay concept mainly as a landing place and a port, to be covered by the Army. Dawnay recalls that the Navy also first said that Suvla was a poor location because of shoals, at which point attention turned to Gaba Tepe, to bite off the toe of the peninsula. However, Suvla was so attractive as an attack point that the Navy revised their idea, and said that an operation at Suvla was possible. Then GHQ's eventual orders followed the Navy's ideas and conceived of Suvla mainly as a port, and only after this was secured would Suvla become an offensive operation. One of the key planners at GHQ for the overall August offensive reveals quite clearly that Suvla was not thought of as an offensive concept. In a letter to his wife on 9 August 1915, Dawnay wrote that the Army would seize Suvla Bay, 'making a good harbour there for the winter in case we want it.' Later in the same letter, Dawnay confirmed again that Suvla was simply seen as a base for the Anzacs and the new army divisions. Orlo Williams, privy to GHQ secrets, put a little more emphasis on Suvla, suggesting that the troops there were to secure two low hills, W Hills and Chocolate Hill, from where Turkish guns could command Chunuk Bair. But, like Dawnay, Williams also considered that the primary mission of the troops at Suvla was simply to secure the area as a base. Only later, in September 1915, did Dawnay claim that he had envisaged a more aggressive role for Suvla if the Anzac offensive failed.[1]

Of course, if the Anzac offensive had succeeded, then Suvla would have been pulled along, and would no doubt have succeeded also. But in the absence of success at Anzac, the critical aspect of the planning that went awry for Suvla was the difference of opinion between GHQ and the newly appointed Lt-Gen. Sir Frederick Stopford, commanding the landing force at Suvla, IX Corps. Hamilton simply assumed there would be a more aggressive stance from Stopford, and told the French on 3 August, that the Anzacs and IX Corps 'will carry out the main attack…'. In contrast, Stopford was doubtful of what he could achieve, writing that 'I fear it likely that the attainment of the security of Suvla Bay will so absorb the force under my command as to render it improbable that I shall be able to give direct assistance to the GOC, Anzac, in his attack on Hill 305 [Koja Cimen Tepe].' So, before the landing, on 31 July, Stopford told GHQ firmly that IX Corps could not help the Anzac attack on Koja Cimen Tepe, although he did aim to capture Chocolate Hill and W Hills, preferably at night. Stopford was clearly informing GHQ that IX Corps' intentions were quite limited. In this, Stopford was encouraged by the CGS, Braithwaite, who again told Stopford that the primary object was to secure Suvla Bay as a base, and that owing to difficult ground, this might take all of IX Corps' troops. If it did not, the next step would be to assist the Anzac attack on Koja Cimen Tepe by advancing on

W Hills and Chocolate Hill. These should be taken, if possible, but without prejudicing the securing of Suvla as a base. Indeed, Neill Malcolm, 11 Division staff, part of IX Corps, thought that Chocolate Hill was really GHQ's furthest objective. Then Braithwaite further devalued the offensive aspect of Suvla in his reply to Stopford's query about artillery by saying that because of the need to land mules, horses and supplies, there would be no more artillery landed until 'at least a week after your disembarkation begins.' So, the idea of Suvla as a port or base was the fundamental concept which prevailed at GHQ and in IX Corps.

Understandably, GHQ did not put nearly as much emphasis on Suvla as they did on the main offensive at Anzac. But it also appears that Hamilton did not fully understand what was going on among his planning staff. Very significantly, Hamilton wrote later to the War Office in November 1915 that 'Our *feints* at ANZAC and HELLES had ensured a minimum of opposition to the IX Corps in their landing at SUVLA BAY.' Taken at face value, this astonishing comment means either that Hamilton thought of Suvla as the main offensive, thus showing himself to be absolutely out of touch with the whole August operation, or he was deliberately diverting attention away from the Anzac failure by emphasizing the problems at Suvla. It is extraordinary that Braithwaite again had to remind Hamilton in 1916 that Suvla was only one of three operations (Helles, Anzac, Suvla), and 'was not even the most important operation…'[2]

Of course, the connection between operations at Suvla and Anzac depended on which vision of Suvla was understood. So when Birdwood declared after the campaign that he knew Stopford might not be able to help him with the Anzac offensive, Hamilton was quick to reject this idea. And when the journalist Ashmead Bartlett also maintained that the operations at Suvla and Anzac were separate, Hamilton rejected that claim, and wrote that the two operations were connected by the hill at Damakjelik Bair. In this he was partly correct, for Aspinall did, at the last minute, send Stopford and IX Corps a message on 6 August which said that Anzac forces hoped to capture Damakjelik Bair before disembarkation at Suvla B Beach began. This was because Stopford complained that B Beach led to the strongest Turkish position, and he would need two brigades to capture it. The intent of Aspinall's message was clearly to reassure Stopford by ordering Anzac to help Suvla, and not the other way around. Similarly, Brigadier-General J.H. du B. Travers' left flanking column at Anzac was also supposed to safeguard the right flank of Suvla. Travers did so, and sent a cable detachment, which reached Suvla by 10.30 p.m. on the night of 6/7 August, but could get no response from the Suvla force. Thus the connection between the two operations was more intent than reality.[3]

Hamilton later argued that success at Suvla would have diverted troops away from the Anzac offensive, and, much more controversially, claimed that success at Suvla would have enabled the forces of Allanson and Baldwin to capture and hold the Sari Bair ridge. Unfortunately for all these arguments by Hamilton, while success at Suvla would undoubtedly have helped the Anzac offensive, this does not alter the fact that before the offensive started, GHQ clearly considered Suvla to be completely subsidiary to Anzac, and understood that Suvla was to be simply a port and base for Anzac, not an equal offensive partner. In fact, when GHQ received the news on 7 August that two divisions had landed successfully at Suvla, Aspinall recalled: 'we [at GHQ] said "The thing is done"', meaning that Suvla's primary task was achieved. In Aspinall's Dardanelles Commission statement, he also wrote that 'Once they [IX Corps] had got ashore without great opposition it had always been thought that the most difficult part of their task would be accomplished.' Stopford also recalled that a GHQ staff member told him verbally before the operation started that the 'security of the harbour should be my first consideration and that this security was not to be forfeited by an advance on Biyuk Anafarta [a village near Koja Cimen Tepe] to Gen. Birdwood's assistance.' Securing a port was clearly the main function of the Suvla landing, and not as support for the Anzac offensive.[4]

Subsequently, senior officers such as Birdwood, Hamilton and Godley, were very quick to blame Stopford and IX Corps for the failure of the entire August operation, including the main offensive at Anzac. It seems there was a conscious effort to cover up the failure at Anzac by focussing attention on Stopford, IX Corps and Suvla, and by selecting Suvla as a scapegoat for the Anzac failure. No doubt there was also simple anger at the opportunities lost at Suvla. Probably both attitudes played a part. However, the predominant attitude seems to have been the need to find a scapegoat for the overall failure of the August campaign. Already by 9 August, Birdwood was critical of Stopford, and on 22 August Birdwood argued that even if his troops had held Chunuk Bair, they would still have been shelled off by Turkish fire from W Hills: 'If only the 9th Corps on the left had shoved along, all would have been well', he wrote. Back in London, key observers soon caught the drift, and so Clive Wigram, private secretary to the king, was already writing to Godley in early September that if 'the 9th Corps had only been able to do a bit more, we should be in a more satisfactory position.' Hamilton himself pinned the blame for the failure of the whole August offensive on Stopford fairly quickly, for example, in messages to Kitchener on 11 and 14 August. Hamilton spread his version of events quite widely, thus in September 1915 he wrote to a senior officer saying that if IX Corps had captured W Hills at Suvla, then the Sari Bair Ridge would have been made good. In various letters home, Godley also blamed Stopford and IX Corps for the August failure, and even acknowledged that Stopford was selected as a scapegoat: 'We are all so dreadfully sorry at F. Stopford having being made the scapegoat – it is so hard to get at the truth or rights of these things, but… the Corps did not push vigorously after it landed…'[5]

Hamilton's own attitude to the Suvla operations was clouded by the belated realization that he and GHQ had neglected Suvla. Hamilton only became fully aware of inactivity at Suvla on 8 August, and tried to explain to Kitchener why this was so. Hamilton started off by telling Kitchener that he arrived at Suvla for an inspection on the first day of landing, i.e. 7 August, but then corrected this to admitting that he actually got on the ground at Suvla only on 8 August at 5.00 p.m. Hamilton explained that this was the earliest he could get to Suvla, either because of heavy fighting there, or because he had to stay at Imbros to oversee the two fronts of Anzac and Helles. Hamilton also argued in his published 'diary' that he wanted to get to Suvla earlier, but was delayed on 8 August in reaching Suvla because the boat he was supposed to use for the journey, *Arno*, needed to draw water to fire up its boiler, and this delayed him for a considerable time. However, the diary of Sergeant Stuart, who kept a log of Hamilton's daily activities, simply recorded: 'In the afternoon about 4 o'clock he [Hamilton] decided to proceed to Suvla Bay. He left in the *Triad* arriving at Suvla Bay about 5 p.m.' The issue is complicated because Hamilton originally intended to send three staff officers to Suvla, rather than go himself. In a message at 8.45 a.m. on 8 August, Hamilton requested this, but *Arno* could not sail because of the need to draw water. Then at 9.39 a.m., Hamilton requested trawler 288, or any another vessel. At 10.33 a.m., the Navy told Hamilton that Trawler 288 was entirely at GHQ's disposal. Possibly because it was slow, Trawler 288 did not suit Hamilton, who alerted *Arno* at 11.45 a.m.: 'I may require her at any moment.' This suggests that Hamilton had not yet decided to go to Suvla. At 12.15 p.m., the Navy repeated that *Arno* was not available, because of watering, but suggested using *Triad* instead, which was leaving at 3.15 p.m. So, at 3.45 the Navy informed *Triad* that Hamilton 'may go in you to Suvla. I am waiting for his reply.' At 3.48 p.m., Hamilton decided definitely to go on *Triad*, which finally got under way at about 4.45 p.m., arriving at Suvla with Hamilton on board by 5.45 p.m.[6]

All this suggests that Hamilton exaggerated the way in which he was delayed in getting to Suvla, especially because Trawler 288 was available, while a destroyer was also available half an hour later. In his correspondence, Hamilton continued to focus on Suvla, especially after the dismissal of Stopford on 15 August. This event unleashed a lengthy battle between Stopford and Hamilton over culpability at Suvla. Stopford hastened to pen a memorandum on 18 August, blaming the eventual Suvla failure on poor instructions from GHQ, secrecy at GHQ, lack of water, strong Turkish opposition, difficulty of terrain and tasks, etc. Eventually, a distinguished War Office Committee, headed by Lt-Gen. A.J. Murray, basically came down on Stopford's side on 21 September 1915, stating that the whole series of tasks assigned to IX Corps was 'somewhat of a risky business and not a thoroughly practical operation of war.' However, this was not the end of the controversy, which continued at full blast through the end of 1915 and into 1916. Through his friend Maj.-Gen. F.S. Robb, the Military Secretary, Stopford requested a hearing from Kitchener, and Robb suggested a Court of Enquiry to settle the argument between the two. Kitchener originally agreed, but then changed his mind, and refused an enquiry because the country was still at war, and because many others would then also want a court of enquiry. Stopford threatened action through the Press or Parliament, and demanded publicity for his case. Finally, Kitchener saw Stopford on 6 March 1916 and told him there were no grounds for complaint, and that he was not to pursue the matter further. As a sop, Robb suggested Stopford be allowed to resume his career as Lieutenant of the Tower of London at the very considerable salary of £400 per annum, and this was agreed. The argument continued through the Dardanelles Commission, when Aspinall, responsible with Dawnay for the overall planning of the August offensive, laid considerable blame on Stopford in his submission. Although Hamilton was basically exonerated in the final Commission Report, Stopford did receive some criticism.[7]

Nevertheless, the attention paid to Suvla then and later has tended to divert attention away from Anzac, so much so that one historian recently considered Suvla to be the main operation in August.[8] But what was the all the furore about? Stopford's task was primarily to capture Suvla as a port, then if possible to advance on the high ground in front of Suvla Bay, including W Hills and Chocolate Hill. Stopford doubted he could help the Anzac plan. Hamilton agreed to this. But why was Stopford so cautious? It is often said of Stopford that he had not commanded in battle, with the implication that he was ignorant of modern warfare, and so relied too much on his chief of staff, Brigadier-General H.L. Reed. In fact, Stopford had accompanied Gen. Sir Redvers Buller as his Military Secretary in the Boer War, and witnessed considerable action there. What is more, like Buller, Stopford learnt there the necessity for an artillery barrage to enable the infantry to advance, and certainly understood the value of trenches in defence, and the importance of reconnaissance before advancing. Also of interest is the fact that Buller, and by association, Stopford, were the object of Hamilton's violent criticism after the humiliation of the siege of Ladysmith in the Boer War, where Hamilton was one of those incarcerated. Further, Stopford and Hamilton were on opposite sides of the famous pre-war Roberts versus Wolseley rings of influence in the British army. How much these earlier situations influenced their relationship at Gallipoli, and in post Gallipoli arguments, is now hard to determine.[9]

Therefore, with extensive Boer War experience just some fifteen years previously, it is understandable that Stopford was cautious when told of the Suvla plan. According to Rear-Admiral A.H. Christian, commanding the naval force at Suvla, both Stopford and Reed reportedly felt that the Suvla plan was not feasible, and feared being driven into the sea. Quite apart from this, Stopford had trouble finding out what the Suvla plan actually was until quite shortly before the operation began. One of Stopford's later complaints was that Hamilton did not enlighten him about the plan when Stopford and Hamilton occupied tents next to each other on the island of Imbros on 11 and 12 July. Hamilton replied that the plan was not specifically worked out at that time, although this was not quite true, since Hamilton roundly condemned Birdwood on 11 July for telling his divisional generals of the plan, which obviously then existed in some form, while Hamilton had not even told the French or Stopford! Even when Stopford did know the plan, it is of interest that Birdwood, some ten days before the Suvla operation, showed Stopford the Suvla Bay area from an Anzac vantage point, and told him there were only some 2,000 men opposing him. Stopford replied that he did not like to advance with only one brigade until he had the others on shore to support the brigade. Stopford also said that his men had done very little night work, probably thinking of the Boer War again, and there were many difficulties in such an unknown country. At this point, Stopford did not yet worry about the lack of artillery, but by 6 August Stopford and Reed had become more concerned about the projected lack of guns at Suvla than any other factor, invoking the lessons of France, where enemy trenches needed howitzer fire before they could be taken. It is often forgotten that Reed was originally a gunner, who had taken part in a courageous attempt to save the guns at the battle of Colenso in the Boer War. Reed had also lately come from France, where the value of artillery was only too obvious, but Stopford, with his Boer War experience, hardly needed to be reminded by Reed of the significance and necessity of artillery. Hamilton later accused Reed of getting his position through royal influence, but regardless, the artillery question made both Reed and Stopford cautious.[11]

The final Suvla plan was for 11 Division, commanded by Maj.-Gen. Hammersley, to land on the evening of 6 August at the south end of Suvla Bay. The first battalions ashore were to capture the low hills of Lala Baba and Hill 10, and also move troops up to the Kiretch Tepe ridge on the northern flank of Suvla Bay. Other battalions of the division would advance and capture Chocolate Hill and W Hills, hopefully by dawn on 7 August. After this, the far Tekke Tepe ridge, overlooking the Suvla plain, was the eventual long range target. Following 11 Division was to be Lt-Gen. Sir Bryan Mahon's 10 Division, which would land at first light on 7 August and capture the entire Kiretch Tepe left flank. The whole operation would be directed by Stopford, initially located with his HQ on board the destroyer *Jonquil*, anchored off Suvla Bay. The primary aim was still to secure Suvla as a port.

From the Turkish point of view, their defenders were actually more numerous than Aspinall's Official History has allowed, in fact some 3,000 men. Of course, this was still a very small figure to be pitted against two British divisions, comprising some 16,000 men, with two further Territorial Divisions, 53 and 54, in reserve. Moreover, Turkish defenders included the less reliable Bursa Gendarmerie, but they were under a very capable German commander, Maj. Willmer. Undoubtedly the Turks were surprised by Suvla, because initial thoughts about possible landing sites varied considerably. In mid-July, Liman von Sanders considered a landing was likely, possibly in the Gaba Tepe area. The Turkish Official History agrees that Liman von Sanders did not expect a landing north of Anzac, but maintains that he also thought of Saros/Bulair, and of the Asian side. In fact, Liman von Sanders did send a message on 6 August to the German chief of staff of the Northern group, Maj. Eggert, stating: 'There are increasing indications of enemy movement against Asiatic coast.' On the other hand, Willmer later asserted that Liman von Sanders did think of Suvla Bay, and also considered that Koja Cimen Tepe was the most dangerous point in the whole Gallipoli peninsula.[12]

The first British forces to disembark at night on 6/7 August, using the newly arrived armoured 'Beetle' landing craft, were the 32 and 33

Brigades of 11 Division. These landed at A and B Beaches respectively, and came ashore relatively unscathed. The 6th Yorkshire Regiment of 32 Brigade captured the small hill of Lala Baba around midnight, but suffered considerable casualties in doing so. The next day, Capt. J.D. Coleridge, staff officer in 11 Division, saw the regiment, and reported: 'The fight for Lala Baba had taken the starch out of them, and the loss of so many officers had much depressed them.' Meanwhile, two battalions of 33 Brigade secured the right flank of the landing. Some difficulties attended the landing of 34 Brigade, which struck shoals in Suvla Bay, and this meant difficult unloading in six feet of water. In the case of the 11th Manchester Regiment, this required two officers to hold a rope, one in the water, one on the lighter, so the men could hand themselves along the rope and land. Because of this, material could not be landed, except for rifles and one machine-gun. The next day, 7 August, due to seawater and sand, the one machine-gun and 300 rifles were unusable. Nevertheless, this battalion made excellent progress north to Kiretch Tepe and performed well for about two days, until at 2.00 a.m. on 8 August, suffering from heat, thirst, and Turkish fire, the battalion was relieved.[13]

Other battalions of 34 Brigade were less fortunate than the 11th Manchesters. The beach master at A Beach was Commander Gibson. His diary shows how the baptism of fire for new and untried troops was so disturbing as to largely incapacitate them. Initially, on 6 August, Gibson remarked on the unsuitability of A Beach: 'Most rotten beach very shelving and lots of sand bars etc couldn't have been worse.' Three of the 'Beetles' got stuck, and Gibson had to borrow boats from *Beagle* to get the troops ashore 'very slowly and very mixed up.' Gibson noticed some twenty soldiers below decks who did not want to land. Gibson forced the men onto the deck and then to land. On 7 August Gibson summarized the problem: 'It was obvious then that a great mistake had been made in sending absolutely raw troops who'd never heard a shot fired in anger to do a difficult job like a night landing under fire.' Most officers had become casualties, and the men lay down on the beach, and 'wouldn't get up or budge and just before daylight began firing, some of them – there seemed to be no officers about... and we couldn't stop these fel-

lows firing – I'm sure they shot some of our own fellows in the back…'
It seems that 32 Brigade did in fact fire on 34 Brigade in the dark. The 11
Division war diary simply reported that the landing at A Beach was
delayed by lighters grounding 200 yards offshore, so that the 'troops had
to wade ashore neck high under fire.' To add to the confusion, some
other 34 Brigade units were landed elsewhere, for example, 68 Field
Company of the Royal Engineers. The propeller of the lighter carrying
this company became fouled, and after being towed around for some
time, the lighter abandoned A Beach, and landed the engineers at C
Beach, south of Suvla Bay, at 5.30 a.m. on 7 August.[14]

Not only was the landing of men a problem, but according to the
rather irascible diary of Capt. Milward, originally GSO 3 of 29 Division,
but seconded to the Q Branch, landing material and supplies was also
very awkward. Milward focussed his displeasure on the Navy: 'As usual,
the Navy had been too sketchy and haphazard, had not supplied enough
small boats, as everyone had foreseen and not a mule had been landed.
Water and food could not be conveyed to the troops.'[15] The Navy was
also very sketchy about details for its landing tasks. Thus, naval Lt H.
Minchin, in charge of two drifters and about ten or twelve tows, was
supposed to pick up his allotted 11 Division troops from two destroyers
and land them at A Beach. Minchin did not know which his destroyers
were, but luckily got that information from a picket boat 'which happened to pass near me…' Minchin then lost contact with his destroyers
due to their greater speed, and also did not know where A Beach was.
He then found B Beach, moved on, and eventually located his destroyers.
They had no troops for him to take on, but they knew where A Beach
was. On arriving there, Minchin found lighters on the shoals, and troops
refusing to land from the rocks. Minchin was at least able to land these
troops. Also, according to Commander Maxwell Lefroy, naval landing
officer at Suvla, all was not well within the naval hierarchy. On 8 August,
Lefroy noted: 'V.A. [de Robeck] in *Triad* & especially C.O.S. [Keyes] very
troublesome giving orders & interfering without telling any one, also
making as many rude signals to R.A. 2 [Christian] as possible…
Christian doing everything himself & situation very difficult and troublesome.'[16]

Quite apart from such naval problems, it was the predictable mix up of troops ashore, at night, which created the most difficulty. One of the features of Suvla was an inland Salt Lake, dry in the summer of 1915, and connected to the sea by a steep gully known as the Cut. The Salt Lake and the Cut were awkward obstacles to troop movement. As it happened, 34 Brigade was concentrated around the Cut, and this concentration prevented 32 Brigade from advancing. Confusion grew as more and more troops landed at night, often late and in the wrong order. Brigadier-General W.H. Sitwell, commanding 34 Brigade of 11 Division, decided to achieve something by ordering an early assault on Hill 10 by the 9th Battalion Lancashire Fusiliers, supported by a few soldiers from 32 Brigade. Because of the darkness, his men did not identify the correct location, and attacked a sand dune instead. An 11 Division HQ staff officer, W.F. Gordon, also related that 34 Brigade thought the bank of the Cut was Hill 10. Consequently, J.D. Coleridge said to Sitwell: 'You haven't even taken Hill 10 yet.' Sitwell disagreed, but Lt-Col. Fishbourne, commanding the 5th Dorset Battalion, confirmed that Hill 10 was still in the hands of the Turks. So Sitwell said to Fishbourne: 'Bones, the 5th will take Hill 10.' So, finally, early on 7 August, Hill 10 was located, and taken.[17]

Meanwhile, 10 Division began landing as planned early the next day, 7 August. Because of problems at A Beach, part of 30 Brigade was landed at A Beach West, inside Suvla Bay, while the rest of 30 Brigade, and 31 Brigade, were landed a considerable distance away, at C Beach, south of Suvla Bay. The division remained separated for several days, contributing to the confusion which was really inevitable, given the landing of two divisions on unfamiliar ground, in a bay which grounded several lighters and forced changes in landing sites, in the face of the enemy, with limited communications, few or no orders because of the secrecy which Hamilton enforced, and either no maps or incorrect maps (some maps were issued of the Asiatic shore as part of the deception plan). Together with the inexperience of troops and commanders, all this produced the sort of results that might have been expected. For example, on 27 July, prior to the landing, Brigadier-General F. Hill, commanding 31 Brigade of 10 Division, was 'discovered on shore' at Mudros, having been in port for some time, but 'No notification of his arrival was sent to the Division… although it was most important for the Divisional Staff to get in touch with him.' Hill also said that two battalions of the Dublin Fusiliers had gone on to the island of Mitylene, but 'Nothing was known about this [at 10 Division HQ] either…'[18] In fact, one brigade of 10 Division had been loaned to the Anzacs, there were six battalions at Mitylene under Hill, and so only three battalions, plus the Pioneers and 10 Division HQ, were with Mahon, the GOC of 10 Division. Mahon tried communicating with Hill via the *Aragon* but failed, and so Hill had no orders for the landing. This was also true for the whole division, as a plaintive message on 6 August from 10 Division to IX Corps showed, complaining of a lack of orders: 'You said you would send anything necessary. AAA. No means of communication. AAA We have received no orders ourselves beyond [original] Order No: One.' At other times, contradictory orders were received from GHQ and the Lines of Communication, or priority messages took four hours to arrive.[19]

Lack of communication was at the root of much of the initial difficulty at Suvla. The Director of Army Signals reported that:

> HQ IX Corps without warning embarked on the *Jonquil* at 2030 on [August] 6th. This boat left harbour very shortly and WT [wireless transmission] only via *Exmouth* was available until morning of 7th when NBS [Nibrunesi Station, south Suvla Bay] reported that *Jonquil* could receive visual from them. At 1730 on 8th, IX Corps HQ left *Jonquil*, and took up position… near the existing beach office.

All of this meant that *Jonquil*, with Stopford on board, was reliant on visual signals until the morning of 8 August, when a phone line was connected to *Jonquil*. Stopford confused matters by not going ashore at 9.00 a.m. on 7 August, as he was supposed to do, but decided to stay on board *Jonquil*. According to Reed, until the phone line was set up on 8 August there was only one yeoman on board *Jonquil* to deal with all signals via semaphore. Added to this was a lack of small boats, so that Reed had to wait for hours on 7 August to get ashore, and even then he was rowed ashore by one seaman. When Stopford and his staff finally got ashore on the evening of 8

August, there was still trouble because of the location of their HQ, which should have been at Lala Baba, but was instead near Suvla Point, at the north end of the bay: 'Very inconvenient as regarding communications, which became precarious, owing to cable along beach crossed by traffic.' Signals problems continued through 9 August, due to the poor IX Corps HQ site and limited personnel, so that operators and linemen had to be sent from GHQ to help. Only at 6.00 p.m. on 9 August was the cable changed from Nibrunesi Point to Suvla. All this explains why IX Corps had difficulty communicating with the Navy and with their own divisions. On the other hand, the lack of information between IX Corps and GHQ that Hamilton complained of during the first two or three days at Suvla has probably been overemphasized, since although there were few formal messages from Stopford, there were other signals. For example, at 6.23 a.m. on 7 August, communication was opened from Suvla to GHQ by Morse, then a formal signal was sent at 8.48 a.m., and even before then GHQ was kept informed of the landing by local signals.[20]

Due to Stopford's isolation and the lack of orders, there were desperate last minute instructions. As the lighters carrying 10 Division approached Suvla Bay at 4.45 a.m. on 7 August, Stopford, who had apparently been asleep at 4.00 a.m., was now awake, and belatedly told Keyes, the naval chief of staff, 'For God's sake stop these people because they do not know where they are.' Thereupon the landing was stopped for an hour as a conference took place between Stopford, Hill, and the Navy representatives, Rear-Admiral Christian and Commander Unwin. Stopford wanted 10 Division to go ashore at A Beach and then go north to Kiretch Tepe. But Christian and Unwin said this was not possible due to the shoals in Suvla Bay, plus the shelling, whereas the preferred C Beach was sheltered by the hill of Lala Baba. So at 5.50 a.m. the decision was made to land at C Beach, and the majority of 10 Division was landed there. Then at 6.30 a.m. Keyes said there were two coves just discovered at new A Beach West that could take the troops. Stopford did not want to alter his decision about C Beach, but the rest of 10 Division did land at A Beach West.[21]

Hamilton blamed Christian for the delay in landing 10 Division, for the casualties suffered by the troops, and for their fatigue at having to march further to reach Hill 10. Christian replied quite effectively:

The real *delay* was due to the Generals of Divisions not having been told one syllable of where their men were to land, Europe or Asia, or the plan of operations – the casualties were unavoidable and as to the fatigue the distance from *C Beach* to… [Hill 10] is only about 1200 yards further than from A West to…[Hill 10]. But we didn't know *A West* existed when my decision was made.[22]

Because of the arrival of 10 Division in two parts, Hill, although commanding 31 Brigade in 10 Division, was instructed early on 7 August to come under the command of Hammersley, GOC 11 Division. Later, this was changed to Hill's 31 Brigade coming under the command of Sitwell, GOC 34 Brigade of 11 Division. The aim of this mixed southern group was to capture Chocolate Hill, but the attack moved very slowly throughout the day, partly because of the need to march around the top end of the Salt Lake and attack Chocolate Hill from the north, due to fear of Turkish artillery facing south on Chocolate Hill. There was also an emerging conflict between Sitwell and Hill, with Sitwell refusing to move, believing that all surprise had been lost. Eventually the assault got under way, then an order was received at 3.00 p.m. to halt the attack for two hours. This was done to arrange for more artillery support, but as the 31 Brigade war diary states 'This order could not be carried out for obvious reasons [since the attack was already in progress] – the attack proceeded and CHOCOLATE HILL [was] in our possession by 5.30 p.m.' This rather bland account hides the fact that Sitwell declined to attack, while Hill argued with Sitwell. So it was not until evening that the Irish Battalions of 10 Division, with the help of 33 Brigade, actually took Chocolate Hill. It seems that Hill was 'difficult', while Sitwell became nervous and excitable.[23]

Sitwell's conduct brings up the question of command abilities. W.F. Gordon recalls finding Sitwell on shore as 34 Brigade was landing. Sitwell told Gordon: 'You are the bloody cause of this.' Gordon naturally asked 'Why and what?' Sitwell explained: 'I mean the bloody division. Look at the situation. Here I have two half-battalions, the Lancashire Fusiliers cut to pieces, and the rest of my brigade in the sea and God knows where.' In fact, Sitwell was mistaken on all counts, and Gordon concluded: 'An excited Brigadier [Sitwell] confronted on landing with a difficult situation failed to appreciate it or solve the problem. He did nothing...'. Another 11 Division staff officer, Neill Malcolm, confirmed that Sitwell was beset by fears, and refused to move his brigade forward unless forcibly convinced. Malcolm also had trouble with Hill, who resisted taking orders from Hammersley, GOC 11 Division, because Hill's brigade was actually in 10 Division. According to Malcolm, Hill returned several times to 11 Division HQ to complain, but he was finally forced to cooperate in using his 31 Brigade for the attack on Hill 10. Malcolm wrote later that Hill was 'difficult by nature, and it was impossible to count on his loyal support in any enterprise in which the 11th Division was concerned.' As J.D. Coleridge stated: 'the truth was that Sitwell was incapable of giving an order, and Hill was incapable of obeying one.' Nor was Hammersley himself a strong commander. After the campaign, Hammersley and Col. J.O'B. Minogue, temporary commander of 32 Brigade after the original commander was wounded, got into an argument over whether Hammersley ordered 32 Brigade to push home the attack on Hill 10 or not. Apparently, Minogue said that Hammersley told him not to push home the attack but to dig in. Hammersley replied that the men of 32 Brigade were not in a fit state to advance. Minogue reminded him that he, Hammersley, had said that 32 Brigade was all right, so Hammersley changed his story, and said that he told 32 Brigade to dig in because otherwise it would upset his plan for the attack next day.[24] Why should these senior officers be so awkward? One explanation is that the pre-war British army suffered from what might be called 'the cult of personality', in which personality and social skills, together with seniority, counted for more than efficiency.[25]

While all this was going on, 30 Brigade of 10 Division, having landed to the north of Suvla Bay at A Beach West, advanced toward Kiretch Tepe and took over from the 11th Manchesters. Unfortunately there was little advance, or rather, according to Capt. T. Verschoyle, 5th Battalion Royal Inniskilling Fusiliers, the brigade sometimes advanced and then moved back. Verschoyle wrote that his battalion had been sitting on Kiretch Tepe since 10.00 p.m. on 7 August, achieving very little, so it was clear that 'something was very much amiss in high places.' Similarly, Lt-

Col. J.A. Armstrong, of the same Battalion, commented 'I knew before I'd been there 24 hours that the whole show was a 'wash-out'. No orders, no scheme, nothing told us what we were expected to do on landing – or anything.'[26] Judging by messages between 10 Division and IX Corps, the inactivity at Kiretch Tepe and further south at Suvla Bay, was caused mainly by both 10 and 11 Divisions refusing to advance without more artillery support. There was also the defensive mentality at Stopford's IX Corps HQ, and exhaustion and water shortages among the troops, especially at Kiretch Tepe. Hence, some IX Corps messages make interesting reading. For example, at 4.30 a.m. on 8 August, IX Corps reported from a plane reconnaissance that Turks were massing in one location, but elsewhere the roads were clear and there were no other Turkish reserves to be seen. Yet IX Corps had no suggestions to make about an advance. The next few messages reveal 10 Division trying hard to arrange artillery support from IX Corps. Yet IX Corps did nothing to assist this process, and instead sent a message at 7.10 a.m. to 10 Division focussing entirely on protecting Suvla:

> The safety of new landing is all important to whole force. The best possible position sea to sea to covering in case of sudden attack should be selected and held by the Battalion you are keeping in reserve. This defence would be quite independent of forces you have further forward.

This message, though, was consistent with what Stopford conceived to be IX Corps' main mission of protecting Suvla as a base. Then at 11.00 a.m., GHQ reminded IX Corps of its duty to advance, and at 11.30 a.m., IX Corps finally issued more aggressive orders to 10 and 11 Divisions, urging a general advance. But the message ended by calling for artillery support if entrenched positions were met with.[27]

It seems that 10 Division did a reasonable job of trying to move forward at Suvla on 8 August, but was stopped by technical and communication problems with the artillery, and especially received very little help from IX Corps. As for 11 Division, 32 Brigade made a move inland, although Lt-Col. Minogue, in temporary command, was given verbal instructions not to fight, but to dig in. Patrols were pushed out, and one of these, the 6th East Yorks, apparently by mistake, went south of Sulajik, a very small village in the central Suvla plain, and took over the unoccupied Scimitar Hill.[28] Meanwhile, Aspinall and Lt-Col. M. Hankey, representative of the Cabinet in London on a fact finding visit to Gallipoli, had been despatched to Suvla from GHQ by Hamilton, with the object of finding out why operations at Suvla appeared to be at a standstill. They arrived about midday on 8 August, and first interviewed Hammersley, who was not optimistic, thinking his troops tired, thirsty, and prone to retire if counterattacked.[29] So the two GHQ envoys then visited Stopford, who was suffering from diarrhoea and a strained knee, and was still on board the *Jonquil*. Stopford emphasized his defensive focus on Suvla as a port, and obviously did not see his task as an aggressive offensive. So Aspinall sent a notorious message to GHQ relating the total lack of action at Suvla, which arrived at 5.30 p.m. However, this message actually had little effect, since Hamilton, as previously related, was already on his way to Suvla. In reality, the first important message came via Roger Keyes, who was already aware of the stalled Suvla offensive on the morning of 8 August, and got a message sent to GHQ to this effect. Meanwhile, evidently now influenced by Aspinall and Hankey, Stopford went ashore to interview Hammersley about a possible advance. As in his interview with Aspinall and Hankey, Hammersley was pessimistic, and ascribed the poor results on 8 August to lack of artillery, loss of officers, exhaustion of troops, and no water. At a higher level, IX Corps explained the failure to capture the high ground at W Hills on 8 August as caused almost entirely by the support of only eight guns, 'whereas the normal allowance should have been at least 100 guns.'[30]

On the other side of the hill, the Turks were as confused about the objectives of Suvla as was Stopford. However, Maj. Willmer prepared the defences with land mines at Hill 10 and Green Hill, because of his lack of wire, and trip wires under water at Lala Baba. Defended localities were dug in, but no extended trench lines. The Turkish weak point was Hill 10, especially when the Salt Lake dried up in July. Interestingly, a Turkish engineer unit at Suvla was ordered to dig a channel to the sea in order to fill the lake, but obviously this did not take place. If it had, the landing would have been even more difficult for IX Corps. Since Turkish reserves could not arrive for some time, Willmer's plan was to delay the landing with a first line of defence at Lala Baba, Hill 10, and Kiretch Tepe, and then retreat with his troops intact to the W Hills. In fact, Willmer got news of the landing at 9.30 p.m. on 6 August. Initially, the Bursa Gendarmerie commander, Maj. Taksin, thought the landing was simply a raid, and focussed on defending Lala Baba. But he soon realized the strength of the British landing, and withdrew his forces to Sulajik and a point north-west of the Salt Lake. According to Turkish reports, Taksin also withdrew his defenders from Hill 10, which made the taking of that hill a simpler proposition for the British 11 Division. Taksin and Willmer also realized the real danger was that the British might outflank their defences by taking the Kiretch Tepe ridge along the northern flank of the Suvla plain. So Capt. Kadri of the Gelibolou Gendarmerie moved a company north to support the defenders there, who had already suffered thirty per cent losses. This move actually prevented the 11th Manchesters from advancing much further along the ridge, and possibly creating a winning situation for IX Corps.[31]

The question then was, what would Liman von Sanders do to protect the Suvla area? At 1.40 a.m. on 7 August, he initially reacted by focussing on Bulair/Saros, but did immediately send one regiment to Willmer from Bulair/Saros. Then at 7.00 a.m. on 7 August, Liman von Sanders firmly grasped the nettle, and instructed 7 and 12 Divisions to march from Bulair/Saros to Suvla forthwith. Since 12 Division was more scattered than 7 Division, it took longer for them to move, and this accounts for the fact that 7 Division arrived first to the east of Suvla and then marched on to the south Suvla area, while 12 Division arrived later, and thus covered the northern Suvla area. Of considerable importance is the fact that 7 Division already arrived at Sivlikoy (to the east of Suvla) by 10.00 p.m. on 7 August, while 12 Division arrived there later, but still during the night of 7/8 August. Then, at 10.00 p.m. on 7 August, in order to coordinate the Turkish defence, Col. Fezi Bey was appointed by Liman von Sanders to command the whole northern group, including Suvla. The most important aspect of all this is that Saros is only some 30 miles from Suvla, and so the two Turkish divisions arrived to the east of Suvla, late on 7 August, in very good time to meet any future Allied attacks on the high ground behind Suvla. In his memoirs, Liman von Sanders claims that the 7 and 12 Divisions arrived on the afternoon of 7 August. This is too early, because they only left the Bulair/Saros area on the morning of 7 August, but they certainly arrived late on 7 August, and Liman von Sanders then gave Fezi Bey orders for an attack at Suvla, using these two divisions, in the afternoon of 8 August, or at the latest, in the evening. However, Willmer reported in the evening of 8 August to Liman von Sanders that the attack had not yet taken place.[32]

This failure to attack was, as Fezi Bey explained to Liman von Sanders, because the 7 and 12 Turkish Divisions needed time to be reorganized and collected together, and time to study the ground. As well, they were exhausted by the heat and the 30-mile march from Bulair/Saros. Thereupon Liman von Sanders dismissed Fezi Bey, and replaced him with Mustafa Kemal at 9.45 p.m. on 8 August. As the Turkish Official History states, and as Kemal's memoirs imply, firing Fezi Bey was actually a mistake. Fezi Bey was absolutely right, the two divisions were in no condition to attack on 8 August. But after another day to recover and reorganize, 7 and 12 Divisions were able to go on the offensive, and Kemal therefore ordered an attack for 4.00 a.m. on 9 August. This was carried out with a force of around 16,000 Turkish soldiers at Tekke Tepe, and at Scimitar and Green Hills (7 Division contained 5,982 men, and 12 Division 10,471 men).[33]

However, this is to get ahead of the story at Suvla, where Hamilton was shortly to make his one decisive intervention in the campaign. On the afternoon of 8 August, Stopford returned to *Jonquil* from his visit ashore. There he received a report from GHQ repeating an air survey which found few Turks around, while GHQ promised future support from the newly arrived 53 Division. Stopford then sat down soon after 4.00 p.m., and wrote orders for a general advance. At the same time, at 3.30 p.m., Hammersley was also working out an attack for dawn the next morning (9 August) on W Hills by 33 Brigade with assistance from 32 Brigade. But at 5.30 p.m., still on 8 August, Hamilton at last arrived on *Jonquil*, and urged Stopford to attack the high ground at Tekke Tepe immediately, before Turkish reinforcements arrived. Stopford demurred and recommended Hammersley's dawn attack the next morning.

Frustrated, Hamilton declared his intent to go ashore to see Hammersley and force 11 Division to attack that night. Later, Stopford complained that Hamilton did not take him ashore, which would have been normal protocol, since Hamilton was going to see one of Stopford's own divisional commanders. But Hamilton claimed that Stopford said he had just been ashore, and was still complaining of his leg. Hamilton declared 'It was not for me to say I wanted Gen. Stopford to come with me: his attendance was one of those things which, in the Service, go without saying, and which, therefore, are not said.' On the other hand, Stopford claimed that Hamilton simply said: 'I must go and see Gen. Hammersley'.[34] Probably both men were at fault here, but it is significant that half an hour after their discussion, Stopford moved his IX Corps headquarters ashore. At Suvla, Hamilton found Hammersley at about 7.00 p.m., and ordered a much enlarged attack from W Hills across to the high ground at Tekke Tepe. Ironically, Stopford had just sent a message to both 10 and 11 Divisions, at 6.45 p.m., urging an immediate attack, as per Hamilton's instructions. True to form, Stopford ended the message by saying that batteries would be landed as quickly as possible – thus hinting that the attack should wait for artillery to arrive before advancing – yet artillery would be useless in the dark.[35] So, now there were three separate orders for an attack on the evening of 8 August, one each from Hammersley, Stopford and Hamilton!

The focus of the attack had also shifted from south to north. Originally Stopford wanted to aim at the W Hills area, but after Hamilton's intervention the attack shifted from W Hills northward to the high ground at Kavak Tepe and Tekke Tepe, in order to forestall the arrival of Turkish reinforcements from the north. Yet, if the intention was to assist the Anzac offensive on the Sari Bair range, then the attack should have focussed first on the W Hills. Another possibility would have been to outflank the Turkish reinforcements by attacking along the Kiretch Tepe ridge with as much force as possible. Nevertheless, Hamilton's intervention focussed on the high ground, and 11 Division, which had issued a preparatory order at 7.00 p.m. on 8 August, for a dawn attack the next morning at 5.00 a.m., now issued a priority order for an immediate attack by 32 and 33 Brigades, plus two battalions of 31 Brigade.[36]

At Hammersley's 11 Division HQ, there was no firm grasp of where their units were located, so when asked about available units for the night attack, Neill Malcolm said the most concentrated force was 32 Brigade, and pointed vaguely in the direction of Sulajik. Subsequently, Malcolm wrote that neither he nor Hammersley had said that 32 Brigade was concentrated. Nevertheless, of the battalions in 32 Brigade, Hammersley named the 6th East Yorkshire Pioneer Regiment as the freshest. (At that time, the Pioneers were regarded as infantry first and pioneers second.) The next urgent matter was to issue orders for the attack. It seems that verbal orders were issued around 7.30 p.m., but written orders were not received at 32 Brigade until 2.15 a.m. on 9 August, although they were issued apparently at 11.30 p.m. on 8 August. The difference in time was due to the extreme difficulty of finding units in the dark. This is something that Hamilton completely ignored when ordering a night advance at such short notice, however desperate the situation. For example, it had taken J.D. Coleridge from 6.30 a.m. to 4.00 p.m. to go around all the positions at Suvla in daylight, and it was obviously going to be far more difficult to find units in the dark. Consequently, Lt John Still, 6th East Yorkshire Pioneer Regiment, later lamented to Hamilton that he only got the orders to advance near dawn on 9 August, at Sulajik, because:

> the Brigade Major was lost! Good God, why didn't they send a man who knew the country. He was lost, lost, lost, and it drives me almost mad to think of it. I know his name.[37]

The unfortunate Brigade Major given the task of finding all the various battalions of 32 Brigade, including the 6th East Yorkshire Pioneers, was actually Maj. B.W. Shuttleworth. Similarly, orders to the 9th West Yorkshire Battalion and the 6th Yorkshire and Lancashire Battalion did not arrive until 4.10 a.m. on 9 August. In the dark, Lt-Col. Minogue decided to wait for his 32 Brigade battalions to concentrate before moving forward. Inevitably, valuable time passed, and eventually the 6th East Yorkshire Pioneers were the first to advance. Shuttleworth's war diary simply says that the other battalions didn't advance sooner because they were scattered and in contact with the enemy. The war diary mentions that messages to the 9th West Yorkshire Battalion never did get through, while the 6th Yorkshire and Lancashire Battalion simply waited. According to Roger Keyes, the Colonel of the 6th Yorkshire and Lancashire Battalion was really too old, and just dithered. Meanwhile, the 6th East Yorkshire Pioneers turned out to be located on the right of 32 Brigade, and so it took some considerable time to find them, collect them and issue orders. Finally, at 4.00 a.m. on 9 August, a few of the 6th East Yorkshire Pioneers, the 67th Field Company RE, and the 8th Battalion Duke of Wellington's West Riding, marched off toward Tekke Tepe, led by just one company of the Pioneers, D company.[38]

It seems that Lt-Col. Moore, commanding the Pioneers, could only get D Company to move because of the 'extreme exhaustion and hunger' of the other companies, plus the lack of explicit instructions, although this latter problem was probably a cover for the exhaustion of the troops, since D Company at least did advance. At 5.00 a.m. on 9 August Shuttleworth reported that the distance to the top of Tekke Tepe was 4,000 yards, and that the Pioneers and the West Riding Battalion were at least one mile forward. As they closed on the Tekke Tepe heights the attack met heavy fire from concealed trenches by elements of Turkish 12 Division, which had probably been patrolling there for at least twenty-four hours, and the Pioneers fell back. John Still and D Company made it to the top of Tekke Tepe with only some thirty men. When that figure was reduced to twenty, these retired. The war diary continues the narrative by saying that the Pioneers then made two stands with the West Riding Battalion, and a defensive line was formed. The war diary of the West Riding Battalion, written a few days later by Capt. V. Kidd paints a more chaotic picture, and it was during this action that Maj. Hugh Price Travers was seen to fall. Kidd assumed command, and when he found Turks going around his flanks, he retired with the remaining 350 men of his battalion, before establishing a line alongside the 11th Manchester Battalion.[39]

Following the failure to capture Tekke Tepe, anxious messages started arriving in daylight on 9 August, for example, at about 9.30 a.m. Shuttleworth sent to 11 Division: 'Our left retiring Turks within a very short distance of Brigade. Report Centre help urgently needed.' Half an hour later, at 10.00 a.m., 32 Brigade sent: 'Being hard pressed can you help.' In another half hour, at 10.30 a.m., 32 Brigade appealed to the 6th East Yorkshire Pioneers: 'Push up here with your Battalion at once to this hut where you left us this morning urgently required come as quickly as possible.' By 11.30 a.m. the crisis had passed, although the battalions sent to support 32 Brigade found various reasons not to reach the forward line.[40] As might be anticipated, IX Corps now became extremely defensive, and were far more worried about the possibility of the Turks breaking through the lines than any ideas of further advance. As a final blow to the disastrous night of 8 August/9, Scimitar Hill was easily occupied by the Turks, since the 6th East Yorkshire Pioneers, as a result of Hamilton's order to attack Tekke Tepe, had abandoned this significant forward position in order to take part in the attack. Hamilton later complained that no one at Suvla knew the Pioneers were on Scimitar, but 11 Division at least did know this fact, although curiously their withdrawal from Scimitar worried Neill Malcolm less than the fact that the Pioneers were distant and hard to contact during the night of 8 August.[41]

It is important to note at this point what none of Hamilton, GHQ, IX Corps or 10 or 11 Divisions knew at the time, namely that the chance to seize the high ground at Tekke Tepe, or to outflank the Turks, had certainly already passed on 8 August because the Turkish 12 Division had already arrived in the Suvla area late on 7 August. What is important here is the timing of the arrival of Turkish 12 Division, because it was later argued by Hamilton and Aspinall, and by future historians, that Hamilton's intervention at Suvla on 8 August resulted in the East Yorkshire Pioneers reaching the top of Tekke Tepe at dawn on 9 August, just half an hour too late to forestall the arrival of the Turks. In other words, if only the East Yorkshire Pioneers and supporting units had reached Tekke Tepe even half an hour earlier then they would have been able to capture the heights before the arrival of the Turks. For this reason, Stopford and Hammersley have been criticized for being far too slow in advancing their forces and capturing Tekke Tepe, while Hamilton's desperate intervention is seen as at least giving the Suvla operation a last chance of success. The tantalizing story of the Turks reaching the summit of Tekke Tepe just half an hour before the arrival of the East Yorkshire

Pioneers at dawn on 9 August is therefore seen as one of those exasperating close chances of success at Suvla being snatched away by the thinnest of margins. Unfortunately for this scenario, it is clear that the Turkish 12 Division actually arrived behind the Tekke Tepe area sometime during the late evening of 7 August or the early morning of 8 August. There was then clearly no race to the summit of Tekke Tepe. Hamilton's intervention was therefore irrelevant, and by extension, Stopford's lack of urgency in handling IX Corps, was also less critical than previously thought. In fact, what Lt John Still and the Pioneers met at dawn on 9 August was either 12 Division patrols, or even the start of 12 Division's dawn offensive, as ordered by Kemal. [42]

Despite the early arrival of Turkish 7 and 12 Divisions at Suvla, there were still several anxious calls from Liman von Sanders for submarines to help stave off the Suvla landing. On 7 August, Kiazim Bey pleaded: 'For God's sake send us submarines.' Certainly, 7 August was the day that German submarines might have been most useful at Suvla, and even though the crisis for the Turks was still very uncertain at both Suvla and Sari Bair, Kiazim Bey still found time on 9 August for a little humour in his messages to Enver Pasa, remarking that the capture of three Allied prisoners by the Bulair/Saros group was as welcome 'as a shepherd's present is pine resin', i.e. useless. Perhaps Allied chances of success were never very strong at Suvla, as J.D. Coleridge wrote later: 'Even if we had taken our objectives (I refer to KAVAK and TEKKE TEPE) I do not think we could have held them, supported as we would have been with only a few guns short of ammunition.' Given the similar experience of Chunuk Bair, and the serious problems of food and water supply already obvious to the troops at Suvla, it seems unlikely, though not impossible, that the Tekke Tepe heights could have been held. [43]

Meanwhile, what was happening to 10 Division, astride the Kiretch Tepe ridge? This division was also expected to attack early on 9 August, and the experience of 30 Brigade was typical of the offensive. The commander of 10 Division, Mahon, arrived at 30 Brigade HQ at 6.00 a.m. on 9 August, and ordered an advance. There was, however, no water and no rations. Brigadier-General Nicol, GOC 30 Brigade, said to Mahon '… what am I to do, I have as yet issued no orders.' Mahon replied: 'You must carry on and do the best you can.' Therefore a general advance began at 7.30 a.m., still without specific orders, although the objective was Kidney Hill, along the Kiretch Ridge. The war diary of the 7th Royal Munster Fusiliers now gives the story of what happened on 9 August. At 6.30 a.m. the naval bombardment of Kidney Hill started. At 8.00 a.m. the battalion received orders to move, although the water bottles were away being filled, so the men had no water. At 9.30 a.m. the battalion actually started the advance. Soon the battalion came under fire, and also encountered the 5th Dorset Battalion of 34 Brigade, 11 Division, apparently also headed for Kidney Hill. The 7th Munster Fusiliers attached themselves to the Dorsets, and quickly adjusted their objective by an angle to the left. At 12.30 p.m., the Dorsets halted, and the 7th Munster Battalion continued alone. Then fire from Turks in trenches on Kidney Hill, plus scattered Turkish snipers, brought the attack to a halt. Probably about this time, Lt S.R.V. Travers, who had been directing the battalion's machine-guns, was shot dead, likely by a sniper. At 1.33 p.m., 30 Brigade HQ urged further advance. But the 7th Munster Battalion war diary simply says: 'Owing to lack of cohesion both in the battalion and with other units, and to the general ignorance of the situation of the enemy and of what was required this was impossible to carry out.' Then at about 3.30 p.m. the order to retire was given, and the advance was over, mainly due to lack of water, and disorganization. As the war diary states: 'During the whole action the men had no water and the heat was intense.'[44]

It is clear that the whole action of 30 Brigade, and of 7th Battalion Munster Fusiliers on 9 August at Kiretch Tepe, was beyond their capabilities, logistically, tactically and administratively. Poor staff work at 10 Division played its part, and behind them, IX Corps did little to help. Naval shelling was used, but not in a consistent way, and the slow timetable of the 7th Munster Battalion precluded much help from this shelling. Mahon himself did not seem vitally interested, and orders from both 10 Division and IX Corps were vague. It would be easy to blame particular individuals, which is the Army habit, but simple inexperience of the intensity and demands of modern war lie at the root of most problems at Suvla. This unexpected intensity affected many officers, for example, in the 7th Munster Battalion, Maj. Drage collapsed by 10

August, and Lt-Col. H. Gore, the CO of the Battalion, 'was a large con-
spicuous object standing up armed only with a cane; but he remained
inert smoking a cigarette in the support line after the action of the 9th.'
Gore was relieved of his command and sent away by Mahon. Finally, the
water shortage in the brutal Gallipoli heat of August was an absolutely
vital factor for 10 Division, and at Suvla generally.[45]

Mention of the critical water shortage raises the obvious question:
why was there very little water, and sometimes no water, available for the
first two or three days of the Suvla landing? Due to its acute importance,
this aspect of the Suvla landing deserves analysis. Despite later attempts
by Aspinall to minimize the water problem, the lack of water showed its
cruel effects, especially in 10 Division. One officer of the 6th Munster
Battalion wrote 'You cannot exaggerate the scarcity of water', another
declared that hundreds of men actually died of thirst, and a later arrival
with 53 Division stated 'I do not think you have any idea of the torments
everyone suffered from thirst…'. Capt. Lord Lifford, staff officer in 34
Brigade, 11 Division, came across a macabre scene in November 1915. He
found fourteen dead men in a clearing, bandaged and sitting up – one
man reading a bible – all from the landing of 6/7 August. Lifford speculated that they had died of starvation or thirst. The chaplain attached to
30 Brigade in 10 Division reported there were stories of men who
sucked their blood to get moisture, and of men 'lying with their tongues
quite swollen for want of water and quite delirious.'[46]

So what went wrong? The plan was for the Director of Works at
GHQ, Col. de Lotbinière, to supply the Navy with four lighters to carry
water to the beaches immediately at the landings, while the Navy supplied a ship, the *Prah*, which carried tanks, troughs, water buckets and
pumps, as well as munitions. It was also presumed that IX Corps' move
inland at Suvla would uncover several wells in the valleys and on the
Suvla plain, which would replenish the supply. GHQ was in overall
charge of the water scheme, which was originally planned by Aspinall at
GHQ. The Navy was in charge of landing the water up to the high water
mark, and at that point IX Corps, in the shape of Brigadier-General
Painter, chief engineer, would take over, to set up water tanks to store the
water on the beach and pumps to fill water carts or bags on mules to

carry the water inland to the front line troops. At this point, an inkling of the basic problem emerges: there were an astonishing number of people in charge of different aspects of the Suvla water plan.

At GHQ, Aspinall made the original plans. Maj.-Gen. Roper, chief engineer at GHQ, was in charge of obtaining canvas bags via the Ordnance department for carrying water inland on mules. Maj. Badcock (Army Service Corps) was in charge of transport and water mules, i.e. actually distributing the water via the mules. Also involved in the planning at GHQ were Brigadier-General Winter, Deputy QMG, and Col. Wallace (Lines of Communication). However, Winter collapsed mentally and physically on 6 August, and was replaced by Lt-Col. L.R. Beadon, Assistant QMG. Prior to the landings, de Lotbinière purchased four water lighters in Alexandria. He also organized the construction of wooden tanks on board these lighters, on the theory that wooden tanks, if holed by shrapnel, could be more easily repaired than metal containers. These tanks were filled with water and sealed. De Lotbinière also provided hoses of 150 feet length, and wooden trestles to keep the hoses above water level when discharging from the lighters, since if the hoses dipped into sea water, the latter would be sucked in and contaminate the fresh water. With these four lighters, plus the *Prah*, and a steam water carrier, the *Krini*, the Navy would then take over the delivery and loading of all materials needed by the Army, including water. The PNTO (Principal Naval Transport Officer) was Commander Ashby, who organized all the transport. There were also naval beach masters at each landing beach, including Capt. Talbot as chief beach master. To provide liaison, the SNO (Senior Naval Officer), Rear-Admiral Christian, was attached to Stopford and IX Corps. The naval chief of staff, Roger Keyes, was responsible for going into naval arrangements, together with Capt. Lambart. Once the water was ashore, up to the high water mark, the Army took over from the Navy, and here the (PMLO) Principal Military Landing Officer, Col. Western, from GHQ, was in overall charge of military arrangements. Under him came the chief engineer of IX Corps, Painter, in charge of piers and local water supplies. However, Painter became dazed and ill on 7 August, and was replaced by Col. Bland on [8] August. Maj. Huskisson, GHQ, was simply listed as being in charge of supplies. Maj.-Gen. Poett,

QMG at IX Corps, was to take over from GHQ on the beach and ensure the distribution of water to IX Corps. Finally, Sir R. Baker was supposed to keep discipline over the distribution of water to the troops.[47]

It is not surprising that things went wrong very quickly with the water supply, given the incredible number of officers involved, plus the two separate services of army and navy. For a start, de Lotbinière claimed that the four water lighters and their sealed water that he provided were lost by the Navy, who insisted it was their duty to tow the lighters from Egypt to Mudros harbour. Eventually, de Lotbinière found one of these lighters at Mudros, and then obtained two more to replace the lost lighters. Confusingly, accounts all mention a fourth lighter, which was aground at Imbros, and so played no part in the landing. Some accounts also include *Krini* as a water lighter. Eventually there were, then, four lighters plus *Krini* and *Prah*. *Prah* was supposed to have water pumps on board, but these apparently could not be extricated in time from the hold of the ship bringing them to Mudros. *Prah* also followed a strangely erratic timetable from Imbros to Suvla and back, arriving at Suvla on 7 August at 6.55 a.m., but leaving again at 7.25 p.m. It arrived once more at Suvla on 9 August at 5.15 a.m., where not much notice was taken of it. Subsequent controversy was also caused by the fact that the lighters landing troops all had water on board in tins, but this was purely for use on board, and for filling water bottles just before disembarkation.[48]

How many water lighters arrived at Suvla, and when? Here, later testimony pits the Navy against the Army, since the Navy, particularly Roger Keyes, insisted that all four lighters turned up, at various beaches, plus *Krini* and *Prah*. Keyes also maintained that those who denied there was any water coming ashore before the afternoon of 8 August, were liars. However, the Army and IX Corps maintained that only two lighters turned up, one at 10.00 a.m. on 7 August, which was cut loose because of Turkish shelling, and then drifted, and came to rest about 200 yards off Lala Baba. A second arrived at A Beach, but grounded about 80 yards from the shore at 2.00 p.m. on 7 August, too far out for the hose to reach. Number three arrived on 9 August and anchored next to the first lighter, while number four never left Imbros. The Navy made various claims, with Roger Keyes the most extreme, arguing that all four lighters arrived on time on 7 August. Integrating all accounts, it seems that the north of Suvla (10 Division) got no water on 7 August, and only partial water supply by the evening of 8 August, while the south of Suvla (11 Division) did a little better because of some water on land, plus the two lighters (though neither could be properly unloaded because they were grounded) and *Krini* located at C Beach.[49]

Undoubtedly there was a severe water shortage at Suvla on 7 August, and through most of 8 August. The problem can be blamed on the astonishingly complicated planning and execution of water supply (too many cooks spoil the broth), on simple inexperience, on the inactivity of responsible army officers ashore, and on the initial lack of interest displayed at GHQ, especially by Aspinall. At the Dardanelles Commission, Aspinall was asked why none of the tables drawn up by GHQ contained specific mention of the water lighters. He replied that he could not explain the omission. Next, he was asked if GHQ considered water to be a vital element of the plan, and Aspinall replied: 'It never was realised that it [water] would be vital. One made every preparation possible in case it were, but we never had any difficulty as to water in landing at Helles, and we hoped we would not have it at Suvla…' Evidently GHQ simply hoped for the best, believing that water would be found onshore at Suvla.[50] Obviously, inexperience was a key factor, which de Lotbinière stressed several times in his evidence at the Dardanelles Commission, as well as army red tape, lack of interest at GHQ and IX Corps, and inflexibility in the Navy. De Lotbinière's robust evidence at the Dardanelles Commission predictably annoyed many senior officers, including Keyes and the CGS Braithwaite. Keyes wrote privately: 'I consider that Joly de Lotbinière is an untruthful, ungenerous, ungrateful, humbug. Apart from the fact that he ought to be tried for perjury!' Braithwaite also considered de Lotbinière 'an arrant humbug', who:

> always thought when he had made a bundobust [arrangement] that it was bound to work, and then when, like that one he made at ANZAC to pump water up the hill, it proved quite inadequate, said people did not know how to work it or use it – and that really is our French Canadian friend all over.

Braithwaite may have had a point, in that Lt-Col. Forster, AAQMG at Mudros, recalled a story told him by Col. Paull, executive engineer for the lines of communication, who explained that piers were very slow in construction because de Lotbinière 'never finished anything.'[51]

A direct reflection of the remarkable number of officers involved in providing water at Suvla meant that no one was willing to take responsibility. This annoyed the Dardanelles Commission, which told Maj.-Gen. Kearns, AQMG at IX Corps: 'it appears to have been rather a fortuitous arrangement as [to] who was responsible for anything. We cannot find out.' Similarly, when interviewing Roper, chief engineer at GHQ, the Commission stated: '… here we had you and Gen. Lotbinière and the Quartermaster General and all sorts of people… fiddling about with regard to the water supply without any of you accepting the responsibility particularly.' Some were quite blatant about their inactivity, for example, Kearns, who, when asked, 'You were there, and you knew there was a shortage of water. What did you do to get it relieved?', answered, 'I personally did not do anything. I had nothing whatever to do with the landing of the water from the water lighters.' Eventually the Dardanelles Commission selected Maj.-Gen. Poett, QMG of IX Corps, as their chief culprit. This was a good choice, since Poett did very little to alleviate the problem of water shortage in his Corps. According to Poett himself, when he arrived at Suvla on board *Minneapolis*, early on 7 August, he took time out for a hair cut before attending to his duties. It soon appeared that one water lighter was grounded, but the hose was too short to reach the beach. Poett did nothing about this, nor did he make any effort to find water inland. Only at 5.15 p.m. on 7 August did Poett point out the water problem to Stopford, and even then did not sufficiently stress the urgency of the matter. Finally, at 7.30 p.m. on 7 August, Poett went on board *Jonquil* to tell Stopford of the serious problem, and asked for mules and water bags to distribute water. Stopford could not help. Nor did Poett do anything to provide for troughs on shore to hold the water when it eventually started to arrive, in fact he actually declined the offer of water tanks on 8 August from a naval officer.[52]

The mention of the naval officer brings up the question of the beach parties. Here it seems that Painter, and his replacement, Bland, should have done much more, as should Kearns and Poett. Commander Gibson, in charge of the naval beach party at A Beach, wrote on 8 August: 'water very scarce RE [Royal Engineers] very futile and their arrangements totally inadequate… Beach Party worked hard on water supply making troughs and helping, otherwise there would have been a disaster.' The next day, 9 August, Gibson remarked: 'RE have gone and no one has relieved them. Beach party running water supply on shore otherwise God knows what would happen.' A naval observation officer told Gibson that inland 'men going half crazy for want of water, only getting ½ bottle a day.'[53]

Ultimately, the water failure really related to, firstly, inexperience, which resulted in a host of officers involved in an unwieldy and over-complicated water plan. Secondly, there existed an army and navy that had not yet grasped the demands of modern warfare. Hence, staff offi-cers, naval officers, and administrative officers, nurtured by years of less demanding service, proved both uninterested in, and strangely incapable of, dealing with the water crisis. In this context, the water problem was an indicator that the Army had not yet grasped the nettle of efficiency at all costs, which could be seen in the gentle treatment afforded many senior officers who failed or were replaced at Gallipoli, especially after Suvla. Lt-Col. Forster, AAQMG at Mudros, commented:

> after the failure of operations, General Officers and Brigadier-Generals were deprived of their commands… and, with very few exceptions, given posts on the lines of communication or in Egypt. Thus after the Suvla fail-ure a number of General Officers appeared on the *Aragon* [housing the Lines of Communication Staff].

Forster produced examples of Maj.-Gen. Wallace, lines of communica-tion, replaced by Maj.-Gen. Altham, where the former was given a newly created and unnecessary job as GOC Mudros. Another officer was appointed GOC School of Instruction although there was no school of instruction; a Colonel commanded a non-existent Rest Camp; and another Colonel commanded dubious Reinforcement Depots. Forster also explained that Lord Dudley, Colonel of Yeomanry, was only fit enough to ride, but when the Yeomanry were dismounted, appeared at

Mudros as Commandant Mudros East, a newly created and unnecessary post. Similarly, Forster claimed that that when Maj.-Gen. Egerton replaced Brigadier-General McGrigor as commandant at Alexandria, McGrigor was given a job with nothing to do on board *Aragon*, as Deputy Commander lines of communication. It is only fair to add that some senior officers were sent home, such as Sitwell, Maj.-Gen. John Lindley (GOC 53 Division) and Stopford. In the case of Stopford, he had only been appointed commander of IX Corps because there were just two candidates available that were senior enough – and the other was too large to get around the trenches. Hence, the seniority system in 1915 dictated Stopford's appointment.[54]

While there were problems at the British senior command level at Suvla, what of lower levels of command? Two junior officer diaries reveal some surprising details, the diary of Lt C.A. Elliott being quite negative, while that of Capt. Drury was more positive. Elliott, 9th Service Battalion, West Yorkshire Regiment, 32 Brigade, 11 Division, wrote a long letter to his mother after being wounded on 9 August. This letter, in the form of a diary, reveals a junior officer shaken by the warfare he was obviously unprepared for. On 6 August, the day the 11 Division was to land at Suvla, Elliott's whole division did physical exercises at 6.00 a.m., followed by a route march from 9.00 to 11.00 a.m. Elliott quite reasonably asked why the division was not rested before landing at Suvla that night, and remarked: 'My idea of a Company route march was to go 500 yards behind a hill, put out a line of sentries, and have a 10 minute halt till it was time to go back to camp.' The division embarked around 5.00 p.m. on 6 August, and landed at Suvla at 10.30 p.m., with the objectives, according to Elliott, being to land at C Beach, then take Baki Baba (Elliott probably meant Lala Baba), then Hill 10. In the confusion of landing at night, the West Yorkshire Battalion charged Elliott's men, so 'We officers rushed up and managed to stop their front rank just as they came up to our rear ranks.' During the night of 6/7 August, Elliott's Battalion helped take Lala Baba, suffering considerable casualties, then crossed the Salt Lake Cut, heading toward Hill 10. Here they were fired on by 34 Brigade, but this was stopped. Then at dawn, with no orders forthcoming, Maj. Wood tried to lead the battalion forward, but hardly a man followed. I went down the line cursing, persuading and even kicking but it was no use. The men were tired out, hungry, thirsty and a little cowed. They had been forward and been driven back, they had lost pretty heavily, they had seen nothing to fire at and had been under pretty heavy fire for 12 hours. They wanted a rest.

Turkish shrapnel then opened on the battalion, and a shell landed near Elliott, mortally wounding a nearby sergeant, 'who was most horribly torn…'. Elliott could not help: 'Among other things I was trying hard to be sick, but I had eaten nothing for 24 hours. When I got myself in hand, the Sergeant was dead.'[55]

At 4.00 p.m. on 7 August, Elliott's battalion dug in on Hill 10, and Elliott led a group to get water from the lighter stranded offshore. They waded out, each man carrying twenty water bottles. There was also food on board the lighter: 'Every scrap had to be fought for in a crowd of naked swearing men.' Bottles were filled, but the water gave out, so some bottles remained empty and others had seawater in them. Elliott and his group got back to the battalion at dark. All night (7 August/8), stragglers were coming in, and on 8 August, the idea was to move forward to the village of Sulajik and dig in. The 6th East Yorkshire Pioneer Battalion was in front of Elliott's battalion, on Scimitar Hill, firing to their right. (This Pioneer Battalion was the one that would withdraw from Scimitar Hill to take part in Hamilton's attack on the Tekke Tepe heights.) Elliott remarked of them: 'Well that was their funeral. We had water and cover and were quite happy.' The men started cooking, and were quite cheerful, but then Capt. Davenport, B Company commander, came up and asked for reinforcements: 'We cursed the East Yorks, B Company, Davenport, the Turks and the Kaiser for 10 solid minutes while the men put out their fires and got into their equipment.' Despite the cursing, the battalion maintained discipline and advanced through thick gorse full of Turks, toward the Tekke Tepe high ground in front, and came under heavy fire. The attack was supposed to be supported by 34 Brigade, but according to Elliott they did not do so: 'We all met once more to curse', while the men got thirstier and thirstier. Men were sent for water, a risky job taking three or four hours.[56]

Elliott's battalion was one of those that were part of Hamilton's plan to take the Tekke Tepe heights on the night of 8 August/9. The plan called for naval supporting fire, and a flank attack by a territorial division, actually 53 Division. Interestingly enough, in the very short time Elliott was on Suvla, he seems already to have caught the prevailing pessimism: 'the naval guns would probably bombard us and it was a cert that the Terriers [Territorials] would fire into us. We were all a bit pessimistic.' Elliott and his battalion did not advance far before they met the Turks at dawn on 9 August. Elliott remembered 'that awful cry. Allah! Allah!' as the Turks came forward. Elliott's men fired blindly away into the scrub, and seemed dazed. Elliott gave the order to retire into the thicker gorse, and then was hit in the leg. His first thought was 'one of elation – I'm wounded I can clear out, and the second of thankfulness, I was not knocked down and I can still walk.' Elliott took the bolt out of his rifle, threw it away, and started down to the beach. Elliott's diary letter reveals a battalion whose morale declined rapidly in the few short days after landing. Elliott remarked of some officers in his battalion that they were keen and aggressive, such as Davenport and Fraser, but he himself and some others seemed pessimistic and apprehensive of the Turks, while the men were worn out and thirsty.[57]

In contrast, the diary of Capt. Drury, 6th Royal Dublin Fusiliers, 30 Brigade, 10 Division, shows a much more confident officer and battalion. Drury thought his troops seemed like a regular army battalion and not a 'Kitchener Crowd' – indeed many officers were regulars. Also, during training, some inefficient officers were sent home for drinking, or simply being too old. After their training in England, the division shipped out to Mytilene, and went on board *Fauvrette* on 7 August, ready for the Suvla landing. There were, however, no orders, no maps, and the wireless was not allowed to be used. The division transferred to the 'Beetles' and landed at 6.00 a.m. on 7 August, at C Beach. Still there was no staff on hand, and no orders, so the battalion came under Brigadier-General Hill, GOC 31 Brigade, and moved north. They crossed the Cut, and stayed in reserve all day, carrying ammunition and becoming thirsty and tired.[58]

Just after midnight on the night of 7 August/8, orders were received first to go to Chocolate Hill, and then later, to go back down again to the

Cut. This was part of the poor staff work in IX Corps, and Drury wrote: 'The men are all talking about the waste of valuable time', watching the neighbouring 11 Division sitting around sleeping and eating. The 6th Dublin Fusiliers then came under the command of Brigadier-General R.P. Maxwell, GOC 33 Brigade, and at 2.30 a.m. on 9 August, marched to the foot of Chocolate Hill and were ordered to take W Hills. The scrub was very thick and the battalion came to a halt in a fire fight with the Turks. Drury went back to 33 Brigade HQ for orders, but this HQ was on the sea side of Lala Baba and could not see what was going on. Moreover, 'Gen Maxwell [was] in the devil of a funk and incapable of giving proper orders.' The staff then gave orders to support the 6th Border Regiment in a further attack on W Hills: 'these orders to reinforce the front line should of course come from the Brig Gen but he seems useless and doesn't know what is going on and doesn't try to find out.'[59]

Back in the firing line, Drury was not impressed by the 6th Lincolns and 6th Borderers of 33 Brigade, who he alleged were 'all over the place lying up in funk holes. Finally, when I got to D Company a whole lot of them started running away like mad, shouting out that they were cut to ribbons etc.' Drury and his fellow officers threatened the men with their revolvers and stopped the withdrawal. A party of twenty Borderers, plus a Company Sergeant Major (CSM) and two officers moved up, but Drury complained they would not 'put their heads up and fire although I showed them good targets. The worst of them was a fat CSM who would only lie down in a ditch and announce: 'We are cut to bits.'' Then a hare got up, and the whole party blazed away at it, although they were 'too afraid to shoot at the Turks.' According to Drury, small parties of Borderers, Lincolns and South Staffordshires were scattered about the western slopes of W Hills, 'lying doggo!'. At 10.30 a.m. heavy Turkish shelling of Hill 70 (Scimitar Hill) pushed the line back, and at 11.30 a.m. Drury noticed some of the Lincolns and Borderers making their way out of the line. Paddy Cox, a 6th Dublins officer, attempted to restore order, and hit one retreating officer over the head with his telescope. Drury also alleged that the 'Queen's West Surreys bolted the minute the heavy shelling started, leaving Bill Whyte [a 6th Dublin's officer] with a mere handful of men.' Finally, the line was withdrawn to a trench 300 yards from the crest of Scimitar Hill at 1.00 p.m. on 9 August.[60]

Drury explained the failure to capture W Hills, and subsequently to recapture Scimitar Hill, through two factors. First was the failure of the staff to prepare proper schemes for W Hills, and then Scimitar Hill, when initially there was little opposition on Scimitar Hill. (Drury apparently didn't know that Scimitar Hill had earlier been occupied by the 6th East Yorkshire Pioneer Battalion.) Drury's second reason for failure was that due to the:

> extraordinarily bad behaviour of the 11th Division troops and some of the 53rd [Division] our day was divided between trying to keep the 33rd Brigade *on*, and the Turks *off* Hill 70 [Scimitar Hill]. The bulk of the 33rd Brigade cleared off early and went the whole way to the beach. I am perfectly sure that if we had had our own 10th Division here complete, we would have smashed the Turk defence and got to our objectives.

Even allowing for partisan reporting, Drury was probably correct. Overall, Drury's diary reflects a good 6th Dublin Battalion, and a division that had high morale, which should have been used more effectively.[61]

The following day, 10 August, was not much better for Drury, with an attack planned for 6.00 a.m. by 53 Division. This Territorial Division did its best, but did not have cover or proper artillery support and so were cut down in the open by machine-gun, rifle and shrapnel fire. Drury commented 'Whoever ordered it [the 53 Division attack] should be shot,' and thought, 'It was a rotten show with no method and devoid of any show of determination.' Drury was probably correct in his criticism of the staff, but overly harsh in his evaluation of a Territorial Division that had landed the previous day, and was given very little chance of success. Meanwhile, 33 Brigade were in support of 53 Division, but according to Drury, some of this brigade went back to the beach and into 31 Field Ambulance lines on A Beach. They were driven out by the 6th Dublins' Col. Shanahan and even by Father Murphy, the Roman Catholic padre, who admitted, 'God forgive me, I hit some of them.' Drury's diary then carries the Suvla story forward, although he was too far south to witness another disaster, when 163 Brigade of 54 Division, including the 1/5 Norfolk Battalion, attacked in the northern Suvla plain area. It was in this operation that some of the 1/5 Norfolk Battalion apparently disappeared into the scrub and forest, and were not seen again. Since one company of this battalion, the Sandringham Company, came from the Royal estate at Sandringham, there has been much publicity about this attack, including a recent film. Turkish evidence shows that the Norfolks advanced too ambitiously, and were caught in a Turkish counterattack. There were a number of 1/5 Norfolk survivors, but the rest were either killed during the action, or possibly bayonetted afterwards, while a few who were wounded survived as prisoners of war.[62]

Then on 15 August a major attack was launched along the Kiretch Tepe ridge by 10 Division. There was good fire support from *Foxhound* and from machine-gun fire at Jephson's Post on the ridge, and the Turks were routed. Nevertheless, the attack slowed down and halted in the thick scrub through exhaustion and lack of water. According to Drury, a supporting flank assault from 54 Territorial Division did not take place at all: 'These Terrier divisions seem hopeless; first the 53rd and now the 54th let us down.' Again, Drury was not quite fair to the Territorials, who did their best, but poor tactics, and being under fire for the first time, under-mined their advance. An eyewitness from the 8th Hampshire Battalion reported that a brigade of 54 Division had to advance across a mile of open ground toward the ridge and were subject to heavy shrapnel fire, with one unfortunate soldier having an arm carried away by a shell which did not burst for another 50 yards. Watching this unpleasant advance caused one company of the 8th Hampshires to refuse to move, and they were sent to the beach. As the rest of the Hampshire Battalion reached the crest of the ridge:

> they could see the fight still going on in front of them but before the lead-ing files could join in, the Turks retired about 100 yards into a strong point and the action ceased. No effort was made to follow them, as no one realised the importance of occupying further ground along the ridge.

This explains Drury's criticism of 54 Division's failure to assist.[63]

On 16 August, Drury went to see Brigadier-General Nicol, GOC 30 Brigade, and complained of lack of support from the plain, i.e. the right flank. Nicol accused the 6th Dublin's of getting the wind up, and the battalion withdrew to a prepared line of defence. The 15 August attack offered a chance of success at Suvla, but on this day Stopford was replaced by de Lisle, who then prepared the final major offensive of 21 August at Suvla, in the southern sector. Involved on 21 August were the 29 Division, 11 Division, and a composite Anzac brigade, with the 2nd Mounted Division and 30 Brigade of 10 Division in reserve. It appears that the main problem in this offensive was weak artillery support, plus technical inability by the artillery to accurately help the infantry. According to Commander Gibson, then in charge of the Suvla left flank naval observation station, there were simply not enough guns: 'We land practically no guns Lord knows why it makes me mad.' Gibson also felt that the Rear-Admiral paid little attention to naval observation for naval shoots.[64] Another observer, Capt. Milward, commented that the artillery could not support the attack because friend and foe were too closely mixed up. On the other hand, the war diary of the 7th Battalion Munster Fusiliers claimed that the bombardment by naval fire and artillery was intense, but a time gap then ensued, allowing the Turks time to man their trenches and bring up reserves.[65] Finally, a particular artillery problem developed at Hill 60, where a New Zealand officer claimed that the Tommies (British) got all the artillery, and the New Zealand Mounted Rifles got none, not a shell. A commander had blundered: 'I know but may not tell.' In fact, the Anzac CRA had received orders to switch his artillery from Hill 60 to support the 11 Division assault at Suvla, 'for which Godley [GOC Anzac] never forgave me...'. The trouble came about because of the very late alteration of artillery plans between IX Corps and the Anzac artillery.[66] The battle for Hill 60 continued in bloody fashion for another week, at the end of which Turks and Allies shared the summit of the hill.

Whether through not landing enough guns, technical inability, inexperience, or poor staff work, the artillery/naval fire did not properly support the large-scale offensive of 21 August on, and was a primary cause of that failure. With this failure, Suvla also came to a halt as an offensive enterprise. Overall, IX Corps' losses during the August Suvla fighting amounted to 5,300 men. Anzac losses during the Sari Bair battles were 12,500. Allied losses from sickness since 6 August were 40,000. In contrast, a preliminary count of Turkish dead and wounded only, without reference to missing or sick, and for only the six days inclusive between 6 August and 11 August, amounted to just 4,373.[67] Despite a grim Allied determination over the next few months at Suvla and Anzac, the troops were decimated by sickness and, although very willing, felt they could do little more. Yet it seems that one key Allied failure at Suvla, and at Gallipoli generally, was the failure of Allied technology. Why was this so?

ALLIED AND TURKISH TECHNOLOGY CREATES STALEMATE

At first glance, the Allies possessed a very significant advantage at Gallipoli in the shape of naval fire power. But this naval superiority was nullified by Turkish countermeasures, and by technical shortcomings. Another potential Allied advantage lay in aviation. But this was undercut by lack of numbers, and again by technical shortcomings. Other areas of technology, such as submarines, artillery, machine-guns, mortars and bombs or grenades, tended to equalize or neutralize Turkish and Allied strengths. Overall, technology at Gallipoli led not to decisive results but to stalemate.

★

In the first years of the war, technology heavily favoured the defence, whether on the Western Front or elsewhere. This was certainly true of the Turkish defensive systems at Gallipoli. To overcome this, the Allies' greatest advantage in technology during the Gallipoli campaign lay in naval support and especially naval fire.[1] This advantage was considered capable of overcoming Turkish resistance on land, especially at Helles. But how effective was naval fire in supporting the Allied troops after the landings had taken place? In fact, naval fire was less useful than expected, due primarily to difficulty with observation. Where observation was good, as was often the case at Helles, naval fire could be devastating against troops in the open, and forced the Turks to attack at night, dawn or dusk. But where fire was indirect, the Navy ran into severe problems.

The first drawback was the inaccuracy of maps. According to Cunliffe-Owen, artillery commander at Anzac, who initially directed naval fire in support of the Anzacs, these maps were prepared from the 1840s version, and did not agree with the ground, and what was most important… the compass bearing was two degrees out, so that if a message came saying 'Fire in 243 D', the ships made the most accurate calculations, and the result was that they were 2 degrees off. Owing to the long range and flat trajectory of the ship' guns, it would be dangerous to shoot too close to our own troops, and they mostly fired AP [armour piercing] shells. Liman von Sanders soon discovered this inaccuracy, and ordered his troops to move their front line trenches as close as possible to the Allied front line trenches, in order to avoid Allied naval shelling.[2]

With poor maps, naval accuracy required other kinds of guidance, and this could come from aerial spotting. The aeroplane was a piece of technology that turned out to be vital, especially at Anzac, because of the difficult ground. It was also an area that gave the Allies another technical advantage in terms of numbers and pilot skills. However, the demands of the Western Front for limited resources, combined with Kitchener's incomprehension of the needs of the Gallipoli campaign, meant that very few Allied planes were available for Gallipoli. Eventually only three Allied squadrons operated at Gallipoli, and few planes were equipped with wireless communication. In early May, for example, there were just three wireless planes for the Army, one for the Navy, and none at all for Anzac. As late as July, a GHQ Report stated that: 'Aeroplane service appears to have broken down. An average of one plane daily is available for work with Army at Anzac and Helles.' Besides lack of numbers, lack of understanding complicated operations of the planes. Pilots complained that they would go up and make the Ready Sign, and then wait an hour or two for the ship to open fire. Then the ship would fire slowly, or simply leave, generally to avoid German submarines or Turkish artillery fire. On the other hand, planes could also leave early, either with engine trouble, or under ground attack. Furthermore, air observers were in short supply and lacked experience in a task that required great skill. Ship–based balloons for observation were also available, although they could only rise to 3,000 feet, and were vulnerable to enemy artillery fire. Cunliffe-Owen summarized aerial spotting at Anzac as follows:

> The aeroplane service was never very good... Officers were sent from Australian and N.Z. Artillery as observers, but there were not enough of them and frequently when observation shoots were being carried out, the good results were thrown away by the ignorance of the Naval observers in 'spotting' properly for land guns, or suddenly going away with the series unfinished.

There was also the difficulty of slow communication between plane and ship or land artillery, while in 1915 communication was one way only, from plane to land or ship. In regard to planes, therefore, a mixture of technical problems, lack of numbers and inexperience undercut efficiency.[3]

The navy also relied on shore based observing officers, and here the process of firing was complicated enough that a memorandum of 10 May ended by stating that for the time being indirect fire would be laid down 'at a safe distance from our forces.' Cunliffe-Owen wrote on 9 May:

> it must be understood that naval guns cannot fire on enemy's guns close to our [Anzac] line. It is too dangerous, because all fire from ships is by compass, as the map is not accurate... the naval guns [should] take outside zones only.

The next day, Roger Keyes noted in a letter that naval fire simply could not help the men if they were close to the enemy. Earlier, Cunliffe-Owen instructed naval observing officers to be careful 'owing to swing of ships and nearness to our own troops & steepness of cliffs.' As a result, Allied troops on shore tended to be critical of naval accuracy, thus one staff officer of 1 Australian Division remarked on 29 May: 'From the moment the *Prince of Wales* opened up on Gaba Tepe's guns, on the first Sunday morning, right through the succession of weeks when they opened up on the Olive Grove battery and the Anafarta villages etc., they seemed to us not able to hit what they aimed at.' Similarly, Lt-Col. Rettie, Field Artillery, simply stated that the Navy could not support the infantry or do counter-battery.[4]

Lest it be thought that naval fire was simple, it is useful to follow the procedure for indirect and unobserved naval fire from an anchored ship. First, the Army asks for fire on a particular Turkish battery at Helles, and gives the map reference. Next, the naval officer fixes the position of the ship exactly, and lays off the angle of the point of aim from some well known point, such as the top of Achi Baba, and measures the range on the chart. The naval officer sets this angle on a sextant, which he gives to the gunnery officer. The gunnery officer takes the sextant to the armoured director, and sits in the trainer's seat. The gunnery officer looks through the sextant to the top of Achi Baba and sees the correct point of aim reflected against it. He orders the gunlayer to train right or left until he has picked up this point. The gunnery officer corrects the range for the height of the point of aim and for the height of the target. He then fires. The first shot usually falls within the deflection scale for direction, and then further rounds are fired at the same point of aim, applying deflection. Remembering that one turn of the training wheel represents 18 minutes of arc, then if the point of aim needed to be altered, say by 5 degrees 30 minutes, then the gunnery officer in the trainer's position shifts the movable graduated ring on the repeat training receiver to zero, and then trains quickly to 5 degrees 30 minutes and reports 'On.' At the word 'On', the director layer takes his point of aim on the shore in line with his cross wire and stays there. This always brought the next shot to within a few yards of the correct deflection. All of this would take about five minutes, sufficient for a fixed target, but obviously too slow for a moving target. If the ship was moving, the procedure got much more complicated, and was usually less accurate.[5]

On the other hand, naval fire, when supported by good observation from plane, balloon or shore, initially proved very destructive of Turkish forces in the open. Capt. Carl Mühlmann, German staff officer, wrote of his own experience on 29 April at Helles, while riding with a small group of officers:

a shell raced close by us… It was an embarrassing moment since we did not know in which direction to seek cover. The only one who saw us was the tethered balloon which, high above us, guided the fire of the ships at Gaba Tepe as well as at Seddulbahir. We spurred our horses and descended into a ravine; after one hour we felt safe enough to continue our journey since the tethered balloon had been hauled down. Then we reappeared in the little forest – and the cannonade began anew. This time a flyer directed the fire – not by telegraph like the tethered balloon, but rather by a series of circles flown over the target. Thus we waited in the forest for darkness…

Later, Mühlmann related how his observation platform at Helles was discovered, and,

Soon, the heavy naval shells roared into our vicinity, so that we had to seek cover in no more than a hole in the ground. The enemy fire was superb. The shells landing in our immediate vicinity covered us with stones and dirt, while the explosives flew over our hole. Around 7 p.m. the fire died down…

Mühlmann was very impressed by the accuracy of Allied naval fire:

The fleet's fire is impressively accurate, even though most times they can only fire indirectly. The English possess incredibly accurate maps [Mühlmann is obviously misinformed here]: the entire peninsula is divided into quadrants, each 1 kilometre long, 1 kilometre wide; these quadrants are again subdivided into certain areas, each marked with a number; and [targets are] thus reported to the fleet by tethered balloons – enemy column in B III 6, and thus an area of 100 square metres is fired upon and decimated in the shortest possible time by countless rapid fire guns.

But the Turks were soon able to adapt, noted Mühlmann: 'At one time, losses were incredibly high – before the troops learned to use even the smallest defile and to move in only the smallest groups…'. Hence, Allied naval support of troops ashore was very effective at Helles when directed by observation, and before Turkish adaptation, while Anzac was always more difficult due to the geography of the place and the fewer Allied observation resources initially applied there.[6]

With the appearance of another piece of technology, the German submarine, Allied naval fire became less effective. In late May, the U21, commanded by Capt. Hersing, sank *Triumph* off Gaba Tepe, and shortly after, sank *Majestic*. This was enough for all Allied battleships to retreat to Mudros and Kephalo harbours, which obviously prevented the battleships' guns from giving land support, although destroyers with their 4ins guns remained. The Allied navy countered with the arrival of monitors in late July, which were flat-bottomed ships with 4ins guns, capable of very accurate fire. These became significant by the end of the campaign, but their impact was too little and too late. In general, even with observation, and especially after German submarines forced the battleships to retire, Allied naval fire was of little value against precise targets like trenches, machine-guns or enemy batteries, due to sheer technical inability. As a post-war report on Gallipoli stated: 'it is clearly proved that the fire of ships' guns cannot be considered an adequate substitute for well-organised support of field and heavy artillery on land.' More clearly, the artillery commander at Anzac following Cunliffe-Owen, Brigadier-General G.G. Winston, stated that the Navy was anxious to help, but was 'incapable of giving much assistance.'[7]

Naval technology, therefore, which promised so much, proved not to be the decisive weapon that the Allies had hoped for. Now, however, with the Allied landings achieved, the focus shifted to land based weapons. The navy still provided support, but it was now the artillery which was chiefly going to enable Allied attacks on land to succeed or not. The generally accepted notion is that shortages of artillery shells and guns spelled failure for the Allies in their attacks at Helles after the landings. A typical assertion is that of Brigadier-General Simpson Baikie, GSO 1 Operations at GHQ:

> The whole story of the artillery at Cape Helles may be summed up in the
> few words: insufficiency of guns, ammunition and howitzers for the oper-

ations undertaken; no high explosive ever available for field guns; no spare parts or spare guns ever available, lack of aeroplanes, and no guns of heavy calibre available to compete with the hostile heavy guns.

Similarly, the artillery officer Lt-Col. Grant, wrote that 'it was a mistake to set out to conquer the Turks with 8 Howitzers and little ammunition…'.[8] There is a good deal of truth in this point of view. However, it is notable that neither Hans Kannengiesser nor Liman von Sanders ascribe the failure of Allied attacks to lack of artillery or shells. Rather, Kannengiesser argued that it was lack of flexibility in the Allied attacks, and too much emphasis on rigid method, which spelled failure. Liman von Sanders even emphasized 'the unlimited [artillery] ammunition of the enemy', compared to lack of Turkish artillery shells, and claimed that British attacks failed for purely tactical reasons. Hence, neither of these German commanders make any mention of Allied material shortages.[9]

The difficulty for historians is that most Allied artillery officers in post-Gallipoli or post-war correspondence tended to compare Gallipoli with Western Front standards, which they experienced *after* Gallipoli. The Western Front was certainly far better supplied with artillery and shells than Gallipoli, and so the emphasis in their remarks is naturally slanted toward an image of scarcity at Gallipoli. Thus Simpson Baikie and Cunliffe-Owen both gave post-war evidence which emphasized throughout the shortage of shells and guns. On the other hand, to argue against this view of scarcity, comments made at the time often praised the artillery, hence Capt. Milward remarked in his diary of the 4 June Allied attack: 'Never had I seen such a bombardment.' This 4 June Helles attack employed over 12,000 shells fired to cover 5,000 yards of trenches, which, apart from the yards covered, compares quite favourably with the 10,000 shells fired at Neuve Chapelle on 10 March 1915 to cover 2,000 yards of trenches in supporting that offensive on the Western Front. Again, in the same attack of 4 June at Helles, there were 102 Allied guns in action, which fired these 12,240 shells in two hours. In addition, there were all the guns of the Allied ships involved, while the Turks could muster but ninety-two guns in reply. This is not to argue that Gallipoli was well supplied with artillery and ammunition. It was certainly not, and there were never enough howitzers or high explosive shells. Obviously, at critical moments abundant supplies of artillery and ammunition would have made a significant difference, especially at Helles. But the key difficulties at Helles may not have been the shortage of munitions, since officers were often satisfied with the artillery preparation.[10]

Western Front experience was invoked at Suvla in August 1915, when Stopford, IX Corps commander, and his chief of staff, Reed, issued orders that enemy trenches were not to be attacked frontally unless sufficient artillery was available, and in general, the painfully slow advance at Suvla was partly defended by Stopford on the grounds that he did not have sufficient artillery. Yet Gallipoli was probably supplied with just enough artillery and ammunition to achieve Allied success. Instead it can be argued that the problem of Allied attacks tended to be, firstly, as noted by Liman von Sanders and Kannengiesser, inexperience. For example, in the early days of April and May 1915, artillery-infantry cooperation was poor, with no conferences, and artillery was not given enough notice of advances. Another example of inexperience relates to the last throw of the dice for the Allies on Gallipoli – the large offensive of 21 August. Here, Cunliffe-Owen wrote in his diary for 18 August that Maj.-Gen. de Lisle, commanding the attack,

> read out a plan of attack, there were no comments or discussions, no questions by Divisional Generals, then Hamilton said a few irrelevant words and at once the plan was accepted. Needless to say it was sketchy in the extreme. There was a good deal of shelling and Gen. Smith [in charge of naval fire support] did not take things very seriously…

Two days later, Cunliffe-Owen again expressed his apprehension:

> The IX Corps orders for the artillery was most vague, for the Navy more so, and allotment of objectives was not settled. Most careful detailed allotment of all guns, with times and objectives by map is absolutely necessary.

The offensive did not succeed, so one problem on 21 August seemed to be inexperience, leading to indifferent staff work, rather than the technology itself.[11]

Secondly, there was a lack of reserves at critical moments. Hence, Lt-Col. Stephenson, Manchester Regiment, made the useful comment that after the 25 April landings, when the Turkish defences were vulnerable to a strong offensive, 42 Division was 'hanging about in Cairo'. Then at the battle of Second Krithia (early May), most of 42 Division was still on transports 'puttering up and down between Cape Helles and Anzac.' Finally at Third Krithia (early June), another division was idly standing by in Mudros harbour. Nothing is certain in war, but these divisions might well have been decisive at critical moments in all three offensives, whatever the technology.[12]

Thirdly, of great importance were the artillery's technical limitations in 1915. Most critically, enemy machine-guns could never all be located and accounted for by the artillery. Yet machine-guns were usually the most significant barriers to the infantry advance. Wire cutting was also in its infancy, and according to the artillery commander of 3 Group Artillery at Helles, was 'quite beyond 18 pounder guns with either HE or shrapnel.' Probably this is too extreme a statement, for wire cutting was achieved, but it was always a problem.[13] Another important Allied difficulty was counter-battery (the destruction of enemy guns), because the Turkish guns had excellent observation due to their location on the high ground, and could be easily concealed behind hill crests, and supplied with many alternative sites. Therefore, it was possible to get line/direction on Turkish artillery, but range was very difficult due to the need for extreme accuracy, since the shells might clear the crests of the hills by only a few feet, but these hills then fell away sharply, and the shells would be wasted. For the same reason, at Anzac, because Allied guns faced steep hills, elevation was a real problem. The solution at Anzac was to have Allied guns on each flank fire at the other flank. But Turkish guns were rarely destroyed by counter-battery, particularly the Olive Grove guns overlooking Anzac. In a post-war visit, Charles Bean, the Australian official historian, discovered that the Olive Grove guns did not seem to have been hit at all. Hence, Allied artillery counter-battery work, particularly at Anzac, was a failure, and the Turkish staff declared post-war: 'As we had only very slight losses in men and guns at Anzac, we knew that our method was very satisfactory.' A further common technical problem was that survey – the accurate location of both the gun and its target on maps and charts – was in its infancy in 1915, and was hardly achieved at Gallipoli. It was often said in 1915 that the error of the gun (each gun fired differently according to wear and tear) 'was so great that accurate maps and charts were unnecessary.' This almost inevitable lack of accuracy in indirect fire, especially against small targets such as enemy batteries, could have costly results, for example when the Australian Lone Pine attack started on 6 August at 5.30 p.m., 'the enemy opened a terrific artillery fire as soon as the Infantry attack was launched and this they have maintained all night and day…'[14]

Apart from failure at counter-battery, Allied artillery also struggled with the preliminary bombardment and with the barrage. For example, the 4 June (Third Krithia) attack was supplemented by six batteries of French 75mm guns. Despite this, and despite pre-registration of the guns to establish accuracy in local conditions, artillery fire could not knock out several enemy machine-guns (no doubt a question of observation here) and there were few Turkish casualties in the trenches as a result of shelling. Moreover, there was some short shooting, naval supporting fire was not accurate and faulty staff work had the 2nd Naval Brigade advancing at 12.15 p.m. when the barrage stopped at 12 noon. This was partly also a matter of inexperience – the troops had not learnt to advance close behind the barrage, while the artillery had not learnt to fire on the enemy trenches until the last possible moment. However, these problems were not unique to Gallipoli, and exactly similar situations occurred on the Western Front. And just as on the Western Front, so at Gallipoli, Allied artillery organization, knowledge and efficiency improved steadily through 1915, especially in responding quickly to the needs of the infantry through involving infantry officers in artillery decision-making. In summary, however, the analysis of Allied artillery is that a mixture of inexperience, technical inability, lack of useful air spotting and Turkish geographical advantages, rather than gun and shell shortages, undercut the value of the Allied artillery at Gallipoli.[15]

Given the failure of the technologically superior Allied naval force, together with the partial failure of the traditional centrepiece of Allied land warfare – the artillery – were there other kinds of technology that might be decisive? And if so, how would the Turks react?

One weapon that was potentially decisive for both sides was the submarine. Both the British official historian, Aspinall, and Liman von Sanders argued that if Allied submarines had closed the Straits to all water transport, then the campaign would have ended, because while Turkish troops could eventually arrive by marching, food and war material had to come by ship. After a British submarine sank a transport at the arsenal dock at Istanbul at the end of May, few Turkish troops went by sea. Besides this, Allied submarines had as much impact as German submarines, for example, in sinking the *Barbarossa* in early August and sending half the Turkish merchant navy to the bottom by the end of the campaign. At one point, in late August 1915, when all Allied options seemed exhausted, Hamilton suggested to Kitchener that doubling or tripling the number of Allied submarines might cut off all Turkish sea supplies to Gallipoli. However, this suggestion was overtaken by Kitchener's hope that instead the French would provide more divisions for Gallipoli. Meanwhile, in reaction to Allied submarines, Turkish anti-submarine defences developed, consisting of booms, mine fields and nets across the Straits, although this did not deter Allied submarines from further results. On the other hand, it is clear that German submarines had a major impact in the early stages because of Allied reliance on naval support. And the sinking of *Triumph* and *Majestic* in May by the German submarine U21, plus the recall of *Queen Elizabeth*, led to the withdrawal of all battleships. This had one key result, which was to leave the Turkish guns on the Asian side free to fire at will, because only the long range battleship guns could reach them. Hamilton was taken by surprise at this turn of events, and so the Asia guns battered Helles and Anzac, and the French beaches in particular, throughout June. However, the arrival of French coastal batteries, and the naval monitors in July, led to some relief from the Asia batteries.[16]

By September, there were fourteen German submarines in the Mediterranean. Yet this array of submarines did not have the decisive impact that might be anticipated from the successes of May. Allied anti-submarine nets, booms, look-outs, and covering light craft were effective, and the inability of German submarines to directly influence the August offensives was reflected in the many desperate Turkish calls for submarine assistance. At the height of the Allied August landings at Suvla, Kiazim Bey, Liman von Sanders' chief of staff, sent a desperate message to Istanbul demanding submarine assistance. On the same day, 7 August, Liman von Sanders sent two messages, both pleading that 'submarines must assist.' Two days later, Liman von Sanders still urged that 'U Boats are very necessary'. Then on 11 August, Kiazim Bey despatched an angry telegram to Istanbul, condemning Turkish losses to Allied submarines (referring to the sinking of *Barbarossa*), and concluded strangely by saying that if anyone wanted 'to hang us' for his critical remarks, they were free to do so. Once more, on 18 and 19 August, Liman von Sanders called directly for submarine help, on the latter day stating that 'Participation of U Boats seems urgently necessary.' Despite all these messages, and apart from the sinking of *Royal Edward* on 13 August with a loss of some 500 lives, German submarines did not help the Turkish land campaign very much. Therefore, the analysis is that submarine technology had the potential to bring the fighting to a halt if submarines had been more technically advanced, and in greater numbers. The Turks were vulnerable due to their essential Sea of Marmora supply lines, but possessed enough merchant ships to continue, despite many losses. The Allies' long supply lines were also open to submarine interference, but this did not happen. Instead, it seems that anti-submarine defences on both sides were just sufficient to maintain operations, given the small number of submarines available, and the technical shortcomings of submarines at the time.[17]

Turning to Turkish land-based technology, it seems that Turkish artillery went through many of the same problems as Allied artillery. There were shortages of shells and guns, neither of which were in adequate supply until August. For example, on 29 April, the Turkish Fifth Army was using 1628 shrapnel shells daily, and running very low. Both Kannengiesser and Liman von Sanders complained of the lack of artillery and shells, argued that the heavy artillery arrived slowly, and complained that the shells produced at the new ammunition factory at

Istanbul only exploded at the rate of one per twenty shells! These artillery shortages especially hurt Turkish counterattacks. For example, it is surprising to note that Mustafa Kemal's attack of 1/2 May at Anzac used only mountain guns for the preparatory barrage and attack, and a crisis of confidence occurred in early May due to very heavy casualties. Indeed, on 4 May, Kiazim Bey reported 15,000 Turkish casualties since 25 April. There was a lull in Turkish attacks, due to shortages of men and material, before another serious Turkish offensive took place at Anzac on 19/20 May with 30,000 troops. This attack was stopped with heavy Turkish casualties by Anzac rifle and machine-gun fire, and by naval fire during the day. Because of artillery shortages, Liman von Sanders later admitted he had not used enough artillery in this attack. After this defeat, the Turks realized that without heavy artillery to blast the Allies out of their trenches, a technical stalemate had developed at Anzac, and so left two weak divisions and their guns at Anzac, and built up their artillery and manpower at Helles. In the middle and later stages of the campaign, artillery shortages were resolved with the arrival of more Turkish field artillery pieces and shells. Thus on 8 August, a secret letter from Kiazim Bey to Enver Pasa, stated that there were now around 16,000 field artillery shells available.[18]

Meanwhile, at Helles, the number of Turkish artillery pieces increased. At Seddulbahir on 25 April there were only twenty-four Turkish pieces, and four machine-guns. Two more field artillery batteries arrived later on 25 April. By early May there were fifty-six guns, and for the Allied attack of 4 June at Helles, the Turks were able to defend with eighty-six guns. By mid-June it was reckoned that the Allied attack had been broken at Helles. Nevertheless, on 6 August, 163 guns were then in place at Helles. It is also noticeable that when the Turks realized in early August that Suvla was a significant area of Allied attack, their artillery there increased very rapidly. Thus on 6 August, only eleven guns were located at Suvla, increasing to fifty-four by 8 August, 100 by 21 August, and finally 140 in October. This certainly shows that the Turkish artillery force could react to crises. But it was the better Turkish artillery locations, and observation at higher elevations than the Allies, that proved extremely valuable at all times.[19]

Hans Kannengiesser also claimed that the Turkish artillery was a well-organized corps. It is true that in the early stages, the Turkish artillery was successful at Anzac on 25 April. But in general, as might be expected, initial inexperience and poor material was a problem for the Turks. For example, on 28 April 1915, according to Lt-Col. Forman, an artillery officer at Helles, Turkish shrapnel burst too high and was totally ineffective. On the same day, Capt. Milward wrote in his diary that the Turks 'shell us now every morning before breakfast, but do no harm with their small guns, bad shells, and bad shooting.' Then, in June, at Helles, Maj.-Gen. de Lisle considered the Turkish artillery 'contemptible' compared to the French. The Turkish official history also stresses the value of machine-guns and rifles in stopping the Allies in their critical May and June Krithia offensives at Helles, rather than artillery. In early August at Suvla, a British artillery officer still reported Turkish shrapnel bursting high, while Lt Heath at Suvla on 12 August wrote that the Turks were shelling, but they must be short of ammunition, or 'they could undoubtedly clear us out of this place in a day...'. Nevertheless, other observers thought that Turkish artillery was improving. Thus, on 7 August, Capt. Elliott wrote that as soon as his unit started to set up a defensive line, Turkish shrapnel burst over their trenches very effectively. During the early August battles at Sari Bair, Lt Reginald Savory reported on the bold use of Turkish mountain guns, and how on 10 August, 'the Turkish artillery had the range to a nicety.' Then, in his diary for 21 August, Cunliffe-Owen remarked that 'The Turkish shrapnel burst very regularly and accurately.' Finally, in October, an Australian report stated that Turkish artillery at Anzac was extremely quick to spot Allied machine-guns firing, and then eliminate them.[20]

However, in the attack, Turkish artillery was less useful, and casualties were traded for lack of guns and experience. Thus, in May 1915, before larger supplies of guns and ammunition started to arrive, the sacrifice of Turkish soldiers in very costly counterattacks, balanced the lack of artillery. Similarly, the early August counterattacks under Mustafa Kemal, were really human wave attacks with the bayonet. Nevertheless, Turkish artillery improved in the later stages, especially in defence. Overall,

Turkish artillery was sufficient, together with other arms, to help produce a technical stalemate.

This technical stalemate was emphasized by the Turkish and German use of machine-guns. Lt-Col. Stephenson, Manchester Regiment, remarked during Third Krithia that 'The Turkish machine-guns were more numerous and better handled than ours.' In fact, according to both the German official history and the Turkish official history, it was clearly the use of machine-gun companies that were decisive in stopping the Allied May and June Krithia offensives. Similarly, at Helles, Lt Savory recalled how the Turks, with their machine-guns, could not be pushed out of trench J13 in early July, and in the steep areas of Anzac, Turkish machine-guns were deadly. Consequently, Savory remarked in early August: 'This mountain warfare is devilish tiring work and is accompanied by large casualties, chiefly from their infernal machine-guns.' However, Turkish machine-guns and ammunition were not in plentiful supply, and so had to be obtained largely from the Straits forts and the German battleships. Evidence for this, apart from the startling incident on 4 May when Turkish soldiers beat up a German machine-gun company by mistake, occurred during the 12/13 July Helles offensive, when an Allied observer noticed some German sailors taken as prisoners, who had been working German machine-guns, but having no ammunition left, had been forced to surrender. Then, on 8 August at Suvla, the German commander, Maj. Willmer, reported that machine-guns from the fleet had only just arrived at his Suvla location. On 10 August, at the critical fight at Chunuk Bair, Kiazim Bey reported there were just eighteen Turkish machine-guns available, but that twelve more were seized from the British. Overall, Turkish and German machine-guns were often in short supply, but were very well served, and were also a very significant factor in helping to create the stalemate on Gallipoli.[21]

Another very important technical Turkish advantage lay in the ready availability of hand grenades. These were a big improvement over the Allied home made jam jar style bombs with a fuse that had to be lit. It is very noticeable how frequently the Turkish forces in June requested grenades, and how often Fifth Army requested bombs. For example, on 7 August, Kiazim Bey urgently requested grenades, and again on 10 August:

'I urgently request, please send hand grenades.' On the other hand, Allied trench reports suggested that Turkish bombs could be smothered and so had limited effect when exploding. Against this is the account of Lt Savory, who found Turkish grenades very effective in July. One further Turkish technical advantage was the establishment of a rifle ammunition making centre on Gallipoli, set up by the German officer, Capt. Pieper, and Turkish women workers. As a result, Turkish forces were rarely short of rifle ammunition, and on many occasions, Allied reports emphasized the power of Turkish musket fire. Once again, it was Lt Savory who wrote during the 4 June Krithia attack that 'The roar of [Turkish] musketry was so intense as to drown all other sounds…'. British and Anzac forces also lacked mortars, apart from a few ancient Japanese mortars. Indeed, at one point in late July, GHQ obtained two Dumezil mortars from the French with 100 rounds each, in exchange for four dozen pots of jam. The Turks also possessed only a very small number of heavy mortars. In only one area do the Allies seem to have been superior in trench materials, and this was the periscope rifle, invented at Anzac. Therefore, it seems that Turkish forces had the technical edge in trench fighting. So, by the end of August, the combination of Turkish artillery, machine-guns, grenades and rifles, was sufficient to halt almost any Allied attack. But in counterattack, the Turkish forces were forced to de-emphasize technology and sacrifice men to achieve their objectives.[22]

In the end, a stalemate developed at Gallipoli. But the stalemate naturally favoured the Turks, who compelled the Allies to withdraw. What were the decisive factors in this technical result?

The initial Allied technical advantages – particularly naval fire support, and then aviation and the artillery – could not achieve superiority because of technical inability, inexperience, adverse geographical conditions, Turkish adaptation, and, in the case of aviation, simple lack of suitable planes equipped with wireless. A weapon that unexpectedly came close to decisive results, the submarine, did not achieve superiority for either side due to lack of numbers and the development of adequate defences against this still evolving weapon. A further major reason that the technologies employed at Gallipoli by the Allies were not decisive is that the Gallipoli campaign took place early in the war, in a period of military experimentation on the Western Front, as well as at Gallipoli, and before any army had really come to grips with the new fire-power revolution. War was thought to be simpler in 1915 than it actually was, while both on the Western Front and at Gallipoli, it took some time before Allied commanders grasped the fact that the Turkish defensive technology of artillery, machine-guns, rifles, and trenches, was good enough to halt almost all offensive possibilities. In the same vein, Turkish and German commanders gradually realized that although they could not throw the Allies into the sea, neither were they likely to be defeated unless caught by surprise. This almost occurred in early August, but once more it was relatively simple for the Turks to re-establish a stalemate. In fact, surprise was the main factor that differentiated Gallipoli from the Western Front. Otherwise, if armies on the Western Front in 1915 could not break through with the benefit of more men and artillery, how could Allied forces on Gallipoli be expected to do so? The only way through was surprise, and this nearly worked.

Turkish forces and their German advisers often suffered from many of the same technical difficulties as the Allies. But the Turks possessed important geographical advantages at Gallipoli in commanding the high ground both at Anzac and Helles, and benefitted greatly from having ready supplies of men and material close at hand. Also, due to their generally defensive form of fighting after May, the technology which the Turks employed at Gallipoli was quite sufficient to produce a stalemate. But there were genuine Allied opportunities at Gallipoli, created by the surprise location of the landings of 25 April, and the surprise of the early August offensive and Suvla landing. What often tipped the scales in favour of the Turks and reinforced the technical stalemate, was better military leadership. Whether in the shape of German commanders like Liman von Sanders, Carl Mühlmann, Maj. Willmer, Hans Kannengiesser, or Turkish staff and commanders like Kiazim Bey, Esat Pasa, Halil Bey, and Mustafa Kemal, the Germans and Turks possessed better higher commanders than the Allies. It was this final factor which overcame Allied naval advantages, and tended to solidify the technical stalemate at Gallipoli. Yet it was this very technology that produced the stress of modern war, as the next chapter shows.

THE EXPERIENCE OF MODERN WAR
AT GALLIPOLI

Stress, Strain and Survival

*Bravery and panic, blood lust and skulking, malingering and heroism — all had
their place at Gallipoli. The emotional intensity of warfare at Gallipoli was mag-
nified by the fact that at Anzac, and later at Suvla, the Allies had their backs to the
sea in small, heavily shelled enclaves. The situation was not much better at Helles,
although the Allied area was larger. On the Turkish side, the lack of diaries and letters make it hazardous to generalize. However, stories from deserters and prisoners
of war, together with some evidence concerning the Turkish medical system, provide
some insights into the Turkish experience.*

*A study of the impact of modern war on those who served at Gallipoli
inevitably leads towards methods of adaptation and survival. Other topics discussed include panic, courage, shell shock, self inflicted wounds, discipline, the distribution of rewards, changing views of the enemy, desertion, prisoners of war, medical
services, nursing, the evacuation, and finally, Christmas Day 1915.*

★

Pte F.E. McKenzie, 3rd Auckland Infantry, kept a diary which reveals
an adaptation to the terrors of war through desensitization and
numbing when it was a question of surviving Turkish shelling and
bombing. At the same time, taking part in attacks had the opposite effect
in arousing his fighting emotions. During the landing of 25 April,
McKenzie noted that his small group advanced too far that day, and only
survived because someone shouted 'retire', which they did or they

would have been wiped out. They also shot most of their Turkish prisoners of war because of their 'treachery'. In the days following, McKenzie soon learnt to distinguish 'every kind of missile and whence it comes, and whose it is by the sound.' Later, on 19 May, McKenzie was road making when a shell landed on his group: 'One saw a head and shoulders, then a few feet away, an arm and then a leg. But such sights are common now and I can look at them without a shudder.' McKenzie also learnt how to survive Turkish bombing, writing in a matter of fact way that 'you cover it [the bomb] with coats or sand bags, if time, and run and fall flat with feet towards the explosion. One's life depends on quickness.' Then on 3 June, McKenzie volunteered for a trench raid. After throwing in his bombs, McKenzie remembered that he:

> sprang in with a roar and the bayonets, and for a wild delirious moment stabbed and cut the demoralised beggars. Twice I drove mine home… Three Turks crawled out from a dugout in the trench and had the cheek to attack us. Carlaw [a fellow Auckland raider] stabbed at one about six times and still he stuck to it and then another one of our chaps got him through the neck. Carlaw was very emphatic when he saw his bayonet was broken and buckled.[1]

McKenzie's feelings might be explained when he wrote that the raid was the best thing they had yet done, and 'wiped out some old scores.' There was then a feeling of revenge. But McKenzie also enjoyed the bayonet charge:

> Can tell you one feels a big fellow in a bayonet charge, with a few bombs in his belt and 10 deaths in his rifle. It is the best and most exciting feeling I've ever had. The old primeval instincts and blood lust, are only thinly buried after all.

There were, therefore, two different responses, high excitement in the attack, and desensitized acceptance in defence. Under Turkish shelling, McKenzie, like many others, also developed fatalism as a coping mechanism. Reflecting on a narrow escape in early July, when some died under shelling and others did not: 'Just luck you see.' Then on 10 August, while taking part in the Sari Bair offensive, a 'shell burst 15 feet in front and blinded me with the flash and explosion and I dropped into the bivouac. Found I was unhurt and 6 bullets had lodged round me… After that I decided I was not to be killed by shrapnel.'[2]

McKenzie's experiences are mirrored to some extent by those of Pte Harry Browne, Wellington Mounted Rifles. Browne also took part in the Sari Bair attack, and actually occupied a trench on the crest of Chunuk Bair. On 8 August, Browne charged up the steep slope toward Chunuk Bair, passing over Anzac dead and wounded. Thus, like McKenzie, Browne had a sense of revenge. After digging the most advanced trench on the crest of Chunuk Bair, just four men were left in it to defend against Turkish counterattacks, since many had left the trench and retired. Browne wrote that he was filled with 'a grim deadliness', and shouted to those who had left the trench 'Come back you —— ', and 'Come on you black ——', for 'men mostly swear in action…'. Despite their critical situation, Browne wrote that 'The fierce joy of battle… was in the air.'[3] Another who described the landing on 25 April as indescribable hell, also remarked that when the bayonets are out, the Turks 'run like hares' and 'squeal like rabbits.' Even late in the campaign, one Gurkha soldier is recorded as cutting off the ears of the Turks that he had shot, drying them, and then hanging them around his neck.[4]

In contrast, there was another reaction that was both quite frequent and certainly understandable at Gallipoli, that of sudden panic. According to the historian Richard Holmes, there are a number of reasons for panic: legitimate action in the face of a disastrous situation; misunderstanding, leading to retreat; blind panic; failure of weapons or meeting up with new weapons; collective panic; a slow dissolution; and helplessness after sitting still under long bombardment.[5] In the case of Gallipoli, there seems to have been one main type of panic – blind, collective panic. Also, there seems to have been a fairly common sequence behind this form of panic: first, preconditions of difficult circumstances; second, and most important, fear of an unknown situation because the panic usually affected a group when that group or unit was *not* in contact with the enemy; third, anonymous shouted warnings that the Turks were attacking the unit ('the Turks are on us'), or anonymous orders to retire; fourth, group or collective panic and rapid retreat, and sometimes, spread of panic to other units (less frequently, an individual would break, but not the unit). For example, an observer described the panic of 13 July at Helles, when 'our men were simply led away by a Major of the battalion line on our right, who came shouting through our lines that we were to retire as the French were about to bombard.' Capt. W.H. Whyte, 6th Battalion, Royal Dublin Fusiliers, remembered that on 8 August at Suvla, a crowd of men 'came rushing through the scrub from [the] N.E.... They were the South Staffordshire battalion yelling 'The Turks are on us." Nearby, the 6th and 7th Platoons of the Royal Dublin Fusiliers also got up and retired, and the remainder of the South Staffordshire battalion also followed them. But there was no sign of the Turks.[6]

Another panic story, also at Suvla, concerns Lt Savory. On 10 August, as the Turks launched a counteroffensive at Sari Bair, Savory was climbing up the Aghyl Dere (gully) with mules, bringing supplies, when:

> a panic-stricken crowd of soldiers, led by an officer with ginger hair and without a hat, came streaming round the corner. He and his men seemed to have thrown away their arms. They were a terrible sight. Screaming and shouting, 'Go back! The Turks are after us!' they tried to pass... I shouted to the officer to stop. He only yelled the louder. 'The Turks are coming. Go back, go back...'. Panic is infectious... something had to be done. I pulled out my pistol and threatened him. He took not the slightest notice, but rushed on. I fired at him and missed. He and his men swept on, down toward the beach. Thank God my own men stood staunch.

Again, there was no sign of the enemy, and so Savory philosophized: 'It is the fear of the Unknown that matters. Most of those who had run, when the panic started, were not at the time engaged directly with the enemy...'.[7] A final group example concerns the Leinster Regiment at Suvla on 11 August. A New Zealand engineer unit was digging trenches, with the Leinsters as cover, when at midnight the Leinsters took fright, fired a volley into the darkness, and rushed back to the working party, which joined the retreat. Then the Wiltshire Regiment came up and fired a volley into the New Zealanders, thinking they were the enemy. Soon after, the Welch Fusiliers came up and also fired another volley into the New Zealanders, wounding fifty or sixty and killing ten others. Here the anxiety brought about by darkness and thus fear of the unknown, was again a key factor, and produced a collective panic.[8]

The French I Division included African troops. These troops, in unfamiliar surroundings, and at night, were susceptible to a similar panic when under pressure. On the night of 3/4 May Turkish attacks caused the Senegalese of 6th Colonial Battalion and the Zouaves of 175th Battalion to bend and break, and flee toward the beach. Maj. Vermusch tried to halt the panic with his revolver and his fists, and it was necessary to put two companies of the Foreign Legion behind them to stiffen their resolve. It seems that the Zouaves continued to have morale problems, and so the French resorted to an old concept – that of the 'amalgames' of the French Revolution. Hence on 21 May 1915, Gen. Gouraud issued the order that the Senegalese and Colonial troops would be split up into mixed battalions with the other French troops. Meanwhile, in order to avoid awkward situations between French and British troops, especially at night, that might also lead to panic and friendly fire, the French command issued orders on 31 May 1915 concerning what to do when the two Allies met. The French should shout out '*halte là*', pronounced in the English style of 'haute.' There should be an immediate halt, with firearms pointed to the ground, then right after, three series of hand claps: 'Pan, pan; Pan, pan; Pan, pan.' Then the head of the unit should approach, and give the password: '*Entente Cordiale*'. It is not clear if this system was properly observed or had the desired effect.[9]

Occasionally, under the influence of direct and stressful events, individuals would panic and retire. A New Zealand soldier, R.J. Speight, noted on 9 August, with astonishment, that his commanding officer got a bullet through the wrist, 'and (very much to my surprise) ran for it.' After the Anzac landing on 26 April, Lt–Col. Malone met an Australian officer 'tearing down the track yelling "Fix bayonets. The Turks are coming."' Malone set up a defensive position with his men, the Turks did not appear, and the panic was then stopped.[10] Another example of individual rather than group panic, occurred at Chunuk Bair. In the most advanced trench were Pte Harry Browne and a very few men of the Wellington Mounted Rifles. On 8 August, reinforcements came up, including an ex-sergeant, named simply as 'A', who did not believe the trench could be held and would not work on improving it. On 9 August, the Turks laid down an artillery barrage, and then attacked with grenades. At this point, 'A' suddenly cried out 'Come on Boys, retire.' Browne and another soldier, Sandy, threatened to kill 'A' if he continued with his actions. Then when a New Zealand counterattack failed, this carried 'A' and others back with them, leaving only four unusually brave men to face the Turks. Here it seems that 'A' had already been predisposed to anxiety, and it was only a matter of time before he would choose a moment of stress to panic and go back.[11]

Much more common than individual panic was simple individual breakdown, normally over a period of time. This was again a completely understandable reaction to the strains of modern warfare, and often this was due to men being too old or unfit. Thus Maj.-Gen. W. Douglas, commanding officer of the 126 Brigade, 42 Division, reported that of his four battalion commanders, one still continued, one had broken down and gone home, and two were invalided out. After the 21 August attack at Suvla, the commander of 86 Brigade broke down and said with tears in his eyes that he did not know war was so ghastly.[12] According to Ian Hamilton, the commander of 88 Brigade was sent home, having collapsed on 4 June, which was a factor in the Helles battle of that day. Hamilton noted that this officer had earlier been sent home from France. During the attack at Chunuk Bair, the commanding officer of the Otago (New Zealand) Battalion foolishly drew up his troops in full view of the Sari Bair heights on 7 August, and his battalion was duly decimated. The commander broke down, 'tears pouring down his cheeks.' In another incident, the New Zealand Infantry Brigade commander was clearly unable to command on 8 August, according to Col. A.C. Temperley, his staff officer.[13] Hence it seems that individual breakdowns were often also due to pre-existing mental or physical conditions of health.

Some officers were sent home from Gallipoli, but many were taken care of in the Lines of Communication staff, or in Egypt, or were sent to

Mudros. This situation was partly due to the fact that the first pick of officers had been sent to France, and thus many at Gallipoli were of lesser calibre. But mainly, this was a striking instance in which some officers, used to a more leisurely existence based on promotion by seniority, found the intensity of modern warfare too difficult to cope with. In these instances, the Army generally reverted to traditional principles, and protected its senior officers.[14] As for the men, there was little choice but to go sick if it was impossible to continue, or to resort to self inflicted wounds, or face disciplinary action. An example of one who had to go sick to survive was Francis Twistleton, Otago Mounted Rifles, who at the end of August took part in the capture of Hill 60. He was on duty for thirty-six hours at a stretch in a fire trench he helped construct:

> In many places the parapet and parados… was built up of dead men, Turks of course; the stench was appalling… I felt as though I could scrape the smell of dead men out of my mouth and throat and stomach in chunks.

Twistleton was forced to report sick although he was not actually sick, but he could keep no food down: 'I seemed to live on the smell of dead men and it was a very hard week.' A rather similar state of affairs of involuntary sickness took place at Helles on 13 July when trenches captured by the Royal Naval Division were full of rotting corpses, hence 'vomiting and sickness very bad.' The next night, 14/15 July, orders could not be carried out because the captured trenches were basically uninhabitable and the men could not carry on.[15]

Prolonged strain could also lead to shell shock, or nervous prostration. The Fleet surgeon of the Royal Naval Division, Arthur Gaskell, already in May 1915 feared the spread of this malady. Quoting from the commander of the Howe Battalion, Gaskell wrote that a small proportion of this Battalion were,

> suffering from nervous prostration. He states that these men have hitherto been able, efficient and courageous but that they have become depressed and frequently give way to attacks of weeping. They are for this reason not only useless but also harmful in depressing the spirits of the men.

The risk was that by appealing to the MO, men with this complaint could be sent 'to a comfortable rest camp. If not carefully guarded against a few such cases will be followed by a big rush of others. I have instilled these views into all the MOs of the Royal Naval Division...'. But in exceptional cases, such as the few in the Howe Battalion, these men should be sent to a rest camp beyond the sound of shell fire, and such a camp should be established at Imbros or a convenient place.[16] Similar arguments were taking place in all other units at Gallipoli, but in most cases the men were allowed to go sick, or were transferred to rear echelons. Yet Allied statistics for shell shock at Gallipoli do not sound excessive for the roughly half million men that served there. No doubt a great many men were not diagnosed for mental stress, but were either misdiagnosed or faced disciplinary action. These statistics show a total of 466 cases in the British and Anzac units and 520 cases in the French units for the campaign. The great majority of cases are listed as Neurasthenia (391 British and Anzac, and 344 French). Other categories were: Traumatic Neurasthenia (ten British and Anzac, and eight French), Hysteria (fifty British and Anzac, but only eleven French), Shock (only fifteen British and Anzac, but 137 French) and Shell Shock (none for the British and Anzacs, but twenty for the French). Obviously, categories were inexact and flexible, and it is curious that the British and Anzacs only acknowledged twenty officers with Neurasthenia, but no officers listed for any of the other categories, while the French listed sixty-five officers with Neurasthenia, but another twenty-five with Shock or Shell Shock.[17]

As far as the men were concerned, outlets for stress included alcohol, malingering, grousing, absence without leave and, at the extreme, self inflicted wounds (SIW). These SIWs were, of course, hard to prove and are now hard to document. Capt. Milward claimed in late August that there were some SIWs, but 'Penalty if caught Death, can't prove it.' However, one specific example does come from the memoirs of Joseph Murray, serving with a mining company at Gallipoli. On 5 June Murray was in a trench with one of his fellow soldiers in the Hood Battalion, nicknamed Tubby. This soldier put his thumb over the muzzle of his rifle and pulled the trigger. Unfortunately, the thumb was still attached, so Murray tried to help him by sawing it off with his sharp jack knife, but this still did not work. By now, Tubby was losing so much blood that Murray 'placed the thumb on the butt of his rifle, inserted the blade, and, with a sharp tap with my fist, the operation was complete.' Tubby explained to Murray that he had done this because 'He was afraid he would have to attack those trenches again and he had the wind up. With tears streaming down his grimy cheeks he pleaded with me not to split on him.' Murray agreed, though angry, and the two concocted the story that just before the attack, someone had fired a rifle as Tubby was climbing out of the trench, and this had taken off his thumb. Tubby was believed, or more likely his officer saw that he would not be much use, and so Tubby was sent to England, and discharged. Murray never heard from him again.[18]

Judging by the reports of the Deputy Judge Advocate on Gallipoli, Capt. Hodgson, few soldiers must have used self inflicted wounds. Indeed, Hodgson only listed three cases of self mutilation up to 3 July 1915. However, as the campaign continued stress increased over time and a new Judge Advocate in October 1915, Capt. Percy, reported that self injury 'is steadily becoming more prevalent.' Nevertheless, under the influence of Ian Hamilton, a lenient and sensible policy was applied to crime and discipline at Gallipoli. Thus nineteen Australian soldiers had been sentenced at Alexandria in March 1915 to three months Field Punishment #1 (being tied to a post or fence for a number of hours per day), but Hamilton reduced this to five weeks in April, which meant immediate release. And while there were eight death sentences at the end of May 1915, Hamilton commuted them all, due to the hardships of the campaign. There were lots of cases of sleeping on duty, but this was due to obvious problems of no rest or sleep. There were also six cases of cowardice by the end of May among the Regulars (i.e. 29 Division), but as Hodgson explained, one had led his platoon in a charge at Seddulbahir and the others, arrested the same night, were willing to carry up ammunition under fire. They all had had no rest for five days, and so their crimes were excused.[19]

The general policy of leniency seems to have worked, for Hodgson remarked at the end of June 1915 that there was not much crime at the front, although drunkenness and robbery were prevalent at Mudros.

Even here there were only four men in prison for theft, and three of them were released on petition. Hodgson noted at the end of July 1915 that the policy of suspending sentences was a good one, as there were very few re-offenders. The exceptions were two Irish men. One was drunk, but this occurred after good conduct for the prior three months. The other exception was more serious, and this individual was condemned to death for neglect of duty. The sentence was carried out at 5.00 a.m. on 2 July 1915. This was the case of Pte T. Davis of the Royal Munster Fusiliers. According to court martial proceedings, Davis had previously been sentenced to be shot in May 1915, and within a week of this sentence being commuted to ten years in prison, Davis reoffended by again being absent from duty, and was then given twenty-eight days Field Punishment #1. Now on 20 June, at 1.00 a.m., Davis was posted as flying sentry at head quarters until 3.00 a.m., but once again, went absent from his duty. The Sergeant in charge had visited the area at 2.30 a.m. and could not find Davis. However, according to Davis's testimony, he had stomach cramps at 2.15 a.m., and spent the remaining 45 minutes of his sentry duty in the latrines. Davis did not cross examine any witnesses, or make any plea for mitigation of his sentence. Strangely enough, neither of the two witnesses (the Sergeant in charge of Davis and a soldier who came on duty at 3.00 a.m.) nor the prosecutor contradicted Davis' story of cramps and latrine, which surely should have been central to the case, since genuine sickness would have been a strongly mitigating factor. Instead the only question asked of the two witnesses was whether Davis had been seen on sentry duty or not. The witnesses were not questioned as to whether Davis had been at his post from 1.00 a.m. to 2.15 a.m., presumably because no one except Davis would have known. Indeed the whole proceeding seems very short and casual, and it may be relevant that the President of this court martial was not of Field rank but only a captain. This was the only death sentence that Hamilton confirmed, and it was obviously carried out because of Davis's previous record.[20]

What was going on in Davis' mind is not clear, and he seems to have been indifferent to his fate. Possibly he was not mentally fit, and he may well have been suffering from dysentery on 20 June, a common complaint. Davis' case was very surprising to Hodgson, who wrote:

He was within a fortnight found guilty of neglecting his duty, and within a month was condemned to death for a second offence of this nature… It is remarkable that a man should have twice within the month after his eleventh hour reprieve committed acts which called for the severest penalty.[21]

The sentences of the other two soldiers who were executed at Gallipoli were both confirmed by Gen. Sir Charles Monro, Commander-in-Chief, Mediterranean Expeditionary Force, late in the campaign. The first was that of Pte Harry Salter, 6th Battalion, East Lancashire Regiment. Salter went absent from his unit on 1 November, at Chocolate Hill, Suvla, and was only apprehended on 11 November at Anzac. Salter was handed over to an escort, Corporal Green, on 16 November at Anzac, but Green got lost on his way to Chocolate Hill in the dark (it was around midnight), and decided to wait on the beach for daylight. Unfortunately, Green fell asleep, and Salter had vanished when Green woke up. On 18 November, Salter was rearrested at Anzac, but managed to escape yet again the same day, before another escort arrived. This time, Salter was recaptured on 19 November, although now he was dressed in Australian uniform. Finally, the resourceful Salter was brought to Battalion Headquarters on 20 November. Salter had nothing to say in his defence at the court martial, and like Davis, had a previous conviction, also for desertion, in August. All Salter's character witnesses were bad – his brigade commander in particular, Lt-Col. O'Dowd, writing that 'His character has no redeeming features, and his persistent efforts to effect his desertion show that he has no intention of serving His Majesty further during the war.' Salter was executed at 7.15 a.m. on 11 December 1915.[22]

It is difficult to explain Salter's actions, but he had evidently decided he could no longer stay in the trenches, and he may have been suffering from shell shock. The third individual executed at Gallipoli was Sergeant Robins. His case is unusual in that his record was good, apart from an alcohol charge in England, and he also held a high NCO rank. Character witness statements were a little suspect, since they had to admit that the battalion (5th Battalion, Wiltshire Regiment) had promoted Robins to the significant rank of Sergeant (twice over, since he had been reduced to Corporal after the alcohol incident in England); but at the same time, also suggest that he was not a good soldier. Robins was charged with not obeying an order by 2nd-Lt J. MacMillan to go out on patrol with him on the evening of 3 December 1915. Robins refused, saying he was not well. MacMillan sent Robins to the medical officer, Lt Thackray, who took his temperature and felt his pulse. These were normal. Robins had no specific complaint, but said he felt unwell. Thackray 'gave him some medicine [unspecified] and told him to carry on.' But Robins again refused to go on patrol, still saying he was not well. The evidence was clear, and Robins did not dispute it, but he made a statement explaining his conduct. Robins said he had served eight and a half years in India and there suffered from fever and ague, and this was his problem on 3 December at Suvla. He had been at Gallipoli nearly five months, and this was his first trouble. Then, before sentencing, the Battalion's acting Adjutant had to admit that he could not produce Robins' record of service form B122 because it had been lost in the recent flood, but that 'to the best of my belief [Robins had] a clean sheet until quite lately.' This was certainly a very casual statement.[23]

Robins was sentenced to death, but the reference to the flood is significant here. At the end of November, storms, floods, and freezing temperatures at Suvla and Anzac created hellish conditions, and caused numerous deaths. This went on for several days. It seems quite likely that Robins, with his earlier health problems, was reacting to this situation. If so, he was an unusually unfortunate victim, since many other soldiers left their posts at this time, and the war was forgotten while the weather took over. Indeed, according to Birdwood, 53 Division left their trenches because of the flood and freezing temperatures, threw down their rifles, went to the hospitals, and nothing could stop them. Why Robins was sentenced to death is not quite clear, his record was good, and his rank spoke of regimental approval. Perhaps his rank told against him, for a barely legible scrawled note by the officer commanding 13 Division, Robins' division, upholding the sentence, stated that Robins' crime was a grave one because on active service, and 'especially when committed by an individual holding the rank of Sergeant…'. Robins' execution was carried out on 1 January 1916, at 8.05 a.m., and the location was carefully detailed as 'a point on the beach 400 yards North of the mouth of the Gully Ravine.'[24]

One other execution occurred on 1 December 1915, that of Pte Downey, 6th Leinster Regiment, for wilful defiance. Downey was actually from Salonika, and a rather chilling comment in the Deputy Judge Advocate's file indicates that Downey was executed because the GOC at Salonika (Monro) wanted this sentence carried out since there was a 'marked tendency toward insubordination… in that command.' Downey was therefore mainly an example to others. The cursory nature of these courts martial are startling, but Gallipoli was actually a relatively safe place to be for those sentenced to death, especially when Hamilton was commanding. Between 25 April and 31 December 1915, 101 men at Gallipoli were sentenced to death, but only three executions were carried out. This is a rate of just under three per cent, while in the British forces generally in the First World War, 3,080 men were sentenced to death, with eleven per cent being carried out.[25] Hamilton's lenient policy continued through his tenure at Gallipoli, so that although there were many cases of sleeping on duty, this was excused because of the hot sun and exhaustion. Also, from 25 July 1915 onward, Field Punishment #1 was suspended on Gallipoli because it exposed men to shell fire, although it was continued on the islands, but only after 6 p.m., because of the heat. During July there were 173 potential court martial cases, 258 in August, mostly men sleeping at their post because of long hours, 307 in September, 427 in November, and 414 in December. This would seem to indicate an increasing frustration with the campaign, probably exacerbated by the weather and increasing sickness, plus the larger size of the Army from July and August. The type of crimes on Gallipoli, via actual British court martial cases up to 3 July 1915, broke down as follows: theft – four; drink – nine; cowardice – twelve; sleeping at post – eighteen; self mutilation – three; and leaving post or absent without leave – fourteen. Up until early July, therefore, there does not seem to have been much dissatisfaction with conditions.[26]

However, beneath the level of officially noted crimes, there did lie a sub-stratum of means by which the men might deal with the strain of war. These could include avoiding the front line by hiding, straggling, malingering, and grousing. Officers would normally try to overlook these problems, and if forced to action, would try to handle problems within their units. For example, Orlo Williams, the cipher officer at GHQ, who inevitably gathered a good deal of information, recorded that on the second night at V Beach, 26/27 April, according to Capt. Richard Neave of the 1st Battalion, Essex Regiment, officers of this battalion in 29 Division had to go up and down with revolvers to keep their men in the trenches. The V Beach people thought that (General Staff) Operations had done a poor job in choosing V Beach, and claimed there was no proper organization.[27] This situation was dealt with by the battalion itself, and in the later stages of the campaign, the situation at Suvla, for example, was so chaotic that nothing could be done about men refusing to attack or men hiding in gullies and undergrowth. Capt. Drury, Royal Dublin Fusiliers, wrote that on 9 August he went around the scrub near Ismail Oglu Tepe at Suvla, and found parties of men who had reached the end of their tether and were hiding.[28]

Although Drury was critical of such men, the lack of organization and leadership at Suvla, plus the stress of conditions for newly arrived and poorly prepared soldiers, produced these reactions. Another word was also used to describe those who drifted back to the beaches, or left the front lines, without permission or reason to do so, and this was 'straggling'. A considerable amount of this took place at Anzac in the late afternoon and evening of 25 April, and has been described in Chapter Four.[29] But straggling took place at other beaches too, for example, at W Beach, on 25 April.[30] The forces at X Beach also allegedly nearly withdrew because they believed they were vulnerable on the night of 25 April.[31] Of course, the forces at Y Beach did withdraw – a form of authorized straggling – and inland from V Beach on 1 May, 'Several men of Y Company, 1st Royal Munster Fusiliers who were driven back from their trenches, were arrested in rear.' These men were 'arrested for being behind the firing line', and were sent for court martial.[32] Straggling occurred in all armies, not only at Gallipoli, and represented one way that men survived critical situations without actually deserting or refusing to fight.

Besides straggling, another word was invented to describe those who avoided duty – malingerers. Strictly speaking this indicated men who feigned sickness in order to avoid duty. Thus Pte F.E. McKenzie was invalided to Malta with dysentery and exhaustion in August. After recovering there, he noted in his diary for 20 September that he wanted to get away from convalescent camp because there were 'Malingerers everywhere.'[33] In August at Anzac, a New Zealand soldier was wounded and spent some time in a hospital ship. He remarked in his diary that only those with courage hang on, while all the wasters got sent away sick, 'and don't we know them all.' Again, Pte McKenzie noted in his diary that when he got typhoid, he came across two of his officers not playing the game in Cairo, 'while we do their work and they draw our pay.' Then, an officer in 13 Division claimed there were lots of malingerers in the 6th Royal Irish Rifles and the 6th Wiltshires, both being 'hopelessly demoralised after the early attack of 10 August 1915.'[34] Maj.-Gen. Godley at Anzac thought medical officers were evacuating men too easily. The men were bored with fatigue work in the heat, this being the end of July, but their health was 'really very good.' Godley was clearly out of touch with conditions, because that very week Birdwood, also at Anzac, remarked that he had only just realized the strain on the men. Later, in October, Godley, perhaps hearing from his wife, declared there was too much drink and fornication in Cairo, so the men should go straight to Mudros, where the climate was bracing, and there were 'no temptations.'[35]

In contrast, Lt-Col. Fenwick, the DADMS for the Anzac Division, recorded what must have been the normal situation for the men. It was not malingering, but the exact opposite – soldiers were too busy to go sick. On 6 May Fenwick recorded that only 21 men of the division went sick over the last seven days, this 'shows how few men have time to get sick…'. When it was necessary to go for a rest, most would echo the words of New Zealander Clutha McKenzie, 6th Manawatu Rifles, that he would do so, but would 'much prefer being in the trenches.'[36] If the soldiers did not have time for sickness, there were always the harmless time-honoured method of grousing and complaining. Examples are too numerous to mention, so one typical comment must suffice. R.J. Speight, on 8 August, after many hours moving up gullies, tired and short of water, was still required to dig a trench: 'We were all just about beat, and growled a bit…'.[37]

In fact, the resilience of officers and men at Gallipoli was astonishing. Prolonged shelling, especially at Anzac, was endured by adapting to an underground existence, learning how to take cover quickly, and applying humour to the situation. Hence, Lt Colvin Algie at Anzac, wrote on 23 May 1915 that he had settled down 'to this rabbit's existence in holes in the ground. Nevertheless, it is the only safe guard against shrapnel.' Another New Zealander also took up the 'men as rabbits' theme: 'the instant they [the shells] started to come we took to earth like rabbits bolting to their holes and no damage was done.' Still another soldier resented being forced to be 'savages or rabbits living in burrows.'[38] Lt-Col. Fenwick spent much time in his diary describing the shrapnel shelling, which, being on the beach at Anzac, he had to endure every day. His anxiety was that shrapnel was very indiscriminate in its effect. Hence on 5 May Fenwick noted 'it is like Hell let loose. One never knows who will be the next to go.' Death is quick here, wrote Fenwick, one is taken and the other left – just a question of providence. On 18 May Fenwick discussed the characteristics of shrapnel. At a certain height, shrapnel covers 30 square yards, but on the ground, about a cricket pitch: 'Spent bullets sound so pretty, just like a bird flying slowly over. Bullets from near range swish and ping like a wasp.' By mid-June, Fenwick had built a wall of sandbags, so the shrapnel would be 'less dangerous.' Fenwick wrote of shrapnel frequently in his diary, and evidently became preoccupied with the daily shelling, which mostly arrived at the evening dinner hour. But he stuck it out and survived until typhoid forced his evacuation in late June. Humour was another defence mechanism, as one of the soldiers tried to adapt – 'I heard tell as how one can make a pet of anything, but I'm blowed if I can make a pet of this blooming shrapnel.' In another darkly amusing episode, Lt-Col. Malone reported on 29 April that a bullet cut the hair on the back of his neck, so the next morning he got his hair cut short by the barber![39]

Similar stories of survival under daily shelling comes from Maj. John Gillam, Army Service Corps, whose job required him to spend much time on the beaches at Helles. Gillam's diary for 13 May records of shelling that:

> The first thing one hears is a noise like the rending of linen, or perhaps the rush of steam… This gets louder and louder, and then… one hears a whine, half whistle, half scream, and then the explosion. If it is very near there is an acrid smell in the air… You duck your head instinctively – you feel absolutely helpless… and as you hear the explosion a quick wave of feeling sweeps over you as you murmur, 'Thank Heaven, not this time.'

Normally, Gillam, Fenwick and others who had daily doses of shelling developed a system of diving for cover, wherever they happened to be, often when a warning whistle went off. Gillam found that hay bales were a good safety barrier, and used them often. But the strain on the nerves was continuous and severe. At Helles, Gillam remarked that 'the continual exposure to high explosive shell [rather than shrapnel at Anzac] is wearing on the nerves, and cases of nervous breakdown here are becoming more and more frequent.' Gillam went sick at one point, and then returned to describe a near miss on 31 July:

> A deafening explosion and dense smoke, dust, and stones, and I find myself locked in the arms of a transport driver with my face buried in the stomach of a fat sergeant, and mules kicking all round. Not a man hit and the shell five yards away. The nearest I have ever had… I look up, and all the others get sheepishly to their feet, and I get out another cigarette… I smoked six of them hard, and tried to… pretend that I did not care…

Despite this, Gillam found the front line troops cheerful: 'For optimists, go to the front line trenches – or the Navy – and for pessimists, go to overworked administrative officers.'[40]

Maj. Gillam survived, and served out the campaign to the bitter end, evacuating Gallipoli with his unit on 8 January. Regardless of the stresses and strains of the campaign, the very great majority of officers and men performed their duties with astonishing bravery and endurance. Were there any rewards for this magnificent effort? The obvious place to look is medals and commendations. As Richard Holmes argues, the question of decorations (an interesting word) generated more discussion than any other topic among officers. There was a curious divide between the accepted public show of indifference by officers on the subject of receiving medals, and the strong private desire for such rewards. Yet the unfair distribution of medals was well known.[41] In this context, one of the fiercest exchange of letters took place in 1916 on the subject of medals for the Navy, who felt that they had been badly let down in not getting enough decorations, compared to the Army. According to Roger Keyes, there was an established convention for the awarding of honours, one medal and one mention in despatches for every 600 men engaged. In regard to the evacuation of Gallipoli, Keyes stated there should be similar awards for every 1,600 men involved. This was easier to compute for the Army than the Navy, claimed Keyes, and so the Army did much better than the Navy in getting awards. Keyes complained to the Admiralty, citing the fact that Military Crosses had been awarded to the chief baker at Rouen, and also to the chaplain at Rouen, who organized concerts, while the Navy was short changed in the Eastern Mediterranean, especially the staff. As Keyes wrote: 'it really means a good deal to so many good fellows…'.[42]

While the Navy complained about their share of the rewards, there were also numerous heroic acts that went unrewarded. Just one example of many must suffice: Pte Wilkin of the 7th Battalion, Royal Dublin Fusiliers, at Kiretch Tepe on 15/16 August, bravely defended his position against a rain of Turkish bombs. He attempted to catch the bombs and throw them back, and 'caught four but [the] fifth unfortunately blew him to pieces.' Yet Wilkin's officer noted there was no recognition for him. Let this short paragraph therefore be Pte Wilkin's only recognition. Inevitably, many others were also not recognized. For example, at the headquarters of 30 Brigade, Brigadier-General Nicol complained: 'Every one of my recommendations for recognition in the Brigade was quashed [by Gen. de Lisle] and not one soul was mentioned.'[43] The previously mentioned New Zealand medical officer, Fenwick, also wrote rather bitterly at the end of May 1915 that it was

1 *Left:* Portrait of
Maj. Hugh Price Travers.

2 *Below:* Maj. Hugh
Price Travers' grave site,
Hill 10 cemetery,
Gallipoli.

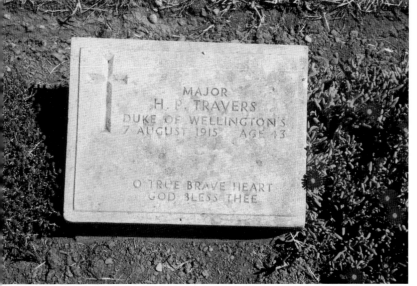

3 Gen. Sir Ian Hamilton, Commander-in-Chief of the Mediterranean Expeditionary Force, outside his command hut on the island of Imbros. Hamilton's body language reveals something of his intelligent but less than ruthless character.

4 *Left:* Portrait of Liman von Sanders, Turkish Fifth Army commander.

5 *Right:* Maj.-Gen. Hunter-Weston, commanding VIII Corps, outside his corps head-quarters on Gallipoli. Indications of his eccentric personality can be seen in his stance.

6 Turkish battery commander Hilmi Bey and lieutenant Fahri stand beside their cannon which, according to Turkish sources, supposedly sank the Bouvet on 18 March. Later, the Turks ascertained that the Bouvet hit a mine.

7 Left to right: Admiral Guido von Usedom, German Commander of the Straits; the German Captain Merten; the Turkish Colonel Djevad Pasa, Commander of the Straits Forts.

8 Turkish cannon preparing to fire during the attempt by the Allied fleet to pass through the Straits on 18 March. As with many Turkish artillery pieces, this cannon remains undamaged by Allied naval fire.

9 *Above:* A crowded trawler carries the 6th Lancashire Fusiliers of 42 Division from the SS *Nile* toward one of the beaches. The picture was taken some time in May 1915.

10 *Left:* The pier at W Beach under Turkish shell fire some time after the landings. Ammunition carts and their horses wait for the shelling to cease before proceeding. A light railway runs around the beach, and a pile of sandbags offers protection on the left.

11 *Below left:* Morto Bay, or S Beach, showing why British troops found this a relatively easy beach to land on.

12 V Beach at Cape Helles, taken from the western headland, with V Beach cemetery in the centre and Fort Seddulbahir in the background. The small ridge behind which the British troops were able to shelter is seen a few yards inland from the water's edge. This was crucial to their survival.

13 The view from the heights above Anzac Cove, showing how difficult it was for the Anzacs to advance uphill, and how easy it was to get lost in the unnamed gullies and valleys.

14 Anzac Cove looking north, with the point known as the Sphinx quite visible above the plateau. The road was a post-war construction.

15 *Above:* Anzac Cove looking south, with Hell Spit Point in the background.

16 *Left:* Mustafa Kemal and his soldiers in a well-fortified trench. Kemal is facing the camera at the far end, with his hands on his binoculars. Note the imam, second from right, who normally accompanied the troops.

17 Unidentified officer at Anzac. The photograph shows the steep nature of the ground and the living quarters dug in to the side of the hill.

18 Turkish soldiers defend a trench in the Anzac sector. Note the well-constructed trench, fire step and sandbags.

19 Some of the dead shown during the truce of 24 May at Anzac, prior to their burial. The figures had begun to bloat, decompose and smell, and the flies attracted to their bodies were leading to medical problems.

20 *Left:* A few Anzac soldiers are taking identification from bodies before burial, during the 24 May truce. The usual debris of war covers the ground, including a stretcher and a rifle.

21 *Below left:* Turkish field artillery in action. The officer standing shows that the enemy must be some distance away.

22 *Below:* Landing horses at V Beach, a photograph taken from the River Clyde. In the background a busy tent city has sprung up, with horses and men everywhere. The scene reveals the logistical demands of the campaign.

٧٨

آرده بوشنه أكله لردا اغنام أوتساذ نذ البر طرخهود
استعملى هطوكسه

23 *Above:* A captured Allied machine-gun. This is a Vickers gun with a belt full of ammunition.

24 *Left:* Three Turkish soldiers who captured an Allied machine-gun. They are, from left to right: Sgt Ismail; Cpl Sukru; Soldier Huseyin.

25 *Left:* A volunteer
bombardier. This Turkish
soldier looks very young but
determined. He wears the
usual 1909 green uniform,
with the enverieh helmet
(so-called because it was
designed by Enver Pasa),
jacket, breeches and khaki
puttees. The shoes are not
regulation issue and he lacks
the normal belt.

26 *Below:* Turkish heavy
machine-gunners in action.
The soldiers disguise
themselves with brush on
their helmets and on the gun.
The soldier on the right has
two stick bombs dangling
from his belt.

27 Anzac staff officers and commanders: on the left with the stick is Maj.-Gen. H.B. Walker, commanding 1 Australian Division, Gen. Birdwood is sitting, and on the right is Maj. C.M. Wagstaff.

28 Esat Pasa, commander of Turkish III Corps, sits at his table, surrounded by his serious-looking staff. Esat Pasa played a key role in the northern sector. His HQ is well camouflaged, but obviously located at a high point.

29 Turkish troops in a well-sandbagged trench at Anzac, facing the Australians. One keeps watch, another is asleep, and the remaining three stay alert with their rifles on their knees.

30 A view of Suvla Bay in the far distance and the Salt lake inland on the right. The picture was taken from Chunuk Bair looking north.

31 Suvla Point, at the end of Suvla Bay. The Kiretch Tepe ridge starts at the top right edge of the photograph.

32 Attacks by Allied submarines during the campaign made the conveyance of war material by sea a dangerous proposition, so the Turks improvised with overland methods such as this ox train. Trench or housing material is waiting to be transported in the foreground.

33 The German Captain (Hauptmann) Lehmann, on the far left, commanding a Turkish artillery unit, accompanied by a useful staff – one man uses a range finder; another studies a map.

34 Cpl Musticep (marked with a cross), who destroyed a French submarine with his artillery piece. This was probably the *Mariotte*, which tried to get through the Straits on 26 July 1915 but was fouled by an obstruction near the Chanak batteries and forced to surface. The captain and crew were made prisoners.

35 *Right:* An Australian soldier, right, using a periscope rifle. His spotter is on the left with a periscope. The periscope rifle was invented by the Australians, with the obvious objective of being able to fire accurately from a trench without exposing oneself to risk.

36 *Below:* Men bathing off Cape Helles. This was a vital way for the troops to refresh themselves and stay healthy, though the danger of Turkish shelling was ever present. On top of the cliff are medical tents, marked with a red cross. These red cross areas were usually respected by the Turks.

37 *Top left:* A typical Anzac trench, with Australian soldiers taking the chance to sleep. Rifles and packs are set neatly aside, and the rifles have mud guards protecting the vulnerable bolt and trigger mechanisms.

38 *Top right:* Inside a narrow and heavily sandbagged Anzac trench. The officer holding up his stick is Maj.-Gen. H.B. Walker, while the closer figure is Gen. Birdwood. On the right is one of the new latrines made from a biscuit box. This system improved the sanitation at Anzac.

39 *Above:* Another view of the beach at Anzac. The usual packing cases and debris of war litter the cove. A number of small piers have been built to allow the unloading of stores and men.

40 *Above:* Mustafa Kemal, with binoculars and outstretched arm, explains the situation to a group of parliamentary deputies. Second from left is Maj. Izzettin Calislar. The battlefield Kemal is describing is the northern area (Anzac to Suvla) and the date is 14 October 1915.

41 *Left: A* group of unidentified Turkish officers. Their strength of purpose comes through in the picture, reflecting Birdwood's argument to the Dardanelles Commission about the Turks being too strong for the Allies.

42 *Below left:* Some of the capable German and Turkish officers that took part in the Gallipoli campaign. First row, sitting from left: Hayder Alkan, Hulusi Bey, Nazim Bey and unknown. Standing behind the sitting group, from left: Rustu Bey, Mustafa Kemal and Esat Pasa. Behind are three officers, standing from left: Maj. Willmer, unknown and Col. Kannengiesser. Behind these are Kemal Ohri Bey, Fahrettin Bey and peering between is Izzettin Calislar Bey. The back two are unknown. Australian War Memorial negative AO 5296.

already known who was to get decorations and Mentions in Despatches, but in any case the despised colonials did not care about such things.[44]

It turned out, however, that at the senior army levels there was much internal competition for rewards. Thus, Godley was disturbed to learn at the end of October 1915 that Hamilton could not get him a KCB (Knight Commander of the Bath) until January 1916. Birdwood consoled Godley that there was great indignation that Godley had not got a KCB in the last Gazette – 'very sorry indeed…', since Birdwood wanted to get all his people 'recognised'. But even in January, Godley did not get his KCB, and Ian Hamilton expressed himself as 'bitterly disappointed…'. However, all was well, for later in 1916 Godley did get his KCB, and was congratulated by Birdwood for it, although Birdwood also complained that because the Lords of the Admiralty wouldn't give de Robeck a baronetcy for the successful Gallipoli evacuation, so Birdwood's name had to be cut out too. Then in what can only be seen as hypocrisy, Godley admonished Maj. Johnston in December 1915 for complaining about not getting honours, and only being made a Brevet [i.e. temporary] Lt-Col. instead of getting a CB (Commander of the Bath). Godley wrote blandly that the aim of every officer should be promotion and not decorations. Your officers, claimed Godley, seemed to look upon honours as a right, and feel a grievance if they did not get them. Still, Godley obviously recognized that they were all part of a system of liberal distribution of decorations for officers, and especially senior officers, and so he promised Johnston that honours and rewards would be forthcoming in the Despatch describing the August 1915 fighting.[45]

Perhaps the most unusual case of the awarding of a medal concerned an officer in the 8th Battalion, Northumberland Fusiliers, whom one may call Captain X. According to Gameson Lane, a brother officer in the same unit, on 9 August, at Suvla, at 6.00 a.m., Captain X:

> gave the order to dig for cover in a ploughed field. He deliberately lost touch with the rest and whilst Passy, Tyrell and Atkins were later fighting, as we should have been, in the front line, Captain X was well dug in, employing half a dozen men in relays with the only shovel available. For

22 hours we lay there whilst the other Battalions passed through us, Captain X point blank refusing to move an inch. At about 4 a.m. on the 10th [August] we moved a few hundred yards to the left…

Then the Turks attacked, and Captain X was not seen again until 6.00 p.m., when he was located hiding in a 'donga', a dry ravine or stream bed. But by 19 August, only two unwounded officers of this battalion remained, one, not surprisingly, being Captain X and the other, the medical officer. Strangely, Captain X escaped detection, reprimand or court martial, perhaps because there was no one left to report on his activities. Again, undoubtedly because there was no one else left to give decorations to, Captain X was awarded the DSO (Distinguished Service Order) for his work at Suvla. After the war Captain X went on to command a regiment in India.[46]

Another potentially dubious award apparently went to the civilian captain of the hay supply ship *East Point*. This captain was discovered by Capt. Unwin, the hero of V Beach, to have been awarded the DSC (Distinguished Service Cross) for his work off Suvla. But Unwin alleged that he discovered this captain hiding behind some boxes on board his ship, admitting that he could not stand shell fire, and doing nothing to put out a hay fire on board his ship. Unwin took over, and organized putting out the fire. Unwin told the Admiralty that this decoration was unjustly awarded and should be rescinded. It seems that the award stood, and de Robeck simply remarked that Unwin had a quick temper.[47]

Decorations were awarded for fighting against the enemy. But what did the Allies think of their enemy, the Turks? Initially, there was suspicion and dislike, even hatred, because of the constant and unpredictable sniping and for what was seen as treachery via 'white flag' tricks. On 12 May, Maj. Coe gave vent to his suspicions, thinking that some Germans were in the Allied trenches, acting as spies, while the Turks were the lowest of the low, using dirty tricks. Unless the case was very much out of the ordinary, wrote Coe, 'I would not make a Turk a prisoner.' No doubt there is a relationship between stress, a new situation, and a paranoid attitude toward the enemy. Hence, there was widespread shooting of snipers who were caught. According to Pte McKenzie, snipers got short shrift;

they also wore Allied uniforms, and there were many Germans amongst them. Percy Doherty, 8th Canterbury Mounted Rifles, similarly remarked that when snipers were caught, they were then generally shot. Strangely, but almost certainly erroneously, this source reported that several women snipers were also caught.[48] Snipers were assumed to be without morality, so that Fenwick was told on 30 April to take the red cross off their hospital tent, since it was a good target for snipers. Sometimes more lurid stories emerged, for example, the Royal Munster Fusiliers machine-gun company said that their platoon sergeant had been caught by the Turks on 25 April, doused and set on fire, and displayed on the rampart. Also 'False orders originating from [the] enemy were continually being passed down [the] line.'[49] It is extraordinary how frequent are references at Anzac to Turkish 'white flag' tricks, and other ruses. This may well have happened, but may also relate to the belief at the time that the Anzacs advanced too far on 25 April, and ran into Turkish traps and ambushes. Or there may simply have been anxiety about an unknown enemy. Hence, Sergeant Chadwick, with the 1st New Zealand Field Ambulance, wrote in his diary on 25 April of Turkish 'white flag' tricks and then, on 29 April, claimed that the Turks pretended to be Indians, carried machine-guns on stretchers and blew retreat on their bugles.[50] Similarly, Lt Colvin Algie remarked that the Turks pretended to be Indians and tried to work the 'white flag' business, but were ignored.[51] Such was the prevalence of these stories that on 26 April an official order was passed along the ranks to ignore the Turkish 'White Flag' efforts.[52]

Lt-Col. W.G. Braithwaite, Anzac Division, even wrote in the war diary that the Turks had three tricks: they shouted out that MacLagan's 3rd Brigade was to retire; shouted that they were a British division advancing; and called out that they were French, 'and danced about shouting.' However, as the campaign went on, a reluctant admiration for the Turks grew. Even Turkish snipers came to be seen as daring and imaginative. According to one source, the Turkish snipers got so daring that one was caught helping British soldiers draw water from a well, while another was only 50 yards from a howitzer. Moreover, the Turks did not shell hospitals or Red Cross areas, unless headquarters or ammunition dumps were nearby.[53] In a strange juxtaposition, Tpr

Hobson remarked on 20 May that the enemy tried white flag schemes, so caution was required, but the very next day he acknowledged that the enemy were fearless and first-class fighters.[54] By and large, the Allies came to think of the Turks as good fighters who would play the game fair. Part of the change in attitude toward the Turks came about because of the 24 May truce at Anzac, to bury the dead of both armies, which lessened the hate between the two sides.[55] Other unofficial armistices took place, for example, on 20 August, when there was an 'Armistice with Turks who brought in 5 W[ounded] of 8/5th [5th Dorsetshire Regiment].' In Joseph Murray's memoirs, a strange incident produced another unofficial armistice on 21 December when, in the Gully area at Helles, a Turk and an Irishman got involved in a bayonet fight in No Man's Land after a Turkish attack. They fought until both were kneeling, exhausted, then:

> we moved forward to collect our man and the Turks did likewise. We were within arm's length of each other but no one spoke… Both parties turned and walked slowly away to their respective trenches. Not a shot was fired from either line even though there were at least a dozen men ambling about at point-blank range.[56]

Apart from such encounters, the only other way the two sides got to know each other was as prisoners of war. Becoming a prisoner of war was obviously not an option that happened easily or safely. There were few Allied prisoners of war, and it was widely believed that the Turks shot or bayonetted both wounded and unwounded prisoners. This belief is reflected in a leaflet issued by Salim Bey Ciftligi, commanding Turkish forces at Helles in June 1915. The leaflet reads, in poor English:

> We hear from prisoners we made lately, that your officers try to make you believe that we Turks kill and massacre our prisoners. Not just the international law, but also our religion as well tell us to treat prisoners and wounded kindly. Be sure English soldiers, that we will receive every single man of you who come to us friendly, that he will return safely home to wife and child.[57]

An investigation of one well-known incident, the disappearance of four-teen officers and 142 men of the 1/5 Norfolk Battalion of 163 Brigade during an attack on 12 August 1915, suggests that the Turks looked after wounded prisoners of war but may have bayonetted unwounded prison-ers of war. During this attack, Maj. Munib, commanding the Turkish force that opposed the 1/5 Norfolks, reported that thirty-five prisoners were taken and that they were all wounded. The Turkish Official History relates simply that the attacking forces of 163 Brigade were all bayonet-ted, without differentiating between prisoners, wounded or those killed in the fighting. A relatively neutral account comes from Capt. Carl Mühlmann, ADC to Liman von Sanders, who wrote in May/June 1915 that 'We do not take many prisoners because the war basically consists of a frontal push, and in the bayonet fight the Turks almost always fatally injure the opponent.'[58]

One who believed the worst of the Turks was Lt John Still, 6th East Yorkshire Regiment. He was captured early on 9 August as his battalion tried to take the Tekke Tepe heights. According to Still, of the three others that were captured with him, one was unharmed, one was beaten and fired at, and the Colonel was bayonetted. Still was hit over the head with a sword at one point, but not otherwise harmed. However, at the point of capture, Still described how a Turkish officer took out his pistol and was about to shoot them when 'an Imam with a turban on… wrestled with him [the officer] and took his pistol away.' Still was then interviewed by Liman von Sanders, who told him that International Law no longer existed, and one of Sanders' German staff said 'they found it almost impossible to get the Turks to take prisoners, or, having taken them, to keep them alive.' Still claimed that of 700 Allied officers and 11,000 men reported missing at Gallipoli, most of whom would have been killed in battle, only 17 officers and 400 men were taken prisoner.[59] However, a dif-ferent record of John Still's interrogation by the Turks exists. As might be expected, Still gives a very different impression in this record. After giving sketchy details of his English address, enlistment, and travels to Suvla, Still said that he was captured at Tekke Tepe early on 9 August, but had no complaints against his captors: 'Really, they [the Turks] treated me well, and I knew that they would do so.'[60] In contrast, in his post-war book, Still exhibits a strong Social Darwinism that tends to undercut his value as an objective observer of Turkish behaviour. According to Still, a wounded soldier 'has about as much chance with the Turks as he would have with a pack of wolves.' This was because a good Turk was as rare as rubies, despite the fact that one Turk, although a violent Moslem, had sent a telegram to Still's wife and another, at Still's surrender, had handed back his wallet with five gold sovereigns in it. However, Still resented being ordered to the rear when captured, although this was for his safety, because 'An order from an Asiatic… is a strange experience. I disliked it.' Still believed that the Ottoman empire produced 'cruelty and unnaturally debased races…', and could only have been run efficiently by non-Turkish groups such as Greeks, Armenians, Jews, slaves or other 'half-breeds and poly-breeds.' On the other hand, the German allies of the Turks were acceptable because they were white men in an Eastern Land.[61]

Still's observations are contradicted by the experience of a fellow officer on 9 August, Capt. Elliott, who was captured at the same time and place as Still. In his interrogation, Elliott remarked that his Turkish captors had the chance to kill him, 'but on the contrary they spared my life. I am especially grateful.'[62] Perhaps the strangest experience was that of Lt Fawkes, of the 1/5 Norfolks. His story also contradicts the Turkish treatment that Still describes, but since Fawkes was wounded when captured, supports the idea of wounded prisoners being preserved and looked after. Fawkes was captured on 12 August at Karakol Dagh, Suvla. According to his interrogation, Fawkes and the 1/5 Norfolks engaged in a fierce fire fight with the Turks, which destroyed his unit. Fawkes was left alive with his Sergeant, Varley, and Fawkes ordered Varley to advance with him for another 100 yards. Then Varley fell, but Fawkes continued on by himself. Then Fawkes also fell, shot in the chest. When he came to, the stars were shining, and the Turks were carrying him. He again lost consciousness, and this time when he came to, he was in a Turkish trench, apparently built into a parapet of sandbags, with a Turk resting his rifle on Fawkes' head. According to Fawkes' interrogation, he then tried to seize the trench, but in another account, he says he simply 'flapped about a bit…' Despite this provocation, the Turks still did not kill him, but gave him food and water, and carried him on their shoulders to the hospital.

Fawkes said that he was grateful for all the help the Turks had given him, and if he had a chance to return to England, he would mention their kind behaviour. Fawkes promised this on his honour.[63] It is not known if Fawkes kept this promise.

Both sides shot or bayonetted their prisoners of war on occasion, and whether the Turks were worse in this regard is hard to evaluate. Probably they were, apart from their preservation of wounded Allied prisoners of war. A recent book details Anzac prisoners who were bayonetted to death, or beaten with rifle butts, or kicked, while one prisoner was even beaten unconscious with a large rock. However, on the Allied side, Birdwood asked one of his brigades at Anzac why there were so few prisoners of war in this brigade. The staff answered that they had a large number, but a heavy Turkish counterattack 'made them feel they could not afford to keep men as prisoners… the Gordons who were on their right, had scruples of the same sort, so they were all polished off! I'm afraid I could only sympathise with them.'[64] But the Allies did capture a number of Turkish soldiers, and also received a number of Turkish deserters, and their stories give a sense of the Turkish experience at Gallipoli. In a parallel to Still's view of Turkish attitudes to Allied prisoners, one deserter claimed that Turkish soldiers would like to desert in larger numbers, but 'have been told that the British shoot their prisoners…'. Another Turkish prisoner claimed that rewards were given to Turkish soldiers, of 1/- for a rifle, 10/- for a machine-gun, and 20/- for a prisoner, although a man who shot a British sergeant got 2/-. If true, this would indicate prisoners were more valuable to the Turks than dead Allied soldiers. Most Turkish deserters initially cited bad treatment from their own officers. For example one prisoner of war claimed the officers had driven the troops on at sword point 'and showed marks on his legs where a Turkish officer had been stabbing him to make him go on.' Then, as the campaign dragged on, and as the weather deteriorated, deserter stories emphasized being fed up with the war, dislike at fighting for the Germans, poor living conditions, cold and hunger, and lack of proper clothing. Also, many deserters were from non-Turkish ethnic groups, mainly Arabs, Greeks and Armenians.[65]

Typical of the complaints of Turkish prisoners/deserters was that of Hakki Mustafa, 126 Regiment, who surrendered on 12 October 1915: 'He himself was so tired of being continually bullied by his officers and so dissatisfied with the bad treatment he had lately received in hospital, that he made up his mind to risk everything and surrender…'. An unusual case concerned a man from the Turkish 28 Regiment who deserted to VIII Corps on 11 November 1915. This man claimed his corporal had a grudge against him because he refused to give the corporal money. Then a shell burst tore off the top of his forefinger. He was accused of self mutilation, and marched off to the hospital by the corporal. There, the doctor was too busy, so the corporal cut off the damaged joint himself. Then he was marched in front of the regimental commander, who gave him fifty blows with a stick. Predictably, this man deserted as soon as he could. In December, Selim Mahomet deserted because 'he was tired of the conditions, i.e. bad food, soup consisting of hot water, no rice, 1,000 to 1 chance of getting any meat.' Pte Theodore, 17th Regiment, came in on 9 October because he was a Greek from Keshan, 'and was always looked upon with contempt by the Turks, who always called him 'Giour' (unbeliever).' Another reason was that supplies were short, and the Greeks in the regiment were always subject to heavy manual labour. Theodore apparently hid in his village when called up in 1914, but was discovered in March 1915 and conscripted. In addition, some Turkish regiments and divisions supplied a particularly high number of deserters, particularly 17 Regiment and 34 Regiment, where low morale and bad treatment seemed to prevail.[66]

Despite their stories, which may have been tailored to the expectations of their captors, Turkish desertions were actually fairly low. A number of Turkish deserters were reported by IX Corps at Suvla in August, i.e. 19 on 13 August, 22 on 16 August and 17 on 17 August, but thereafter the numbers dropped off, and soon became one or two per day. Meanwhile, in regard to Turkish prisoners of war, the number captured at Anzac up to 10 July 1915 was 117, with 985 captured at Helles by the British, and 238 by the French.[67] It is impossible to tell how many of these might have been deserters. However, given what appeared to be much tougher living and food conditions on the Turkish side, poor treatment by Turkish and German officers, and ethnic dissatisfaction by non-Turks, the Turkish desertion rate does not seem especially high. On the other hand, desertion may not have been a very safe option. According to Clutha McKenzie, who conversed in limited fashion with Turkish soldiers during the ceasefire of 24 May:

Many of the Turks expressed a wish to surrender to us but of course the conditions of armistice do not permit of deserters being accepted during its existence. They can't come across to us in the day time as their own side would shoot them, and if they approached us at night, they would meet a similar fate from us. So they find it difficult to desert.

However, in the French sector, at Kereves Dere, on 13 July, some 200 Turkish troops did desert, and this was because they were Greeks enrolled against their will, but also because their officers had been killed or wounded, and this made it safe to desert, which, according to the French, they did 'with joy.'[68]

Desertion was therefore not an easy option for the Turks, and according to the historian Niall Ferguson, this option was not safe for any soldier on the Western Front either. However, for those Turks that did become Allied prisoners of war, one area of their service that caused complaint was the indifferent Turkish medical service. There was poor treatment in hospital, apparently unpleasant medical officers, and an evacuation system as poor as that of the Allies. Early in the campaign, on 28 April, the German staff officer, Capt. Carl Mühlmann, wrote of seeing:

many, many wounded, in part wandering the streets [of Maidos], in part carried from the battlefield at Ari Burnu to the field hospital over cobblestones on rigid two-wheel carts… no moaning and groaning; no complaining; the troops bore their sufferings in manly fashion. Naturally, the field hospital is much too small for the masses of wounded.

Then Mühlmann headed towards Krithia and soon met Turkish wounded streaming in from Helles 'most with hand or foot wounds;

any and all medical services were missing, so that the poor wounded had covered the 20 kilometres… alone on their way to the hospital at Maidos.' A Turkish member of the medical corps later recalled that at the hospital in Canakkale, many cases were suffering from dysentery, as in the Allied army, and the diet for all was a bowl of rice and some meat. Water was a problem for the Turks as well as for the Allies, and this soldier saw Turkish soldiers drinking from puddles on the ground, the unfortunate result being leeches stuck in their throats.[69]

Medical evacuation was as great a problem for the Turks as for the Allies. A poem written by a Turkish soldier who was wounded on 19 May tells a harrowing tale of his journey to hospital. This soldier was wounded in eight places at Anzac during the big Turkish night attack of that date. He managed to crawl back to the Turkish trenches over a period of three hours and then, after another few hours, he was put on the back of a soldier who took him to the divisional gathering point for wounded, and put in a tent filled with straw. Here he appeared to get no treatment. In the evening, medics placed the wounded on horse carts, 'one on top of another, Like empty wheat bags… Ten, fifteen wounded on a cart. Some cry out, Some die that minute… The roads of Ari Burnu are bumpy.' By the next morning they had arrived at the pier, ready to tranship to Istanbul.

> Someone shouts from inside the [medical officers] tent: 'Where are you from?… What is your father's name?… Driver throw him down.' The pain is unbearable. I swore at the driver… he said 'Swear my brother, As much as you like.' We were laid on the sand… Maybe a thousand wounded on the beach…'

In the afternoon a ship appeared:

> They loaded us on to it, Shouting, swearing, Again like empty bags. Inside the ship it was hell. Blood squelching… We sailed, Seven days, seven nights. Maggots appeared in my wounds… If Allah doesn't kill, he doesn't. The Turk is strong, he can endure.

Finally, in Istanbul, the wounded poet is put on a comfortable trolley, and 'I prayed for the state then…'. It seems that the author had to wait until he reached Istanbul before he was treated, thus it was survival of the strongest in the Turkish army.[70]

On the Allied side, medical systems proved initially to be grossly inadequate, due partly to Hamilton's decision to leave the director of medical services back in Alexandria when GHQ arrived at Mudros in early April, before the landing. GHQ focussed on the landing itself, and paid insufficient attention to problems of evacuation of the wounded, so there were only two hospital ships available on 25 April, plus the last minute addition of seven converted transport ships. Meanwhile treatment of the wounded on shore was predicated on success leading to sufficient sheltered space for field ambulances, casualty clearing stations, and three stationary hospitals, which did not occur. Nor were arrangements in Egypt much better, where unsuitable, hot hospitals and poor medical treatment existed. There was also a certain amount of indifference, judging by the story of one medical officer, Fenwick, who reported sick to *Aragon*, where the lines of communication staff lived in some luxury. No one was interested, and he tried another ship, where an officer refused to bring the wounded up with a sling, and the wounded were compelled to get themselves aboard. At Mudros, another field ambulance officer alleged that the Army Service Corps was selling milk to the troops. When investigated, the ASC QM went sick.[71] Inexperience of modern war, and the sheer difficulty of managing a landing and maintaining medical services in limited space, also played their part. Fenwick also recalled the muddle and chaos at Anzac on 25 April, treating 400 wounded on the small beach, being swept by shrapnel fire: 'It seemed impossible for men to live under the hail of bullets… I certainly was very astonished that I was alive.' Around 1,500 wounded men were evacuated that day. Also on 25 April at Anzac, a sergeant, actually a vet, was pressed into service on board *Lutzow*. On the day of the landing, he felt sick at the smell of so much blood, with 104 wounded on the ship. Mostly, the men were quiet, but one Australian lieutenant, wounded in the temple, kicked up a row: 'He wants me to hold his hand all the time and never leave him.' On 9 May, two men went mad, one thought he had been robbed of £10,000 and tried to kick the ship to pieces to get it back.[72]

A New Zealand nurse, Lottie LeGallais, served on the hospital ship *Maheno*. Lying off the Anzac beach, LeGallais remembered how a bugle blew when the lighter carrying wounded men left the beach for the ship. When full, the ship flew the Blue Peter, and sailed for Malta, Alexandria or England. In September, LeGallais wrote: '... we all had awful wounds [to treat], it was dreadful, and what with fleas and crawlers my skin at present is nearly raw, but we all scratch, – scratch – except the men patients poor devils, they are used to them.' For those who died during the night, a lighter and tug would arrive in the morning: 'Any trade this morning?' would be the call, and bodies would be taken away for burial. Then in November 1915, a transport with wounded and nurses aboard was struck by a torpedo, and LeGallais recorded the nurses' stories:

> Fox they say her back was broken, another nurse both legs; Rattray had two nurses keeping her up for hours, they were holding on to spars & with hands crossed these girls kept Rattray up until she became mental & died of exhaustion… Hilyard sang 'Tipperary' and 'Are We Downhearted' until she died; those girls were mostly together 5 o'clock were picked up by minesweeper & French destroyers… The officers on the minesweeper were splendid to them, put hot bottles in their beds, gave them their dry clothes…

LeGallais' later letters in November now showed a different problem at Anzac, enteric (typhoid) was rife, and huge barges carrying 450 men each operated a regular service, leaving the beach at 10.30 a.m. and 3.30 p.m. every day.[73]

LeGallais' mention of enteric points up the problem of disease, which, with dysentery and diarrhoea, began to have a serious impact on the troops, especially at Anzac, as the summer heat increased. A host of flies invaded every space and spread disease, feeding off faeces and the decomposing bodies of the dead from both sides. Indeed, it was the absolute necessity of burying the dead that caused the 24 May armistice at Anzac, where pits were dug 'to put the awful things into.' On the other hand, Ian Hamilton earned considerable criticism for rejecting a Turkish offer of an armistice to bury the dead at Helles in July, 'on purely military grounds.' Another source of disease was the insanitary condition of the trenches. Men, horses and mules relieved themselves where they could, producing an ever present plague of flies. Latrines were dug, but there was initially no sanitation system of dealing with the flies that also invaded these pits and spread disease. Latrines could also be a dangerous place to be, as one unfortunate soldier discovered when, hit by shrapnel while sitting on the latrine, 'the poor beggar fell back into the pit and was quite dead when pulled out a few minutes after.' Hygiene was only properly dealt with when a new system was introduced in September, of biscuit tins and a close fitting wooden box, with the lid used as a seat. Contents were treated with kerosene and put into a deep pit and fired weekly. Despite this, disease had got too strong a hold, and by September a thousand men each day were being evacuated sick from Gallipoli to Mudros.[74] One other aspect of medical treatment is usually overlooked – the veterinary service. Horses and mules were wounded and killed also, and vets strove to repair the wounded. Often, the demand for men was so strong that not enough dressers were left to deal with horse wounds. Similarly, horses weren't always well looked after. In one case, while being transported from Egypt to Gallipoli in July, the heat killed the horses on board, especially because the water for the horses was brown Nile water, already used on a previous voyage, and the horses wouldn't drink, despite their thirst.[75]

With all the problems of a stalled campaign, evacuation still came as a surprise, but for the Allied soldiers at Anzac, Suvla and Helles, this was a moment of deeply mixed emotions. Men pinned notes to the wall: 'Goodbye, Johnnie, we will see you again soon, probably on the Suez Canal', and 'Remember you didn't push us off, we simply went.' Others were more angry, so that news of the evacuation 'was not received with joy. I took photos of graves of dear friends.'[76] At Helles, Joseph Murray, too, admitted to a feeling of anger: 'I could not admit, even to myself, that we had been beaten after the sacrifice of so many men.' Yet for some it was obviously a relief. Lt Masterman, New Zealand Mounted Brigade, wrote that news of the evacuation was received 'with glee as we were anticipating a very bad winter… [this] was the best thing that could have happened…' At Helles, Maj. Gillam also felt relief on 8 January: 'Phew! The relief. 'W' Beach the last few weeks! Let's forget about it!'[77] Probably most men felt a mixture of anger, sadness at leaving dead comrades behind, and relief. After the evacuation, the soldiers of Anzac, who were evacuated before Christmas, found a last unhappy memory of the campaign. Pte Francis Humphreys, 5th Field Artillery, at Lemnos on 25 December, wrote that 'Xmas Dinner was awful. Biscuits and jam and cheese that had to be chaind [sic] up'. A more bitter memory came from Pte McKenzie, 3rd New Zealand Mounted Infantry, who recalled that he spent Christmas Day in harbour on an Indian trading boat, with no rations, but the officers had cake, fowl and champagne. At night he cursed the 'Kaiser and the war and our officers in their drunken luxury.' A slightly more optimistic note comes from an anonymous soldier of the Auckland Battalion, who reported bully beef and biscuits for Christmas dinner at Mudros on a ship, but still had to pay sixpence for a half-full dixie cup of tea. Even better was the Medoc wine that Frederick Varnham bought and had with his Christmas dinner on board the *Huntsgreen*. After that though, Christmas day was uneventful: 'Loafed badly. Caught 1 flea, 14 lice.'[78]

For most officers and men of both sides, the intensity of the Gallipoli/Canakkale campaign was a severe shock to their expectations of war, and of course, was often deadly. But the great majority of men engaged in combat found ways to adapt and, if they were lucky, to survive. Some 85 years later, the physical legacies at Gallipoli/Canakkale are the neatly kept Allied cemeteries, the Turkish monuments and museums, and the haunted ground of Gallipoli/Canakkale itself.

But what led to the Allied evacuation, and how was it achieved?

EVACUATION

The Allied decision to evacuate from Gallipoli occurred because of events in the Balkans, the visit to England by Guy Dawnay from GHQ, and a series of negative reports on the progress of the Allied campaign. Surprisingly, it seems that the Turks were not deceived, and even anticipated the Allied evacuation. Still, the Allied departure from both Anzac/Suvla and then Helles was well planned and proved very successful.

*

A t Hamilton's GHQ, hope turned to the desperate search for solutions in late August, September and October. Birdwood told Kitchener in October that only an unlimited supply of heavy ammunition or extensive mining could break the log jam. Hankey suggested several wild schemes in early October, such as flooding Turkish trenches by pumping sea water into them, or destroying Turkish trenches with water jets, or using Greek fire against Turkish ships. Other plans included using the newly developed Stokes mortars, or applying liquid fire to Turkish trenches, or employing smoke bombs to screen attacks. But none of these came to fruition (in particular the Stokes mortar was not available for Gallipoli), while winter weather began causing severe problems. This was at its worst when men from 53 Division, frozen and flooded out of its trenches in early December, threw down their rifles and left their trenches for the hospitals. These were all symptoms of a stalled campaign.

But when and where did the idea of evacuation first arise? The initial portent of doubts occurred already in July, when first Glynn, and then Hankey, were despatched to Gallipoli by Kitchener and the Cabinet respectively, to provide reports on operations. When Glynn returned to London, Kitchener learnt for the first time of the severe problems in Gallipoli, and belatedly began to free up troops and ammunition for the campaign. Meanwhile, Hankey became an unofficial referee and liaison officer on Gallipoli for Prime Minister Asquith, the War Office and the Admiralty. Churchill was also supposed to accompany Hankey on his fact finding mission, but Lord Curzon, Lord Privy Seal, among others, vetoed Churchill's trip, and so Hankey went alone in late July. Hamilton was naturally suspicious of Hankey's errand, and wrote to de Robeck on 21 July, asking whether Hankey had come to report on de Robeck or himself. If Hankey had come on Hamilton's job, then:

> I would not at all like him to be allowed to run about Mudros before I had got hold of him and set his feet firmly on the right path. Whether we think him doctrinaire, narrow and academic (as I do) or whether we believe him to have a real practical grip of naval and military matters – there is no doubt at all he has the ear of the Cabinet, and especially of the PM [Prime Minister] – My idea would be to give him a shake down in the sand together with a few centipedes and flies. Then to send him in charge of a trusty staff officer to Anzac & Helles to be shelled, and then he will be anxious to get back as quickly as he can without hearing too much naval and military irresponsible gossip.

As luck would have it, Hankey accompanied Aspinall to Suvla on 8 August, and witnessed the lack of activity that day by IX Corps. Partly as a result of this, Hankey's letters and ultimate report to Cabinet painted a rather dismal picture of Gallipoli, particularly of IX Corps and the Territorial divisions, although Birdwood's Anzac Corps came in for praise. In consequence of this information, Birdwood was promoted to Lt-Gen., and Egerton, commanding 52 Division, recalled.[1]

Then, on 12 August, after the failure of the August offensive, Dawnay put forward the idea of evacuation at GHQ, or at least evacuation of the northern wing. Predictably, this aroused stiff resistance, and even Dawnay's ally at GHQ, Aspinall, thought Dawnay 'was 'overdone', and due for a rest!!' But by late August, Dawnay got GHQ to think in terms of evacuation as a remote possibility under certain circumstances, although this was still strongly resisted by Hamilton and Braithwaite. Aspinall wondered about evacuating Suvla and Anzac, and thought about setting up a Torres Vedras style line of defence at Helles.[2] In fact, there was a ferment of discussion at GHQ during late August, as drafts of strategic options testify. In one draft, unsigned and undated, but probably by Dawnay, and probably on 21 or 22 August 1915, the writer argues that the advantage of gaining Chunuk Bair would be 'so small' if there was no further objective in prospect. In blue ink margin comment, Hamilton strongly disagreed: 'the effect of our gaining Chunuk Bair… would be immense…', while withdrawal would be disastrous. The draft writer concluded it was necessary to re-embark the northern wing, and Hamilton wrote: 'I agree, but not till we have tried to defeat the Turks on Sari Bair.' Then in an unsent draft despatch by Dawnay, dated 22 August 1915, he argued for either a reduced line at Suvla/Anzac, or withdrawal of the northern wing, because there were not enough men to defend both Helles and Anzac/Suvla. On 29 August an Aspinall situation report noted that Allied casualties had been 89,000, that it might be necessary to evacuate Suvla, and most unusually, stated that Turkish morale was up, while Allied morale was down. The conclusion was that to get on, 50,000 new rifles were needed, plus submarines and a French landing on the Asian shore. Another draft of a Hamilton despatch, written by Aspinall and undated (but in September), admitted that the capture of Koja Cimen Tepe 'might not be decisive', although this could cut the isthmus in two in one operation, while the same effect could only be achieved at Helles in three operations. On the other hand, Aspinall now believed that a landing on the Asian side would not be decisive.[3]

Back in London, a flow of unofficial reports and reporters turned the official line against Gallipoli. Stopford prepared his own report in late August, critical of Hamilton, which was essentially accepted by the War Office. An Australian journalist who had been on Gallipoli, Keith Murdoch, arrived in London in late September, and gained the ear of

Asquith, who circulated his report to the Dardanelles Committee. Murdoch's report was highly coloured and exaggerated in its criticism of Hamilton and GHQ, but there was enough truth in it to raise serious doubts, and it became clear that the Allied army had failed. On the other hand, Hankey, trying to rescue the campaign, referred to Murdoch as 'a horrible scab'. There was also trouble with the French, for example, Gen. M. Bailloud, the French commander in Gallipoli since July, wrote to the French Minister of War on 16 August 1915, reporting the failure at Anzac and then Suvla. Hamilton had apparently told Bailloud that the failure was due to the inexperience of the soldiers and the feebleness of their commanders. Bailloud reported that Hamilton did not use French troops in the August diversionary attacks at Helles, but even if he had wanted to, Bailloud told the War Minister he would not have agreed, 'given your orders to me. I have not thought it necessary to inform Hamilton of your ulterior projects.'[4]

As this message strongly implied, France was losing interest in the campaign, and was focussing elsewhere. But there was a resurgence of interest on 1 September, when France surprisingly offered four new divisions for a landing on the Asian shore, in order to finish the campaign. Hamilton was jubilant, but it turned out to be mainly a political stunt to find a position for Gen. M. Sarrail, who was dismissed from his job by Gen. J.J.C. Joffre but was too important a Republican to be left out of the jockeying for a top command. The offer was also conditional on the results of Joffre's offensive in late September, and nothing came of this initiative.

Quite apart from this, a major new development occurred in September, in fact the most significant factor in the eventual Gallipoli evacuation, when Bulgaria joined the Central Powers, signalling the failure of the Allies' Balkan and Gallipoli strategy. As a result, Germany could now directly supply the Turks with heavy artillery and ammunition by rail to Istanbul, thus threatening the very existence of the Allies on Gallipoli. Then Greece and Serbia appealed for help, and on 24 September the Allies agreed to support them with one French division from Helles, and the British 10 Division from Suvla. According to Stephen Gaselee of the British Foreign Office, it was this Balkan situation that forced the British government to focus on Salonika and abandon the Gallipoli campaign.[5]

As an unintended part of this refocusing on the Balkans, Dawnay was sent home from GHQ on 2 September. Dawnay's trip occurred because in the second half of August, Dawnay originally wanted Aspinall sent home from GHQ to get the true facts out in London. The CGS Braithwaite resisted doing this for ten days, as did Hamilton. But Hamilton realized the serious difficulty of GHQ's position and at last agreed. Ironically, Hamilton then chose to send Dawnay to London instead of Aspinall, thinking Dawnay less pessimistic than Aspinall, whereas the reverse was actually true. In England, Dawnay saw Kitchener, the Director of Military Operations, and everyone else of consequence, pointing out the grave situation in Gallipoli, and he particularly stressed the need for a new overall policy in the Balkans. This last piece of advice coincided with Bulgaria joining the Central Powers, and this was what specifically undercut the Gallipoli campaign. According to Bonar Law in the War Cabinet, there were three options at a crucial meeting of the Dardanelles Committee on 12 October: defend Serbia; leave the whole theatre; or send more divisions to Gallipoli. Apparently it was Lt-Gen. Sir William Robertson, the CIGS, who finally convinced the Dardanelles Committee at the same meeting that abandoning Gallipoli was the best choice. Hankey was among those very reluctantly convinced by Robertson's arguments to evacuate Gallipoli, as was Bonar Law, although Hankey changed his mind a few days later. According to Hamilton, however, it was Lord Northcliffe, the newspaper magnate, who master minded the Gallipoli evacuation. Regardless, it was decided in London on 14 October to recall Hamilton because he was 'generally reported to have lost the confidence of the troops.' Kitchener tried to protect Hamilton by recalling the CGS Braithwaite and replacing him with Lt-Col. L.E. Kiggell, Haig's future chief of staff on the Western Front, but Hamilton defended Braithwaite, and so they were both brought home.[6]

Hamilton's replacement was Gen. Sir Charles Monro, whom Hankey described as having the strange habit of slapping his listener on the arm while shouting the word 'Ja'. Monro, a convinced Westerner, spent only a few days on Gallipoli at the end of October, with his chief of staff, Maj.-Gen. A.L. Lynden-Bell. Monro visited all three fronts in just one day, 30 October, while Lynden-Bell managed to avoid stepping foot on land at all. Instead Lynden-Bell was provided with extracts from all relevant war diaries, highlighting the failings of various units and head quarters. Monro was strongly impressed by the Allied problems at Gallipoli, especially the anticipated arrival on the Turkish side of heavy guns and ammunition from Germany, and recommended withdrawal the next day, 31 October. At the time this advice was received, the Cabinet was also losing confidence in Kitchener, and wanted to remove him from the War Office, since he refused to 'tell them the whole truth' about operations. There was also the fear that he might break down. Still, it was decided to send Kitchener out to Gallipoli to confirm or reject Monro's advice. Kitchener, though, had received from Aspinall just a few days earlier, an 'Appreciation', dated 22 October 1915, which predicted that a Gallipoli withdrawal would result in the loss of fifty per cent of the Allied force and sixty-six per cent of the guns. This, plus a new naval proposal by Roger Keyes to force the Straits, galvanized Kitchener into action. Before going to Gallipoli, he sent a message to Birdwood on 3 November that reflected a certain instability in Kitchener's character: 'Decipher yourself. Tell no one', he cabled. Kitchener then proposed a new combined naval and military operation at Gallipoli, including a landing at Bulair, with Birdwood in charge, and added: 'I absolutely refuse to sign an order for evacuation, which I think would be the greatest disaster, and would condemn a large percentage of our men to death or imprisonment.' Birdwood replied at once, quickly realizing that such a venture would likely fail. Ever astute politically, Birdwood said he could not do a new landing. On the other hand, he felt he could hang on at Gallipoli.[7]

However, Kitchener was not yet done, and he unilaterally appointed Birdwood as GOC Gallipoli, replacing Monro, who was now in disgrace. Monro was shuffled off to command at Salonika. Aspinall was to be chief of staff to Birdwood. Thus there were now two camps – those who wanted to hang on at Gallipoli: Birdwood, Godley, Wemyss, Keyes, and of course, Kitchener and Hamilton at home – and those who favoured evacuation: Monro, Lt-Gen. Sir Julian Byng (GOC IX Corps), de Robeck and 'Joey' Davies (Lt-Gen. Sir Francis Davies, now GOC VIII Corps at Helles). Reportedly, Kitchener tried to shift Byng into the 'hang on at Gallipoli' camp by offering him two new divisions for IX Corps. But Byng held firm, unless plentiful artillery ammunition for a three day offensive became available, and this Kitchener could not provide. However, Kitchener got help from the 'Egyptians', Lt-Gen. Sir John Maxwell and Sir Henry McMahon (High Commissioner for Egypt), who feared a negative Muslim reaction to defeat at Gallipoli, a particular obsession of Kitchener's, and supported Kitchener's desire to stay. If there was to be evacuation, then Maxwell and McMahon desired another blow at the Turks, which led to the futile and deliberately unworkable schemes of attacking Alexandretta and Ayas Bay. Finally, Kitchener left for Mudros on 6 November and inspected Gallipoli. There ensued heated discussions for a week, with Kitchener ultimately, but very reluctantly, accepting the need for evacuation. According to Dawnay, it took him three weeks to convince Kitchener of this. Even so, Kitchener only agreed to the evacuation of Anzac and Suvla, and not Helles – 'oh, he has much to answer for!', wrote Dawnay. Kitchener was apparently swayed by Wemyss and Keyes, who in December again wanted a new naval attack, with Helles being defended by the Navy. To resolve the now complicated command problem, Monro was appointed overall commander of the Mediterranean area, except for Egypt, Birdwood was to command at Gallipoli, and Maxwell at Salonika. Hankey commented that Monro was now a sort of Pope at Gallipoli, but Kitchener was still the super Pope. In this time of wavering decision making, Birdwood, Dawnay and Aspinall were all seriously concerned that the winter weather, which washed away piers, might actually prevent evacuation. In London, further wavering took place, but the Cabinet finally agreed on 7 December to evacuate Suvla and Anzac. This was really the beginning of the end, and after the completely successful evacuation of these areas on 18 and 19 December, the Helles evacuation, again pushed forward by the new CIGS, Robertson, was decided on 23 December. Final orders were sent on 28 December, and the actual evacuation of Helles took place on 8 and 9 January 1916.[8]

In all this political manoeuvring, did the Turks suspect anything? Certainly, after the evacuation of Anzac and Suvla, the chances were very good that Helles would also be evacuated. In addition, Allied security was poor, despite disinformation schemes. In one instance, Birdwood noted on 1 December that "Communications' has distinguished itself by wiring in clear to Bungo [Byng] about 'Evacuation being prepared for' etc !!!'. After the war, Hamilton wrote that the Turks knew that evacuation would take place, but they were in poor condition and were happy to see it happen. Judging by one important message, written in French, from Liman von Sanders to Mustafa Kemal in late November 1915, the Turks were well aware of changing conditions among the Allies, and recognized the strong likelihood of withdrawal. In this message, Liman von Sanders told Mustafa Kemal that the strong attack which Kemal proposed for that same day, 29 November, at 3.00 p.m. did not conform to the current aims of the Turks. Liman von Sanders stated that Kemal knew very well that the enemy was *at the moment* still in considerable strength, while the Turkish artillery preparation was not strong enough to protect against heavy infantry casualties. But Liman von Sanders expected a radical change in the Allied situation very shortly, because there were clear signs that the enemy wished to withdraw (*s'éloigner*). When there were further clear signs of a change in the enemy situation, wrote Liman von Sanders, then another attack was possible. So, in late November, Liman von Sanders' message already anticipated an Allied withdrawal. Kannengiesser had also heard rumours of a withdrawal before the Suvla/Anzac evacuation, and anticipated the evacuation from Helles because he discovered that only one or two Allied guns per battery were firing. Thus, the Allied evacuation was expected, as was confirmed by Liman von Sanders' message to Kemal, but obviously Fifth Army did not know exactly when this would happen. If the Turks had known this specifically, then Turkish infantry attacks might or might not have been launched, but Turkish artillery and infantry fire would certainly have been employed during the Allied evacuation.[9]

Meanwhile, the actual means of Allied evacuation was a matter of controversy. There were two basic plans at Anzac/Suvla. The first envisaged a fighting retreat by degrees to a second, and even a third line. The second plan aimed to maintain the normal front lines, employ a small rearguard on the last night, and evacuate everyone in two nights. The second plan was proposed and strongly supported by Godley, despite opposition from Reed and to a lesser extent from Byng, Maj.-Gen. F.S. Maude (GOC 13 Division), and others. As Godley reasonably argued, if the withdrawal was advertised by a fighting retreat, as in the first plan, then 'the Turk must attack us and we must then fight a very difficult rearguard action.' But if the trenches were maintained until the last moment, then the Turks could not tell if they were opposed by 10,000 or 40,000 troops. In fact, on the last night at Anzac, 10,000 troops were taken safely off in three parties. There were trick rifles left behind, firing after water or candle devices ran down and allowed the rifle to fire, and a mine was set off at the Nek at the last moment. This killed about seventy Turks, but assisted the evacuation because it was thought by the Turks that this might signal an Allied attack. Fifty of the worst mules and donkeys were left behind, plus five guns which could not be moved, otherwise almost everything useful, except for food, was taken off. The last man left Anzac around 4.00 a.m. on 20 December, but the Turkish artillery only began bombarding the beaches at 5.30 a.m. The next day, the Allied navy came in to fire at the stores left behind but did little damage. Much the same situation occurred at Suvla, although two officers set fire to two large piles of stores there at 4.00 a.m., giving the Suvla evacuation away, but this still did not prevent the last boats from leaving safely at 5.00 a.m.[10]

Surprisingly, the success of the evacuation was repeated at Helles, where the main problems were not so much the Turks, as the weather and the lack of piers. The weather was just a matter of luck, while the piers were quickly built under the able direction of Capt. Matthews, RE, employed before the war as a foreman of works. As for the Turks, there seems to have developed something of a 'live and let live' policy at Helles. For example, Lt-Gen. Davies, commanding at Helles, instituted a soccer competition to keep up morale. The Turks used to watch the matches, but they never fired – it was rumoured they were betting on the results. However, the Turks had a very good idea that Helles would soon be evacuated after the Anzac/Suvla withdrawal, and when the Turkish defenders at Helles criticized the Anzac defenders for letting the Allies get away, the retort was, according to Zeki Bey: 'Well, you know now there will be a withdrawal from Helles. So – do what you want to do there.' In fact, the Turkish infantry were not keen to attack, and the Turkish attack at Gully Spur of noon on 7 January, the eve of the first night of evacuation, was a half-hearted affair, and strongly resisted. The usual trick effects and booby traps were organized at Helles, and then there was nothing else to do but wait for the last night, 8 January. In order to calm the nerves of his staff, Davies ordered them to play bridge on the afternoon of 8 January, and then again on board ship after the evacuation. The evacuation was a complete success, and the last boat left Helles at about 4.00 a.m. Then, as luck would have it, a gale began to get up. That night Davies' ship, *Triad*, 'plunged about like a bucking horse and I was nearly chucked out of my bunk. What a [close] shave of a [potential] bust up.'[11]

And so the Gallipoli campaign came to an end. But arguments over the campaign did not, with post-war discussion in the Turkish Army over the ease of the Allied evacuation, and in Britain through the investigations of the Dardanelles Commission (1916–1917).

11

IAN HAMILTON AND THE
DARDANELLES COMMISSION

Collusion and Vindication

Following the Allied evacuation from Gallipoli, rumours began to spread about the Allied failure at Gallipoli, while Hamilton and Stopford got into a long running argument over the Suvla operation. As a result of questions in the House of Commons, a Royal Commission was appointed in 1916 to investigate the Gallipoli campaign.

★

I t is a curious fact that the only Royal Commissions set up during or after the First World War to investigate campaign problems dealt with campaigns outside the Western Front – and Gallipoli fitted this pattern. It is true that the Kirke Commission looked at the lessons of the First World War, but this was not a parliamentary commission. What then was the purpose of the Royal Commission on Gallipoli? Certainly to discover the reasons for Allied failure, although according to Sir Ian Hamilton, the real objective of the Commission was not to whitewash Churchill, but to blacken Kitchener, whose performance was under attack in 1916. But for many participants it was a welcome chance to tell their story and be vindicated. On the other hand, for many staff and senior officers, it was a shocking situation, since Allied generals and staff were rarely called upon to account for their failures. The most prominent witness was obviously going to be Sir Ian Hamilton, who, since his recall from Gallipoli in mid-October 1915, naturally sought vindication for his actions as commander-in-chief. He was even promised further employ-ment by Lord Derby after the Dardanelles Commission finished its work, but Lord Derby failed to actually offer Hamilton a job.[1]

Due to the thorough nature of the Royal Commission, often called the Dardanelles Commission, this has become one of the key documents for understanding the Allied campaign. Gathered in several bulky vol-umes are the replies of witnesses to questions, as well as the written evi-dence that they also provided. As might be expected, the replies and the statements all need to be evaluated carefully. And in the case of key wit-nesses, caution is particularly required, for the evidence shows that a good deal of predictable collusion went on before the witnesses made their statements. Thus, the first order of business is to try and winnow out the reliable statements from the unreliable among the many hundreds of pages of the Dardanelles Commission.

First of all, Hamilton went energetically to work in 1916 to prepare for the Commission. His first action was to attempt to influence the mem-bership of the Commission. In particular, Hamilton wanted to avoid the presence of Lord Nicholson, the former CIGS, who was antagonistic to both Lord Kitchener and Hamilton. Therefore Hamilton wrote and asked that Nicholson not be appointed, but, despite this, Nicholson was appointed to chair the Commission. Nicholson's appointment caused Hamilton to 'shiver', although he believed that Nicholson 'hates Kitchener a great deal worse than he hates me… [and is] jealous of me…'. Later on, in May 1917, Hamilton argued that, 'Had it not been for Lord Nicholson's presence on this Commission I would have been absolutely vindicated… Temperamentally he is at the opposite pole from me – my hidden enemy – and the enemy of all 'Neck or Nothing' enter-prises.' Despite Hamilton's explanation, the enmity between Nicholson and Hamilton seems to have stemmed from the South African War, when Hamilton got himself made senior to Nicholson by ante-dating his Maj.-Gen. rank to the date of his arrival in South Africa, although Hamilton was still only a Colonel at the time of the siege of Ladysmith (1899–1901). It also appears that Hamilton blocked some of Nicholson's promotion recommendations in the pre-war era, when Hamilton was on the Army Selection Board.[2]

Thus, the die was cast, and Hamilton would have to muster all his resources to escape the criticism of Nicholson, and emerge from the Commission as unscathed as possible. Hamilton then tried to influence matters by suggesting to the Secretary of the Dardanelles Commission, Grimwood Mears, who to summon as witnesses. Next, Hamilton tried to anticipate the probable key areas of investigation by the Commission. He was considerably helped in this process by developing a secret source in the Commission, who told him what was being said, and which line of questioning the members were pursuing. He told Braithwaite, his chief of staff on Gallipoli, that this could put them in prison 'if it is known that we know.' Part of the information that Hamilton obtained secretly from this source was Hankey's evidence, and also Winston Churchill's paper concerning the naval part of the Dardanelles operation. This latter evidence caused Hamilton to suggest to Braithwaite that they discuss Churchill's paper together because their case was, to a point, similar to Churchill's case.[3] Using this source, Hamilton began to prepare replies to the most important issues with Braithwaite. Initially, the two key problem areas seemed to Hamilton to be, firstly, why couldn't the land campaign have started right away after the naval failure of 18 March, instead of waiting for the actual landing date of 25 April? And secondly, why was GHQ apparently detached from the Suvla Bay operation of August 1915, and so why was more energy and leadership not shown there? Hamilton suggested answers already – to the first question, the answer was that it was necessary to wait for the arrival of 29 Division before launching the invasion, and there were also problems with the faulty loading of ships. (Ironically, the French also had problems with loading and they too had to reload their ships.) Hence, GHQ was not properly organized until mid-April, and small craft were also not available until then. As for Suvla, the IX Corps commander, Stopford, and his chief of staff, Reed, were responsible for the slow progress there, and this was the more important because divisional, brigade and battalion commanders were all inexperienced. Braithwaite responded to the first question by saying that although Birdwood wanted to attack straight away, there were serious ordnance, medical and logistic problems before an immediate attack could take place. Then, in regard to Suvla, Braithwaite reminded Hamilton that Suvla was only one of three operations at the time, 'was not even the most important operation…', and that once the commander-in-chief gives the orders, it is up to the commander on the spot (Stopford) to take over. Besides, the Anzac operation was not successful either, and the lack of success at Anzac hindered the Suvla operations.[4]

Hamilton was interviewed by the Commission for the first time in October 1916, and in a long letter told Braithwaite the questions and his answers. One question bothered Hamilton – how many troops were readily available after the naval defeat on 18 March? Hamilton had answered: the Royal Naval Division, one French Division, 5,000 Australians and 25,000 Australians in Egypt. Was this correct, he asked Braithwaite? Hamilton had actually hurt his case by estimating such a large number available for an immediate landing, but Braithwaite replied that there were actually only 27,000 troops available directly after 18 March, and 'all upside down on their ships – packed 'anyhow'!', plus the usual problems of supplies, water, artillery, transport, etc. However, Hamilton's letter also cleared up a question that not only the Dardanelles Commission but later historians have puzzled over. The Commission wanted to know whether Hamilton had pressured Vice-Admiral de Robeck to give up on naval operations and let the Army land? Hamilton strongly denied this, for when:

> we [Hamilton and Braithwaite] were in the launch going over to the second conference [on 22 March] you and I had agreed that this was a purely naval point and that we would leave it entirely to the sailors. Further, I said that there was no voice raised at the conference in opposition to de Robeck. The only difference… was that Birdwood preferred a landing at once…[5]

Just three days later, in a letter to de Robeck, Hamilton confirmed that at the conference on 22 March (Hamilton erroneously dated this 23 March), de Robeck had said that the time had come for a joint Army-Navy operation, and no one objected. After 18 March, the Navy wanted to go on, but during the next two days the Navy saw this as impossible.[6]

This was, in fact, a key point, for now the die was cast for an army land-ing, but it is important to note that originally the plan was for a *joint* Army-Navy operation. In fact, de Robeck told Churchill on 26 March 1915 that combined operations were essential after 'having heard Ian Hamilton's proposals.' It is often overlooked, therefore, that the whole 25 April operation called for a combined Army-Navy advance, with the Navy bombarding the forts at the Narrows on the second and third days of the landings (26 and 27 April), plus the sweeping of the Kephez mine-field after the forts had been silenced. This would then leave the way open for the Navy to advance into the Sea of Marmora. Of course, the difficulty of the landings and the slow advance of the Army meant that the naval side of the operation soon faded into a supporting action for the Army.[7]

Hamilton's letter, after giving his evidence, also contained reference to the long running feud between himself and Stopford over the Suvla landing in August. The Dardanelles Commission had not heard of the Report that Stopford sent in, nor the War Office conference over it, in September 1915. Somewhat naturally, Hamilton wanted a copy of Stopford's Report, but did not know how to get it: 'If Woodward [AG at GHQ] were a good chap I would write him now and get him to have it done in the AG's office.' Unfortunately Hamilton and Woodward were at loggerheads over relations between GHQ and the AG's office in 1915, so this couldn't be done. Braithwaite had not seen Stopford's Report either, but Archie Murray [Sir Archibald Murray, CIGS in 1915], a member of the committee that received Stopford's Report, said that GHQ had given Stopford a very difficult task at Suvla. Braithwaite in reply wanted to explain 'in detail why Stopford hadn't been given too much to do…'.[8] The Stopford affair would heat up later, but for now, Hamilton turned his attention to his primary defence. This evolved into the argument that the Gallipoli campaign failed due to shortages of men, artillery, ammuni-tion, and material. Since these shortages were generally outside Hamilton's control, this would exonerate him from error. Hence, in November 1916, Hamilton pressed Gen. Stockdale (Artillery) to stress the shortages of artillery and ammunition. Similarly, Col. Forman (Artillery) told Hamilton in a letter of November 1916 that with more men, more Howitzers and more ammunition, they would have got through. In November, Hamilton told Birdwood that the real vital point of the enquiry was the shortage of ammunition.[9] Later, in 1917, Hamilton tended to emphasize shortages of troops. He told Roger Keyes 'My strong card is the continual shortage of drafts to my British Divisions…', and in commenting on Birdwood's Commission evidence, Hamilton wrote that the major errors in London were the delay in sending drafts, an almost 100,000 deficit by October 1915; the delay in sending reinforcements; and delay in sending trench mortars, bombs and grenades, requested a month before the landing.[10]

Having decided on a general line of defence, it was then necessary for Hamilton and other senior officers to coordinate their testimony with that of other senior officers. Among those who relied on Hamilton for this was Maj.-Gen. de Lisle, who wrote that he wanted to call on Hamilton because 'I particularly want to be clear on certain points…' Other senior officers that coordinated their testimony included Godley and Birdwood. When Godley was first called to testify, this seemed to him an 'awful bombshell…', but he wanted Birdwood's advice before sending in his report on the conduct of operations as requested by the Commission. Birdwood counselled him to follow a 'know nothing' strategy:

> Personally I should feel inclined to give the very shortest and evasive or
> rather non-committal answers [as] possible, and base this on the fact that
> you have no detailed information beside you, and have neither the time
> nor the opportunity to go into details at present…

One other device was to try to actually physically avoid the Commission altogether, as Birdwood explained to Godley. Birdwood had gone home to England from France on leave, but when the Commission called him, this 'made me come back sharp [to France]. They are now shouting for me again, and I suppose will get me one of these days, but I do not mean to be in a hurry about it.' Godley also managed to temporarily put off the Commission, and was hopeful that 'I may still evade it alltogether [sic].'[11]

In the meantime, realizing that the Commission would probably catch up with them sooner or later, Hamilton, Godley and Birdwood coordinated their testimony. It was a curious relationship. They needed each other for mutual defence, yet they all naturally desperately wanted to preserve their own individual reputations. For example, Birdwood wrote to Hamilton in late November 1916, saying that the Commission wanted to know about supplies. In line with his 'know nothing' strategy, Birdwood said that he would tell the Commission he had no records, and would give 'a very short and colourless reply, but before doing anything… if you could tell me what you think or anything you have said that could help, and so that our replies would not be at variance.' Hamilton stressed shortage of ammunition, and Birdwood wrote back, saying that he and Godley had coordinated their evidence, and emphasized his 'know nothing' strategy: '… I propose starting by telling the commissioners that I have no notes of details whatever by me, and could therefore only answer their questions in generalities. In this I shall entirely follow the line you have taken, and bring out the extreme shortage of ammunition…'. Birdwood reassured Hamilton that he would:

> refuse to discuss the 'conduct of operations' – except in so far as they were concerned with my own small show at ANZAC, and state that the conduct of the big operations was for you, and it is not for me or anyone else to presume or criticise.

Of course, Anzac was not a small show, but Birdwood was actually issuing an implicit warning to Hamilton against criticizing him (Birdwood), for he concluded by doubting that the Commission would get any valuable information or opinions: 'It is of course all right if we agree with and confirm what you say, but it would be a nice kettle of fish if we went in for criticising what you have done!'[12]

Hamilton certainly took the strong hint from Birdwood that mutual criticism would be disastrous. Replying to Birdwood, Hamilton carefully soothed him: 'Not a word shall I say which will in any tiniest respect reflect on you or our views or actions. No matter how cunningly questions may be framed, you may feel quite safe of my replies.' Hamilton did however, suggest to Birdwood that he continue the Hamilton line of the need for more men, material and small craft. Of course, the last point needed careful handling to avoid hurting naval feelings. But in a separate letter to Godley, Birdwood was less complimentary about Hamilton's assistance:

> Ian Hamilton does not, as a matter of fact, give me much information to help me: He tells me that he considers the really vital point of the enquiry to be 'shortage of ammunition' and has enclosed a long report from Simpson Baikie (who was at Helles) about this.

Added in the margin, in pencil, is the comment: 'I [Birdwood] am not sending this report on [to Godley] as it doesn't help us at all – but it does show that we are saying nothing *contrary* to his views.' The report was not helpful to Birdwood and Godley mainly because it dealt with Helles and not Anzac. So Birdwood continued:

> What you have said on this subject is I think quite right, viz., that there was no shortage of rifle, but a great shortage of gun and howitzer ammunition – I shall only send in my remark on a general line to the effect I have mentioned to you, viz., that the conduct of operations lay with Sir Ian, and it is not for me to criticise them – that we, like probably every army in the world, constantly suffered from shortage of reinforcements and ammunition –.[13]

Meanwhile, Godley's evidence at the Commission was favourable to Hamilton. He did, however, stress a new factor, that not only were the Anzacs short of men at the right moment, perhaps needing two more divisions, or even 150,000 men, but that the Turks were too strong for them. This meant that it was not poor plans, lack of material, bad orders, lack of water, or naval problems, that caused failure, but an external factor outside the control of Godley or Birdwood, i.e., the Turks. There were, therefore, two slightly different defences, Hamilton's, which basically stressed shortages of men and material, and that of Godley and Birdwood, stressing similar shortages plus the idea that the Turks were too strong.[14] In any case, Hamilton was pleased with Godley's testimony, but he still feared Birdwood. At one point he asked Braithwaite what would happen if the Commission 'asked him [Birdwood] in a leading sort of way if he did not think the whole force should have been landed at Anzac and Suvla in the first instance [on 25 April], I really don't know what Birdie [sic] might not answer.' However, Birdwood was prepared to help by following the Hamilton line of stressing shortages of ammunition, trench mortars, men, and another shortage, canteen stores. Consequently, Hamilton was grateful: 'I am glad indeed to learn that our ideas are marching into the Commission to the same tune.' This was not so difficult, for after giving evidence, Hamilton intended to show Birdwood his Commission papers when the latter arrived in England, and urged him to 'lose not a moment in coming to my house and ask to see the papers left for you to look over. It is vital and will help you enormously.' Of course, all this was strictly illegal: 'The fact of such papers being in existence is, of course, deadly secret.'[15]

However, friction between Hamilton and Birdwood did emerge in January 1917. This occurred when Hamilton tried to get Birdwood to say that he, Birdwood, was against the evacuation of Gallipoli because Gen. Sir Charles Monro was hustled for time and visited Gallipoli only once, while his chief of staff, Lynden-Bell, never got off the ship at all. 'Be sure you say this', wrote Hamilton, since this would also help Birdwood. But Birdwood returned a frosty reply, sensing a political trap, and wrote saying that he would not make any statements about Monro, and would not talk against others. Hamilton again smoothed things over, and simply replied that the key question was whether Birdwood stood for evacuation (Monro's view) or not (Hamilton's view). Hamilton appeared to be following a strategy of protecting himself against both the Commission and Birdwood by involving Birdwood in Hamilton's evidence and papers. Hamilton continued this line in mid-February 1917, when he wrote that he was now allowed to see all the evidence from the Commission, and although this was confidential material, Hamilton was making a digest of key points for Birdwood 'on which they are likely to hang you…' One of the key points was the supply of water for the Suvla landing. Hamilton asked Birdwood to find out for him how many tins of water were available on 6/7 August: 'Like a dear fellow don't forget this.' Another request in the same letter was for Birdwood to let Hamilton know what one member of the Commission, Fisher, thought about Hamilton, then 'I will burn the letter on receipt and treat the tip as secret.'[16]

However, another problem appeared in mid-1917 when Birdwood told Hamilton he had seen a member of the Commission privately, Sir Thomas Mackenzie. Mackenzie had said that Lord Nicholson was out to whitewash Stopford and take a critical attitude to Hamilton, and had inserted a sentence in the Report to this effect. Hamilton replied in a panic, asking Birdwood to use his influence with Mackenzie to remove the anti-Hamilton sentence which had been inserted by Nicholson. Hamilton wanted Birdwood to send a telegram to Mackenzie, suggesting rather pompously that the Anzacs would be upset if Hamilton was criticized. To stress his anxiety, Hamilton underlined his plea to Birdwood, asking Birdwood to use the following wording: '*Since you have got back [to France] and have had some chance of sounding them [the Anzacs in France], you feel more confident than ever that a censure of that sort would not be backed by the sentiments of the ANZACS.*' Loyally, Birdwood did write to Mackenzie twice, and told Hamilton that the problem was a sentence of general censure, rather than anything specific. Hamilton wrote again, asking Birdwood to use Lt-Gen. 'Joey' Davies, VIII Corps commander at Gallipoli, who was a friend, to help erase the offending sentence. Birdwood responded in July 1917, saying that it was too late to intervene with Davies, and ended with a rather grating self-compliment: 'I was fortunately able to do so [intervene], owing to the fact of Mackenzie having mentioned it to me and if I have succeeded in what I attempted, I shall be happy in the consciousness of having done my best, not only for a real old friend, but in the cause of justice.'[17]

The cautious but still relatively harmonious relationship between Birdwood and Hamilton became much less friendly with the publication of Hamilton's book, *Gallipoli Diary*, in 1920. In this book, Hamilton described for the first time the problems at Anzac during 25 April, and Birdwood's message recommending re-embarkation of the Anzac forces that same evening. Stung by this, Birdwood wrote to Charles Bean, trying to put the best interpretation on this revelation. Birdwood said that, although he had always liked Hamilton,

> I cannot help recognising that the publication of this book now is quite on a par with his character, for he is full of vanity, and has absolutely no ballast. A man of judgement (which he is not) would not have published a book of this description at the present moment [perhaps referring to the emerging Chanak crisis], reflecting, as it does so much, upon Lord Kitchener and the whole administration generally; while it rather damns the writer if no other reason than that a man in his position should never have spent anything like the time which a diary of this nature must daily have occupied...

In fact, *Gallipoli Diary* was a *post facto* construction from 1916 rather than a 1915 diary, but Birdwood's comment probably reflected his deepest feelings about Hamilton. Birdwood's reaction to the book confirmed the fears of Lady Hamilton, who thought the book would make her husband's friends shiver, and his enemies rejoice.[18]

Ironically, in the same year, 1920, Hamilton was in touch with Godley, trying to get him to intervene in Hamilton's current argument with Lt-Gen. Sir John Maxwell. This argument had to do with Hamilton's contention that Maxwell, Commander-in-Chief in Egypt, held back troops in Egypt that were destined for Gallipoli. Hence, Hamilton wanted Godley to write to the press to say that if Cox's 29th Indian Infantry Brigade had arrived from Egypt on 25 April, instead of early May, this 'would have in your opinion got us the high ridge [Achi Baba].'[19] Whether this was true or not, Hamilton was obviously willing to use all his influence to get his side of the story across. But to do this, he needed the key players at Gallipoli on his side. This naturally included Braithwaite, his chief of staff. But Braithwaite had been accused by Lady Hamilton of being very unpopular and dragging Hamilton down with him, and there were certainly tensions between Hamilton and his former chief of staff. Unfortunately, Braithwaite was angry at Hamilton for ignoring him in the commander-in-chief's final Dispatch: 'Though I am sure you don't realise the fact it is nevertheless true that your omission of all reference to my work in your final Dispatch was much commented on in military circles, and did me much harm…'. However, as with Hamilton and Birdwood, Braithwaite and Hamilton needed each other, because in the same letter, Braithwaite said that he relied on Hamilton to save him from their Gallipoli enemies, 'snarling dogs who are yapping at my heels.'[20]

Hamilton certainly needed Braithwaite when another crisis emerged over the question of GHQ's relations with IX Corps before the Suvla operation. According to Lt-Col. L.R. Beadon, AQMG at GHQ, there were no formal conferences between the staff of IX Corps and the Q staff at GHQ before the Suvla operation started. Beadon claimed to have personally made the necessary arrangements with the AQMG of IX Corps. Beadon's comments obviously indicated a lack of contact between GHQ and IX Corps, and a danger point for Hamilton and Braithwaite. Hamilton diverted Beadon by saying he could not place his letter before the Commission because then the letter of Maj.-Gen. Winter (QMG at GHQ), who was suffering from a mental breakdown, would also have to be produced, and Winter had 'let himself fire off some curses at the Great Tribunal.' However, to Braithwaite, Hamilton gave an entirely different explanation:

> Had I sent this in [Beadon's letter], Nick [Lord Nicholson] and one or two of the Commission would have got right home at you, for this is the very point they have been urging, that the Administration Staff were not freely enough taken into your confidence. Thus, for the moment I have averted this danger, but the Commission may write to Beadon, or Beadon may insist on making his point when he sees the copy of what I have said. Therefore I warn you so that, just if you meet Beadon, you could (without saying anything about this, *which you must not on any account do*) get on the right side of him.[21]

To Hamilton's surprise, Braithwaite was not worried by Beadon's letter:

> We had at that time 'Mothers Meetings' every week (on Thursdays) which Winter… attended and not Beadon. These 'Mothers Meetings'

were discontinued after a time because our friend Woodward [Brigadier-General, AG at GHQ] would never take the trouble to come to them. But, I personally, was in close touch with Winter about all Administration matters connected with the Suvla Bay landing, and Beadon was in daily touch with Aspinall and Dawnay over the same matter… Then when Winter got worse… I not only saw Beadon every day, but many times every day.

This, incidentally, shows that either Hamilton did not know what was going on, or else had forgotten. Braithwaite concluded that if Woodward said we were not in touch, he is 'a liar, pure and simple…'. Braithwaite followed this up in his next letter by criticizing Woodward (who turned out to be an enemy of Hamilton and Braithwaite at the Commission), by noting that Woodward, from the day he arrived, wrote to GHQ in France abusing both Hamilton and especially Braithwaite. Hamilton replied by focussing on Woodward as well as Beadon and the relations of GHQ and IX Corps. Hamilton wanted Braithwaite to write to Grimwood Mears, saying two things: that Woodward had not asked for a delay of two days before operations started on 25 April, in order to improve the woeful medical arrangements; and secondly, that there was good coordination between GHQ and IX Corps.[22]

Braithwaite was not impressed by Hamilton's request, and would have nothing to do with writing to Mears at the Commission. He did however agree to take an oath, if necessary, denying that Woodward had wanted a two day delay of operations. But Braithwaite also told Hamilton sharply:

> Whether you knew about the discontinuance of 'Mothers Meetings', owing to Woodward's defection, I do not know, but you know it now – and you certainly knew we had 'Mothers Meetings' because I remember telling you so.

Furthermore, Braithwaite argued he was not opposed to Woodward at the time, but only after the campaign, and so on Gallipoli tried to get Hamilton to see more of Woodward. 'In fact I remember your very words the last time, which were these: "All right, I'll be good and I'll ask him to tea this very afternoon."' This obviously put Hamilton on the defensive, but he merely remarked that 'Woodward was hurt by my not listening with sufficient interest to his yarns…'. However, if Braithwaite was not going to help, Hamilton decided to turn to Winter, despite the latter's loss of memory. In a rather self-serving request, Hamilton told Winter in September 1917 that it might be wise for him to put in black and white the story that came out in Lt-Col. Beadon's testimony. This was that there was a 'luncheon party between you, Elliott, Maxwell and Woodward whereat Woodward strove to come to some understanding as to the course to be adopted before the Commissioners with a view to downing the General Staff.' Apparently Winter withdrew from this joint attempt at collusion, so Hamilton wanted Winter to either give the story to the Commission, or have the fact witnessed and kept privately. It is not clear what Winter did, but it is unlikely to have influenced the Commission.[23]

Besides pressuring Winter, Hamilton was not above pushing other individuals to produce stories favourable to himself. For example, he suggested to a certain England, probably Lt-Com. Hugh England, commanding *Chelmer*, that he write again to Grimwood Mears, after thinking the matter over, and 'say then, that you had it on your conscience that perhaps you ought to have said something about the delay and hesitation of the 9th Corps when first they landed at Suvla…'. Then when Col. Allanson testified that regular troops would have captured Hill Q without any reference to what was happening at Suvla (whereas Hamilton's line was to blame Suvla for the failure at Anzac), Hamilton said that Allanson's testimony would have to stand for 100 years, but that he was content with it. However, Hamilton added that although he knew Allanson was shortly leaving London, couldn't Allanson have lunch with the Hamiltons on Friday at 1.30 p.m.? One wonders what suggestions might have been made about Allanson's further testimony during that lunch! Another person who apparently followed Hamilton's suggestions was Col. Unsworth, who gave evidence on the medical situation at Gallipoli, and told Hamilton that 'I was able to work a lot in the direction you so very kindly advised.' It seems Col. Unsworth was also confident that Birdwood would help very much 'in the right direction.'[24]

The result of all this manoeuvering was that all seemed set fair for Hamilton's vindication, and in Birdwood's words, a 'mild' verdict. But then the Mesopotamian Report was published, which according to Birdwood made the Commission scent blood, and led to further investigation of the medical situation at Gallipoli. Here Hamilton had a problem with Col. N. Howse (DDMS at Anzac and later, DMS at Anzac), who 'gave rotten evidence. He spoke... with one eye on the political gallery in Australia'. However, Hamilton was saved by the evidence of Courtauld Thompson, an Australian medical surgeon, who came in at the last moment and gave favourable evidence 'at the last stride.' Also helpful were Hamilton's own arguments that Howse's evidence was hearsay, or an indictment of war in general, while Howse should have stayed on the hospital ship and done more for the campaign that way. Finally, leaving nothing to chance, Hamilton got two Australians to offer positive evidence, the famous Capt. A. Jacka, VC, and Lt-Gen. McCay, commanding 2 Australian Division, on the good work done on the beaches by the medical staff.[25]

Hamilton conducted his defence during the Dardanelles Commission hearings like a military campaign. He had written letters almost every day from late 1916 until late 1917 to ward off criticism, turn away his enemies, and make sure his Gallipoli friends, officers and staff all more or less followed the same line. He was helped by the fact that most of his associates had something to hide, so it was better to stick together rather than hang separately. He also managed to find out secretly what was going on in the Commission, which made planning his strategy much easier. It is difficult to blame Hamilton for all this, for he, like the rest, were naturally anxious to preserve their reputations. But what was it that Hamilton felt were his weak points where he might with some justice be criticized? This is of interest because these are the areas which he himself acknowledged to be problematic, rather than any areas chosen by later historians. Initially, Hamilton found out there were six points on which he was to be attacked, particularly from the accusations of Keith Murdoch, the Australian journalist. These were: that Hamilton was never seen by the troops; that he hardly ever went to visit Anzac; that he was but a spectator at Suvla Bay in August; that GHQ did not provide water for the troops at Suvla; that he left on 21 August in the middle of a battle; and that GHQ left a lot of artillery in Egypt. Most of these accusations were deflected or rebutted by Hamilton over the period of the Commission until there were three main questions left. These were, firstly, the one area where Hamilton obviously felt most vulnerable, namely his personal intervention at Suvla with Stopford on 8 August, leading to the failed attack early on 9 August. Hamilton did not feel he ever properly rebutted this question, and believed this was his weakest point. So when he heard that a sentence of censure had been included in the Commission's Report, he jumped to the conclusion that this was the problem area. Secondly, there was the problem of water at Suvla. Here, although GHQ was clearly vulnerable, Hamilton believed that Roger Keyes had defeated the Commission, who came to feel that Stopford had exaggerated the difficulty. Hamilton also justifiably diverted criticism onto individuals such as Col. de Lotbinière. Third, was the question of the split between the Administrative staff and the rest of GHQ, which included serious medical evacuation mistakes. Once again GHQ was clearly part of the problem, but accusations were again diverted onto individuals such as Surgeon General W.A. Birrell.[26]

Besides these main questions, there were secondary criticisms. One of these once again related to Suvla, and this was, why weren't more guns landed earlier at Suvla? Braithwaite provided the answer – guns could not be landed until the infantry had made space for them. Hamilton also felt he disproved the accusations that he did not visit the troops, wrote poetry all day, and lived on potted meat and champagne on *Arcadian*, and presumably at Imbros. Overall, it is curious that Hamilton believed he had been vindicated in areas about which later historians would be more critical, such as isolation from what was really going on, but he was most worried about his intervention at Suvla, where most future commentators would applaud a decisive attempt to assert leadership. Also, as recounted in Chapter Seven, Hamilton's intervention which produced the failed attack at dawn on 9 August at Suvla was in any case too late to take the high ground before the Turks arrived, since the Turks had already been there since the night of 7/8 August. So Hamilton's intervention did not actually have a material impact on the Suvla operation: the game was already lost. Similarly, the area that Hamilton expected to be his strongest defence, the lack of men, again would attract later criticism for his weakness in dealing with Kitchener over this issue.

The conclusion on Hamilton and the Dardanelles Commission is that this was an arena in which Hamilton's particular skills came to the fore – his charm, his persuasiveness, his letter writing ability, his extensive social and military contacts, his coordination of lines of defence with his chief military and naval colleagues, his clever collusion with witnesses, his pressure on subordinates, and his quick intelligence in dealing with Commission questions. Hamilton escaped some criticisms that could justly be levelled against him, and the Commission did not query other key areas, such as Hamilton's fixation on Achi Baba. Probably the Commission did not have the military expertise, or sufficient evidence, or perspective, to deal with strictly military tactical and strategic matters. Hamilton was also apparently able to prevent the Commission from looking into the allegation that he had lost the confidence of his men.[27]

The general conclusions of the Dardanelles Commission basically laid blame on the government in London:

> We are of the opinion that, with the resources then available, success in the Dardanelles, if possible, was only possible upon condition that the Government concentrated their efforts upon the enterprise and limited their expenditure of men and material in the Western theatre of war. This condition was never fulfilled.

As far as Hamilton himself was concerned, the Commission did have two rather specific complaints, despite Birdwood's mention of a general criticism. The first, anticipated and feared by Hamilton, was that Hamilton unjustly criticized Stopford's orders on the morning of 8 August, and that on the evening of 8 August, 'we think that Sir Frederick Stopford's difficulties were increased by the intervention of Sir Ian Hamilton.' This criticism seems unfair – Hamilton was simply trying to inject some enthusiasm into the moribund Stopford. The second complaint criticized Hamilton for not realizing the 'strength and the fighting qualities of the Turkish troops' immediately after the landing, when the Allied advance was first checked. It would have been well, wrote the Commissioners, had Hamilton 'examined the situation as disclosed by the first landings in a more critical spirit… and submitted to the Secretary of State for War a comprehensive statement of the arguments for and against a continuance of the operations.' In other words, Hamilton was over-optimistic right at the start. This criticism was more telling. However, Hamilton's optimism and misjudgement of the Turks seems to be mainly based on his allegiance to the orders of Kitchener, and his unwillingness to let Kitchener down. In addition, it was part of the ethos of the British Army at the time that commanders should always maintain a cheerful disposition and ignore set-backs, as also happened on the Western Front.[28]

Overall, it seems that Hamilton, because of all the limitations and difficulties he faced on Gallipoli, emerged more favourably from the Commission than might be expected. This was to a certain extent because Hamilton manipulated the Commission, and made sure that the results of the Commission were as favourable to him as possible, and engineered as much collusion with his viewpoint as could be achieved. He also made all possible use of his many army and social contacts. And clearly some of his defensive arguments were justified. But he was never employed again by the Army.

CONCLUSION

The Turks, Hamilton, and the Riddle of Gallipoli

Can the riddle of Gallipoli be solved? General conclusions regarding the Gallipoli campaign must reflect both sides of this conflict. Turning first to the Turkish defenders, it is obvious that they were ultimately successful, although their performance was sometimes uneven. On the one hand, Turkish forces and their commanders were occasionally misguided. For example, there was the strange case of the capture of Lt Palmer before the Allied landings, with its likely influence on Liman von Sanders' miscalculation regarding Bulair/Saros from 25 to 27 April; there was a considerable amount of Turkish confusion at Kum Kale on the Asian side on 25 and 26 April; and an erratic display at Anzac on 25 April by the Arab regiments of 19 Division, which initially performed poorly. This was compounded by false information of a landing further south at Kum Tepe on 25 April, which temporarily took Mustafa Kemal out of the command structure. At Helles on 25 and 26 April initial stout resistance at V Beach led subsequently to a disorganized withdrawal. Then, in early May, there was a serious crisis in the German/Turkish high command at Helles, more critical than previously understood, in which Turkish troops came very close to being withdrawn behind Achi Baba. At the same time, Turkish attacks at Helles at the beginning of May were much more costly and disorganized than originally supposed. Once more, a potential collapse was narrowly averted. Allied naval fire against Turkish troops at Helles also seems to have been more successful in late April and May than is generally realized.

On the other hand, Turkish defenders scored a decisive success early in the campaign on 18 March, when mines in Eren Keui Bay, and artillery fire, defeated the Allied naval attack. Turkish sources show there to have been more mines laid in Eren Keui Bay than previously thought. As a result of this attack, Churchill, and historians subsequently, believed that the Turkish artillery at the Straits had run out of shells, especially heavy shells, but Turkish evidence shows this to be incorrect. Hence, another Allied naval attack would very likely not have succeeded. On land, after late April, Turkish troops and their commanders, with the overwhelming defensive power of artillery, machine-guns, magazine rifles, wire and trenches, proved more than a match for Allied offensives. Liman von Sanders, Carl Mühlmann, Hans Kannengiesser, Maj. Willmer, Mustafa Kemal, Esat Pasa and many others, all showed decision and strength of will at crucial times. This was particularly true of Mustafa Kemal on 25 April at Anzac, of Liman von Sanders on 6/7 August, when he sent two divisions south from Bulair/Saros very quickly. This action by Liman von Sanders pre-empted the potential of the Suvla landing, and negated the intervention by Hamilton at Suvla on 8 August. Despite later assertions regarding the very narrow margin by which British forces failed to take the Tekke Tepe heights at Suvla early on 9 August, they were in fact already too late by at least one day due to Liman von Sanders' quick reaction. Meanwhile, Mustafa Kemal recognized the critical nature of the Chunuk Bair situation in early August and was willing to sacrifice troops to regain the initiative, which he and his troops achieved at dawn on 10 August at Chunuk Bair.

Yet there were times when Allied break throughs were possible. During the naval attacks of February and March, more efficient minesweeping efforts by using navy destroyers would have delivered a much better chance of naval success. Directly after the landings of 25 April, the Turks were in disarray and a more efficient command system would have enabled a much stronger immediate push inland at Helles. Exploitation of the Turkish crisis in early May was also possible at Helles. During the August offensives, despite severe difficulties, a more efficient Allied command system would have given the tired but still capable troops better chances of success at Sari Bair and Suvla.

How much then does the failure of Allied arms at Gallipoli rest with its commanders, how much with systemic/structural factors, how much with prevailing technology and tactics, and how much with Turkish defenders? Evaluating Allied commanders first, it seems that in so far as Hamilton and senior Allied commanders acted with freedom of action, then they might be judged critically. But how much freedom did Hamilton have? Hamilton was certainly tied into a traditional understanding of command that limited his options very considerably. There is no doubt that Hamilton and his CGS, Walter Braithwaite, both entered the campaign with a theory of war which downplayed technology in favour of human will and character. In 1910, Hamilton wrote:

> Blindness to moral forces and worship of material forces inevitably lead in war to destruction. All that exaggerated reliance placed upon chassepots and mitrailleuses by France before '70; all that trash written by M. Bloch [the pre-war Polish theorist who warned that war might become impossible due to modern weapons] before 1904 about zones of fire across which no living being could pass, heralded nothing but disaster. War is essentially the triumph, not of a chassepot over a needle-gun, not of a line of men entrenched behind wire entanglements and fireswept zones over men exposing themselves in the open, but of one will over another weaker will.

Walter Braithwaite propounded much the same theory in 1913, when he gave a lecture entitled: 'For the conduct of an army character weighs more than knowledge or science.' In this lecture, Braithwaite remarked: 'How often do we hear such expressions as "It is impossible to attack over such open ground." Surely none of us will ever acquiesce in such statements.' Braithwaite put forward the example of various battles to contradict these statements, including the Japanese at Shaho in 1904, carried out under modern conditions. 'There should be no such word in the dictionary of a soldier as "impossible". Mobility, power of manoeuvre and the offensive spirit are the requisites for success and, these elements being present, nothing is impossible.' Braithwaite continually stressed the power of the offensive, and stated that 'war is intensely human... all war is more a struggle for the mastery between two men – that is, the two commanders – than it is between the masses of men who serve under their command.'[1]

There was nothing unusual about these attitudes, they were common-place in the British officer corps at the time. It was understood that the offensive was the key to success, and that high morale and character would always carry the day. Unfortunately for Hamilton and Braithwaite, their appointment to high command occurred just as war-fare was radically changing, and the old verities were no longer a safe bet. At the same time, the Gallipoli campaign took place early enough in the war so that such sentiments were still generally held, while the learning curve and technology had not yet provided any solutions to the trench stalemate. But perhaps the Hamilton/Braithwaite approach to war might still have worked at Gallipoli since there were occasions, for example at Suvla, where old fashioned dash and morale could have succeeded. Yet the defensive technology of modern war employed by the Turks was usually strong enough for the older Allied style to fail. Hamilton did not realize this was a problem for some time, and still thought warfare was running along predictable lines until around June. In fact, according to Lt-Gen. Sir Stanley von Donop, Master General of Ordnance, Hamilton's GHQ did not recognize that it was trench warfare until July, when suitable materials such as corrugated iron were ordered. In addition, Hamilton was influenced by the common Social Darwinism of the time, which only too easily fitted into the 'win through morale and character' theory. Thus when writing of the Turks in early May 1915, Hamilton theorized that 'this high strung discipline [of their German commanders] cannot be natural to the Turkish character, and I hope myself we may soon be able to strain it to the breaking point.' Hamilton simply assumed that the Turkish character inevitably possessed a lower breaking point than European (German and British) character. Hamilton held the same view of some of his allies, especially the French colonial Zouaves, who were untrustworthy because of their racial origins.[2]

So far, it is hard to fault Hamilton for simply being part of a common British officer corps world view, although he was perhaps slow to recognize change. But Hamilton also faced the question whether he had the right to interfere with subordinates, or to remove senior officers, and here his command style begins to diverge from that of some other

British commanders on the Western Front at the time. When Hamilton failed to intervene with Hunter-Weston over Y Beach on 25 April, he justified himself afterwards by saying that he was dissuaded by Braithwaite: 'My inclination was to take a hand myself in this affair [Y Beach] but the Staff are clear against interference when I have no knowledge of the facts...'. This was reasonable except that Hamilton could clearly see V Beach was failing, while reinforcements at Y Beach would have reinforced success there. On another occasion, Hamilton also failed to intervene with Hunter-Weston over a possible night advance at Second Krithia. Then, when Hamilton thought that Byng, new commander of IX Corps, was too passive in September 1915, Hamilton only gave him 'very gentle hints as I think, with a man of Byng's reputation, one must leave him to himself for as long as possible.' Hamilton believed that 'Once a Commander-in-Chief has given his instructions and made sure that those... are fully seized with his ideas, he must leave to those subordinates the task of transmitting his ideas to their subordinates.' Of course this was sensible, a commander who continually interfered with his subordinates would certainly be impossible to work with. But, at Gallipoli, Hamilton was only called upon to intervene in a small number of critical situations.[3] Consequently, the historian R.R. James was justified when he criticized Hamilton for basically handing over command to his subordinates. Ironically, the only time when Hamilton did intervene decisively was at Suvla on 8 August, yet this was the particular action he felt guilty about during the Dardanelles Commission hearings. Hamilton was, therefore, bound into a mental universe that prevented him from taking decisive actions at certain times, and his age (62) and previous military and social experience worked against him. This, combined with a sense that Hamilton was something of a social general, meant that he was reluctant to get into conflict with senior officers such as Kitchener, Byng and Hunter-Weston.

In this context, Roger Keyes' evaluation of Hamilton is of interest. Already in early April, Keyes wrote in his diary that Hamilton was charming, and a good friend of Keyes' mother, but was also a 'humbug'. Humbug means imposter or fraud, and Keyes repeated the characterization in May: 'He may be a humbug but he *is* a charmer.' At another point, Keyes illustrated his concern about Hamilton by recounting the story that when the two of them were on board ship at the beginning of May, Hamilton acted rather like a school boy in suggesting in a whisper that the two of them should visit Anzac, when it was obviously important to do so.[4] Keyes did not fully spell out his view of Hamilton, but he evidently saw him as a charming general with useful social contacts, but lacking toughness.

Others who commented on Hamilton were Maj.-Gen. Godley and his wife. Godley felt sorry for Hamilton and blamed Braithwaite, who was Hamilton's 'evil genius.' Lady Godley was more forthright. Reporting from Cairo, she wrote that no one was surprised at Hamilton's recall, with officers saying 'he has made a hash of things & a great mistake in going on hammering at Cape Helles and that he should not have stuck himself at Imbros.' For his part, Godley simply commented that Monro had arrived and was very solid – a great contrast to Hamilton. A few days later, Godley mentioned that all were down on Hamilton at Gallipoli, but he again blamed Braithwaite. It seems that Godley was more generous to Hamilton than Lady Godley, but he obviously had misgivings about Hamilton, even apart from Braithwaite's influence.[5]

Two members of GHQ who had an intimate view of Hamilton and his command style were Orlo Williams, the cipher officer, who also helped draft Hamilton's reports and despatches, and Guy Dawnay, a staff officer responsible for much of the planning at Gallipoli. Orlo Williams felt that Hamilton was over-optimistic and obstinately unwilling to face facts and report unpleasant truths. After Hamilton's recall, Orlo Williams wrote 'The truth is that Sir Ian never did anything himself at all; as Dawnay said… "if ever we had had to ask his advice on anything, imagination faints at the probable result."' Orlo Williams did not think highly of Braithwaite either: 'The CGS also was no real use: he had not the necessary brain for this job.' Meanwhile, Dawnay argued that Hamilton did not really do anything, and did not have any new ideas or schemes. When Kitchener proposed recalling Braithwaite, but not Hamilton, Dawnay wrote: 'the man who was really out of his element was Sir Ian himself, from whom the CGS never had one note of help or guidance or reasonable advice since the day we started out.' Dawnay was anxious that Braithwaite should not be recalled without Hamilton also departing: 'It is Sir Ian who is really Stellenbosched…'. Dawnay summed up his view by admitting that Hamilton was badly used by his subordinates, referring correctly to several senior officers who failed: 'But the salient fact is that he [Hamilton] is *no use*…'.[6]

In Hamilton's defence, it is clearly the case that Dawnay was correct: there were many senior officers who let Hamilton down. Hunter-Weston, Stopford, Reed, Poett, Hammersley, Godley, Lindley, Hill, Sitwell, Johnston, Braithwaite himself – the list is a long one and by no means complete. Many of these were dug outs, or left over from the British Expeditionary Force in France. Yet, a common thread in views of Hamilton suggest that he was seen as something of a lightweight, with a journalist mentality, charming and well connected socially, but increasingly detached from events, and above all, not a strong and decisive commander. In fact, Hamilton had become something of a figure head, a commander-in-chief who did not really command. Another close observer, Aspinall, voiced common post-war criticisms that Hamilton was over-optimistic in his reports to London, and submissive to Kitchener over men and munitions. A further general criticism was that Hamilton isolated himself from his command on the island of Imbros. Although Hamilton rightly defended himself from this charge by pointing out he had two widely separated fronts to deal with, there is a suspicion that, at least subconsciously, he did detach himself from the campaign. Hence some officers like Stopford and Woodward felt that Hamilton simply ignored them, and others like Orlo Williams considered Hamilton to be out of touch and a figure head. It is also true that some senior officers just did not see Hamilton very often, for example, Birdwood at Anzac, who on 9 August reported that he saw Hamilton that day, but this was the 'first time for a very long time…'.[7]

Indeed, it was just this sense of isolation of Hamilton and his GHQ that was one of two main criticisms in Kitchener's wire to Hamilton in October, suggesting the replacement of Braithwaite. Kitchener wrote that criticisms from unofficial sources in England focussed on 'the staff work [of] your HQ and complaining of the members [of the staff] being much out of touch with the troops in Gallipoli.' Staff work at GHQ did overlook some problems, especially in giving Hunter-Weston too much freedom during the Krithia offensives, where attacks assumed a ritualistic quality. GHQ planning of major operations, especially the August offensives, also became far too complicated and ambitious. But, given the conditions on Gallipoli and the poor quality of some commanders and troops, GHQ staff work was of reasonable quality, unlike that of VIII Corps under Hunter-Weston or IX Corps under Stopford. And of necessity, the running of a large command like Hamilton's at Gallipoli meant a certain unavoidable separation between Hamilton's GHQ and the troops on the ground. On the other hand, there was a certain detachment from reality in Hamilton's case, and his reply to Kitchener that he was unavoidably isolated by the sea, that there was a lack of liaison officers, and that GHQ was small, while largely true, may not have been the strongest answer.[8]

Of course, Kitchener himself deserves much criticism in the organization and running of the strategy of the Gallipoli campaign.[9] Clearly, he was absurdly optimistic, he seriously under-estimated the Turks, he hung on to 29 Division for too long at the beginning of the campaign, he operated secretively as chief war planner, he relied far too heavily on the Navy, he thought of Gallipoli as a subsidiary campaign, he did not release men and munitions to Gallipoli in timely fashion, he sent poor quality officers and divisions to Gallipoli, and he changed his mind over very important factors, such as whether Allied forces could land on the Asian side. On the other hand, Kitchener was just one member, albeit a significant one, of the War Cabinet; he did have to consider the Western Front as the major theatre, and he was permanently under pressure from those who favoured the Western Front; there was a British shell shortage in 1915; and although it turned out that Britain was quite safe from invasion, this was something Kitchener had to keep in mind. When it became apparent to him in May 1915 that he had miscalculated over Gallipoli, Kitchener found himself in a cleft stick – in 1915 it was not possible to properly supply two major theatres, yet withdrawal from Gallipoli was unthinkable due to his apprehension about the effects of this in the East.[10]

So, the question arises, did Kitchener effectively doom the Gallipoli campaign? It is clear that Kitchener hindered the expedition to a considerable extent with poor planning, preparation and judgement, but he did not condemn it to failure, since there were some chances for Allied success. Kitchener and the War Office were frequently criticized, not least by Hamilton, for failing to provide sufficient men and munitions. Was there justification for this? First of all, Hamilton argued that he never knew Kitchener told Maxwell to supply men from Egypt to Gallipoli, yet Kitchener told Maxwell on 6 April to let Hamilton have what troops he wanted and could be spared, and this was communicated to Hamilton on 7 April. Then, Kitchener's telegram of 27 April to Hamilton was clear enough. If Hamilton needed more troops, 'Maxwell will give you any supports from Egyptian Garrison you may require.' On 17 May, asked for an estimate of troops needed, Hamilton told Kitchener he wanted two more Corps, but there was no room at Gallipoli for them. Kitchener replied, worried by this request, but he was surprised that the extra 4,500 men from Egypt were not required. On 19 June, Col. Fitzgerald, Kitchener's military secretary, wrote to Braithwaite at GHQ: 'Do not be shy of asking for troops; we have large numbers trained and ready here now, only held back by the ammunition supply, but that is improving fast.' If anything, Kitchener and London were ahead of Hamilton in asking for men from Egypt and suggesting that troops were available. Of course, asking and getting were two different things, and Maxwell in Egypt fought selfishly to retain as many troops as he could. Hamilton also did not like to press Kitchener too hard for troops, although it has recently been argued that Hamilton was more demanding in this regard than previously thought. Yet it seems the problem was not always so much lack of men as lack of room, the timing of their arrival, and the astonishing Allied casualty rate.[11]

In regard to timing, 29 Indian Brigade landed on 1 May, just too late for the First Krithia attack of 28 April. Would it have been worth waiting for these troops? Next, some troops of 42 Division were used at Second Krithia (6–8 May), but the majority landed during Second Krithia. Why not wait for them before launching the offensive? Then 52 Division arrived a few days after Third Krithia (4 June). Why not wait for them before launching this offensive, especially as the Turkish defence wilted under this attack, and might have crumbled with another attack the next day? It is also the case that in the August offensive, Anzac could not contain any more troops, while at Suvla the landing of four divisions should certainly have been enough men. It can also be argued that shortage of men was not the real problem, but rather the incredible wastage of men during Allied offensives. Previous chapters have detailed the casualties of some attacks, but by the end of Third Krithia, Allied casualties amounted to some 60,000 troops. Most of these had been caused by the unimaginative tactics of Hunter-Weston confronting trench warfare – casualties were inevitable, but not at this rate. More attacks in June and July at Helles then cost several thousand more Allied casualties. Turkish casualties were even higher, but these could more easily be replaced.

If shortage of men was not so much the problem as the timing of their arrival, and subsequently, their wastage, then was lack of munitions a crucial factor? Although there were shortages of Allied artillery and shells, especially howitzers and high explosive shells, it was really technical inability and inexperience that was the problem rather than shortages.[12] If this is so, can Allied failure be explained by structural or systemic factors? This appears to be largely the case. First of all, the systems and attitudes of the Navy and the Army were very often incompatible. Hamilton complained to Birdwood in mid-June 1915 that the British Navy:

> have no business methods whatever: keep no copies of their letters or orders, & are, generally speaking, as unbusinesslike as they are brave. We shall never get this supply matter fairly squared out until the transport part of the Naval show is separate from the Admiral and his operations, or fighting branch. Just as you get into [the] swing [of things] there comes a signal 'All ships coal' – or 'all ships report to the Admiral' – & then you are fairly knocked out for the day.[13]

Another inherent cause of friction between Army and Navy was the failure of the Navy to provide sufficient lighters and small craft, which de Robeck refused to admit were in short supply. Hamilton also complained that the PNTO (Principal Naval Transport Officer) did not consult the Army, while only in mid-June did the Navy and the War Office pool their resources in regard to hospital ships. Most important, Hamilton felt he could not issue orders to the Navy, as he noted in July 1915: 'What would it not be to me were the whole Fleet to attack as we land at Suvla! But obviously I cannot go out of my own element to urge the Fleet to actions...'.[14] Reflecting on Gallipoli and the relations between Navy and Army, Admiral J.H. Godfrey wrote in his post-war memoirs: 'I fancy that at times during the Dardanelles Campaign close cooperation on the [naval] Commander-[army] GSO 1 level was discouraged. The principals were too intent on getting their own way and didn't want staff officers interfering with their plans.' In general, Godfrey believed that 'There was the land war and the sea war and that was that.'[15]

These were structural problems, not likely to be easily changed. Such structural factors were repeated in other realms, for example, indifferent relations between GHQ and the Administrative/QMG staff, the ill organized Lines of Communication, and the persistent problem of identifying the contents of ships at Mudros, where 'Ships lay loaded at Mudros for weeks and even months.' In the latter case, for example, Lt-Col. T.H.B. Forster found that a motor roller, badly wanted ashore, had been for some weeks lying undiscovered aboard a ship at Imbros. After describing various problems at Mudros, such as the order of timbers for large piers which instead wound up as a chimney for the hospital at Lemnos, and in mine props at Anzac, Col. G.S. Elliott wrote: 'There seemed to be no system [at Mudros], no central control or direction. We were sheep without a shepherd...'. Hamilton was well aware of the situation, but powerless:

at Mudros, with its water and food supply for thousands upon thousands; with its arrangements for thousands of wounded; with its forwarding of personnel, ammunition and food to at least five different landing places... with its vital necessity for working hand in glove with the Navy; with every sort and description of huge vessel breaking bulk there... all these fill the ordinary person with despair... I am in despair myself about it.[16]

Other structural problems relate to the inexperience, and sometimes inability, of many commanders, staff and senior officers. This was particularly true, through no fault of their own, of the new Territorial Divisions. Despite the remarkable courage and sacrifice of the men and officers at Gallipoli, there was an underlying lack of competence among the directors of operations. Previous chapters have adduced several examples of this, so here one or two instances must suffice. At the lower level, Lt A.M. Laing, 1/Essex, 88 Brigade, 29 Division, remarked that staff work was terrible, and the staff never went near the front line. At the higher level, Brigadier-General Monash, CO 4th Australian Brigade, admitted that staff work in August was 'more or less a muddle.' According to Brigadier-General H.C. Frith, CO 125th Brigade, 42 Division, the commander of his division did not go into the front trenches for some five or six weeks, although his staff did. Lt-Gen. Sir W. Marshall complained of the same thing – the commander of 87 Brigade never went near the front lines. Added to this trend was the rather rigid hierarchy of the British army at the time. Only a few officers, such as Capt., later Lt-Col., Guy Geddes, 1st Royal Munster Fusiliers, dared to challenge the system. All of this was a structural problem of trying to fight and learn the art of war at the same time. By 1917 and 1918 there was a different atmosphere, but this was 1915.[17]

The final conclusion on the Allied side of the campaign at Gallipoli must be that it is wrong to focus on the mistakes of particular individuals. It is also an error to declare that the Allied campaign was doomed. Instead, the solution to the riddle of Gallipoli seems to rest with four conclusions. The Allies failed primarily because of their inexperience of modern war, especially because the 1915 campaign took place early in the war, before the learning curve, greater experience, and vastly improved technical ability provided solutions to the trench stalemate later in the war. In fact, tactics ate strategy at Gallipoli. Essentially, the failure of Allied naval and army tactics prevented strategy from succeeding. There were also, secondly, Allied structural and systemic problems, alluded to above, which were generally beyond the control of individuals. Thirdly, just as on the Western Front, the technology of modern war heavily favoured the defence, and this usually prevented Allied break throughs. In fact, exactly the same situation was occurring on the Western Front in 1915. If Allied forces could not break through on the Western Front – with more men and munitions – how could Allied forces be expected to break through on Gallipoli? The answer is that they could not, except as mentioned previously, through surprise. That is why there were genuine opportunities for Allied success during the naval attack in March on land, in late April at Helles, in early May at Helles, and in August at Anzac and Suvla.[18] Fourth, and lastly, Allied failure occurred because of a much stronger Turkish defence and greater Turkish numbers than anticipated. And here it was not just an efficient command system and large numbers, but also, what is often overlooked, the very strong nationalism of the Turkish troops. As an example, Hasan Ethem, a soldier in the 57th Regiment of Kemal's 19 Division, wrote a letter on 17 April to his mother, a few days before his death:

> 'My God, all that these heroic soldiers want is to introduce Thy name to the French and English. Please accept this honourable desire of ours and make our bayonets sharper so that we may destroy our enemy!… You have already destroyed a great number of them so destroy some more.' After praying thus I stood up. No one could be considered luckier and happier than I after that.

Ethem continued: 'If God wills, the enemy will make a landing and we will be taken (to the front lines), then the wedding ceremony will take place, won't it?' Here Ethem refers to the belief among Muslims that martyrdom means the chance to meet God after death as in a wedding ceremony. As Carl Mühlmann wrote about the Turkish soldier: 'all is possible with this raw human material.'[19]

*

According to the British Official History, casualties, including the sick in the campaign, amounted to some 205,000 British, 47,000 French and 251,000 Turks. Turkish casualty figures are disputed, and are almost certainly higher. Another source gives Turkish casualties as '2,160 officers and nearly 287,000 other ranks', for a total of approximately 289,160 men. This may be close to the reality.[20] To remember these casualties, the Turkish soldiers have a very large monument at Seddulbahir, and a small cemetery with a few grave sites; the French have their own cemetery at Seddulbahir, where each soldier has his own cross; Anzac and British soldiers either have their own grave sites in several cemeteries or, if the bodies were not recovered, there is a memorial at Helles, listing all those who died. Returning to the three officers who started this book, Hugh Price Travers is buried in Hill 10 cemetery, while Spenser Robert Valentine Travers and Hugh Eaton Frederick Travers are remembered on the Helles memorial. Their story and that of Gallipoli is a story of remarkable sacrifice and bravery on both sides. How best to remember them all? Perhaps the most emotional memorial is to be found on the beach at Anzac Cove, where a monument bears words spoken in 1934 in the Meclis (Turkish Assembly) by Atatürk, President of Turkey, formerly Mustafa Kemal:

> Those heroes that shed their blood and lost their lives... You are now lying in the soil of a friendly country. Therefore rest in peace. There is no difference between the Johnnies [Allied soldiers] and the Mehmets [Turkish soldiers] to us where they lie side by side here in this country of ours... You, the mothers, who sent their sons from far away countries, wipe away your tears, your sons are now lying in our bosom and are in peace. After having lost their lives on this land they have become our sons as well.[21]

ABBREVIATIONS

AAQMG	Assistant Adjutant and Quartermaster General.
ADC	Aide de Camp
AG	Adjutant General
ANZAC	Australian and New Zealand Army Corps
AQMG	Assistant Quarter Master General
ASC	Army Service Corps
CGS	Chief of the General Staff
CIGS	Chief of the Imperial General Staff
CRA	Commander Royal Artillery
CSM	Company Segeant Major
DADMS	Deputy Assistant Director of Medical Services
DMS	Director of Medical Services
DDMS	Deputy Director of Medical Services
FOO	Forward Observation Officer
GHQ	General Head Quarters
GOC	General Officer Commanding
GSO	General Staff Officer
HQ	Head Quarters
IGC	Inspector General Lines of Communication
MG	Machine Gun
NCO	Non Commissioned Officer
PNTO	Principal Naval Transport Officer
PMLO	Principal Military Landing Officer
QM	Quarter Master
QMG	Quarter Master General
RA	Rear Admiral
RE	Royal Engineers
SIW	Self Inflicted Wound
SNO	Senior Naval Officer
VA	Vice Admiral

NOTES

Abbreviations used in the footnotes for documentary sources:

AMA	Auckland Museum, Auckland, New Zealand
AWM	The Australian War Memorial, Canberra, Australia
BL	British Library, London, England
CCC	Churchill College, Cambridge, England
FAV	The French Army Archives, Vincennes, France
GSA	General Staff Archives, Ankara, Turkey
IOW	County Record Office, Newport, Isle of Wight, England
IWM	Imperial War Museum, London, England
KAM	Kippenberger Army Museum, Waiouru, New Zealand
KCL	Liddell Hart Centre for Military Archives, King's College, London, England
MLS	Mitchell Library, Sydney, Australia
NAM	National Army Museum, London, England
NAW	National Archives, Wellington, New Zealand
PRO	Public Record Office, Kew Gardens, London, England
TLW	Turnbull Library, Wellington, New Zealand
Turkish Official History	TC Genelkurmay Baskanligi, *Birinci Dunya Harbi: V Nci Cilt, Canakkale Cephesi Harekati*, 3 volumes, June 1914 – January 1916.

Prologue

1. Capt. V. Kidd, War Diary, 8th West Riding Regiment, 17 August 1915, War Office 95/4299, Public Record Office, Kew Gardens [hereafter PRO].
2. Capt. H. Aplin, War Diary, 7th Royal Munster Fusiliers, 10th Division, 29 August 1915; Lt-Col. G. Drage to Gen. Aspinall, 1 February 1931; War Office 95/4296, PRO.
3. Military Secretary, War Office, to Robert Travers [father], Timoleague, Co: Cork, 9 February 1916, personal officer file, War Office 339/20103, PRO.

Private letter, Robert Travers, Timoleague, County Cork, 9 March 1998, to Tim Travers. Among S.R.V. Travers' effects was a photo locket of his fiancée, Winifred Draper, of Bandon, County Cork, to whom he left the contents of his bank account. A memorial to him now exists in Timoleague Church.

4. War Diary, 9th Battalion Lancashire Fusiliers, War Office 95/4299; personal officer file, War Office 339/9582; PRO.

5. Ironically, in two of the personal officer files in the PRO, one theme appears to be financial. Thus, the father of Capt. Hugh Eaton Frederick Travers, Brigadier-General Joseph Oates Travers, knowing that his own death was near, wrote the War Office saying that because Hugh was still only listed as missing, the family solicitor wanted 'urgently' to know Hugh's actual date of death, since 'it is of considerable importance whether he was of age on that date or not', Brigadier-General Travers to War Office, 8 June 1933, War Office 339/9582, PRO. Meanwhile, the father of Lt Spenser Travers, Robert Travers, wrote the War Office on 15 December 1916, requesting payment of the balance of his son's account, perhaps for the benefit of his son's fiancée, or for Spenser's brother Arthur, who inherited Spenser's estate, War Office 339/20103, PRO. Thus did the Great War spread its deadly tentacles into the field of family inheritance.

Preface

1. Since this manuscript was completed, there has appeared Edward Erickson's book, *Ordered to Die: A History of the Ottoman Army in the First World War*, Greenwood Press, Westport, Connecticut, 2000). It is fair to say that Erickson presents a more positive picture of the Ottoman army at Gallipoli than the present author would fully agree with.

2. Capt. Carl Mühlmann, Bundesarchiv-Militärarchiv (Freiburg), RH 69 Kriegsgeschichtliche Forschungsanstalt des Heeres (formerly, Military Archive of the German Democratic Republic), W 10-51475 [hereafter Mühlmann, *Letter*]. I owe a very considerable debt of gratitude to my superbly supportive colleague Holger Herwig for locating this document, and then generously translating the obscure and illegible German into English.

3. A limited review of the literature follows. For internal factors, see Brigadier-General C.F. Aspinall-Oglander, *History of the Great War, based on Official Documents: Military Operations: Gallipoli, Volume 2, May 1915 to the evacuation*, William Heinemann, London, 1932, pp. 387, 479 ff. Although Robert Rhodes James avoids a specific conclusion, he tends to focus on internal factors in his *Gallipoli*, London 1965; Pimlico edition with new preface, London, 1999. James' book remains probably the best overall view of the

campaign. Michael Hickey, *Gallipoli*, John Hickey, London, 1995, while avoiding outright criticism, seems to emphasise both internal and external factors. The recent focus on external factors (Kitchener and London) is most evident in Nigel Steel and Peter Hart, *Defeat at Gallipoli*, Macmillan, London, 1994, and John Lee, *A Soldier's Life: General Sir Ian Hamilton, 1853–1947*, MacMillan, London, 2000. Edward Erickson would also argue that the key to the Allied failure was the Ottoman army. The conclusions of the Turkish official history in regard to morale and leadership are in TC Genelkurmay Baskanligi [Turkish General Staff], *Birinci Dunya Harbi: V Nci Cilt, Canakkale Cephesi Harekati, 3 Nci Kitap, Haziran 1915 – Ocak 1916*, Ankara, 1980, pp. 557 ff. [hereafter *Turkish Official History*, vol. 3].

4. Michael Tyquin, *Gallipoli: the Medical War: The Australian Army Medical Services in the Dardanelles Campaign of 1915*, New South Wales University Press, Kensington, 1993

The Origins of the Military Campaign and the Naval Attack at Gallipoli

1. Much of this material is covered in James, *Gallipoli*, chapter 2; Steel and Hart, *Defeat at Gallipoli*, chapter 1; and Hickey, *Gallipoli*, chapter 5. Also, Fisher to Churchill, 9 January 1915, Chartwell Papers, 13/56, Churchill College, Cambridge [hereafter CCC]. Admiral Lord Fisher, Evidence at the Dardanelles Commission, pp. 205, and Fisher to Lord Cromer, 11 October 1916, Cabinet 19/33, PRO.

2. Churchill to Carden, 3 January 1915, Carden to Churchill, 5 January 1915, Carden to Churchill, 11 January 1915, Chartwell Papers, 13/65, CCC. On Carden, see A. J. Marder, *From the Dreadnought to Scapa Flow. The Royal Navy in the Fisher Era, 1904–1919. Volume II, The War Years: To the Eve of Jutland*, Oxford University Press, London, 1965, p. 231. On Limpus, Lord Wester Wemyss, *The Navy in the Dardanelles Campaign*, Hodder & Stoughton, London, 1924, p. 18. On staff officers, Paul Halpern ed., *The Keyes Papers, vol. 1, 1914–1918*, London, 1979, pp. 153–4, and Roger Keyes, *The Naval Memoirs of Admiral of the Fleet Sir Roger Keyes: the Narrow Seas to the Dardanelles, 1910–1915*, London, 1934, p. 188.

3. Naval Intelligence Department, *Turkey Coast Defences, 1908: Part II, Coast Defences*, pp. 8, 11, Admiralty 231/49, PRO.

4. 'Military Expedition to Zealand in Support of the Danes against German Invasion', 30 June 1908, p.768, Admiralty 116/1043B, PRO.

5. Churchill to Maj. John Churchill, 19 April 1915, Chartwell Papers, 13/65, CCC. Admiral F. Tudor, Evidence at the Dardanelles Commission, p. 178; Col. Hankey, Evidence at the Dardanelles Commission, p. 22; Col. Charles Callwell, Evidence at the Dardanelles Commission, p. 218; Cabinet 19/33,

PRO. Roger Keyes to Eva (wife), 17 March 1915, 2/9, Keyes Papers, 13484, British Library [hereafter BL]. Kitchener to Maxwell, 27 February 1915, General Staff copies of telegrams, 1915, War Office 158/574, PRO.

6. De Robeck, Order #16, 'Preparations for Battle', 9 February 1915; HMS *Vengeance*, 'Remarks on #16', 14 February 1915; 'Second Remarks on #16', 17 February 1915; de Robeck Papers, 4/2, CCC. Commodore Charles Bartolome, navy secretary to 1st Lord, Evidence at Dardanelles Commission, p. 124, Cabinet 19/33, PRO.

7. Wemyss, *The Navy in the Dardanelles Campaign*, p. 15. Lloyd George, Evidence at Dardanelles Commission, p. 005, Cabinet 19/33, PRO. Kitchener to Maxwell, 23 February 1915, Maxwell to Kitchener, 24 February 1915, Kitchener to Maxwell, 24 February 1915, War Office Telegrams, Cabinet 19/31, PRO.

8. Maxwell to Kitchener, 26 February 1915, War Office Telegrams, Cabinet 19/31, PRO. Kitchener to Maxwell, 5 March 1915, War Office 158/574, PRO.

9. Churchill to Carden, 24 February 1915, Chartwell Papers, 13/65, CCC. Carden, Evidence at the Dardanelles Commission, p. 162; Hankey, Evidence at the Dardanelles Commission, p. 18, 26; Cabinet 19/31, PRO. Carden to de Robeck, 26 February 1915, de Robeck Papers, 4/37, CCC. Lady Hamilton, Diary, 22 October 1915, 44, Hamilton Papers, Liddell Hart Centre for Military Archives, King's College, London University [hereafter KCL]. Lady Hamilton's source was May Spender, wife of the editor of the *Westminster Gazette*.

10. Carden to Churchill, 13 January 1915, Chartwell Papers, 13/65, CCC.

11. Commander Gibson, Diary, 25 February 1915, 26 February 1915, Rear-Admiral I. W. Gibson Papers, 87/32/2, Imperial War Museum [hereafter IWM]. Robert G. Blackie, Lt, *Triumph*, 'One of the Black Squad, 1914–1918', p. 8, unpublished manuscript in possession of Mr Peter Blackie.

12. Commander Gibson, Diary, 1 March 1915, 2 March 1915, 3 March 1915, 5 March 1915, 6 March 1915, Gibson Papers, 87/32/2, IWM. Marder, *Dreadnought to Scapa Flow*, p. 240. Wemyss, *The Navy in the Dardanelles Campaign*, p. 27. Carden to de Robeck, 3 March 1915, 4/37, de Robeck Papers, CCC. Roger Keyes to Eva (wife), 8 March 1915, 2/9, Keyes Papers, BL.

13. Carden to Admiralty, 4 March 1915, Carden to Churchill, 6 March 1915, Carden to Churchill, 10 March 1915, Churchill to Carden, 11 March 1915, Chartwell Papers, 13/65, CCC. Wemyss, *The Navy in the Dardanelles Campaign*, pp. 28–29. Gibson, Diary, 12 March 1915, Gibson Papers, IWM. Churchill, Evidence at the Dardanelles Commission, p. 98, Cabinet 19/33, PRO. Roger Keyes to Eva (wife), 8 March 1915, 2/9, Keyes Papers, BL.

14. Martin Gilbert, *Winston Churchill, Volume 3, The challenge of war 1914–1916*, Heinemann, London, 1971, p. 337. Gibson, Diary, 15 March 1915, Gibson Papers, IWM.

15. Roger Keyes to Eva (wife), 12 March 1915, 2/9, Keyes Papers, BL. Carden to Churchill, 14 March 1915, Churchill to Carden, 15 March 1915, Chartwell Papers, 13/65, CCC. Gibson, Diary, 13 March 1915, 14 March 1915, Gibson Papers, IWM.

16. Capt. Dent, 'Notes when in command of HMS *Irresistible*, 25 June 1925, War Office 95/4263, PRO. Carden to Churchill, 14 March 1915, Churchill to Carden, 15 March 1915, Carden to Churchill, 15 March 1915, Malta to Churchill, 20 March 1915, 13/65, Chartwell Papers, CCC. Roger Keyes, *Naval Memoirs*, pp. 229, 247, 254, 257. Carden to Admiralty, 14 March 1915, Carden to French CinC, 14 March 1915, French CinC to Carden, 15 March 1915, Carden to Malta, 19 March 1915, 5/11, Keyes Papers, BL. De Robeck, Diary of Events, 19 March 1915, 4/6, de Robeck Papers, CCC.

17. Aspinall, Letter book, Box 111, re: mines/mine sweeper committee not meeting, OG 113/3, Aspinall-Oglander Papers, County Record Office, Newport, Isle of Wight [hereafter IOW]. Carden to Churchill, 14 March 1915, Carden to Churchill, 16 March 1915, 13/65, Chartwell Papers, CCC. Wemyss, *The Navy in the Dardanelles Campaign*, p. 43. De Robeck, Meeting of Captains, 19 March 1915, 4/5, de Robeck Papers, CCC.

18. Gibson, Diary, 16 March 1915, IWM. Roger Keyes to de Robeck, no date, but probably 16 March 1915, 4/39, de Robeck Papers, CCC.

19. Gibson, Diary, 17 March 1915, IWM.

20. Gilbert, *Churchill*, pp. 338 ff. Hankey, Diary, 12 March 1915, Hankey Papers, 1/1, CCC. Churchill to Carden, 15 March 1915, two messages, Chartwell Papers, 13/65, CCC. Hankey, Evidence at Dardanelles Commission, pp. 20 ff., Cabinet 19/33. Birdwood to Maxwell, 4 March 1915, and Kitchener to Maxwell, 11 March 1915, War Office 158/574, PRO.

21. Gilbert, *Churchill*, p. 347. Vice-Admiral P-E. Guépratte, *L'Expédition Des Dardanelles, 1914–1915*, Paris: 1935, pp. 58–60. See also Sir Julian Corbett, *History of The Great War: Naval Operations*, vol. 2, Longmans, London, 1921, pp. 213–215.

22. George Schreiner, Associated Press of America, 19 March 1915, Ischanak Kelessi, War Office 106/1465, PRO.

23. Guépratte, *L'Expédition Des Dardanelles*, pp. 66–74.

24. Gibson, Diary, 18 March 1918, IWM. Schreiner, *op cit*.

25. Carden to de Robeck, 21 March 1915, 4/37, de Robeck Papers, CCC. Wemyss, *The Navy in the Dardanelles Campaign*, p. 41.

26. Kemal to Ministry of War, 24 March 1915, Cabinet 105, Record 780, Shelf 5, File 182; German report on Allied Attack, 4 April 1915, Archive 1/1; Record 553/509, File 118, General Staff Archives, Ankara [hereafter GSA].

27. *Ibid.*, p. 5. Mines Report, 1914–1918, Map 1/13, File 4659, Archive 6/1666, Record 230–375, GSA. Unfortunately, Map 1/13 does not give a date when the mines *across* the Straits at Eren Keui were laid. However, since the same map also shows the twenty-six mines laid parallel to the shore as listed in the 4 April 1915 German report, *op cit.*, some of which were obviously detonated on March 18, implying that this was a pre March 18 map, it is quite possible that the mines across the Straits were also laid before March 18.

28. It seems that Room 40 of British Naval Intelligence intercepted a message from the Kaiser to von Usedom on 12 March, saying that ammunition would reach the Straits in time, but this message was handed to Fisher and Churchill on 19 March, *after* the naval attack, giving them the wrong impression of ammunition troubles as a result of the attack, Geoffrey Penn, *Fisher, Churchill and the Dardanelles*, Leo Cooper, Barnsley, South Yorkshire, 1999), p. 153. TC Genelkurmay Baskanligi, *Birinci Dunya Harbinde Turk Harbi, V Nci Cilt, Canakkale Cephesi Harekati, 1 Nci Kitap (Haziran 1914 – 25 Nisan 1915)*, 2nd ed., Ankara 1993, pp. 267–269 [hereafter *Turkish Official History*, vol. 1]. Corbett, *History of the Great War: Naval Operations*, p. 224. Gilbert, *Churchill*, pp. 354, 357.

29. Roger Keyes, *Naval Memoirs*, p. 248, *The Naval Memoirs of Admiral J.H. Godfrey*, vol. 2, p. 2, unpublished ms., 74/96/1, IWM. De Robeck to Wemyss, 18 March 1915, Naval messages, 17/7/25/4, Hamilton Papers, KCL. De Robeck to Hamilton, 19 March 1915, 5/4, Hamilton Papers, KCL. Hamilton to de Robeck, 19 March 1915, 4/40, de Robeck Papers, CCC.

30. Hamilton to Kitchener, 18 March 1915, and 19 March 1915, Kitchener to Hamilton, 19 March 1915, pp. 63–64, Dardanelles Commission, Cabinet 19/31, PRO.

31. De Robeck, Meeting of Captains, 19 March 1915, 4/5; Carden to de Robeck, 21 March 1915, 4/37; de Robeck Papers, CCC. Roger Keyes, *Naval Memoirs*, pp. 256 ff.

32. Aspinall, 'Chapter 14 Difficulties', Letter book, OG 113/3, in Box 111, Aspinall-Oglander Papers, IOW. A number of conflicting sources look at de Robeck's change of mind: Churchill, Evidence at the Dardanelles Commission, p. 120, Cabinet 19/33, PRO. Corbett, *History of the Great War: Naval Operations*, pp. 227–228. Marder, *From the Dreadnought to Scapa Flow*, pp. 251–252. Gilbert, *Churchill*, pp. 360 ff. Wemyss, *The Navy in the Dardanelles Campaign*, pp. 43 ff. Kitchener, Instructions of 12 March 1915, 'Buckley's Draft', 5/4, Hamilton Papers, KCL. Gilbert, *Churchill*, p. 363.

33. Roger Keyes to Ev. (wife Eva ?), 26 March 1917, 5/38, Keyes Papers, BL.
34. Roger Keyes, Evidence at Dardanelles Commission, 16/8/3, Hamilton Papers, KCL. Hankey, Diary, 20 March 1915, Hankey Papers, 1/1, CCC.
35. De Robeck to Churchill, 23 March 1915, Churchill to de Robeck, 25 March 1915, de Robeck to Churchill, 11 April 1915, and Churchill to de Robeck, 13 May 1915, 13/65, Chartwell Papers, CCC. De Robeck to Admiralty, 27 March 1915, Admiralty to de Robeck, 28 March 1915, de Robeck to Admiralty, 29 March 1915, 5/11, Keyes Papers, BL. Admiral Jackson, 'Note on the Passage of the Dardanelles', 11 May 1915, in Box 111, Aspinall-Oglander Papers, IOW. De Robeck, Memorandum, 23 April 1915, War Office 106/705, PRO. Hankey, Diary, 12 May 1915, 1/1, Hankey Papers, CCC. Godfrey, *Naval Memoirs*, vol. 8, p. 65, 74/96/1, IWM.
36. Hamilton to de Robeck, no date, but probably 26 March 1915, since Hamilton had just received Churchill's 140 of 25 March 1915, Naval Signals, 17/724/1, Hamilton Papers, KCL. Aspinall, Appreciation for CGS, 23 March 1915, Box 116/4, Aspinall-Oglander Papers, IOW. Hamilton to Kitchener, 23 March 1915, Dardanelles Commission, Cabinet 19/31, PRO. Dr O.C. Williams, Diary, 21 March 1915, vol. 1, 69/78/1, IWM.
37. Hankey, Diary, 6 April 1915, 7 April 1915, 8 April 1915, 1/1, Hankey Papers, CCC. Hence the Admiralty on 28 March simply stated that it had been hoped not to involve the Army, but now the Army was necessary.
38. Wemyss, *The Navy in the Dardanelles Campaign*, p. 51. Godfrey, *Naval Memoirs*, vol. 2, pp. 30, 22, vol. 8, pp. 23–24, 74/96/1, Godfrey Papers, IWM. Hamilton, pencil notes on 12 March draft instructions, 17/4/1/31, Hamilton Papers, KCL. One who afterwards spoke of the problems of divided control between land and sea, and lack of mutual understanding, was Maj. Guy Dawnay, GS GHQ, 'Dardanelles', Staff Lectures, Dawnay Papers, 69/21/1, IWM. Admiralty to de Robeck, 28 March 1915, 5/11, Keyes Papers, BL. On Kitchener's verbal instructions to Hamilton, see Edmonds to G.W. Lambert (Admiralty, 1905–1915), 26 Feb. 1940, Cabinet 103/58, PRO.
39. Kitchener to Maxwell, 20 February 1915, and 23 February 1915, pp. 54 ff., War Office Telegrams, Cabinet 19/31; and in War Office 158/574; PRO. Appreciation of Kitchener, unsigned, undated, Box 116/9, Aspinall-Oglander Papers, IOW.

Turkish Expectations of the Allied Landings

1. Liman von Sanders, 'Appreciation', 26 January 1915, 180-304-774, in 'Sea and Beach reports to Fifth Army,' Cabinet 176, Record 1, Shelf 1, File 3432, GSA.
2. *Ibid.*

3. Liman von Sanders, *Five Years in Turkey*, US Naval Institute, Annapolis, 1927, pp. 59–60, 56.

4. Turkish Consul to GHQ, 22 March 1915, Index 20; and Military Attaché in Rome to Supreme Military Command, Index 13; Cabinet 105, Record 780, Shelf 5, File 182, GSA. This file contains many other similar reports.

5. Re: Palmer in Athens, Malta to Vice-Admiral EMS, 4 March 1915, 5/11, Keyes Papers, BL. Information on Palmer in Gallipoli in Roger Keyes, *The Naval Memoirs of Admiral of the Fleet Sir Roger Keyes*, pp. 288–290. Palmer is listed as Temporary Lieutenant in Admiralty files on the E15, 'Loss of Submarine E15 on 18 April 1915', Admiralty 1/8418/90, PRO. Information on the end of E 15 in Prisoner of War statements, Charles Stratford, serving on E 15, 26 August 1915, Cabinet 113, Record 2115, Shelf 5, File 542, GSA. Col. Djevad Bey to Supreme Command, 20 April 1915, Cabinet 105, Record 774, Shelf 4, File 180, Index 30, GSA.

6. Col. Djevad Bey to Supreme Command, 20 April 1915, *op cit*. Palmer did become a prisoner of war, and as far as can be discovered, survived the war.

7. Col. Djevad Bey to Supreme Command, 21 April 1915, *op cit*. The message from Supreme Command requesting this further explanation was not located in the archives, but is evident from Djevad Bey's reply.

8. The 25 April intercept of Allied numbers by Fifth Army is in 'First landing on Canakkale…', Cabinet 105, Record 776/325, Shelf 4, File 180, GSA.

9. Fethi Bey (probably Fezi Bey, then commanding in the Saros area) to Enver Pasa, 22 April 1915; Correspondence between Fifth Army and Supreme Command, 20 April 1915, Cabinet 9–105, Record 304–774, Shelf 13–4, File 180, Index 30; GSA. Also, Liman von Sanders to Enver Pasa, 24 April 1915; and Kesan Gendarmerie to Enver Pasa, 25 April 1915; 'Logistics and Attacks at Gallipoli/Canakkale', Cabinet 105, Record 775, Shelf 4, File 180; the two messages of 25 and 26 April are in: 'First landings on Canakkale and sea attacks', Cabinet 105, Record 776/325, Shelf 4, File 180; GSA. *Turkish Official History*, vol. 1, p. 253. Mühlmann, *Letter*.

10. Mühlmann, *Letter*.

11. Mühlmann, *Letter*. Canakkale Forts to Istanbul, 25 April 1915, and Merten Pasa to Istanbul, 26 April 1915, Cabinet 105, Record 776/325, Shelf 4, File 180, GSA.

12. Mühlmann, *Letter*. Hickey, *Gallipoli*, p. 145, sees the *Queen Elizabeth* as sinking a fully laden troop ship. However, there is no doubt that it was extraordinarily accurate shooting. Liman von Sanders, *Five Years in Turkey*, p. 67.

13. Mühlmann, *Letter*.

14. Birdwood's original plan had been to land at Bulair, GOC Egypt to Vice-Admiral EMS, 6 March 1915, 5/11, Keyes Papers, BL.

The Allied Landings at Helles and Kum Kale

1. Hamilton to Kitchener, 18 March 1915, 5/1, Hamilton Papers, KCL. Hamilton to Kitchener, 23 March 1915, Cabinet 19/31, PRO.

2. Hunter-Weston to wife, 7 April 1915, and Appreciations, 48364, BL.

3. Birdwood to Col. Callwell, 10 April 1915, and Birdwood to Col. Fitzgerald, 19 April 1915, 60, Birdwood Papers, AWM. Hamilton to Kitchener, 3 April 1915, 5/1, Hamilton Papers, KCL.

4. Braithwaite to Fitzgerald, 10 April 1915, Dardanelles Commission, Cabinet 19/28, PRO.

5. Commander Gibson, Diary, 5 April 1915, 7 April 1915, 25 April 1915, 87/32/2, IWM. Blackie, 'One of the Black Squad, 1914–1918' p.11. Wemyss to de Robeck, Sunday morning, perhaps 25 April; and Friday evening, perhaps 30 April; 4/32, de Robeck Papers, CCC.

6. Unsigned and Undated Note, 5/37, Keyes Papers, 13484, BL. Birdwood to Hamilton, 1 April 1915, Hamilton to Birdwood, 2 April 1915, 5/10, Hamilton Papers, KCL. Hamilton, comments on Hunter-Weston Dardanelles Commission testimony, p. 99, 16/8/6, Hamilton Papers, KCL.

7. Aspinall, Appreciation for CGS, 23 March 1915, Box 116/4, Aspinall-Oglander Papers, IOW.

8. Hamilton to Kitchener, 10 April 1915, 5/1, Hamilton Papers, KCL. Aspinall, hand written notes, in Da Costa to Aspinall, 9 February, 1931, Cabinet 45/241, PRO. De Robeck thought the Anzac landing was a feint in 11 April 1915 to Admiralty, Dardanelles Commission, Cabinet 19/30, PRO.

9. Hamilton to Kitchener, 15 April 1915, and 23 April 1915, 5/1, Hamilton Papers, KCL.

10. Hunter-Weston to wife, various letters on 27 April 1915, BL.

11. Aspinall, hand written comments, in 'C', Cabinet 45/241, PRO.

12. Aspinall to Bean, 17 December 1929, 3DRL 7953/27, Bean Papers, AWM. Evidence of Lt-Col. H.E. Street, GSO 2, 29 Division, 17 December 1916, p. 25, Cabinet 19/31, PRO. Capt. Milward, GSO 3, 29 Division, Diary, 24 April 1915, Cabinet 45/259, PRO.

13. Cf. Steel and Hart, *Defeat at Gallipoli*, p. 86.

14. Roger Keyes to Vice-Admiral (Personal), 31 May 1915; Davidson, Letter of Proceedings, 29 May 1915; in Chief of Staff Minutes, 4/23, de Robeck Papers, CCC.

15. Duties of attendant ships are noted in *Naval Memoirs of Admiral J.H. Godfrey, 1915–1919*, vol. 2, p. 6, 74/96/1, IWM.

16. *Ibid*.

17. De Robeck for GOC MEF [Hamilton], 12 April 1915; de Robeck, 'Orders for Combined Operations,' 12 April 1915; War Office 106/705, PRO.

Maj.-Gen. Alex Godley, GOC Anzac Division, 24 April 1915, to Col. the Honourable Sir James Allen (New Zealand Minister of Defence), Godley Papers, WA 252/2, National Archives, Wellington, New Zealand [hereafter NAW].

18. Discussion of range systems is in Jon Sumida, *In Defence of Naval Supremacy: Finance, Technology and British Naval Policy, 1889–1914*, Routledge, London, 1989. Capt. Hughes Lockyer, 'The Battle of the Beaches,' unpublished, no date, but post 1936, and Brigadier Alan Thomson, *Albion*, to John North (historian), 20 April 1937; Lockyer Papers, 75/56/1, IWM. Col. Braithwaite, 'Notes on the Landing,' in Braithwaite, Diary, WA 1/1, Godley Papers, NAW. De Robeck, 'Memorandum,' 23 April 1915, War Office 106/705, PRO.

19. Wemyss, *The Navy in the Dardanelles*, pp. 62–63, 78. Eric Bush blames the frightened Greek crew who fled below decks as the attached ships approached the shore, *Gallipoli*, Allen and Unwin, London, 1975, pp. 120–121. Capt. Geddes, 1st Bn. Royal Munster Fusiliers, 'The Landing from the 'River Clyde' at V Beach, April 25, 1915,' War Office 95/4310, PRO.

20. *Ibid.* Capt. Unwin to Capt. Lockyer, 21 June 1936, Capt. Lockyer to Keble Chatterton, 28 April 1915, Roger Keyes to Capt. Lockyer, 2 January 1937, Brigadier Alan Thomson to John North, 20 April 1937, Eric Bush to Capt. Lockyer, 21 March 1970, 75/56/1, Lockyer Papers, IWM. Log of *Cornwallis*, 25 April 1915, ADM 53/38708, PRO. For Sgt. Ryan, Capt. Edwardes Report, 25 April 1915, HQ 86 Brigade, War Office 95/4310, PRO.

21. Director of Army Signals, War Diary, 25 April 1915, War Office 95/4268; Aspinall, GHQ War Diary, 25 April 1915, War Office 95/4263; PRO. Log of *Albion*, 25 April 1915, ADM 53/33216, PRO. Lt-Col. Tizard, C.O. 1st Royal Munsters, 'Report on the Landing from the Collier *River Clyde*,' 28 April 1915, War Office 95/4310, PRO. Brigadier Alan Thomson, *Albion*, to John North, 20 April 1937, 75/56/1, Lockyer Papers, IWM. Capt. Geddes, 'The Landing from the River Clyde…,' War Office 95/4310, PRO.

22. Commander Gibson, Diary, 25 April 1915, Gibson Papers, 87/32/2, IWM. Milward, Diary, 25 April 1915, *op cit*.

23. Roger Keyes to Capt. Lockyer, 2 January 1937, 75/56/1, Lockyer Papers, IWM. Hunter-Weston, Diary, 25 April 1915, BL. Director of Army Signals, War Diary, 25 April 1915, War Office 95/4268, PRO. GHQ War Diary, 25 April 1915, War Office 95/4263, PRO.

24. Admiral J.H. Godfrey, *Naval Memoirs*, pp. 5–6, 9–10, 15, 74/96/1, Godfrey Papers, IWM.

25. Milward, *op cit*. 'First landing on Canakkale, and naval attacks,' messages #4, #6, #7, 25 April 1915, Cabinet 105, Record 776/325, Shelf 4, File 180, GSA. Captured Turkish Orders, Krithia, 25 April 1915; Turkish papers relative to

April 24 and 25, 1915, 5/14, Admiralty Orders and Letters, Keyes Papers, 13484, BL. Col. Mahmut, 'Memoirs of the Battalion Commander who opposed the first landings at dulbahir,' no date, K34980, IWM.

26. Mahmut, 'Memoirs,' pp. 2–12. IWM.

27. Mahmut, Memoirs, IWM. Milward, *op cit.*

28. Milward, *op cit.* Letter by James Brightmore, rating on *Euryalus*, in J.J. Fallon, 'HMS *Euryalus* at W Beach,' *The Gallipolian*, #77, Spring 1995. Daily Reports, Fifth Army, 25 April 1915, #2–21, and #2–28, GSA.

29. F. Hyde Harrison, 1st Battalion Border Regiment, to Aspinall, 27 April 1926, Box 116/1, Aspinall-Oglander Papers, IOW. War Diary, 2nd Battalion, Royal Dublin Fusiliers, 25 April 1915, War Office 95/4310, PRO. Questions put to the Turkish General Staff, 1919, Question and Answer #169, Cabinet 45/217, PRO.

30. F. Aylwyn to Aspinall, no date, Cabinet 45/241, PRO. Southern Landing, de Robeck for GOC MEF *Queen Elizabeth*, 12 April 1915, War Office 106/705, PRO.

31. Col. Matthews, Testimony at Dardanelles Commission, Cabinet 19/33, PRO. Milward, Diary, 26 April 1915, *op cit.* Report of the CID Official History Committee, 15 February 1928, Cabinet 16/52, PRO. Aylwyn to Aspinall, no date, Cabinet 45/241, PRO. Roger Keyes to wife Eva, 26 April 1915, 2/10, Keyes Papers, BL. Stirling Cookson to Aspinall, 12 February 1926, Box 112; Admiralty letter and R.D. Lough to Aspinall, 12 April 1927 and 30 March 1927, Box 112; Capt. Koe, R.N., to Aspinall, 8 February 1932, Box 111; Stirling Cookson to Aspinall, 12 February 1926, Box 112; Aspinall-Oglander Papers, IOW. Aspinall, Evidence of witnesses at Dardanelles Commission, 16/1/4, Hamilton Papers, KCL.

32. Log of HMS *Sapphire*, 25 April 1915, Admiralty 53/59129; Log of HMS *Amethyst*, Admiralty 53/33548; PRO. Col. Matthews, Testimony at Dardanelles Commisssion, Cabinet 19/33, PRO. 87 Brigade, War Diary, 25 April 1915, War Office 95/4310, PRO. Milward, Diary, 26 April 1915, *op cit.* Report of the CID Official History Committee, 15 February 1928, Cabinet 16/52, PRO. F. Aylwyn to Aspinall, no date, Cabinet 45/241, PRO. GHQ, War Diary, 25 April 1915, War Office 95/4263, PRO.

33. Aspinall, Evidence at Dardanelles Commission, 16/1/4, Hamilton Papers, KCL.

34. D'Amade to Minister of War, 8 March 1915; d'Amade to Carden, 15 March 1915; d'Amade to War Cabinet, 30 March 1915; Dossier du Chef d'Etat Major, Compte Rendu, 20 N 27; Confidential, Compte Rendu, 15 March–23 April 1915, #8A; Journée du 27 April 1915, in fact the liaison offi-

cer, Capitaine de Putron, persuaded d'Amade not to send this telegram, 20 N 28; French Army Archives,Vincennes [hereafter FAV].

35. C.E.O. Compte Rendu, #2A, 20 N 28; Rapport du Col. Ruef, on board *Savoie*, 28 April 1915, in XVII, 'Pieces Justification du Journal des Marches des Operations du C.E.O.,' 26 N 75; FAV.

36. Compte Rendu, *op cit.* Aspinall-Oglander, *History of the Great War, based on Official Documents: Military Operations: Gallipoli, Volume 1, Inception of the Campaign to May 1915*, Heinemann, London, 1929, p. 261. 'First Landing and Sea Attacks,' Canakkale to CinC, 25 and 26 April 1915, Cabinet 105, Record 776/325, Shelf, 4; File 180, GSA. TC Genelkurmay Baskanligi, *Birinci Dunya Harbinde Turk Harbi, V Nci Cilt, Canakkale Cephesi Harekati, 2 Nci Kitap (25 Nisan 1915 – Mayis 1915).*, Ankara, 1978, pp. 88–89 [hereafter *Turkish Official History*, vol. 2]. Roger Keyes, Report on Operations of 25 and 26 April 1915, 1 July 1915, Admiralty Orders and Letters, 5/14, Keyes Papers, BL.

37. Hamilton to Roger Keyes, 15 June 1917, 17/4/2/96, Hamilton Papers, KCL. Braithwaite to Fitzgerald, 7 July 1915, Letters between Gen. Braithwaite and Col. Fitzgerald, Evidence at Dardanelles Commission, Cabinet 19/28, PRO.

38. Compte Rendu C.E.O, #2A; Compte Rendu Debarquement, 26 April 1915, 9.15 p.m., d'Amade to Minister of War; Rapport… les operations C.E.O., 25 Avril – 13 Mai 1915; 20 N 28; 1st Division War Diary, 26 Avril 1915; Rapport du Col. Ruef, 28 Avril 1915, #17; 26 N 75; FAV. Hunter-Weston, Diary, 26 April 1915, BL.

The Anzac Landing

1. Birdwood to Aspinall, 8 May 1926, and 30 August 1926, Box 116, Aspinall-Oglander Papers, IOW. Maj.-Gen. Bridges, GOC 1 Australian Division, 'Orders for landing at Anzac 1915', 18 April 1915, 3DRL 8042/4, Bean Papers, AWM. Lt-Col. W.G. Braithwaite to GOC Anzacs, 13 April 1915; Birdwood Order #1, 17 April 1915; Maj. Gen. Walker, BGGS Anzacs to GOC Australian Division, 18 April 1915; Evidence at Dardanelles Commission, Cabinet 19/29, PRO. Lt-Col W.G. Braithwaite, Diary, 21 April 1915, WA 1/1, Box 1, NAW. According to Denis Winter, *25 April 1915: The Inevitable Tragedy*, University of Queensland Press, Lucia, 1994, there were three different and sequential plans for the landing. It seems more likely that there was one basic plan modified over time.

2. Lt Colvin Algie, Diary, 21 April 1915, 1374, Algie Papers, Turnbull Library, Wellington, New Zealand [hereafter TLW]. Hamilton to Kitchener, 23 April 1915, in Hamilton, Evidence at the Dardanelles Commission, Cabinet 19/29; and Hamilton, Evidence at the Dardanelles Commission, Cabinet

19/32; PRO. Dawnay to Aspinall, 7 July 1926, Gallipoli Correspondence, Box 112, Aspinall-Oglander Papers, IOW. Hamilton, Comments on Dardanelles Commission Evidence, Birdwood Question 21360, p. 108, 16/8/6, Hamilton Papers, KCL. Birdwood to Fitzgerald, 19 April 1915, 60, Birdwood Papers, AWM.

3. Birdwood to Callwell, 10 April 1915, Birdwood to Fitzgerald, 19 April 1915, 60, Birdwood Papers, AWM. Dawnay to Aspinall, 7 July 1926, Box 112, Aspinall-Oglander Papers, IOW. Turkish guns at Anzac, 25 April 1915, Archive 6/1666, Cabinet 205, Record 274-490, Shelf 5, File 4668, GSA.

4. Cunliffe-Owen, BGRA Australian Division, 15 April 1915, Indian Mounted Brigades Summary of Events, 367/82, 228 Files, AWM. Godley to Allen (New Zealand Minister of Defence), 24 April 1915, Godley Allen letters, Godley Papers, WA 252/2, NAW.

5. Maj. Coe, 12 Australian Field Artillery, to Father, 21 April 1915, L/12/11/3286, 2 DRL 491, AWM. Winter, *25 April 1915*, p. 81.

6. Birdwood, Diary, 19 April 1915, 21 April 1915, 22 April 1915, 29a, Birdwood Papers, AWM. Steel and Hart, *Defeat at Gallipoli,* p. 53. Anzac War Diary, 25 April 1915, cited in Aspinall Letter Book, Box 113/3, Box 111, Aspinall-Oglander Papers, IOW. *Turkish Official History*, vol. 1, pp. 95 ff.

7. Lt-Col. Braithwaite, Diary, 24 April 1915 [sic]; and Birdwood to CGS MEF (Braithwaite), 8 May 1915; WA 1/1, Box 1, NAW. Algie, Diary, 25 April 1915, 1374, TLW. Maj.-Gen. Bridges, Despatch, 7 May 1915, in Aspinall Letter Book, 113/3, Box 111; Sketch map of Force Order #1, 13 April 1915, Box 112; Aspinall-Oglander Papers, IOW. Birdwood to Fitzgerald, 19 April 1915, 60, Birdwood Papers, AWM. Thursby, Naval Operations Orders, 17 April 1915, 25/367/26, AWM. Capt. Dix, 'Impressions of Anzac landing,' 25/367/5, AWM.

8. De Robeck to Churchill, 5 May 1915, 13/65, Chartwell Papers, CCC.

9. Among modern sources, the fullest accounts of why the landing was too far north are in Winter, *25 April 1915*, passim, James, *Gallipoli*, pp. 104 ff.; Bush, *Gallipoli*, pp. 110 ff.; Steel and Hart, *Defeat at Gallipoli*, pp. 53 ff. and 421-422. Birdwood to CGS MEF (Braithwaite), 8 May 1915, 60, Birdwood Papers, AWM.

10. Corporal William Guy to Gus (Tanner), 4 May 1915 and 10 May 1915, Ms C254, Guy Papers, Rare Books Archive, University of Calgary.

11. Lt-Col. John Luxford, Diary, 25 April 1915, 4454/2, TLW. Lt-Col. Fenwick, Diary, 25 April 1915, 1497, Auckland Museum, Auckland, New Zealand [hereafter AMA]. Capt. Rhodes, ADC to Gen. Godley, Diary, 25 April 1915, 1690-1691, TLW. New Zealand Brigade, Another War Diary Account, 25 April 1915, in Braithwaite, Diary WA1/1, Box 1, NAW. James,

Gallipoli, p. 269, fn. Bean, Extract Book, Interviews with Maj. Brand, Maj. Salisbury and Lt Derham, 3 DRL 1722/2, Bean Papers, AWM. Winter, *25 April 1915*, p. 188 and fn. 16, p. 270. Lt-Col. Malone, New Zealand Wellington Battalion, Diary, 25 April 1915, 1998.1755. Kippenberger Army Museum, Waiouru, New Zealand [hereafter KAM]. Bean, Notes from interviews, Brand, 25/9, 3DRL 1722/2, Bean Papers, AWM. Col. Rosenthal, Diary, 25 April 1915, Ms. 2739, Mitchell Library, Sydney [hereafter MLS].

12. Bean, Notes of interview with Brigadier McCay, CO 2nd Brigade, 3DRL 1722/2, Bean Papers, AWM.

13. Maj. (later Col.) A.C. Ferguson, CO 21 Kohat Mountain battery, 'Gallipoli 1915', early 1916, *The Gallipolian*, no. 85, Winter 1997, p. 21. Blackie, 'One of the Black Squad, 1914–1918', p. 12. Charles Bean, Notebook, 25 April 1915, 38/3DRL 606/223 (1), Bean Papers, AWM. Log of *Bacchante*, 25 April 1915, ADM 53/34645, PRO. 2nd-Lt Aylmer Green,
    12 Battalion, AIF, to Aspinall, 2 January 1932, Box 111, Aspinall-Oglander Papers, IOW. Col. J.J.T. Hobbs, CO 1 Australian Division Artillery, War Diary, 25 April 1915, Item 1a, 3DRL 2600, AWM.

14. Comments by Edmonds and Aspinall in 'Gallipoli Correspondence File, Box 112, Aspinall-Oglander Papers, IOW. Bean, *The Story of Anzac*, vol. 1, pp. 314 ff.

15. *Ibid*. Anzac HQ Messages, April 25 to April 28, 1915, 25/367/213, AWM. Bean, Interview with Maj. Bennett, 2nd in command, 6th Battalion, 3 DRL 1722/2, Bean Papers, AWM.

16. Anzac HQ Messages April 25 to April 28, 1915, 25/367/213; Royal Naval Signals April 1915 at Anzac, 25/367/26; AWM. Brigadier A.C. Temperley to Aspinall, 20 February 1927, Box 112, Aspinall-Oglander Papers, IOW.

17. Account out of New Zealand War Diary, 25 April 1915, WA 1/1, Box 1, NAW.

18. Indian Mountain Artillery, Summary of Events, 25 April 1915, 367/82, AWM. Aspinall, hand written note on Edmonds' comments of Aspinall's chapter 8, Gallipoli Correspondence File, Box 112, Aspinall-Oglander Papers, IOW

19. Rosenthal, Diary, 25 April 1915, Ms. 2739, MLS. Account out of War Diary, NZ War Diary, WA 1/1, Box 1, NAW. Signal Log of Queen, 25 April 1915, Box 116, Aspinall-Oglander Papers, IOW. Col. Hobbs, War Diary, 25 April 1915, 27 April 1915, Item 1a, 3DRL 2600, AWM. Extracts, War Diary, 8th battery, 3rd Field Artillery Brigade, 25 April 1915, Part 1, 224, AWM. Anzac HQ Messages 25 April to 28 April, 1915, 25/367/213, AWM.

20. War Diary, 8th battery, 3rd Field Artillery Brigade, 25 April 1915, Part 1, 224, AWM. Maj. Smith, letter to Mother, 2 June 1915, recounting 25 and 26

April, 1915, PR 84/365, AWM. Col. Hobbs, Diary, 26 April 1915, PR 82/153/1, AWM. Information on batteries on 26 April in Maj. Sinclair-Burgess, Australian Field Artillery, War Diary, Mss 48, part 1, 224, AWM.

21. George Tuck, Diary, 25 April 1915, MS 3879, TLW. Anonymous Diary, 25 April 1915, Ms 95/25, AMA. Maj. A.C. Temperley to Aspinall, 20 February 1927, Box 112, Aspinall-Oglander Papers, IOW.

22. Birdwood to Kitchener, 3 May 1915, 47, Birdwood Papers, AWM. Brudenell-White to Bean, 7 February 1923, 3DRL 7953/2, Bean Papers, AWM. Bean to Aspinall, 9 June 1927, citing White in comments on Aspinall's chapter; Bean to Edmonds, enclosing Aspinall draft, 26 March 1928; and Aspinall to Bean, 22 May 1928; 3DRL 7953/27, Bean Papers, AWM. Aspinall, Appreciation, 23 March 1915, p. 8, Box 116/4, Aspinall-Oglander Papers, IOW.

23. Malone, Diary, 25 April 1915, KAM. Braithwaite, Diary, 25 April 1915, Another account, 25 April 1915, WA 1/1, Box 1, NAW. Vice-Admiral de Robeck, Landing of Army on the Gallipoli Peninsula, Evidence at Dardanelles Commission, Cabinet 19/29, PRO. Roger Keyes, Report on Operations of 25 and 26 April 1915, onboard *Triad*, 1 July 1915, 5/14, Keyes Papers, BL. Birdwood to Kitchener, 3 May 1915, 47, Birdwood Papers, AWM. Lt Francis Levenson-Gower West, Auckland Infantry, Diary, 26 April 1915, 9300990, KAM. On 4th Brigade, Anzac HQ Messages 25 April to 28 April 1915, 25/367/213; Col. A Graham Butler, medical officer of 9th Battalion, to Bean, 16 August 1927, 3DRL 7953/27, Bean Papers; AWM.

24. 'Straggling' may be defined as unwounded men going down to the beach without orders to do so, or unwounded men gathering in gullies or valleys without purpose. The story is in 3DRL 7953/27, Bean Papers, AWM.

25. Gellibrand to Bean, 27 June 1927, mentioning Howse, and Gellibrand to Bean, 13 October 1927, 3DRL 7953/27, Bean Papers, AWM. A.C. Temperley to Aspinall, 20 February 1927, and 10 August 1926, Box 112, Aspinall-Oglander Papers, IOW. Birdwood, Diary, 25 April 1915, 29a, Birdwood Papers, AWM.

26. Bean to Aspinall, 9 June 1927, 3DRL 7953, Bean Papers; Anzac HQ Messages, 25 April to 28 April 1915, 25/367/213; Birdwood, Diary, 25 April 1915, 29(a); AWM.

27. Braithwaite, Diary, and Notes on the landing, War Diary, 25 April 1915, WA1/1, Box 1, NAW. Birdwood to Bean, 24 July 1920, 3DRL 8042/2, Bean Papers, AWM. Dawnay to wife, 30 June 1915, 40/1/7; Ashmead Bartlett, Evidence at Dardanelles Commission, 16/8; Hamilton Papers, KCL. AQMG, War Diary, 25 April 1915, WA1/1, Box 1, NAW. Rhodes, Diary, 25 April 1915, vol. 4, Ms 1690–1691, TLW. On the *Lutzow*, see AQMG War

Diary, 25 April 1915, WA1/1, Box 1, NAW. Anzac HQ Messages, 25 April to 28 April 1915, 25/367/213, AWM. E.Y. Daniel to Aspinall, 8 December 1928, Box 111; Signal Log of *Queen*, 25 April 1915, Box 116; Thursby to Aspinall, 10 March 1927, Box 116; Aspinall to Godley (re: Wemyss), 3 March 1927, Box 116; Aspinall-Oglander Papers, IOW. Aspinall, *Military Operations: Gallipoli*, vol. 1, p. 269. According to Sapper T.C. Farrier, NZ Engineers, Diary, 25 April 1915, the Admiral (Thursby) advised withdrawal, but Birdwood refused, '3 Months in Gallipoli', Cabinet 45/251, PRO.

28. A.J. Withers, Australian Department of Defence, to Bazley, staff of Australian Official History, 23 June 1927, containing the Aspinall pages of chapter 12, and substituted section, 3DRL 7953/38, AWM.

29. Roger Keyes to wife Eva, 26 April 1915, 2/10, Keyes Papers, BL. Orlo Williams, Diary, 25 April 1915, vol. 1, 69/78/1, IWM. Dawnay to wife, 30 June 1915, and Mrs George Shields' comment dated August 1969, 40/1/7, Hamilton Papers, KCL. Bean, *The Story of Anzac*, vol. 1, University of Queensland Press edition, 1981, pp. 460–461. Thursby seems to have felt that the Anzacs were a sorry lot at 1.30 a.m. but recovered during the 26th, Thursby to de Robeck, 26 April 1915, 4/35, de Robeck Papers, CCC.

30. Hamilton to Aspinall, 25 March 1927, Box 116, Aspinall-Oglander Papers, IOW. Malone, Diary, 25 April 1915, KAM.

31. Birdwood to Bean, 3DRL 8042/2, Bean Papers, AWM.

32. Bean to Ross, 28 July 1925, 3DRL 7953/7, Bean Papers, AWM. File on Birdwood's Message, a series of some thirty letters between Aspinall, Godley and Birdwood, dated 1927, Box 116, Aspinall-Oglander Papers, IOW.

33. Godley to Aspinall, 20 February 1927, Birdwood to Aspinall, 4 May 1927, Aspinall to Godley, 9 April 1927, Aspinall to Godley 13 April 1927, Aspinall to Birdwood, 23 May 1927; Box 116, Aspinall-Oglander Papers, IOW. Bean, *The Story of Anzac*, vol. 1, pp. 452 ff.

34. *Turkish Official History*, vol. 2, pp. 97 ff. Mustafa Kemal (Atatürk), *Memoirs of the Anafartaler Battles*, pp. 4 ff., 76/75/1, IWM. Zeki Bey, cited in Charles Bean, *Gallipoli Mission*, 1948, Canberra ABC edition, 1990, chapters 11 and 12, and Appendix 3.

35. *Ibid.*

36. *Ibid.*

37. Birdwood, Diary, 29 April 1915, 1 May 1915, 29 (a), Birdwood Papers, AWM. Fifth Army (Kiazim Bey, Chief of Staff) to Commander of the Straits, 27 April 1915, Cabinet 135, Record 11, Shelf 3, File 1562, GSA. Mustafa Kemal, *Memoirs*, p. 11, 76/75/1, IWM. A group of 500 stragglers noted by Lt Gatcliffe, the FOO of 2nd Australian Field Artillery Brigade on 28 April, in 2nd FAB to Divisional Artillery HQ, 28 April 1915, 1.27 p.m., 25/367/186, AWM.

38. Mustafa Kemal, *Memoirs*, pp. 14 ff., 76/75/1, IWM.
39. War Diary, 1st Battalion, Wellington Rifles, Messages, 27 April 1915, WA 73/3, NAW.
40. Malone, Diary, 26–28 April, 1915, KAM.
41. Malone, Diary, 28 April 1915, 7 May 1915, KAM. Bean, *The Story of Anzac*, vol. 1, pp. 513 ff.
42. Levenson-Gower West, Diary, 28 April 1915, 30 April 1915, 1 May 1915, vol. 1, 1993.990, KAM
43. Malone, Diary, 2 May 1915, *op cit*. War Diary, Anzac Division, 2 May 1915, WA 1/1, Box 1, NAW.
44. War Diary, Col. Hobbs, for April and May, 3 DRL 2600, 1(a), and 'General 3/6/15', 3; 1st Division Artillery Brigades, Reports, April and May 1915, 25/367/186; AWM.
45. Roger Keyes to Eva, 3 May 1915, 2/11, Keyes Papers, BL. Birdwood, Diary, 8 and 10 May 1915, 29 (a), Birdwood Papers, AWM. Malone, Diary, 10 May 1915, 14 May 1915, KAM. Steel and Hart, *Defeat at Gallipoli*, p. 217.
46. New Zealand Brigade War Diary, WA 1/1, Box 1, NAW. Mustafa Kemal messages, 13 May 1915 and 21 May 1915, in 19 Division war reports, Cabinet 227, Record 1-185, Shelf 1, File 5382; Turkish Cease Fire File, Cabinet 175, Record 116-316, Shelf 5, File 3426; GSA.
47. New Zealand Brigade War Diary, WA 1/1, Box 1, NAW.
48. Blackie, 'One of the Black Squad, 1914–1918', pp. 14–15.

The Fighting at Helles and the May Turkish Crisis

1. War Diaries: 1st Battalion, Lancashire Fusiliers, 26 and 27 April 1915; 2nd Battalion Royal Dublin Fusiliers, 26 and 27 April 1915; 1st Battalion Royal Munster Fusiliers; War Office 95/ 4310, PRO. For Turkish confusion, see Mühlmann, Letter.
2. Hunter-Weston letters to wife, 27 April 1915, BL.
3. Maj. D.E. Forman, B Battery, 15 Brigade, 29 Division, evidence at Dardanelles Commission, p. 46, Cabinet 19/29, PRO.
4. Journée du 27 Avril 1915, File 8a, 20 N 28, FAV.
5. Maj. Forman, *op cit*. War Diary, 28 April 1915, HQ 86 Brigade, 29 Division; 28 April 1915, 1st Battalion, Royal Munster Fusiliers, War Office 95/4310, PRO. Hunter-Weston, Diary, 28 April 1915, BL. Hamilton to wife, 30 April 1915, 25/12/2/3, Hamilton Papers, KCL.
6. Hamilton to Lady Hamilton, 29 April 1915, 25/12/2/2, Hamilton Papers, KCL. Fifth Army messages, Cabinet 105, Record 775, Shelf 4, File 180, GSA. Col. Mahmut, Memoirs, K 34980, IWM. Mühlmann, Letter.

7. Von der Goltz to Liman von Sanders, 1 May 1915, Cabinet 105, Record 775, Shelf 4, File 180, GSA. Mühlmann, Letter.

8. Mühlmann, Letter.

9. Mühlmann, Letter. Commander-in-chief to Fifth Army, 9 May 1915, Cabinet 105, Record 775, File 180, Index 98, GSA.

10. Mühlmann, Letter.

11. Mühlmann, Letter. James, *Gallipoli*, p. 147; Hickey, *Gallipoli*, pp. 161–162, Steel and Hart, *Defeat at Gallipoli*, p. 151.

12. 1 French Division War Diary, 1 – 4 May 1915, File 11, 26 N 75; Messages in Report on Operations, 27 April – 14 November 1915, 20 N 27; FAV.

13. Orlo Williams, Diary, 4 May 1915, IWM. Capt. C.A. Milward, Diary, 2 and 3 May 1915, National Army Museum, London [hereafter NAM]. Report of Operations, 25 April – 13 May 1915, File 8a, 20 N 28; 21 May 1915, Gouraud to French Corps d'Orient, 3rd Bureau, Operations, 20 N 27; FAV.

14. Mühlmann, Letter.

15. Kiazim Bey to Enver Pasa, Urgent and Private, 4 May 1915; Enver Pasa to Fifth Army, 4 May 1915; Liman von Sanders to 1st Administration Department, 4 May 1915; Kiazim Bey to Enver Pasa 5 May 1915; Liman von Sanders to Enver Pasa, 5 May 1915; Maj. Gen. von Bronsart, Supreme Command, to Liman von Sanders, 5 May 1915; Liman von Sanders to Enver Pasa, 9 May 1915; Cabinet 105, Record 180, Shelf 4, File 775, GSA.

16. Mühlmann, Letter.

17. Mühlmann, Letter.

18. Mühlmann, Letter. It is fair to add that R.R. James does mention the poor state of the Turks in early May, though, following Kannengiesser, he ignored Thauvenay and put the blame on Weber for initiating the withdrawal idea, James, *Gallipoli*, pp. 150–151. Others followed suit, Hickey, *Gallipoli*, p. 166, Steel and Hart, *Gallipoli*, p. 154.

19. R.R. James, *Gallipoli*, pp. 142–143.

20. Hamilton, Diary, Second Version, 5 May 1915, 6/9/4, Hamilton Papers, KCL. Hunter-Weston to wife, 6 May 1915, BL. John J. Goate, 5th Royal Scots, Diary, 6 May 1915, *The Gallipolian*, no. 91, Winter 1999, p. 26. War Diary, 1st Battalion, Royal Munster Fusiliers, 6 May 1915, War Office 95/4310, PRO.

21. Kannengiesser, *Campaign in Gallipoli*, pp. 138 ff. James, *Gallipoli*, pp. 150–151. War Diary, 1 French Division, 6 May 1915, File 11, 26 N 75, FAV.

22. Wolley Dod, *op cit*. Bean, *The Story of Anzac*, vol. 2, pp. 22–41.

23. Gen. Masnou, GOC 1 Division, to d'Amade, no date, but 9 May 1915, Annexe 170; Col. Nogues, GOC Metropolitan Brigade, to 1 Division, no date, but 8 May or early 9 May 1915, Annexe 171; FAV. Ministère de la

Guerre, *Les Armées Françaises dans la Grande Guerre*, Tome 8, Vol. 1, Annex 1, Paris, 1924.

24. Aspinall, reported in E.Y. Daniel to Gaselee, 3 May 1927, Box 111, Aspinall-Oglander Papers, IOW. Milward, Diary, 8 May 1915, NAM. Sholto Newman to Aspinall, 9 March 1922, Cabinet 45/261, PRO. Hamilton, Diary, Second Version, 9 May and 10 May 1915, 6/9/4, Hamilton Papers, KCL. Orlo Williams, Diary, 9 May 1915, IWM. Hunter-Weston, letter to wife, 11 June 1915, Diary, 15 May 1915, BL.

25. Hamilton to wife, 3 May 1915, 25/12/2/4, Hamilton Papers, KCL. Hunter-Weston, Letters to wife, 27 April 1915, 6 May 1915, second letter, 6 May 1915, 15 May 1915, 25 May 1915, 11 June 1915; Diary, 4 July 1915; letter to Wigram, 6 May 1915; BL.

26. Brigadier Charles Bonham-Carter, 'Memoirs,' BGGS GHQ, pp. 26 ff.; F.L. Freeman to Bonham-Carter, 25 August 1958; Bonham-Carter to 'My dear Joan', 27 August 1918; and Bonham-Carter to Father, 13 September 1918; Correspondence, Bonham-Carter Papers, CCC.

27. Hamilton to Kitchener, 7 June 1915, 2 July 1915, 21 September 1915, 5/1; Hamilton to Churchill, 18 June 1915, Hamilton to Asquith 7 July 1915, 5/6; Hamilton Papers, KCL. Birdwood to Hamilton, 1 July 1915, 3 DRL 3376/62, Birdwood Papers, AWM. Further emphasis on bayonet fighting by Hamilton, and distress at 'this trench method', in Hamilton to Kitchener, 9 May 1915, 10 May 1915, GS GHQ, War Office 95/4264, PRO. Godley to Sir Ronald Graham, 23 July 1915, WA 252/6, Godley Papers, NAW.

28. Hunter-Weston to GHQ, 29 May 1915, GS War Diary, War Office 95/4264, PRO. Re: Somme, Tim Travers, *The Killing Ground*, Allen and Unwin, London, 1987, pp. 158–159.

29. Very good French ideas, derived from Joffre, are in 'Notes sur les Attaques', 2 June 1915, 20 N 27, FAV. For timetable, Milward, Diary, 4 June 1915, NAM. Ashmead-Bartlett, quoting Col. Wilson, evidence to Dardanelles Commission, 3 May 1917, 16/1/2, Hamilton Papers, KCL.

30. Report on operations of 4 June 1915, File 8a, 20 N 28; Report by Gen. Simonin, GOC 4th Mixed Brigade, 4 June 1915, File 6, 20 N 27; FAV. Milward, Diary, 4 June 1915, NAM.

31. Paris, Report on operations, to GHQ, 6 June 1915, Naval Division, War Office 95/4290, PRO. TC Genelkurmay Baskanligi, *Turkish Official History*, vol. 3, pp. 48, and 44–51 generally.

32. *Turkish Official History*, vol. 3, pp. 48 ff. Lt-Col. A.E.F. Fawcus, 1/7 Manchester Battalion, 42 Division, Dardanelles Commission, Cabinet 19/29, PRO.

33. Kannengiesser, *The Campaign in Gallipoli*, p. 178. De Lisle to Aspinall, 10 October 1928, Cabinet 45/241, PRO.

34. Hunter-Weston, Letter to wife, 5 June 1915, 8 June 1915, 11 June 1915, BL. Orlo Williams, Diary, 4 June 1915, 5 June 1915, 6 June 1915, 8 June 1915, 29 July 1915, IWM. Hamilton to Lady Hamilton, 5 June 1915, 25/12/2, Hamilton Papers, KCL. Col. H.F. Grant to Aspinall, 2 March 1929, Cabinet 45/241; Brig. Gen. Stockdale to Aspinall, 13 February 1929, Cabinet 45/244; PRO.

35. Egerton, marginal notes, in Egerton to Aspinall, 15 December 1929, and Egerton to Aspinall, 8 June 1929, PRO. G.C. Wynne to Aspinall, no date, Box 111, Aspinall-Oglander Papers, IOW. R.R. Thompson to Aspinall, 7 July 1931, Cabinet 45/245, PRO.

36. Maj. Forman, 12 July 1915, Dardanelles Commission, Cabinet 19/29, PRO. Lt Wills, Diary, 12 July 1915, in 'Extract from Capt. H.C. MacLean's History of the 7th Cameronians', Cabinet 45/243; Lieut. D.E. Brand, 5th HLI, Diary, 12 July 1915, in Brand to Aspinall, 26 October 1929, Cabinet 45/241; PRO.

37. George Blake to Aspinall, 4 September 1929, Cabinet 45/241, PRO. Maj. Gen. Paris, Report on Operations, 13–16 July 1915, dated 18 July 1915; Brig. Gen. Trotman, Report on Operations, 13 July 1915, dated 18 July 1915; war diary, Royal Naval Division, 14 July 1915; War Office 95/4290, PRO. Ashmead-Bartlett, Evidence at Dardanelles Commission, 3 May 1917, in 16/1/2, Hamilton Papers, KCL.

38. Hamilton to Aspinall, 20 or 29 July 1916, in plain envelope containing Dardanelles Commission material, Box 115/9, Aspinall-Oglander Papers, IOW.

39. A. Chaudeigne, Report of the attack of July 13 by 2nd Battalion, 6th Colonial Regiment, EMA Section Historique, 8a; Report on operations of July 12 and 13, 8a; 20 N 28, FAV. Milward, Diary, 14 July 1915, NAM.

40. Liman von Sanders, *Five Years in Turkey*, p. 79. Mühlmann, Letter.

41. Orlo Williams, Diary, 8 May 1915, 2 June 1915, 5 June 1915, 21 July 1915, IWM. Orlo Williams was a useful independent observer of Hamilton, but Dawnay also had serious doubts about Hamilton, expressed later, Dawnay to wife, 19 October 1915, 69/21/2, Dawnay Papers, IWM.

42. Hamilton to Birdwood, 14 June 1915, re: Anzac operations, and morale attacks at Helles, Letters to Birdwood, 5/10, Hamilton Papers, KCL.

43. See the unpublished paper by Lt-Col. Edward Erickson, 'Strength Against Weakness: Ottoman military effectiveness at Gallipoli, 1915', kindly lent me by Lt-Col. Erickson.

44. Hamilton to Churchill, 30 June 1915; Hamilton to Asquith, 30 September 1915; 5/6, Hamilton Papers, KCL. Hamilton to Birdwood, 14 June 1915, 5/10, Letters to Birdwood, Hamilton Papers, KCL.

The Anzac Breakout

1. Malone, Diary, 14 May 1915, KAM. Thursby to Birdwood, 3 May 1915, copied to de Robeck, 3 May 1915, 4/42, de Robeck Papers, CCC. Aspinall-Oglander, *Military Operations: Gallipoli*, vol. 2, p. 23.
2. James, *Gallipoli*, pp. 219–220. Tpr Clutha McKenzie, Diary, 28–31 May 1915, 79/23, AMA.
3. Atatürk, 'Memoirs of the Anafartaler Battles', p. 28, IWM.
4. Mustafa Kemal, 'Memoirs', pp. 23 ff., 76/75/1, IWM. Skeen Memorandum, 30 May 1915, in 63, Birdwood Papers, AWM. Orlo Williams, Diary, 5 June 1915, 6 June 1915, 23 June 1915, 28 June 1915, 3 July 1915, 21 July 1915, 69/78/1, IWM. Hamilton to Birdwood, 18 May 1915 and 14 June 1915, Letters to Birdwood, 5/10, Hamilton Papers, KCL. Aspinall to Bean, 3 June 1929, 3 DRL 7953/27, Bean Papers, AWM. Birdwood to Kitchener, 9 July 1915, Kitchener Letters, 47, AWM. Interview with Lord Kitchener on 11 July 1915, in Ellison's handwriting, 17/4/2/84; Ellison to Hamilton, 2 June 1917, 17/4/2/85; Hamilton to Mears, 12 May 1917, 17/4/2/51; Correspondence regarding Dardanelles Commission, 17/4/2, Hamilton Papers, KCL.
5. Dawnay to wife, 15 July 1915, 69/21/1, Dawnay Papers, IWM. Orlo Williams, Diary, 21 July 1915, IWM.
6. Maj. Curry, 1st Battery, NZFA, Diary, 6–12 August 1915, Ms 858, AMA. Maj.-Gen. Smyth to Bean, 8 March 1931, 3DRL 7953/27, Bean Papers, AWM.
7. Curry, *op cit*.
8. *Ibid*. Bean, *Gallipoli Mission*, pp. 185, 187, and for the counterattack, 195–197. Atatürk, 'Memoirs', p. 30, IWM.
9. Brudenell White to Bean, 21 May 1924, 3DRL 7953/2, Bean Papers, AWM. Bean, *The Story of Anzac*, vol. 2, chapter XXI, 'The Feints of 7 Augustth'.
10. White to Bean, 21 May 1924, 3DRL 7953/2, Bean Papers, AWM.
11. Artillery and Naval orders for Third Phase of operations against Chunuk Bair and Baby 700, 7 August 1915, 25, Artillery files, 367/75/5, AWM. *Endymion* log, ADM 53/40874; *Colne* log, ADM 53/38208; *Chelmer* log, ADM 53/37629; PRO. Bean to Hobbs, 29 January 1923, 3DRL 7953/2, Bean Papers, AWM.
12. War Diary, 1st New Zealand Field Artillery Brigade, Appendix 2, New Zealand Artillery timetable, 7 August 1915, p. 26, WA 51/1, NAW. Clyde McGilp, War Diary, 7 August 1915, TLW. Re: navy, an official naval report stated that the Army rejected the idea of ships directing fire on enemy front line trenches which were close to Allied trenches, 'Report of the Committee appointed to investigate the attacks delivered on, and the

enemy defences of, the Dardanelles Straits', Admiralty, Naval Staff, Gunnery Division, April 1921, p. 265, AWM 51/39 (hereafter *Mitchell Report*). Capt. Mitchell was the naval advisor at GHQ on Gallipoli.

13. Bean to Hobbs, 28 February 1923, 3DRL 7953/2, Bean Papers, AWM.

14. Lt-Col. Brazier, 10th Light Horse, to Bean, 19 March 1931 and 13 April 1931, 3DRL 7953/27, AWM. Lt-Col. Johnston, New Zealand Artillery, Appendix 2, p. 24, 5 August 1915, and 7 August 1915, WA 1/1, War Diary 1st New Zealand Field Artillery Brigade, NAW. Col. Hobbs, Diary, 24 August 1915, 28 August 1915, PR 82/153/1, AWM.

15. War Diary, 69 Brigade Field Artillery, War Office 95/4301, PRO. War Diary, HQ 3rd Australian Light Horse Brigade, 7 August 1915; 10th Light Horse, 7 August 1915; 8th Light Horse, 7 August 1915; all in War Office 95/4288, PRO. War Diary, General Staff, Anzac Corps, 7 August 1915, War Office 95/4282, PRO. General Staff, 2nd Anzac Corps War Diary, 7 August 1915, WA 1/1, Box 4, NAW. See also Greg Kerr, *Private Wars: Personal Records of the Anzacs in the Great War*, Oxford University Press, Melbourne, 2000, p. 139.

16. Lt-Col. Brazier to Bean, 13 March 1931 and 19 March 1931, 3DRL 7953/27, AWM.

17. Col. Antill to Bean, 21 March 1931, Maj.-Gen. Hughes to Bean, 24 March 1931, Bean to Edmonds, 17 June 1931; 3DRL 7953/27, Bean Papers, AWM. See Bean, *The Story of Anzac*, vol. 2, pp. 611 ff. for his sanitised but accurate overview of the Nek attack.

18. Atatürk, 'Memoirs', pp. 31–32, IWM.

19. Lt-Col. Bolton, CO 4th Worcesters, to Aspinall, 5 November 1930, Cabinet 45/241; Col. Wolley Dod, CO 86 Brigade, 29 Division, to Aspinall, 30 October ?, Cabinet 45/245; PRO.

20. Tuli (Col. Geddes) to Dear Charles (Aspinall), 8 November 1930, Cabinet 45/245, PRO.

21. Reports sent by military attachés and from Intelligence Reports, 14 July 1915, landing at Saros expected, information from island of Lesbos; 21 July 1915, landing at Saros expected; 22 July 1915, landing at Saros expected, or possibly Anatolia, information via German HQ; Cabinet 105, Record 780, Shelf 5, File 182, GSA. Also *Turkish Official History*, vol. 3, pp. 386–390. Liman von Sanders to Supreme Command, 18 July 1915, in German, received 19 July 1915, Cabinet 105, Record 782; Shelf 4, File 182, and Asim, Director of Operations, Supreme Command, to Fifth Army, 5 August 1915, Cabinet 105, Record 782; Shelf 4, File 182, GSA.

22. Percy Doherty, 8th Canterbury Battalion, Diary, 6 August 1915, KAM. Leonard Leary, Wellington machine-gun section, 'Attack on Chunuk Bair –

August 1915', recorded on 26 October 1960, TLW. Malone, Diary, 30 July 1915, 4 August 1915, KAM. James, *Gallipoli*, p. 237.

23. Malone, Diary, 4 August 1915, KAM. Maj. Temperley, Brigade Major, New Zealand Brigade, 'A Personal narrative of the Battle of Chunuk Bair, August 6–10, 1915', p. 11, 1994.3315 KAM. Others believed Johnston was drunk on 7 August, James, *Gallipoli*, footnote, p. 269.

24. Tpr Law, 4th Waikato Regiment, Diary, 6 August 1915, AMA. Doherty, Diary, 6 August 1915, 7 August 1915, 1989.943 KAM. Harry Ernest Browne, Wellington Mounted Rifles, Diary, 6 August 1915, TLW.

25. Lt-Col. Bishop, then commanding 8th Company, Otago Battalion, 'The August Battle for Chunuk Bair as seen by a subaltern', 6 August 1915, TLW. Temperley, *op cit.*, p. 5.

26. Temperley, 'A Personal narrative…', pp. 7–11, *op cit.*; Maj.-Gen. Young, CO Auckland Brigade, to Aspinall, March 1931, Cabinet 45/245, PRO. Lt H. Stewart, Canterbury Battalion, to Aspinall, 28 March 1933, Box 111, Aspinall-Oglander Papers, IOW.

27. Col. Temperley to Aspinall, 27 October 1930, and 1 January 1930, Cabinet 45/245, PRO. Temperley, 'A Personal Narrative…', pp. 5 ff., *op cit.*; Lt H. Stewart to Aspinall, 28 March 1933, Box 111, Aspinall-Oglander Papers, IOW.

28. For example, Fifth Army messages of 7 August 1915 to Supreme Command, Cabinet 105, Record 782, Shelf 4, File 182, messages #s 60 – 63, GSA. Col. Hans Kannengiesser, *The Campaign in Gallipoli*, London, 1927, pp. 206 ff. Atatürk, 'Memoirs of the Anafartalar Battles', pp. 32–34, IWM. Lt-Col. Bishop, 'Ten Years After: Gallipoli in Peace and War', TLW.

29. Brigadier-General Andrus, commanding 2nd column, to Aspinall, 6 December 1930, Cabinet 45/241, PRO. Anonymous Hauraki engineer or pioneer, Diary, 7 August 1915, 1998.32, KAM.

30. Atatürk, 'Memoirs', pp. 34–40, IWM. *Turkish Official History*, vol. 3, p. 406. Zeki Bey in Bean, *Gallipoli Mission*, p. 224.

31. Daily Journal of Fifth Army, 8 August 1915, Cabinet 4, Record 30, Shelf 8749, File 3407, GSA. Bill Cunningham to Col. Hughes, 23 February 1916, Robert Hughes Papers, TLW. War Diary, 8th Battalion Welch Regiment, Pioneers, 8 August 1915, War Office 95/4301, PRO. Leary, 'Attack on Chunuk Bair…', 26 October 1960, p. 6, TLW.

32. Malone, Diary, 20 May 1915, KAM. Temperley, 'A Personal Narrative…', pp. 13 –15, KAM. Maj. Fowles, HQ New Zealand Mounted Brigade, Summary of Events, 8 August 1915, 9 August 1915, WA 40/3, Item 6, NAW. Bishop, 'The August Battle for Chunuk Bair as seen by a subaltern', c: 1925, TLW. Christopher Pugsley, *Gallipoli: the New Zealand Story*,

Hodder, Auckland, 1984, pp. 291 ff. Pugsley's excellent book contains a very full defence of Malone.

33. Browne, Diary, 8 August 1915, TLW. Luxford, Diary, 8 August 1915, 4454–2, TLW. Law, Diary, 8 August 1915, 9 August 1915, ms 90/20, AMA.

34. Browne, Diary, 9 August 1915, 3519, TLW. Harry Browne survived Gallipoli, and later served in France. See chapter 9 for an expanded version of Browne's experience.

35. Lt-Col. Allanson, Testimony at Dardanelles Commission, pp. 615 ff., Cabinet 19/33, PRO. Ship's log of *Bacchante*, ADM 53/34645, PRO. Details of the Allanson affair are in Godley to Birdwood, 14 February 1917; Birdwood to Godley, 15 February 1917; Godley to Birdwood, 27 February 1917; Godley-Birdwood Correspondence, Godley Papers, WA 252/10, NAW. Godley, Birdwood and Cox all saw Allanson as an unreliable witness and excitable. Temperley, 'A Personal narrative…', p. 22, *op cit.*, thought it was Anzac howitzers that did the damage.

36. Godley-Birdwood Correspondence, Godley Papers, *op cit.* R.A. Savory, 14th Sikhs and 6th Battalion, South Lancashire Regiment, Memoirs, 9 August 1977, 7709-22, NAM.

37. Godley to Aspinall, 26 November 1930, cabinet 45/242, PRO.

38. Bean believed it was bringing down the wounded that was critical in stopping Baldwin's column, Bean to Butler, 20 August 1925, 3DRL 7953/35, Bean Papers, AWM. Capt. Hicks, 10th Battalion, Hampshire Regiment, Diary, 8 August – 10, 1915, Cabinet 45/254, PRO. Capt. Hicks to Aspinall, 18 January 1931, in 10th Hampshires War Diary; 6th Battalion Royal Irish Rifles, War Diary, 9 and 10 August 1915; War Office 95/4296, PRO. Temperley, 'A Personal narrative…', pp. 20–22, *op cit.*

39. 19 Division report, afternoon of 8 August 1915, in Maps and Sketches of Fifth Army, Cabinet 175, Record 21, Shelf 2, File 3405; Fifth Army Journal, 8 August 1915, Cabinet 4, Record 30, Shelf 8749, File 3407, Index 5/30; Kiazim Bey, chief of staff, Fifth Army, to Supreme Command, sent on morning of 9 August, received 10 August 1915, Cabinet 105, Record 782; Shelf 4, File 182, GSA.

40. Zeki Bey in Bean, *Gallipoli Mission*, p. 224, mentions 23 and 24 Regiments of 8 Division, and 25 and 64 Regiments of 9 Division. The Turkish General Staff indicates that Kemal's attacking force consisted of 23 and 24 Regiments of 8 Division, and 26 Regiment of 13 Division, Answers to Questions, Question #78, Cabinet 45/236, PRO. Fifth Army Journal, 8 August 1915, Cabinet 4, Record 30, Shelf 8749, File 3407, Index 5/30; Anafarta Group to 8 and 9 Divisions, 9 August 1915, Cabinet 203, Record 4-127, Shelf 3, File 4557, Index 20; GSA.

41. Liman von Sanders telegraphed Enver Pasa on 10 August that he collected men from all groups in order to mount the counterattacks that day, Liman von Sanders to Supreme Command, 10 August 1915, Cabinet 105, Record 782, Shelf 4, File 182, Index 77, GSA. Capt. Hicks, 10th Hampshire Regiment, Diary, 10 August 1915, Cabinet 45/254, PRO.

42. Sketch map, 10 August 1915, in Maps and Sketches of Fifth Army, Cabinet 175, Record 21, Shelf 2, File 3405, GSA. Casualty Report, 6 to 11 August, 1915; and Liman von Sanders to Supreme Command, 10 August 1915; Cabinet 105, Record 782, Shelf 4, File 182, GSA. *Turkish Official History*, vol. 3, p. 425.

43. The diary of Capt. Tahu Rhodes, ADC to Godley, shows how much Godley's staff stayed at their HQ over these critical days, 7 – 10 August 1915, Ms 1690–1691, TLW.

Operations at Suvla and the Turkish Reaction

1. Edgar Anstey to Aspinall, 6 June 1929, Cabinet 45/241, PRO. Dawnay to Aspinall, 6 March 1929, Box 116, Aspinall-Oglander Papers, IOW. Hamilton to de Robeck, 4 July 1915, and de Robeck to Hamilton, 10 July 1915, Suvla Landing Operations, War Office 158/889, PRO. Braithwaite to Stopford, 29 July 1915, and Stopford to GHQ, 31 July 1915, GHQ Orders for Operations 6 August 1915, War Office 95/576PRO. Dawnay to wife 9 August 1915, and Dawnay to Straps ?, War Office, 1 September 1915, in Letters to wife, March 1915–January 1916, 69/21/1, IWM. Orlo Williams, Diary, 6 August 1915, 69/78/1, IWM.

2. Braithwaite to GOC IX Corps, 29 July 1915, Stopford to GHQ, 31 July 1915, Hamilton to GOC French Corps, 3 August 1915, Braithwaite to GOC IX Corps, 5 August 1915, GHQ Orders for Operations 6 August 1915, War Office 158/576, PRO. Neill Malcolm to Aspinall, 1 March 1931, 11 Division war diary, War Office 95/4297, PRO. Stopford to GHQ, 31 July 1915; Hamilton to Kitchener, 20 November 1915, War Office 138/40, PRO, my underlining. Braithwaite to Hamilton, 25 August 1916, 17/4/1/5, Hamilton Papers, KCL.

3. Birdwood, testimony at Dardanelles Commission, and Hamilton's reply notes, 16/8, Hamilton Papers, KCL. Hamilton, Evidence at Dardanelles Commission, responding to Ashmead Bartlett, pp. 138–139, Cabinet 19/32, PRO. Orders for attack of 6/7 Augus, re: Gen. Travers' column, 63, Birdwood Papers, AWM. Stopford, GOC IX Corps to GHQ, 31 July 1915, and Aspinall to GOC IX Corps, 6 August 1915, GHQ Orders for Operations 6 August 1915, War Office 158/576, PRO.

4. James, *Gallipoli*, p. 283. Aspinall, 'Statement', no date, 17/3/1/81, Hamilton Papers, KCL. Stopford, 'Statement in connection with... Hamilton's

Despatch on 11 December 1915', 16 February 1916, War Office 138/40, PRO.

5. Birdwood to Maxwell, 9 August 1915, and Birdwood to Kitchener, 22 August 1915, 63, Birdwood Papers, AWM. Hamilton to Kitchener, 24 August 1915, 5/1, Hamilton Papers, KCL. Clive Wigram to Godley, 8 September 1915, Godley microfilm, 32577, in Alex Godley Papers, Hamilton Papers, KCL. Hamilton to Kitchener, 11 and 14 August, 1915, Hamilton Papers, 5/1; Hamilton to Lawson, 8 September 1915, in Statements of Dardanelles Commission witnesses, p. 35, 16/8, Hamilton Papers; KCL. Godley to Col. Streatfield, Grenadier Guards, 25 August 1915, Godley Papers, WA 252/6, NAW.

6. Hamilton to Kitchener, 11 August 1915, Hamilton Papers, 1/5, KCL. Hamilton, *Gallipoli Diary*, 8 August 1915, vol. 2, pp. 58–61. Commander-in-chief's Diary, 8 August 1915, typed by Sergeant Stuart, 6/10; cf. Hamilton to Hankey, 8 March 1917, in which Hamilton wonders whether it was Hankey's message that stirred him into going to Suvla, 17/3/1/143; *Exmouth* and *Triad* logs, 17/7/26/6; Hamilton Papers, KCL. Ships logs and messages entered in Dardanelles Commission documents by Hamilton, Cabinet 19/32, p. 69, PRO.

7. Stopford memorandum, 18 August 1915, 17/7/13/4, Hamilton Papers, KCL. Hamilton to War Office, 20 November 1915, War Office 138/40, PRO. War Office Committee Recommendations on Suvla Bay Operations, 7 October 1915, War Office 95/4264, PRO. Stopford, Statement, 16 February 1916, War Office, 138/40, PRO. Hamilton to Mears, Secretary, Dardanelles Commission, 26 July 1917, 17/4/3/18, Hamilton Papers, KCL. The whole rather sordid argument between the two men, involving the War Office, Kitchener, Robb, Sclater, etc., is in War Office 138/40, PRO. This file was closed until 1993.

8. Philip Haythornthwaite, *Gallipoli 1915*, London, 1991, p. 71.

9. Thomas Pakenham, *The Boer War*, London, 1979, pp. 210, 213, 230, 368–370, 457. Of course, Stopford was not Hamilton's pick for the job as IX Corps chief, since Hamilton wanted either Byng or Rawlinson. Ironically, Byng arrived later at Gallipoli to take over IX Corps, too late to achieve anything.

10. Stopford, Evidence at Dardanelles Commission, and Hamilton's rebuttal, in 16/8, Hamilton Papers, KCL. GHQ War Diary, 11 July 1915, War Office 95/4264, PRO. Re: Christian's comment, Capt. Maxwell Leroy to Aspinall, 20 July 1929, Box 116, and repeating Christian's comment, Capt. Maxwell Lefroy to Aspinall, 13 February 193, Box 115, Aspinall-Oglander Papers, IOW.

11. Birdwood to Kitchener, 22 August 1915, 63, Birdwood Papers, AWM. Aspinall, 'Statement', 17/3/1/81, Hamilton Papers, KCL. On Reed at

Colenso, W. Baring Pemberton, *Battles of the Boer War*, Pan edition, London, 1969, p. 137; Pakenham, *The Boer War*, pp. 230, 236, 346. On Reed's royal influence, Hamilton to Capt. Still, 16 January 1924, 6/7, Hamilton Papers, KCL.

12. Fifth Army, Liman von Sanders, to Supreme Command, 18 July 1915, Cabinet 105, Record 782, Shelf 4, File 182, Index 13, GSA. Re: numbers, and anticipations of landing sites, *Turkish Official History*, vol. 3, pp. 386 ff. Willmer to Aspinall, 15 January 1930, and 16 February 1930, Box 112; Liman von Sanders to Maj. Eggert, 6 August 1915, in M. Cornwall to Aspinall, 24 June 1930, Box 116; Aspinall-Oglander Papers, IOW.

13. J.D. Coleridge, Notes, C, in Coleridge to Aspinall, 26 March 1919, 'Account of 33 Brigade', in War Diary, 11 Division, War Office 95/4297, PRO. War Diary, 11th Battalion Manchester Regiment, 34 Brigade, 11 Division, War Office 95/4299, PRO.

14. Commander Gibson, Diary, 6 and 7 August 1915, IWM. Administration, 11 Division, war diary, 7 August 1915, and 68 Field Company Royal Engineers, 11 Division, war diary, 6 August 1915, War Office 95/4298; [on friendly fire] Maj. M. Ferrers-Guy to Aspinall, 16 January 1931, War Office 95/4299; and A. Beecroft, Signals, to Aspinall, 9 February 1931, Cabinet 45/241; PRO.

15. Milward, Diary, 6 August 1915, 6510/143/3, NAM.

16. *Ibid.* Commander Minchin to Aspinall, 11 July 1929, Cabinet 45/243, PRO Maxwell Lefroy to Aspinall, 19 February 1929, Diary, Box 116, Aspinall-Oglander Papers, IOW.

17. Accounts in John Duncan to Aspinall, 15 February 1915, Cabinet 45/24; Brigadier-General Haggard, GOC 32 Brigade, Dardanelles Commission, p. 75, Cabinet 19/29; J.D. Coleridge to Aspinall, Note A, 26 March 1919, 11 Division war diary, War Office 95/4297; 59 Brigade RFA, 11 Division, war diary, War Office 95/4298; PRO. W.F. Gordon to Aspinall, 10 March 1930, Box 116, Aspinall-Oglander Papers, IOW.

18. 10 Division war diary, A & Q, 27 July 1915, War Office 95/4294, PRO.

19. Statement by Gen. Sir B. Mahon, Dardanelles Commission, Cabinet 19/30, PRO. A & Q Branch, 4 – 6 August 1915; 10 Division to 9 Corps, 2000 hours, 6 August 1915, GS 10 Division, War Office 95/4294, PRO. Naval memoirs of Admiral Godfrey, vol. 2, p. 21, 74/96/1, IWM.

20. War Diary, Director of Army Signals, 7 – 9 August 1915; Narrative of Signal Work (GHQ and IX Corps), 6 – 7 August 1915; War Office 95/4268, PRO. Reed's comments reported in Aspinall to Maxwell Lefroy, 3 January 1931, Miscellaneous Correspondence, Box 115, Aspinall-Oglander Papers, IOW.

21. Birdwood, answers to questions at Dardanelles Commission, p. 1094, Cabinet 19/33, PRO. Series of letters in 1915 and 1916 from Rear-Admiral Christian to

Vice-Admiral de Robeck, 4/34, de Robeck Papers, CCC. Keyes, reported in Aspinall letter book, OG 113/3, in Box 111; G. Winton to Aspinall, 4 February 1930, Miscellaneous letters, OG 116/8; Aspinall-Oglander Papers, IOW.

22. Christian to de Robeck, 19 January 1916, 4/34, de Robeck Papers, CCC.

23. HQ 31 Brigade, 10 Division, war diary, summary for 7 August 1915, War Office 95/4296; GS, 10 Division, messages, 7 August 1915, War Office 95/4294; IX Corps War Diary, 7–8 August 1915, War Office 95/4276; R.G. Coleridge, Comments on '11 Division at Suvla Bay', pp. 14–16, Cabinet 45/227; Brig. Gen. Hill to Hammersley, January 1916; Cabinet 45/242; Extract of letter from Capt. Atkins to Gen. Moberly, 26 September 1915, in Cabinet 45/241; Brig. Gen. Sitwell, evidence at Dardanelles Commission, p. 1226, Cabinet 19/33; PRO.

24. Neill Malcolm, staff officer, 11 Division, 'The 11th Division at Suvla Bay', War Office 95/4297; Minogue's story reported in letters from B.W. Shuttleworth to Aspinall, 20 February 1926 and 9 October 1931, Cabinet 45/244; PRO.

25. See Part 1 of Tim Travers, *The Killing Ground, op. cit.*

26. Capt. T. Verschoyle, 5th Battalion Royal Inniskilling Fusiliers, to Aspinall, 6 February 1931, Lt-Col. J.A. Armstrong to Aspinall, 17 February 1931, 10 Division, War Office 95/4296, PRO.

27. Messages between IX Corps and 10 Division, 8 August 1915, War Office 95/4294; IX Corps War Diary, 8 August 1915, War Office 95/4276; PRO.

28. War Diary, HQ 32 Brigade, 8 August 1915, War Office 95/4299, PRO.

29. Hammersley, Dardanelles Commission, p. 153, Cabinet 19/29, PRO.

30. Account by GSO of Corps at HQ 11 Division, 8 August 1915, IX Corps War Diary, War Office 95/4276, Appendix 4, PRO. Roger Keyes to Hamilton, 27 April 1917, 17/3/2/34; Ironically, Hamilton could not remember who had sent messages that day, Hamilton to Hankey, 8 March 1917, Hankey to Hamilton, 9 March 1917, 17/3/2/1; Hamilton Papers, KCL.

31. Willmer to Aspinall, 15 January 1930 and 12 April 1930, Box 112, Aspinall-Oglander Papers, IOW. *Turkish Official History*, vol. 3, pp. 386 ff.

32. *Turkish Official History*, vol. 3, pp. 398–402. Willmer to Aspinall, 12 April 1930, Box 112, Aspinall-Oglander Papers, IOW. Liman von Sanders, *Five Years in Turkey*, p. 84.

33. *Turkish Official History*, vol. 3, pp. 398–410. Willmer to Aspinall, 15 January 1930, Box 112, Aspinall-Oglander Papers, IOW. Atatürk, 'Memoirs of the Anafartaler Battles', p. 41, IWM.

34. Hamilton, comments on Statements of Witnesses at Dardanelles Commission, 16/8; Stopford, Statement at Dardanelles Commission, 16/7;

'The Dispute as to whether my intervention on the 8th August was too
strong or not strong enough…', 17/7/9/1; Hamilton Papers, KCL.

35. IX Corps to 10 and 11 Divisions, 6.45 p.m., 8 August 1915, War Diary, 11
Division, War Office 95/4297, PRO.

36. War Diary, 11 Division, 8 August 1915, War Office 95/4297, PRO.

37. Neill Malcolm, reporting Coleridge's journey, 'The 11th Division at Suvla
Bay', War Office 95/4297, PRO. Lt John Still, Adjutant, 6th East Yorkshire
Regiment, to Hamilton, 19 September 1923, 6/7, Hamilton Papers, KCL.

38. War Diary, HQ 32 Brigade, 8–9 August 1915, Shuttleworth messages, War
Office 95/4299; Roger Keyes to Aspinall, 15 December 1930, Cabinet
45/243; PRO.

39. War diary, East Yorkshire Pioneers, 9 August 1915, in War Office 95/4298;
War Diary, 32 Brigade, Shuttleworth messages, 9 August 1915, War Office
95/4299; Lt V. Kidd, War Diary, 8th Duke of Wellington's West Riding
Battalion, 9 August 1915, War Office 95/4299; PRO. John Still, *A Prisoner in
Turkey*, London and New York, 1920, pp. 30–32.

40. War Diary, 9 August 1915, Shuttleworth messages, War Office 95/4299,
PRO.

41. IX Corps to 10 Division, 9.45 a.m., 9 August 1915, IX Corps to 10, 11 and
53 Divisions, 10.10 a.m., 9 August 1915, IX Corps to 10 Division, 1600, 9
August 1915; 10 Division HQ, War Office 95/4294, PRO. Hamilton to Hill,
3 November 1923, and Hamilton to Hill, 7 November 1923, 6/7; Hamilton
comments on 32 Brigade War Diary, 2 March 1918, 6/5; 'The Dispute as to
whether my intervention on the 8th August 1915 was too strong…',
17/7/9/1; Hamilton Papers, KCL. Neill Malcolm, 'The 11th Division at
Suvla Bay', War Office 95/4297, PRO.

42. *Turkish Official History*, vol. 3, pp. 398–410. According to Kiazim Bey, 7 and
12 Divisions reached Suvla by midnight on the night of 7 August/8,
Kiazim Bey to Supreme Command, 8 August 1915, Cabinet 105, Record
782, Shelf 4, File 182, Index 65, GSA. Hamilton to Hill, 3 November 1923;
Lt John Still to Hamilton, 19 September 1915; 6/7, Hamilton Papers, KCL.
Aspinall-Oglander, *Military Operations: Gallipoli*, vol. 2, p. 288, Steel and
Hart, *Defeat at Gallipoli*, p. 268, Hickey, *Gallipoli*, p. 292, R.R. James,
Gallipoli, p. 296.

43. Kiazim Bey to Supreme Command, 7 August 1915, and 9 August 1915,
Cabinet 105, Record 782, Shelf 4, File 182, Indexes 63 and 75, GSA.
Liman von Sanders, messages on 7 August 1915, in M. Cornwall to
Aspinall, 24 June 1930, Box 116, Aspinall-Oglander Papers, IOW. J.D.
Coleridge, staff officer, 11 Division, comments on Neill Malcolm, 'The
11th Division at Suvla Bay', p. 28, War Office 95/4297, PRO. Coleridge's

verdict is strongly supported by Lt-Col. Edward Erickson, 'Strength Against Weakness', p. 20.

44. Brig. Gen. Nicol to Aspinall, 21 January 1931, in HQ 30 Brigade 10 Division War Diary; 9 August 1915, 7th Battalion Royal Munster Fusiliers War Diary; War Office 95/4296, PRO. Lt S.R.V. Travers' body was recovered and he was buried on A Beach West, the grave marked with a wooden cross. This has now disappeared. When Lt S.R.V. Travers left his home in Timoleague, County Cork, it is recorded that he told his mother: 'Goodbye, mother, you won't see me again.' Recalled by the author's father, Lt-Col. Hugh Travers, who was present on the occasion.

45. See similar comments by Brig. Gen. Nicol to Aspinall, 21 January 1931 and 2 February 1931, Cabinet 45/243; Lt-Col. Drage to Aspinall, 28 January 1931, War Office 95/4296; PRO.

46. Capt. Small, 6th Munsters to Aspinall, 21 February 1931, Frank Silk to Aspinall, 5 February 1930; Cabinet 45/244; A. Linderg to Aspinall, 13 March 1931; Col. (then Capt.) Lord Lifford to Aspinall, 31 January ?, Cabinet 45/243; PRO. Aspinall, as a GHQ planner of Suvla, usually sought to find confirmation that water was available in wells at Suvla, so when Maj. R.H. Scott, 6th Irish Fusiliers, wrote to him on 16 February 1931, saying that there was never a shortage of water, Aspinall noted in the margin: 'Important. Contradicts Hill and Cooke Collis, agrees with my personal knowledge. CAO', Cabinet 45/243, PRO. Reverend Canon R. McLean, Protestant chaplain to 30 Brigade, testimony to Dardanelles Commission, p. 934, Cabinet 19/33, PRO.

47. Testimony at Dardanelles Commission, from all the above named, in Cabinet 19/33; plus further testimony from Roger Keyes, Rear-Admiral Christian, and de Lotbinière, in Cabinet 19/29; and from Poett to Aspinall, no date, in Cabinet 45/244; PRO.

48. De Lotbinière, testimony at Dardanelles Commission, Cabinet 19/29, Cabinet 19/33, PRO. Aspinall, 'Note on water', Secret Private Papers, Box 115/9, Aspinall-Oglander Papers, IOW. *Prah*'s log, p. 189, Cabinet 19/28, PRO.

49. See various statements by Roger Keyes, Christian, several naval officers, de Lotbinière, Poett, Roper, the Rev. McLean, and especially Stopford on pp. 517–518, in Cabinet 19/33, and Poett in Cabinet 45/244; PRO. Roger Keyes, evidence at Dardanelles Commission, p. 1443, Cabinet 19/33, PRO.

50. Lt-Col. Aspinall, evidence at Dardanelles Commission, p. 734, Cabinet 19/33, PRO.

51. Written comments by Roger Keyes, on evidence given by de Lotbinière, in 16/8/6, p. 61; Braithwaite to Hamilton, 15 January 1917, 7/4/2/1; Hamilton

Papers, KCL. Lt-Col. Forster, evidence at Dardanelles Commission, p. 741, Cabinet 19/33, PRO.

52. Maj. Gen. Kearns, AQMG IX Corps, evidence at Dardanelles Commission, p. 1244; Brig. Gen. Roper, RE, GHQ, evidence at Dardanelles Commission, p. 641; Maj. Gen. Poett, evidence at Dardanelles Commission, pp. 1126–1138; Cabinet 19/33, PRO. Maj. Gen. Poett to Aspinall, no date, Cabinet 45/244, PRO.

53. Commander Gibson, Diary, 8 and 9 August 1915, IWM.

54. Lt-Col. T.H. Forster, AAQMG, evidence at Dardanelles Commission, pp. 740–744, Cabinet 19/33, PRO. The *Aragon* was the ship that contained the Lines of Communication staff.

55. Lt Elliott, 9th Service Battalion, West Yorkshire Regiment, to mother, no date, except 'Tuesday', probably therefore 10 August 1915, 8403–63, NAM.

56. *Ibid*.

57. *Ibid*.

58. Capt. Drury, 6th Royal Dublin Fusiliers, 30 Brigade, 10 Division, Diary, 7 August 1915, 7607 – 69, vol. 1, NAM.

59. *Ibid*., 8 August 1915.

60. *Ibid*., 9 August 1915.

61. *Ibid*.

62. *Ibid*., 10 August 1915. On the 1/5 Norfolks, see Reports by Col. Munib, the commander of 36th Turkish Regiment that opposed the Norfolks attack, 12 August 1915, Record H2, File 5359, Index F1.16 – F1.19, GSA. On the Norfolks being bayonetted, *Turkish Official History*, vol. 2, pp. 213–214. It is significant that all the 1/5 Norfolk prisoners of war captured by the Turks who survived, were wounded, Record 2115, File 542, Indexes 5 ff., GSA. The BBC film was *All the King's Men*, 1999.

63. Drury, Diary, 15 August 1915, NAM. '8th Bn. Hampshire Regiment (Isle of Wight Rifles) at Suvla Bay' in War Office 95/4325, PRO.

64. Gibson, Diary, 22 August 1915, and 15 August 1915, 19 August 1915, IWM.

65. Milward, Diary, 21 August 1915, NAM; War Diary, 7th Munster Fusiliers, War Office 95/4296, PRO.

66. Twistleton, Otago Mounted Rifles, 'Gallipoli', vol. 2, p. 3, TLW. G.G. Winston, CRA, Anzac, to Aspinall, 11 December 1930, Cabinet 45/245, PRO. C.E.W. Bean, *The Story of Anzac*, vol. 2, pp. 728–730. It was during this 11 Division attack that Capt. Travers, 9th Battalion, Lancashire Fusiliers, went missing between 21 and 22 August 1915, Casualties, 11 Division, War Office 95/4298, PRO.

67. Aspinall-Oglander, *Military Operations: Gallipoli*, vol. 2, pp. 354–356, 366. Turkish Fifth Army Losses, 6 August – 11 August 1915, Cabinet 105, Record 782, Shelf 4, File 182, Index 49, GSA.

Allied and Turkish Technology Creates Stalemate

1. The most useful document in this area is the *Mitchell Report*.

2. Cunliffe-Owen, 'Extracts from a lecture on Artillery at ANZAC', Royal Artillery Institution, 22 January 1920, Cabinet 45/246; and Cunliffe-Owen, Diary, end April – early May, 1915, Cabinet 45/246; PRO. Cunliffe-Owen, 'Artillery at ANZAC in the Gallipoli Campaign', *Royal Artillery Journal*, vol. XLVI, no. 12 (1919–1920), passim. Liman von Sanders, *Five Years in Turkey*, p. 71.

3. *Mitchell Report*, pp. 243, 244, 525, AWM. Cunliffe-Owen, Diary, 12 May 1915 [no planes at Anzac], vol. 2, p. 26 [for spotting], Cabinet 45/246, PRO. Brig. Gen. C.F. Aspinall-Oglander, *Military Operations, Gallipoli*, vol. 2, p. 17, for planes available in May.

4. RA Nicholson, *Swiftsure*, 'Arrangements for directing fire…', 10 May 1915, #134, Box 112, Aspinall-Oglander Papers, IOW. Maj. Casey, Diary, 29 May 1915, cited in Winter, *25 April 1915*, pp. 227–228. Brig Gen. Cunliffe-Owen, 'For Artillery Observation Officers for Ships', 28 April 1915, 367/49/25; Brig Gen. Cunliffe-Owen to GOC Anzac, 9 May 1915, 'Memo CRA #1, 367/229/25; AWM. Roger Keyes to Eva (wife), 10 May 1915, 2/11, Keyes Papers, BL. Lt-Col. Rettie to Aspinall, 16 July ?, and Rettie, 'With the Field Artillery Brigade at Suvla Bay Landing', no date, p. 6, Cabinet 45/244, PRO.

5. *Mitchell Report*, pp. 525–526.

6. Mühlmann, Letter.

7. 'Replies to questions put by Australian Official Historian on fighting in Gallipoli,' Question 168, Cabinet 45/217, PRO. *Mitchell Report*, p. 402 (and on the positive and negative value of Monitors, p. 528). Brig. Gen. G.G. Winston, CRA Anzac, to Aspinall, 11 December 1930, Cabinet 45/244, PRO. According to Hunter-Weston at the Dardanelles Commission, de Robeck told both Ian Hamilton and the Admiralty that naval guns could not do much, especially against trenches and machine-guns, Hunter-Weston, Evidence, Dardanelles Commission, p. 912, Cabinet 19/33, PRO.

8. Simpson Baikie, 'Notes by Brigadier-General Simpson Baikie on the Artillery at Cape Helles in the Dardanelles Expedition,' 1916/1917, p. 67/4, Dardanelles Commission, Cabinet 19/28; Lt-Col. Grant to Aspinall, 2 March 1929, Cabinet 45/242; PRO.

9. Kannengiesser, *The Campaign in Gallipoli*, p. 268; von Sanders, *Five Years in Turkey*, pp. 75, 79.

10. Milward, Diary, 4 June, 6510/143/3, NAM. Simpson Baikie, 'Notes', *op cit.*; Cunliffe-Owen, 'Artillery at ANZAC in the Gallipoli Campaign,' *op. cit.*; Robin Prior and Trevor Wilson, *Command on the Western Front: the Military Career of Sir Henry Rawlinson, 1914–1918,* Blackwell, Oxford and Cambridge,

1992, pp. 111–113. *Mitchell Report*, p. 234. Hamilton to Kitchener, 29 June 1915, War Committee minutes, Dardanelles Commission, pp. 95–96, Cabinet 29/31, PRO. Satisfaction with the artillery was expressed by several officers at Third Krithia, while Kannengiesser admired the preparation at Second Krithia.

11. On Stopford and artillery, Questions to Stopford at Dardanelles Commission, Question 9734, pp. 22–24, Hamilton Papers, 16/7/2/1, KCL; and 'Report on Operations of 9th Army Corps', 26 October 1915, pp. 5, 7–8, War Office 106/707, PRO. On poor cooperation, Brig. Gen. Stockdale, 15 Bde. Artillery, Statements to Dardanelles Commission, p.14, Cabinet 19/31, PRO. Cunliffe-Owen, Diary, 18 and 20 August 1915, Cabinet 45/246, PRO.

12. Lt-Col. Stephenson, 8th Manchester Regiment, to Aspinall, 16 January 1929, Cabinet 45/245, PRO.

13. For inability to destroy machine-guns, Lt-Col. Grant to Aspinall, 2 March 1929, Cabinet 45/242; for wire, Brig. Gen. Wylie, commanding 3 Group Artillery, Helles, to Aspinall, no date, Cabinet 45/245; PRO. But Col. Hobbs, 1st New Zealand Field Artillery, claimed to do effective wire cutting, Diary, 6 August 1915, PR 82/153/1, AWM.

14. 'Replies to question put by Australian Official Historian on fighting in Gallipoli', Questions 208 and 209, Cabinet 45/217, PRO. Col. Hobbs, 1st New Zealand Field Artillery, Diary, 6 August 1915, PR 82/153/1, AWM. Bean, *Gallipoli Mission*, p. 260. On survey, *Mitchell Report*, p. 524.

15. Lt-Col. Grant to Aspinall, 2 March 1929, Cabinet 45/241, PRO; *Mitchell Report*, p. 234; for inexperience, Col. Dare, CO 14th Bn., Australian Division, to Bean, 16 July 1931, 3 DRL 7953/28, Bean Papers, AWM; for Naval Brigade, Aspinall-Oglander, *Military Operations: Gallipoli*, vol. 2, p. 47. Improvement in artillery through 1915 can be followed in the diaries of artillery officers, such as Col. Rosenthal (MLS) and Col. Hobbs (AWM).

16. Liman von Sanders, *Five Years in Turkey*, p. 73; Hickey, *Gallipoli*, p. 193. Aspinall, *Gallipoli,* vol. 2, pp. 35, 37–38. Hamilton to Kitchener, 30 April 1915, p. 140, Cabinet 19/29, PRO. On more submarines, see Hamilton to Kitchener (Draft telegram), 31 August 1915, and War Office to Hamilton, 11 September 1915, Box 112, Aspinall-Oglander Papers, IOW.

17. Kiazim Bey, Chief of Staff, Fifth Army, to Director of Military Operations, Constantinople, 7 August 1915, and 11 August 1915, Cabinet 105, Record 782, Shelf 4. Files 63 and 93 C; GSA. Translated Turkish telegrams, Liman von Sanders to Enver and Bronsart, 7 August 1915; to Enver, 9 August 1915; to Bronsart, 18 and 19 August 1915; in Marshall Cornwall to Aspinall, 24 June 1930, Box 116, Aspinall-Oglander Papers, IOW. Aspinall-Oglander,

Military Operations: Gallipoli, vol. 2, p. 38. However, fear of German submarines at Bulair/Saros did deter the Allies from landing there in August 1915, Haythornthwaite, *Gallipoli*, p. 70.

18. Liman von Sanders to 1st Department, Constantinople, 29 April 1915, 'Logistics and Attacks at Gallipoli', Cabinet 105, Record 775, Shelf 4, File 180, GSA. Petter, *Dokumentation*, Bundesarchchiv-Militärarchiv (Freiburg), passim, for shortages of artillery and shells until August. Kannengiesser, *Campaign in Gallipoli*, pp. 142, 166; Liman von Sanders, *Five Years in Turkey*, pp. 75–76. For mountain guns in Kemal's 1/2 May 1915 attack, 'Atatürk's Memoirs of the Anafartaler Battles', p. 14, 76/75/1, IWM. Kiazim Bey to Enver, 4 May 1915, *Turkish Official History*, vol. 2, pp. 177–178. Kiazim Bey to Enver, 8 August 1915, Cabinet 105, Record 782, Shelf 4, File 182, GSA. 'Replies to Questions…', Question 201, Cabinet 45/217; Questions 37–44, 45–52, Cabinet 45/236; PRO.

19. 'Replies to Questions…', Questions 191, 172, 236, re: guns at Suvla, Cabinet 45/217; Questions 61–72, and 32–36 re: attack broken by mid-June, Cabinet 45/236; PRO. Aspinall has only 94 Ottoman guns at Helles on 6/7 August, Aspinall-Oglander, *Military Operations: Gallipoli*, vol. 1, p. 171. Re: observation at Helles, Lt-Col. Forman, RHA, Diary, October 1915, p. 47, Dardanelles Commission, Cabinet 19/29, PRO.

20. Kannengiesser, *The Campaign in Gallipoli*, p. 142. Lt-Col. Forman, RHA, Diary, 28 April 1915, Dardanelles Commission, Cabinet 19/29, PRO. Milward, Diary, 28 April 1915, Cabinet 45/259, PRO. Re: machine-guns rather than artillery, *Turkish Official History,* vol. 3, pp. 45–46, 48, 51. Col. W.F. Gordon, 34 Bde. Staff, re: Ottoman artillery bursting high, to Aspinall, Box 116, Aspinall-Oglander Papers, IOW; Lt Heath, RN, re: Ottoman artillery at Suvla, Diary, 12 August 1915, Cabinet 45/253, PRO. Gen. de Lisle, 'My Narrative of the Great War,' vol. 1, p. 75, in 17/4/3, Hamilton Papers, KCL. Cunliffe-Owen, Diary, 21 August 1915, Cabinet 45/246, PRO. Capt. Elliott, Letter to his mother, p. 11, 8403–63, NAM. Lt-Gen. Sir Richard Savory, 14th Sikhs, 'Some Gallipoli Memories,' *The Gallipolian*, no. 15, Autumn 1974, pp. 16–17, and no. 18, Autumn 1975, p. 14. 'Notes on Machine-guns', section #1, 367/129, Record Group 25, AWM.

21. Lt-Col. Stephenson to Aspinall, 16 January 1929, Cabinet 45/245, PRO. Re: German machine-gun companies, Petter, *Dokumentation*. Mühlmann, *Letter.* The observer on July 12/13 was Lt-Col. J.H. Patterson, *With the Zionists in Gallipoli*, London, 1916, p. 201. Kiazim to Enver, 9 August 1915, Cabinet 105, Record 782, Shelf 4, File 75, GSA. Maj. Willmer to Aspinall, 12 April 1930, Box 112; Harun el Raschid, *In remembrance of Liman von Sanders…*, p. 9, Box

111; Aspinall-Oglander Papers, IOW. Lt-Col. Grant, RA, to Aspinall, 2 March 1929, Cabinet 45/242, PRO. Savory, 'Some Gallipoli Memories,' *The Gallipolian*, no. 10, Winter 1972, p. 17, and no. 16, Winter 1974, p. 11. Admiral Souchon to Commander-in-chief, 3 May 1915, on sending 8 machine-gun batteries and 41 men to 5th Army on Torpedo Boat *Samsun*, Cabinet 105, Record 775, Shelf 4, File 180, GSA.

22. Petter, *Dokumentation*, for making rifle ammunition on site. On grenade requests in June, '19 Division War Reports, 6 March–10 June 1915,' 8 June 1915, 57 Regiment to 19 Division, and 10 June 1915, 57 Regiment to 19 Division, Cabinet 227, Record 1-185, Shelf 1, File 5382, GSA. For grenade requests in August fighting, Kiazim Bey to Enver (Extremely Urgent), 7 August 1915, and 10 August 1915, both in Cabinet 105, Record 782, Shelf 4, File 182, GSA. Doubts about Turkish bombs is in Steel and Hart, *Gallipoli*, pp. 340–341. Savory, 'Some Gallipoli Memories', *The Gallipolian*, no. 10, Winter 1972, p. 14. On Dumezils, Orlo Williams, Diary, 31 July 1915, IWM. An example of Turkish guns, machine-guns and rifles stopping an attack is 53 Division's attack on 10 August, Capt. Drury, Diary, 10 August 1915, NAM.

The Experience of Modern War at Gallipoli

1. F.E. McKenzie, Diary, 26 April 1915, 19 May 1915, 2 June 1915, 3 June 1915, Ms. 96/13, AMA.
2. *Ibid.*, 3 June 1915, 5 July 1915, 10 August 1915.
3. Browne, Diary, 8 August 1915, 9 August 1915, Ms. 3519, TLW.
4. George Albert Tuck, Diary, 27 April 1915, 8 May 1915, Ms. 2164-2166, TLW. Gurkha story in Capt. Drury, Diary, 24 August 1915, 7607-69, vol. 1, NAM.
5. Richard Holmes, *On the Firing Line*, London, 1985, pp. 225 ff.
6. George Blake to Aspinall, 4 September 1929, Cabinet 45/241, PRO. Capt. W.H. Whyte, 6 Battalion Royal Dublin Fusiliers, to Aspinall, no date but 1929 or 1930, Cabinet 45/245, PRO.
7. Savory, 'Some Gallipoli Memories', *The Gallipolian*, Winter 1974, no. 16, pp. 11–12; and Autumn 1975, no. 18, p. 13.
8. Anonymous Hauraki engineer, Diary, 11 August 1915, Box 007, KAM.
9. Report from evening of 3 May – 10 May 1915, to Minister of War, 20 N 28; 1 French Division war diary, 4 May 1915, 26 N 75; Gouraud, 'Note de service Concernant les Signaux… entre les Troupes Allies', 31 May 1915, 5a, Operation Orders, 3rd Bureau, 20 N 27; FAV.
10. R.J. Speight, Diary, in letter to Katie, 6 July 1916, 92/34, AMA. Malone, Diary, 26 April 1915, KAM.
11. Browne, Diary, 8 and 9 August 1915, TLW.

12. Maj.-Gen. W. Douglas, giving evidence at the Dardanelles Commission, p. 32, Cabinet 19/32, PRO. Tuli (Maj. Geddes, Royal Munster Fusiliers) to Aspinall, 15 November ?, Cabinet 45/245, PRO.

13. Ian Hamilton, no date, Correspondence concerning Dardanelles Commission, 17/4/1/40 and 41, Hamilton Papers, KCL. Col. A.C. Temperley, 'A personal narrative of the battle of Chunuk Bair, August 6–10, 1915', in Brigadier Braithwaite Papers, Ms. 005, pp. 6, 10, 18, KAM.

14. Lt-Col. T.H.B. Forster, evidence at Dardanelles Commission, p. 48, Cabinet 19/29; and further evidence, pp. 740, 744, Cabinet 19/33; PRO.

15. Twistleton, Gallipoli file #2, Ms. 1705, TLW. Brigadier-General Trotman, 'Report of operations on 13 July…', 18 July 1915; Maj.-Gen. Paris, 'Report of operations July 13–16 inclusive', 18 July 1915; Royal Naval Division War Diary, War Office 95/4290, PRO.

16. Fleet Surgeon Arthur Gaskell, ADMS to RN Division, 25 May 1915, to DMS, GHQ, RN Division war Dairy, War Office 95/4290, PRO.

17. Sir William Macpherson et al (eds.), *History of the Great War: Medical Services*, vol. 3, HMSO, London, 1923, p. 1.

18. Milward, Diary, 23 August 1915, 6510/143/3, NAM. Joseph Murray, *Gallipoli 1915*, London, 1965, NEL paperback edition, 1977, pp. 105–106.

19. Reports of the Deputy Judge Advocate, 31 May 1915, 30 June 1915, 31 October 1915, War Office 154/116, PRO.

20. *Ibid*. Davis court martial, War Office 71/431, PRO.

21. Reports of the Deputy Judge Advocate, 31 July 1915, War Office 154/116, PRO.

22. Salter court martial, War Office 71/439, PRO.

23. Robins court martial, War Office 71/442, PRO.

24. *Ibid*. Birdwood to Kitchener, 2 December 1915, 65, Birdwood Papers, AWM.

25. Capt. Percy, Deputy Judge Advocate Report, 31 December 1915, War Office 154/116, PRO. For execution rates, Joanna Bourke, *Dismembering the Male: Men's Bodies, Britain and the Great War*, Chicago, 1996, pp. 94–95.

26. Reports of the Deputy Judge Advocates, War Office 154/116, PRO.

27. Orlo Williams, Diary, 11 May 1915, vol. 1, 69/78/1, IWM.

28. Capt. Drury, Diary, 9 August 1915, vol. 1, 7607–69, NAM.

29. See Chapter 4.

30. Milward, Diary, 25 April 1915, 6510/143/3, NAM.

31. F. Hyde Harrison, 1st Battalion Border Regiment to Aspinall, 27 April 1926, Box 116/1, Aspinall-Oglander Papers, IOW.

32. Lt-Col. Tizard, 1st Battalion Royal Munster Fusiliers, 'Report on the landing from the Collier River Clyde', War Diary, War Office 95/4310, PRO.

33. F.E. McKenzie, Diary, 20 September 1915, Ms. 96/13, AMA.
34. Benoni Sandilands, New Zealand Mounted Infantry, Ms. 1405, TLW. F.E. McKenzie, Diary, 5 July 1915, Ms. 96/13, AMA. F.H. Fountaine to Aspinall, 28 November 1928, Cabinet 45/242, PRO.
35. Godley to Birdwood, 30 July 1915, and Godley to Birdwood, 22 October 1915, WA 252/9, Godley-Birdwood correspondence, NAW. Lady Godley was in Cairo, and ran a convalescent home. Birdwood to Braithwaite, 24 July 1915, 64, Birdwood Papers, AWM.
36. Lt-Col. Fenwick, DADMS, Diary, 6 May 1915, Ms. 1497; Clutha McKenzie, Diary, 12–20 June 1915, Ms. 79/23; AMA.
37. Speight, Diary, 8 August 1915, Ms. 92/34, AMA.
38. Lt Colvin Algie, Hauraki Battalion, Diary, 23 May 1915, 1990.595 KAM. Twistleton, Ms. Papers, 1705, p. 6, TLW. Doherty, Diary, 3 November 1915, KAM.
39. Fenwick, Diary, 5 May 1915 (also shrapnel pet story), 7 May 1915, 9 May 1915, 18 May 1915 (for characteristics of shrapnel), 1 June 1915, 15 June 1915, 18 June 1915, Ms. 1497, AMA. Malone, Diary, 29 April 1915, KAM. Godley claimed that Fenwick broke down at Anzac, and was not right in Egypt, Godley to Allen (New Zealand Minister of Defence), 10 October 1915, Godley-Allen correspondence, WA 252/2, NAW.
40. Maj. John Gillam, diary entries for 13 May 1915, 27 July 1915, 20 August 1915, in *Gallipoli Diary*, London, 1918, 1989, pp. 85, 173, 201.
41. Holmes, *On the Firing Line*, pp. 355 ff.
42. Letters between Keyes, de Robeck, Bartolomé, and others, in 1916, on the subject of medals, 5/39 and 5/40, Keyes Papers, 13484, BL.
43. R.G. Kelly, 7th Battalion Royal Dublin Fusiliers, to Aspinall, 11 May 1931, HQ 29 Brigade; Brig. Gen. L.L. Nicoll to Aspinall, 21 January 1931, HQ 30 Brigade; 10 Division War Diary, War Office 95/4296, PRO.
44. Fenwick, Diary, 31 May 1915, *op cit.*, AMA.
45. Hamilton to Godley, 30 October 1915, and 17 February 1916, and 23 February 1916, Godley Letters, Z 5083, NAW. Birdwood to Godley, no date, Godley-Birdwood letters, WA 252/9, NAW. Birdwood to Godley, 7 January 1915, and Birdwood to Godley, no date, and Birdwood to Godley, 4 May 1916, Godley-Birdwood letters, WA 252/10, NAW. Godley to My Dear Johnston (possibly Maj. H.H. Johnston, of the 2nd Australian Light Horse Brigade), 3 December 1915, Godley semi-personal letters, WA 252/6, NAW.
46. A. Gameson Lane to Aspinall, 22 May 1931; H.I. Powell to Aspinall, 13 April 1931; Honours Awarded; War Diary, 34 Brigade, 11 Division, War Office 99/4299, PRO. At the highest level, according to Field Marshal 'Wully' Robertson, Byng, who served at Gallipoli, was eventually awarded the rank

of field marshal because he was always a nice fellow. On the other hand, Cavan was always a joke, and got his field marshal's baton because of court and political influence, Robertson to Godley, 30 November 1932, Z 5083, Godley Papers, NAW.

47. Unwin to Admiralty, 15 September 1915, de Robeck to Keyes, 4 November 1916 and 23 September 1916, 5/39 and 5/40, Keyes Papers, 13484, BL.

48. Maj. Coe, Australian Field Artillery, to Father, 12 May 1915, L/12/11/3286, Coe Papers, 2 DRL 491, AWM. F.E. McKenzie, Diary, 26 April 1915, AMA. Doherty, Diary, 9 August 1915, KAM.

49. Fenwick, Diary, 30 April 1915, *op cit.*, AMA. Levenson-Gower West, Diary, 7 May 1915, 26 April 1915, vol. 1, KAM.

50. Sergeant R. Chadwick, 1st New Zealand Ambulance, Diary, 25 April 1915, and 29 April 1915, 1996/1820, KAM.

51. Algie, Hauraki Battalion, KAM.

52. Fenwick, Diary, 26 April 1915, *op cit.*, AMA.

53. 'Another account out of war diary', in Diary of Events of Gen. Braithwaite, Anzac Division, 26 April 1915, WA 1/1, Box 1, NAW. Twistleton, Ms Papers 1705, p. 7, TLW.

54. Tpr Frank Hobson, Diary, 20 May 1915 and 21 May 1915, Ms. 94/50, AMA.

55. Corporal McMillan, Canterbury Mounted Rifles, *40,000 Horsemen*, pp. 30, 32, unpublished memoirs, 1997/503, KAM.

56. War Diary, 20 August 1915, 9 Bn. Lancashire Fusiliers, 34 Brigade, 11 Division, War Office 95/4299, PRO. Joseph Murray, *Gallipoli*, p. 206.

57. Salim Bey Ciftligi, commander Turkish forces near Seddulbahir, 6 June 1915, Record 75, File 3451, Index 20-8, GSA.

58. Maj. Munib, 36th Regiment, after action report, 12 August 1915; and Maj. Munib to GOC 12 Division, 13 August 1915; Record H2, File 5359, Index F.1.16/1.17, and 1.19; GSA. *Turkish Official History*, vol. 3, pp. 213–214. Nigel McCrery, in his book *The Vanished Battalion*, London, 1992, makes the case for the 1/5 Norfolk prisoners being shot after capture by the Turks. Mühlmann, *Letter*.

59. John Still, *A Prisoner in Turkey*, London and New York, 1920, pp. 30–34, 37.

60. Interrogation of Prisoners of War, Lt John Still, Cabinet 113, Record 2115, Shelf 5, File 542, GSA.

61. Still, *A Prisoner in Turkey*, pp. 30–40, 123–125, 247.

62. Interrogation of Prisoners of War, Capt. Derek Elliott, Cabinet 113, Record 2115, Shelf 5, File 542, GSA.

63. *Ibid.*, 2nd-Lt William Fawkes. Still also wrote of Fawkes' experiences in *A Prisoner in Turkey*, p. 107, without mentioning Fawkes' name, and later wrote about Fawkes in Still to Aspinall, 10 May 1932, Box 111, Aspinall-Oglander

Papers, IOW. According to Lt-Col. Fountaine's letter to Aspinall, 11 December 1930, War Office 95/4296, PRO, the 1/5 Norfolks were all shot after capture.

64. Greg Kerr, *Lost Anzacs: The Story of Two Brothers*, Melbourne, 1997, paperback edition, 1998, pp. 3–4, 99–101. Birdwood to Hamilton, 11 October 1917, Birdwood Correspondence, 1917–1925, 1/14, Hamilton Papers, KCL.

65. Turkish prisoner of war captured near Ari Burnu, 20 September 1915, in prisoner of war statements in Sir Gerard Clauson Papers, 80/47/2, IWM. In 1915, Clauson was an Intelligence Officer at IX Corps HQ. All of the forty odd interrogations are from the September to December 1915 time period. On the stabbing story, Doherty, Diary, 30 June 1915, KAM.

66. *Ibid.*

67. *Ibid.*, IX Corps Intelligence Bulletin, 14 October 1915; Prisoners Captured in Southern Zone to 10 July 1915.

68. Clutha McKenzie, Diary, 24 May 1915, 79/23, AMA. 'Report on the operations of 12 and 13 July, 1915', 8(a), 20 N 28, FAV.

69. Niall Ferguson, *The Pity of War*, New York, 1999, chapter 13, 'The Captor's Dilemma'. Mühlmann, *Letter*. 'Iskender Mericli: Memories of a Turkish soldier', *The Gallipolian*, #75, Autumn 1994, pp. 14–18. 70. Anon, 'Human Landscapes from my Country', in Kevin Fewster, Vehici Basarin and Hatice Basarin, *A Turkish View of Gallipoli/Canakkale*, Hodja Press, Richmond, Victoria, 1985, pp. 127–129. On Allied problems, see Michael Tyquin, *Gallipoli: the Medical War: The Australian Army Medical Services in the Dardanelles Campaign of 1915*, Kensington, NSW, 1993.

71. Analysis of the medical system in Tyquin, *op cit.*, and in Dardanelles Commission, especially Cabinet 19/31 and Cabinet 19/32, PRO; and in all studies of the Gallipoli campaign. Fenwick, Diary, 7 June 1915, MS 1497, AMA. Lt-Col. Stoney-Archer, evidence at Dardanelles Commission, p. 15, Cabinet 19/31, PRO.

72. *Ibid.*, 25 April 1915. Sergeant A.E.M. Rhind, New Zealand Vet Service, 1993.1001; KAM.

73. LeGallais, letters to Sonnie, 25 September 1915 and 17 November 1915, Folder 6, 95/11, AMA. On removing the dead, Twistleton, vol. 1, p. 9, TLW.

74. Sandilands, Diary, 4 August 1915, TLW. 35 Field Ambulance, 11 Division, war diary, September 1915; 22 Sanitary Section, 11 Division, war diary, 6 September 1915; War Office 95/4298, PRO. Hamilton to Weber Pasa, 9 July 1915, Cabinet 175, Record 115-316, Shelf 5, File 3426, GSA. Col. McMunn to QMG, 14 October 1915, Private letters from Dardanelles, War Office 107/44, PRO. Lt-Gen. Altham, Dardanelles Commission, p. 8, Cabinet

19/28, PRO.

75. ADVS war diary, 11 Division, 23 August 1915, War Office 95/4298; ADVS war diary, 10 Division, 16 and 17 July 1915, War Office 95/4294; PRO.

76. Chadwick, Diary, 16 December 1915, 1996/1820, KAM. F.E. McKenzie, Diary, 19 December 1915, Ms. 96/13, AMA.

77. Lt Masterman, New Zealand Mounted Infantry, Diary, no date, KAM. Joseph Murray, *Gallipoli*, p. 217, from his Diary for 6 January 1916. Maj. John Gillam, *Gallipoli Diary*, p. 321, Diary entry for 8 January 1916.

78. Pte Humphreys, 5th Field Artillery, Diary, 25 December 1915, Ms. 1623, TLW. F.E. McKenzie, Diary, 25 December 1915, Ms. 96/13, AMA. Anonymous, Diary, 25 December 1915, Box 007, KAM. Frederick Varnham, Diary, 25 December 1915, TLW.

Evacuation

1. Hankey to Birdwood, 9 October 1915, Birdwood to Hankey, 20 October 1915, 46, Birdwood Papers, AWM. On Glynn, Dawnay to wife, 15 July 1915, 69/21/1, IWM; Orlo Williams, Diary, 29 July 1915, IWM. Birdwood to Kitchener, 21 October 1915, 48; Birdwood to Kitchener, 2 December 1915, 65; Birdwood Papers, AWM. Hankey, Diary, 17 July 1915, 19 July 1915, 29 August 1915, 1 September 1915, 9 October 1915, Hankey Papers, CCC. Hamilton to de Robeck, 21 July 1915, 4/40, de Robeck Papers, CCC. Hankey to Asquith, 12 August 1915, in Dardanelles Commission, pp. 6 – 13, Cabinet 19/29, PRO.

2. Orlo Williams, Diary, 21 August 1915, 2 September 1915, 3 September 1915, IWM. Dawnay to wife, 21 December 1915, 2 January 1916, Letters to wife, 69/21/1; Dawnay, 12 August 1915, 21–22 August 1915, Various Papers, April–December 1915, 69/21/2; Dawnay Papers, IWM.

3. Draft, Lt-Col. G.S., no date or author; G.P. Dawnay, draft telegram for War Office of 22 August 1915, not despatched; Aspinall, Situation, 29 August 1915; Aspinall draft of Hamilton despatch re: July and August fighting, no date, but September 1915; Box 115/4, Aspinall-Oglander Papers, IOW.

4. Stopford, Report of Operations, 9th Army Corps, 26 October 1915, War Office 106/707, PRO. Keith Murdoch to Andrew Fisher, Australian Prime Minister, 23 September 1915, copied to Asquith and Dardanelles Committee, 5/5, Hamilton Papers, KCL. Hankey, Diary, 29 September 1915, Hankey Papers, CCC. Bailloud to Minister of War, 16 August 1915, File 6, 20 N 27, FAV. The French also wanted to attack the Asian side instead of at Helles or Anzac.

5. Hankey, Diary, 22 September 1915 to 24 September 1915, 30 September 1915, Hankey Papers, CCC. Stephen Gaselee, Foreign Office, to E.Y. Daniel,

secretary to Official History Committee, 10 October 1931, Box 111, Aspinall-Oglander Papers, IOW.

6. Orlo Williams, Diary, 3 September 1915, 6 October 1915, IWM. Dawnay to wife, 16 October 1915, 18 October 1915, 19 October 1915, 21 December 1915, 27 October 1915, 10 November 1915, 31 December 1915, 2 January 1916, 69/21/1, IWM. Hamilton, copy 2 of chapter 2, 'The Commander', no date but post war, 19/8-9, Hamilton Papers, KCL. Hankey, Diary, 12 October 1915, 13 October 1915, 21 October 1915, 24 October 1915, Hankey Papers, CCC. Kitchener to Hamilton, no date, 17/7/10, and Hamilton to Kitchener, no date, 17/7/11, Hamilton Papers, KCL.

7. Monro, Report, 31 October 1915, in Dardanelles Commission, Cabinet 19/33, PRO. Monro to Kitchener, 2 November 1915; Aspinall, Appreciation, 22 October 1915; War Office 158/575, PRO. Kitchener to Birdwood, 3 November 1915, Birdwood to Kitchener, 4 November 1915, Kitchener to Birdwood, 6 November 1915, War Office 158/581, PRO. 'Notes for Maj.-Gen. A.L. Lynden-Bell', no date, Box 116, Aspinall-Oglander Papers, IOW. Hankey, Diary, 1 October 1915 (for Kitchener break down), 1 November 1915 (for Kitchener leaving War Office), 6 November 1915 (for Keyes' naval plan and Birdwood wanting to hang on), Hankey Papers, CCC.

8. Note by Aspinall, enclosing letter from Dawnay to Aspinall, 21 November 1915, Box 111, Aspinall-Oglander Papers, IOW. Dawnay to wife, 2 January 1916, 69/21/1, IWM. Charles Callwell, Proposed Evidence, p. 107, Cabinet 19/28, PRO. 23 December 1915, Notes of War Committee meeting, p. 51, Cabinet 19/31, PRO. (The Dardanelles Committee was renamed the War Committee at the beginning of October 1915). Hankey, Diary, 13 November 1915, 7 December 1915, Hankey Papers, CCC. Re: naval plan, de Lisle, Diary, 6 December 1915, 9 December 1915, Cabinet 45/241, PRO; and Godley to Lady Godley, 20 December 1915, WA 252/12, NAW, also for the pro- and anti-evacuation groups. Dawnay to Aspinall, 1 February 1932, Cabinet 45/241, PRO, for the Alexandretta and Ayas schemes. Re: Kitchener's offer to Byng, G.S. Clive, Diary, 16 May, 1916, Clive Papers, Cabinet 45/201/2, PRO.

9. Zeki Bey, commanding 1st Battalion, 57th Regiment, in Bean, *Gallipoli Mission*, pp. 247–251. Birdwood to Godley, 1 December 1915, WA 252/9, NAW. Hamilton, notes for chapters, 1931, 19/10, Hamilton Papers, KCL. Liman von Sanders to Mustafa Kemal, 29 November 1915, 'Appointment of Mustafa Kemal' file, Archive 5/8810, Record 53/126, File 4568, Index 16–7, GSA (my underlining). Kannengiesser, *The Campaign in Gallipoli*, pp. 245–246, 256–258.

10. Godley to Birdwood, 10 December 1915, 12 December 1915, 20 December 1915, WA 252/13; Godley to Robertson, 24 December 1915, postscript in Godley to Earle, 24 September 1915, WA 252/6; NAW.

11. Zeki Bey, in Bean, *Gallipoli Mission*, p. 253. Lt-Gen. Davies, GOC VIII Corps, to Aspinall, 7 November 1931, Cabinet 45/241, PRO.

Ian Hamilton and the Dardanelles Commission

1. Hamilton to Braithwaite, 12 December 1916, 17/3/1/64, Correspondence with witnesses at the Dardanelles Commission, 17/3/1; Hamilton to Birdwood, 22 March 1918, Correspondence with Birdwood 1917–1925, 1/14; Hamilton Papers, KCL.

2. Hamilton notes, 6/1; Hamilton to Braithwaite, 17 August 1916, 17/4/1; Hamilton to Roger Keyes, 5 May 1917, 17/3/2/41, Correspondence with witnesses, 17/3/2; Hamilton Papers, KCL. On Hamilton versus Nicholson, Aylmer Haldane, Diary, 26 April 1901, 28 October 1908, Haldane Papers, Diary 1875–1913, 20247, National Library of Scotland, Edinburgh.

3. Hamilton to Braithwaite, 21 September 1916, 17/4/1/9, and Hamilton to Braithwaite, 5 October 1916, 17/4/1/16; Correspondence concerning Dardanelles Commission, 17/4/1, Hamilton Papers, KCL.

4. Hamilton to Grimwood Mears, 22 November 1916, 17/3/1/5, Correspondence with witnesses, 17/3/1; Hamilton to Braithwaite, 21 September 1916, 17/4/1/9, and 22 August 1916, 17/4/1/4, and Braithwaite to Hamilton, 25 August 1916, 17/4/1/5; Correspondence concerning Dardanelles Commission, 17/4/1, Hamilton Papers, KCL. For Hamilton's private source in the Commission, Hamilton to Braithwaite, 4 August 1917, 17/4/3/28, and re: Kaye, 'Summary of conversation between xxx and xxx', 12 July 1917, 17/4/3/8; Correspondence concerning Dardanelles Commission, 17/4/3, Hamilton Papers, KCL. On French repacking ships, d'Amade to Captain of Ports and Communications, 21 March 1915, File 3, 20 N 28, FAV.

5. Hamilton to Braithwaite, 14 October 1916, 17/4/1/21, and Braithwaite to Hamilton, 16 October 1916, 17/4/1/24; Correspondence concerning Dardanelles Commission, 17/4/1, Hamilton Papers, KCL.

6. Hamilton to de Robeck, 17 October 1916, 17/4/1/28, Correspondence concerning Dardanelles Commission, 17/4/1, Hamilton Papers, KCL.

7. De Robeck to Winston Churchill, 26 March 1915, Dardanelles, Chartwell Papers, 13/65, CCC. De Robeck, from *Queen Elizabeth*, Memorandum to Fleet, 23 April 1915, Orders for Combined Operations, War Office 106/705, PRO.

8. Hamilton to Braithwaite, 14 October 1916, *op cit.* Braithwaite to Hamilton, 14 October 1916, 17/4/1/23, Correspondence concerning Dardanelles Commission, 17/4/1, Hamilton Papers, KCL.

9. Hamilton to Stockdale, 21 November 1916, 17/3/1/4, Correspondence with witnesses, 17/3/1; Col. D. Forman to Hamilton, 7 November 1916, 17/4/1/59, and Hamilton to Birdwood, 27 November 1916, 17/4/1/75; Correspondence concerning Dardanelles Commission, 17/4/1; Hamilton Papers, KCL.

10. Hamilton to Roger Keyes, 5 May 1917, 17/3/2/41, Correspondence with witnesses, 17/3/2; Comments on Birdwood testimony, Questions 21366–9, p. 114, 16/8/6; Hamilton Papers, KCL.

11. De Lisle to Hamilton, 14 December 1916, 17/3/1/53, Correspondence with witnesses, 17/3/1, Hamilton Papers, KCL. Godley to Birdwood, 20 November 1916; Birdwood to Godley, 22 November 1916; Birdwood to Godley, 21 January 1917; Godley to Birdwood, 26 January 1917; Godley-Birdwood Correspondence, 1916–1917, Godley Papers, WA 252/10, NAW.

12. Birdwood to Hamilton, 23 November 1916, 17/4/1/73, Correspondence concerning Dardanelles Commission, 17/4/1; Birdwood to Hamilton, 4 December 1916, 17/3/1/14, Correspondence with witnesses, 17/3/1; Hamilton Papers, KCL.

13. Hamilton to Birdwood, 8 December 1916, 17/3/1/14, Correspondence with witnesses, 17/3/1, Hamilton Papers, KCL. Birdwood to Godley, 30 November 1916, Godley-Birdwood Correspondence, Godley Papers, WA 252/10, NAW.

14. Godley to Birdwood, 14 February 1917; Birdwood to Godley, 15 February 1917; and Godley to Birdwood, 27 February 1917; Godley-Birdwood Correspondence, Godley Papers, WA 252/10, NAW.

15. Hamilton to Braithwaite, 14 November 1916, 17/4/1/64, Correspondence concerning Dardanelles Commission; Birdwood to Hamilton, 14 December 1916, 17/3/1, and Hamilton to Birdwood, 16 December 1916, 17/3/1/57, Correspondence with witnesses, 17/3/1; Hamilton to Birdwood, 19 January 1917, 17/4/2/16, Correspondence concerning Dardanelles Commission, Hamilton Papers, KCL.

16. Hamilton to Birdwood, 27 January 1917, 17/3/1/90; Birdwood to Hamilton, 31 January 1917, 17/3/1/94; Hamilton to Birdwood, 3 February 1917, 17/3/1/99; Hamilton to Birdwood, 14 February 1917, 17/3/1/118, Hamilton to Birdwood, 7 March 1917, 17/3/1/42; Correspondence with witnesses, 17/3/1, Hamilton Papers, KCL.

17. Birdwood to Hamilton, 21 June 1917, 17/4/2/106, Hamilton to Birdwood, 25 June 1917, 17/4/2/107, Correspondence concerning

Dardanelles Commission, 17/4/2; Birdwood to Hamilton, 28 June 1917, 17/4/3/2, Hamilton to Birdwood, 3 July 1917, 17/4/3/3; Correspondence concerning Dardanelles Commission, 17/4/3; Birdwood to Hamilton, 7 July 1917, Birdwood Correspondence, 1/14; Hamilton Papers, KCL.

18. Birdwood to Charles Bean, 24 July 1920, 3DRL/8042/2, Bean Papers, AWM. Lady Hamilton, Diary, 29 March 1920, Reel 4, 44, Hamilton Papers, KCL. It seems quite possible that Hamilton did keep an intermittent private diary during 1915, besides Sergeant Maj. Stuart's appointment diary. If he did, this has disappeared.

19. Hamilton to Godley, 29 May 1920, Z 5083, Godley Letters, Godley Papers, NAW.

20. Braithwaite to Hamilton, 14 March 1917, 17/3/2/6, and Braithwaite to Hamilton, 19 March 1917, 17/3/2/14, Correspondence with witnesses, 17/3/2; Lady Hamilton, Diary, 22 October 1915, Reel 3, 44; Hamilton Papers, KCL.

21. Lt-Col. Beadon to Hamilton, 2 August 1917, 17/4/3/25, Hamilton to Beadon, no date, 17/4/3/26, Hamilton to Braithwaite, 4 August 1917, 17/4/3/28; Correspondence concerning Dardanelles Commission, 17/4/3, Hamilton Papers, KCL.

22. Braithwaite to Hamilton, 9 August 1917, 17/4/3/30, Braithwaite to Hamilton, 13 August 1917, 17/4/3/33, Hamilton to Braithwaite, 15 August 1917, 17/4/3/36; Correspondence concerning Dardanelles Commission, 17/4/3, Hamilton Papers, KCL.

23. Braithwaite to Hamilton, 18 August 1917, 17/4/3/39, and Hamilton to Braithwaite, 20 August 1917, 17/4/3/40, Correspondence concerning Dardanelles Commission, 17/4/3; Hamilton to Winter, 26 September 1917, 17/3/2/80, Correspondence with witnesses, 17/3/2; Hamilton Papers, KCL. On Winter's mental state, Hamilton to Mears, 24 May 1917, Statements to the Dardanelles Commission, p. 80, Cabinet 19/32, PRO.

24. Hamilton to England, 19 December 1916, 17/3/1/67A, Allanson to Hamilton, 6 February 1917, 17/3/1/100, and Hamilton to Allanson, 7 February 1917, 17/3/1/101, Correspondence with witnesses, 17/3/1; Hamilton Papers, KCL.

25. Birdwood to Hamilton, 11 October 1917, Hamilton to Birdwood, 7 August 1917, and Hamilton to Birdwood, 28 September 1917; Birdwood Correspondence, 1917–1918, 1/14 Hamilton Papers, KCL.

26. Hamilton to Braithwaite, 14 November 1916, 17/4/1/64; Hamilton to Braithwaite, 4 June 1917, 17/3/2/47; Hamilton to Birdwood, 25 June 1917, 17/4/2/107; Hamilton to Braithwaite, 15 August 1917, 17/4/3/36;

Correspondence concerning Dardanelles Commission, Hamilton Papers, KCL.

27. Hamilton to Birdwood, 3 July 1917, 17/4/3/3, Hamilton to C.M. Stephen, Artillery, 25 July 1917, 17/4/3/17, Braithwaite to Hamilton, 29 July 1917, 17/4/3/22; Correspondence concerning Dardanelles Commission, 17/4/3, Hamilton Papers, KCL. On preventing the Commission from looking into losing the confidence of his men, Hamilton to Aspinall, 10 February 1931, Box 115, Aspinall-Oglander Papers, IOW.

28. The Final Report of the Dardanelles Commission. (Part II – Conduct of Operations &c.), Command Paper 371, HMSO, 1919, pp. 86 – 88.

Conclusion

1. Gen. Sir Ian Hamilton, *Compulsory Service*, London, 1910, pp. 121–122; Brigadier-General Walter Braithwaite, 'For the conduct of an army character weighs more than knowledge or science', lecture delivered at Simla, 30 July 1913, *Journal of the United Service Institution of India*, vol. 42, 1913, pp. 366–367. It is fair to add that Braithwaite was puzzled over how aviation might influence the modern battlefield.

2. Hamilton to Kitchener, 5 May 1915, and 26 May 1915, 5/1, Hamilton Papers, KCL. Von Donop, evidence at Dardanelles Commission, p. 5, Cabinet 19/29, PRO.

3. Hamilton, *Gallipoli Diary*, vol. 1, pp. 132–133, 147; Hamilton to Aspinall, 24 December 1929, Cabinet 45/242, PRO. Hamilton to Kitchener, 8 September 1915, 5/1, Hamilton Papers, KCL. Examples of British commanders who intervened with their senior officers would be Haig and Allenby.

4. Roger Keyes to Eva (wife), 13 April 1915, 2/10; 10 May 1915, 3 May 1915, 2/11; Keyes Papers, BL.

5. Godley to Lady Godley, 22 October 1915, and 7 November 1915; Lady Godley to Godley, 23–25 October 1915; Godley-Lady Godley correspondence, WA 252/12, NAW.

6. Orlo Williams, Diary, 2 September 1915, 16 October 1915, IWM. Dawnay to wife, 19 October 1915, 10 November 1915, Letters to wife, Dawnay Papers, IWM. 'Stellenbosched' refers to the town in South Africa where failed officers were sent during the Boer War.

7. Aspinall-Oglander, *Military Operations: Gallipoli*, vol. 2, p. 387. Orlo Williams, Diary, 21 July 1915, IWM. Birdwood to Maxwell, 9 August 1915, 63, Birdwood Papers, AWM. Much later, J.E. Edmonds argued that Hamilton could not have succeeded at Gallipoli with the Divisional COs and staff available to him, Edmonds, unpublished 'Memoirs', chapter XX, p. 18, Edmonds Papers, III, 2/11, KCL.

8. Kitchener to Hamilton, no date, message #8515, and Hamilton to Kitchener, no date, #732, Hamilton Papers 17/7/10 and 11, KCL.

9. See the statement concerning Kitchener's faults by the AG, Sclater, p. 1, Cabinet 19/31, PRO. There was also the 1906 War Office evaluation, which argued that naval guns guaranteed the landing, 'The Possibility of a Joint Naval and Military attack upon the Dardanelles', 20 December 1906, 17/7/22, Hamilton Papers, KCL. Aspinall pointed out that Callwell's memo for Kitchener in February 1915 was very optimistic, and this influenced Kitchener, Aspinall-Oglander, *Military Operations: Gallipoli*, vol. 2, fn. p. 417. The defence of Hamilton by John Lee, *A Soldier's Life: General Sir Ian Hamilton*, also generally censures Kitchener.

10. See previous footnote, and just one example of criticism, de Lisle criticised Kitchener for sending poor troops and leaders, and for thinking that 500 men and 500 horses made a regiment, de Lisle to Aspinall, 15 May 1932, Box 111, Aspinall-Oglander Papers, IOW.

11. Kitchener to Maxwell, 6 April 1915, Hamilton to Maxwell, 7 April 1915, War Office 158/574; Kitchener to Hamilton, 27 April 1915, Hamilton to Kitchener, 17 May 1915, Kitchener to Hamilton, 18 May 1915, Cabinet 19/31; Fitzgerald to Braithwaite, 19 June 1915; PRO.

12. See chapter 8.

13. Hamilton to Birdwood, 17 June 1915, Letters to Birdwood, 5/10, Hamilton Papers, KCL.

14. Re: small craft, Hankey to wife, 7 September 1915, 3/20, Hankey Papers; Admiral Douglas Gamble to de Robeck, 17 August 1915, 4/39, de Robeck Papers; CCC. On PNTO, Hamilton to Kitchener, 15 July 1915, 5/1, Hamilton Papers, KCL. On hospital ships, 'Transport Report on Hospital Ships', II, no date, p. 45, Cabinet 19/30, PRO. Hamilton, 27 July 1915, *Gallipoli Diary*, vol. 2, p. 32.

15. 'The Naval Memoirs of Admiral J.H. Godfrey', vol. 8, 'Afterthoughts', p. 24, 74/96/1, IWM.

16. Lt-Col. Forster, p. 48; Col. Elliott, p. 8; Evidence at Dardanelles Commission, Cabinet 19/29, PRO. Hamilton to Cowans (A.G.), 2 July 1915, IGC Letters, War Office 107/43, PRO.

17. A.M. Laing, 1/Essex, to Aspinall, 26 October 1930; Brig. Gen. J. Monash to Aspinall, 22 September 1931, Lt-Gen. Sir W. Marshall to Aspinall, 6 January 1929; Cabinet 45/243, PRO. Brig. Gen. Frith, Evidence at Dardanelles Commission, p. 49, Cabinet 19/29, PRO. Lt-Col. Geddes, 1st Munster Fusiliers, 86 Brigade, 29 Division, to Aspinall, 8 November

18. In this context, one aspect of the Allied campaign that deserves another look is the basic strategy on land: there seems to have been an underlying

assumption that capturing the high ground was essential. Naturally, high ground was important for observation and control, yet in retrospect, another strategy might have been an outflanking left hook at Suvla, or a right hook from the Anzac area to cut the peninsula across the Maidos plain.

19. Hasan Ethem to his mother, 17 April 1915, 'Last letter of a Turkish martyr killed in the Gallipolian War', translated by Dr Erkan Turkmen, *The Gallipolian*, Winter 1994, p. 6. Mühlmann, *Letter*.

20. Aspinall Oglander, *Military Operations: Gallipoli*, vol. 2, p. 484. Lt-Col. C.C.R. Murphy, *Soldiers of the Prophet*, London, 1921, p. 151, citing the careful investigation of Djevad Pasa, the Turkish commander of the Straits.

21. Reportedly, Atatürk used these words as part of a speech in the Meclis to assuage the families of Anzac soldiers who had died on Gallipoli, who felt that the Turkish government was not paying enough attention to their grave sites.

BIBLIOGRAPHY

I. Unpublished Sources

Auckland War Memorial Museum Library, Auckland, New Zealand
Anonymous Diary
Maj. Curry Papers
Lt-Col. Fenwick Papers
Tpr Frank Hobson Papers
Tpr Law Papers
Nurse LeGallais Papers
Tpr Clutha McKenzie Papers
Pte F.E. McKenzie Papers
R.J. Speight Papers

Australian War Memorial, Canberra, Australia
C.E.W. Bean Papers
Lt-Gen. Sir William Birdwood Papers
Military Records: 1 Australian Division, 2 Australian Division, Anzac Division

British Library, London
Maj.-Gen. Aylmer Hunter-Weston Papers
Commodore Roger Keyes Papers

Bundesarchchiv-Militärarchiv (Freiburg), Germany
Capt. Carl Mühlmann Letter
Petter Dokumentation

Churchill Archives Centre, Churchill College, Cambridge
Maj.-Gen. Bonham-Carter Papers
Sir Winston Churchill Chartwell Papers
Lord Fisher correspondence
Dardanelles correspondence

Vice Admiral De Robeck Papers
Lt-Col. Hankey Papers

County Record Office, Newport, Isle of Wight
Brigadier-General Cecil Aspinall-Oglander Papers

French Army Archives, Vincennes
Gallipoli Records: 3rd Bureau Operations Papers; G.Q.G. Papers

General Staff Archives, Ankara, Turkey
Fifth Army Papers

Imperial War Museum, London
Atatürk Papers (Col. Mustafa Kemal 'Memoirs')
Sir Gerard Clauson Papers
Maj.-Gen. G.P. Dawnay Papers
Rear Admiral I.W. Gibson Papers
Admiral J.H. Godfrey Papers
Capt. H.C. Lockyer Papers
Col. Mahmut Papers
Dr. Orlo C. Williams Papers

Kippenberger Army Museum, Waiouru, New Zealand
Lt Colvin Algie Papers
Anonymous Hauraki Battalion Papers
Brigadier-General W.G. Braithwaite Papers
Sergeant R. Chadwick Papers
Percy George Doherty Papers
Lt Francis Levenson-Gower West Papers
Lt-Col. Malone Papers
Lt Masterman Papers
Corporal McMillan Papers
Sergeant A.E.M. Rhind Papers
Col. A.C. Temperley Papers

Liddell Hart Centre for Military Archives, King's College, London★
Gen. Sir Ian Hamilton Papers

★The references to the Hamilton collection have changed since the research was done for this book. Please consult the concordance available at the Liddell Hart Centre for Military Archives for the new references.

Bibliography

Mitchell Library, Sydney
Col. Rosenthal Diary (Papers)

National Archives, Wellington, New Zealand
Maj.-Gen. Alex Godley Papers
Military Records: New Zealand Brigades

National Army Museum, London
Capt. Drury Papers
Lt Elliott Papers
Capt. C.A. Milward Papers
Lt R.A. Savory Papers

National Library of Scotland, Edinburgh
Aylmer Haldane Papers

Privately Held Manuscripts
Lt Robert G. Blackie, 'One of the Black Squad, 1914–1918',
    unpublished manuscript in possession of Mr Peter Blackie.

Public Record Office, Kew Gardens, London
Admiralty Files
Cabinet Office Files
War Office Files

Turnbull Library, Wellington, New Zealand
Lt Colvin Algie Papers
Lt-Col. Bishop Papers
Harry Ernest Browne Papers
Robert Hughes Papers
Pte Humphreys Papers
Leonard Leary Papers
Lt-Col. John Aldred Luxford Papers
Clyde McGilp Papers
Capt. Tahu Rhodes Papers
Benoni Sandilands Papers
George Albert Tuck Papers
Francis Morphet Twistleton Papers
Frederick Varnham Papers

University of Calgary, Calgary, Alberta, Canada
Corporal William Guy Papers

II. Government Publications

The Final Report of the Dardanelles Commission. (Part II – Conduct of
    Operations &c.), Command Paper 371. (London: HMSO, 1919)

III. Primary Sources

Bean, C.E.W., *Gallipoli Mission* (1948, Canberra: ABC edition, 1990).
Callwell, C.E., (ed.), *Campaigns and their lessons.* (London: Constable & Co,
    1911–1931).
Callwell, C.E., *The Dardanelles.* (London: Constable & Co, 1919).
Cooper, Bryan, *The Tenth (Irish) Division in Gallipoli.* (London: 1918). Reprinted
    by Irish Academic Press, Dublin, 1993.
Gillam, Maj. John, *Gallipoli Diary.* (London: 1918). Republished by Strong Oak
    Press, Stevenage [England], 1989.
Guépratte, Vice Admiral P-E., *L'Expédition Des Dardanelles, 1914–1915.* (Paris:
    1935).
Halpern, Paul, (ed.), *The Keyes Papers: 1914–1918,* Volume 1. (London, 1979).
Hamilton, Sir Ian, *Compulsory Service.* (London: 1911)
Hamilton, Sir Ian, *Gallipoli Diary,* 2 Volumes. (London: Edward Arnold, 1920).
Hamilton, Sir Ian, *Listening for the Drums.* (London: 1944).
Kannengiesser, Col. Hans, *The Campaign in Gallipoli.* (translated by Maj. C.J.P.
    Ball), (London, 1927).
Keyes, Admiral of the Fleet Sir Roger, *The Naval Memoirs of Admiral of the Fleet
    Sir Roger Keyes: Volume 1, the Narrow Seas to the Dardanelles, 1910–1915.*
    (London, 1934).
Lushington, R.F., *A Prisoner With The Turks 1915–1918.* (London: Simpkin,
    Marshall, Hamilton, Kent & Co. Ltd, 1923).
Carl Mühlmann, *Der Kampf um die Dardanellen,* Volume 16. (Oldenburg: 1927).
Carl Mühlmann, *Das deutsch-turkische Waffenbündnis im Weltkrieg.* (Leipzig:
    1940).
Murphy, Lt-Col. C.C.R., *Soldiers of the Prophet.* (London: John Hogg,
    1921).
Murphy, Lt-Col. C.C.R., *A Mixed Bag.* (London: William Clowes, 1921).
Murray, Joseph, *Gallipoli 1915* (London: 1965). NEL paperback edition, 1977
Patterson, Lt-Col. J.H., *With the Zionists in Gallipoli.* (London: Hutchinson,
    1916).

Samson, C.R., *Fights and Flights.* (London: Ernest Ben, 1930).

Still, John, *A Prisoner in Turkey*. (London and New York: The Bodley Head, 1920).

Von Sanders, Liman, *Five Years in Turkey.* (1920, Annapolis, Maryland: United States Naval Institute, 1927)

Wemyss, Admiral of the Fleet Lord Wester, *The Navy in the Dardanelles Campaign* (London: Hodder & Stoughton, 1924).

IV. Official Histories

Aspinall-Oglander, Brigadier-General C.F., *History of the Great War, based on Official Documents: Military Operations: Gallipoli: Inception of the Campaign to May 1915*, Volume 1. (London: William Heinemann, 1929)

Aspinall-Oglander, Brigadier-General C.F., *History of the Great War, based on Official Documents: Military Operations: Gallipoli: May 1915 to the evacuation,* Volume 2. (London: William Heinemann, 1932)

Bean, C.E.W., *Official History of Australia in the War of 1914–1918: The Story of Anzac from the outbreak of war to end of the first phase of the Gallipoli campaign, May 4, 1915*, Volume 1. (St. Lucia: University of Queensland Press, 1981; a reprint of the edition first printed in 1921)

Bean, C.E.W., *Official History of Australia in the War of 1914–1918: The Story of Anzac from May 4, 1915 to the evacuation of the Gallipoli Peninsula*, Volume 2. (St. Lucia: University of Queensland Press, 1981; a reprint of the edition first printed in 1924)

Corbett, Sir Julian, *History of The Great War: Naval Operations*, Volume 2. (London: Longmans, 1921).

Macpherson, Sir William *et al* (eds), *History of the Great War: Medical Services,* Volume 3. (London: HMSO, 1923).

Ministère de la Guerre, *Les Armées Françaises dans la Grande Guerre*, Tome 8, Vol. 1, Annex 1. (Paris, 1924).

TC Genelkurmay Baskanligi [Turkish General Staff], *Birinci Dunya Harbinde Turk Harbi, V Nci Cilt, Canakkale Cephesi Harekati, 1 Nci Kitap, Haziran 1914 – 25 Nisan 1915*. (Ankara: 2nd edition, 1993). [The Turkish War in the First World War, Gallipoli Front Operations, Volume 1, June 1914 – 25 April 1915.]

TC Genelkurmay Baskanligi [Turkish General Staff], *Birinci Dunya Harbinde Turk Harbi, V Nci Cilt, Canakkale Cephesi Harekati, 2 Nci Kitap, 25 Nisan 1915 – Mayis 1915*. (Ankara: 1978). [The Turkish War in the First World War, Gallipoli Front Operations, Volume 2, 25 April – May 1915.]

TC Genelkurmay Baskanligi [Turkish General Staff], *Birinci Dunya Harbi: V Nci Cilt, Canakkale Cephesi Harekati, 3 Nci Kitap, Haziran 1915 – Ocak 1916.*

(Ankara, 1980). [The Turkish War in the First World War, Gallipoli Front Operations, Volume 3, June 1915 – January 1916.]

V. Secondary Sources

Bourke, Joanna, *Dismembering the Male: Men's Bodies, Britain and the Great War.* (Chicago: University of Chicago Press, 1996).

Bush, Eric W., *Gallipoli.* (London: Allen & Unwin, 1975).

Derham, Rosemary, *The Silent Ruse: Escape from Gallipoli.* (Australia: Cliffe Books, 1998).

Erickson, Edward, *Ordered to Die: A History of the Ottoman Army in First World War.* (Westport, Connecticut: Greenwood Press, 2000).

Farrar-Hockley, A. (ed.), *Sir Ian Hamilton, The Commander.* (London, 1957)

Ferguson, Niall, *The Pity of War.* (New York, 1999).

Fewster, Kevin, Vehici Basarin and Hatice Basarin, *A Turkish View of Gallipoli/Canakkale.* (Richmond, Victoria: Hodja Press: 1985).

French, David, *British Strategy and War Aims, 1914–1916.* (London: Allen and Unwin, 1986).

French, David, *The Strategy of the Lloyd George Coalition, 1916–1918.* (Oxford: Clarendon Press, 1995).

Gilbert, Martin, *Winston Churchill: The challenge of war 1914–1916*, Volume 3. (Heinemann: London, 1971).

Hankey, Lord, *The Supreme Command 1914–1918.* (London: Allen & Unwin, 1961).

Haythornthwaite, Philip, *Gallipoli 1915* (London: 1991)

Hickey, Michael, *Gallipoli.* (London: John Murray, 1995).

Holmes, Richard, *On the Firing Line.* (1985 – Harmondsworth: Penguin edition, 1987)

James, Robert Rhodes, *Gallipoli* (London 1965; Pimlico edition with new preface, London, 1999)

Kerr, Greg, *Lost Anzacs: The Story of Two Brothers.* (Melbourne, 1997 – paperback edition, 1998).

Kerr, Greg (ed.), *Private Wars: Personal Records of the Anzacs in the Great War.* (Melbourne: Oxford University Press: 2000).

Laffin, John, *Damn the Dardanelles!* (Sydney: Doubleday, 1980).

Lee, John, *A Soldier's Life: General Sir Ian Hamilton, 1835–1947.* (London: MacMillan, 2000).

Liddle, Peter, *Men of Gallipoli: the Dardanelles and Gallipoli Experience August 1914 to January 1916.* (London: Allen Lane, 1976).

Liddle, Peter and Hugh Cecil (eds), *Facing Armageddon. The First World War experienced.* (London: Leo Cooper/Pen and Sword, 1996).

Marder, A. J., *From the Dreadnought to Scapa Flow. The Royal Navy in the Fisher Era, 1904–1919: The War Years: To the Eve of Jutland*, Volume 2. (London: Oxford University Press, 1965).

McCrery, Nigel, *The Vanished Battalion*. (London: Simon and Schuster, 1992).

Moorehead, Alan, *Gallipoli*. (New York: Ballantine Books edition, 1958).

Pakenham, Thomas, *The Boer War* (London, 1979).

Pemberton, W. Baring, *Battles of the Boer War*. (London: Pan edition, 1969).

Penn, Geoffrey, *Fisher, Churchill and the Dardanelles*. (Barnsley, South Yorkshire: Leo Cooper 1999).

Prior, Robin and Trevor Wilson, *Command on the Western Front: the Military Career of Sir Henry Rawlinson, 1914–1918*. (Oxford and Cambridge: Blackwell, 1992).

Pugsley, Christopher, *Gallipoli: the New Zealand Story*. (Auckland: Hodder, 1984).

Smith, Paul (ed.), *Government and the Armed Forces in Britain, 1856–1990*. (London and Rio Grande: The Hambledon Press, 1996.

Steel, Nigel and Peter Hart, *Defeat at Gallipoli*. (London: Macmillan, 1994).

Sumida, Jon, *In Defence of Naval Supremacy: Finance, Technology and British Naval Policy, 1889–1914*. (London: Routledge, 1989).

Thomson, Alistair, *Anzac Memories: Living with the Legend*. (Melbourne: Oxford University Press Australia, 1994).

Tuncoku, A. Mete, *Anzaklarin Kaleminden Mehmetcik, Canakkale 1915*. (Ankara: 1997)

Travers, Tim, *The Killing Ground: The British Army, the Western Front and the Emergence of Modern Warfare, 1900–1918*. (London: Allen and Unwin, 1987)

Trumpener, Ulrich, *Germany and the Ottoman Empire, 1914–1918*. (Princeton: Princeton University Press, 1968).

Tyquin, Michael, *Gallipoli: the Medical War: The Australian Army Medical Services in the Dardanelles Campaign of 1915*. (Kensington: New South Wales University Press, 1993).

Winter, Denis, *Making the Legend: The War Writings of C. E. W. Bean*. (St. Lucia: University of Queensland Press, 1992)

Winter, Denis, *25 April 1915: The Inevitable Tragedy*. (St. Lucia: University of Queensland Press, 1994)

VI. Articles

Braithwaite, Brigadier-General Walter, 'For the conduct of an army character weighs more than knowledge or science', *Journal of the United Service Institution of India*, vol. 42, 1913.

Cunliffe-Owen, F., 'Artillery at ANZAC in the Gallipoli Campaign', *Royal Artillery Journal*, vol. XLVI, no. 12 (1919–1920).

Erickson, Lt-Col. Edward, 'Strength Against Weakness: Ottoman military effec-
    tiveness at Gallipoli, 1915,' forthcoming article.

Fallon, J.J., 'HMS *Euryalus* at W Beach,' *The Gallipolian*, No. 77, Spring 1995.

Ferguson, Maj. (later Col.) A.C., CO 21 Kohat Mountain battery, 'Gallipoli
    1915', *The Gallipolian*, no. 85, Winter 1997.

Goate, John J., 5th Royal Scots, 'Diary,' *The Gallipolian*, no. 91, Winter 1999

Hasan Ethem to his mother, 17 April 1915, 'Last letter of a Turkish martyr killed
    in the Gallipolian War', translated by Dr. Erkan Turkmen, *The Gallipolian*,
    Winter 1994.

'Iskender Mericli, Memories of a Turkish soldier', *The Gallipolian*, #75, Autumn
    1994.

Okse, Col. Necati, 'Atatürk in the Dardanelles Campaign,' *Revue Internationale
    d'Histoire Militaire*, No. 50, 1981.

Savory, Lt-Gen. Sir Reginald, 14th Sikhs, 'Some Gallipoli Memories,' *The
    Gallipolian*, no. 15, Autumn 1974, and no. 18, Autumn 1975.

Stevens, D.M., 'Naval Support at Gallipoli,' *Australian Defence Force Journal*,
    Volume 117, March/April 1996.

Travers, Tim, 'Command and Leadership Styles in the British Army: The 1915
    Gallipoli Model,' *Journal of Contemporary History*, Volume 29, No. 3, July 1994.

Travers, Tim, 'The Other Side of the Hill,' *MHQ: The Quarterly Journal of Military
    History*, Volume 12, No. 3, Spring 2000.

Travers, Tim, 'The Ottoman Crisis of May 1915 at Gallipoli,' *War in History*,
    Volume 8, No. 1, January 2001.

Trumpener, Ulrich, 'Suez, Baku, Gallipoli: The Military Dimensions of the
    German-Ottoman Coalition, 1914–18,' in Keith Neilson and Roy A. Prete
    (eds) *Coalition Warfare: An Uneasy Accord*. (Waterloo: Wilfrid Laurier
    University Press, 1983).

Trumpener, Ulrich, 'Liman von Sanders and the German-Ottoman Alliance',
    Journal of Contemporary History, Volume 1, No. 4, October 1996

APPENDIX I

Select Chronology

1 November 1914	Britain and France declare war on Ottoman empire (Turkey).
2 November 1914	Russia declares war on Ottoman empire (Turkey).
2 January 1915	Duke Nicholas of Russia appeals to Britain for assistance.
3 January 1915	Winston Churchill requests advice from Vice Admiral Carden regarding a naval attack at the Dardanelles.
5 January 1915	Vice Admiral Carden cautiously replies to Churchill.
26 January 1915	Liman von Sanders considers possible Allied landing sites on Gallipoli.
19 February 1915	Vice Admiral Carden's naval attack on the Dardanelles commences.
12 March 1915	Sir Ian Hamilton appointed to command Mediterranean Expeditionary Force.
18 March 1915	Vice Admiral de Robeck launches final Allied naval attack at the Dardanelles.
24 March 1915	Liman von Sanders appointed to command Turkish Fifth Army on Gallipoli.
17 April 1915	Destruction of British submarine E 15, and capture of Lt Palmer.
25 April 1915	Allied landings at Helles, Anzac and Kum Kale.
28 April 1915	First Battle of Krithia
1–4 May 1915	Turkish attacks at Helles and Turkish crisis emerges.
6–8 May 1915	Second Battle of Krithia.
19–20 May 1915	Mass Turkish attacks at Anzac lead to heavy Turkish losses.
24 May 1915	Truce at Anzac to bury dead.
25 May 1915	Sinking of battleship *Triumph* by German submarine.
4 June 1915	Third Battle of Krithia.
12–13 July 1915	Allied attacks at Helles.
6–7 August 1915	Diversionary attacks at Helles.

6 August 1915	Diversionary Australian attack at Lone Pine.
6–7 August 1915	Main Anzac offensive toward Sari Bair range com mences.
6–7 August 1915	Two Allied divisions land at Suvla.
7 August 1915	Australian attack at the Nek takes place.
7 August 1915	Liman von Sanders send two divisions south from Bulair area they arrive in Suvla area over night of 7–8 August 1915.
8 August 1915	New Zealand forces capture Chunuk Bair.
8 August 1915	Mustafa Kemal appointed overall commander of northern area.
9 August 1915	Allied units, including Gurkhas, briefly capture part of Hill Q.
9 August 1915	British forces at Suvla fail to capture high ground due to earlier arrival of Turkish forces.
10 August 1915	Mustafa Kemal and mixed Turkish forces recapture Chunuk Bair.
12 August 1915	Attack of 1/5 Norfolk Battalion at Suvla.
12 August 1915	Dawnay at GHQ first puts forward idea of partial evacuation.
15 August 1915	British attack at Kiretch Tepe in Suvla area.
21 August 1915	Large scale Allied attack at Suvla.
29 August 1915	Partial Allied capture of Hill 60 in south Suvla area.
2 September 1915	Dawnay departs for London.
6 September 1915	Bulgarians agree to invade Serbia in conjunction with Germans and Austrians.
15 October 1915	Hamilton and Braithwaite replaced by Kitchener.
28 October 1915	Monro arrives at Gallipoli, and three days later recommends evacuation.
29 November 1915	Liman von Sanders aware of probable Allied withdrawal.
7 December 1915	London decides on Anzac/Suvla evacution
23 December 1915	London decides on Helles evacuation also.
19–20 December 1915	Evacuation of Anzac and Suvla.
8–9 January 1916	Evacuation of Helles.

APPENDIX II

Allied Order of Battle: First Landings, April 1915

Commander-in-Chief	Gen. Sir Ian Hamilton, GCB
Chief of the General Staff	Maj.-Gen. W.P. Braithwaite, CB
Deputy Adjutant-General	Br.-Gen. E.M. Woodward
Deputy Quartermaster-General	Br.-Gen. S.H. Winter.

29TH DIVISION
Maj.-Gen. A.G. Hunter-Weston, CB

86th Brigade:

2/Royal Fusiliers	1/R. Munster Fusiliers
1/Lancashire Fusiliers	1/R. Dublin Fusiliers

87th Brigade:

2/S. Wales Borderers	1/R. Inniskilling Fusiliers
1/K.O.S.B.	1/Border Regt

88th Brigade:

4/Worcestershire Regt	1/Essex Regt
2/Hampshire Regt	1/5th Royal Scots (TF)

XV Bde RHA (B, L & Y Btys)

XVII Bde RFA (13th, 26th & 92nd Btys)

CXLVII Bde RFA (10th, 97th & 368th Btys)

460th (Howitzer) Bty RFA

4th (Highland) Mountain Bde RGA (TF)
    (Argyllshire Bty and Ross & Cromarty Bty)

90th Heavy Bty RGA

14th Siege Bty RGA

1/2nd London, 1/2nd Lowland &
    1/1st W. Riding Field Coys RE (TF)

Divisional Cyclist Coy

ROYAL NAVAL DIVISION
Maj.-Gen. A. Paris, CB

1st (Naval) Brigade:
 Drake Bn   Deal Bn RMLI
 Nelson Bn
2nd (Naval) Brigade:
 Howe Bn   Anson Bn
 Hood Bn
3rd (RM) Brigade:
 Chatham Bn RMLI   Plymouth Bn RMLI
 Portsmouth Bn RMLI
Motor Maxim Squadron (RNAS)
1st & 2nd Field Coys Engineers
Divisional Cyclist Coy

AUSTRALIAN & NEW ZEALAND ARMY CORPS
G.O.C. Lieut.-Gen. Sir W. Birdwood, KCSI

1ST AUSTRALIAN DIVISION
Maj.-Gen. W.T. Bridges, CMG

1st Australian Brigade:
 1st (N.S.W.) Bn   3rd (N.S.W.) Bn
 2nd (N.S.W.) Bn   4th (N.S.W.) Bn
2nd Australian Brigade:
 5th (Victoria) Bn   7th (Victoria) Bn
 6th (Victoria) Bn   8th (Victoria) Bn
3rd Australian Brigade:
 9th (Queensland) Bn   11th (W. Australia) Bn
 10th (S. Australia) Bn   12th (S. & W. Austr. and Tasm.) Bn
I (N.S.W.) FA Bde (1st, 2nd & 3rd Btys)
II (Victoria) FA Bde (4th, 5th & 6th Btys)
III (Queensland) FA Bde. (7th, 8th & 9th Btys)
1st, 2nd & 3rd Field Coys Engineers

Maj.-Gen. Sir A.J. Godley, KCMG

New Zealand Brigade:
    Auckland Bn   Otago Bn
    Canterbury Bn   Wellington Bn
4th Australian Brigade:
    13th (N.S.W.) Bn   15th (Queensland & Tasmania) Bn
    14th (Victoria) Bn   16th (S. & W. Australia) Bn
New Zealand FA Bde (1st, 2nd & 3rd Btys)
New Zealand Field Howitzer Bty
Field Coy New Zealand Engineers

CORPS TROOPS

7th Indian Mountain Artillery Bde
    (21st (Kohat) Battery and 26th (Jacob's) Battery)
Ceylon Planters Rifle Corps

CORPS EXPÉDITIONNAIRE D'ORIENT
Commander Gen. d'Amade

1ST DIVISION
Gen. Masnou

Metropolitan Brigade:
    175th Regiment
    Régt de marche d'Afrique (2 Bns Zouaves, 1 Bn Foreign Legion)
Colonial Brigade:
    4th Colonial Regt (2 Bns Senegalese, 1 Bn Colonial)
    6th Colonial Regt (2 Bns Senegalese, 1 Bn Colonial)
    6 Batteries of artillery (75-mm)
    2 Batteries of artillery (65-mm)

APPENDIX III

Allied Order of Battle: August 1915

Commander-in-Chief	Gen. Sir Ian Hamilton, GCB
Chief of the General Staff	Maj.-Gen. W.P. Braithwaite, CB
Deputy Adjutant-General	Br.-Gen. E.M. Woodward
Deputy Quartermaster-General	Br.-Gen. S.H. Winter.

VIII CORPS
G.O.C. Lieut.-Gen. Sir F.J. Davies, KCB
Br.-Gen., Gen. Staff Br.-Gen. H.E. Street

29TH DIVISION
Maj.-Gen. H. de B. de Lisle, CB

86th Brigade:
    2/Royal Fusiliers   1/R. Munster Fusiliers
    1/Lancashire Fusiliers   1/R. Dublin Fusiliers
87th Brigade:
    2/S. Wales Borderers   1/R. Inniskilling Fusiliers
    1/KOSB   1/Border Regt
88th Brigade:
    4/Worcestershire Regt   1/Essex Regt
    2/Hampshire Regt   1/5th Royal Scots (TF)
XV Bde RHA (B, L & Y Btys)
XVII Bde RFA (13th, 26th & 92nd Btys)
CXLVII Bde RFA (10th, 97th & 368th Btys)
460th (Howitzer) Bty RFA
4th (Highland) Mtn Bde RGA (TF) (Argyll Bty, Ross & Cromarty Bty)
90th Heavy Bty RGA
14th Siege Bty RGA
1/2nd London, 1/2nd Lowland & 1/1st W. Riding Field Coys RE (TF)
Divisional Cyclist Coy

42ND (EAST LANCS.) DIVISION (TF)
Maj.-Gen. W. Douglas, CB

125th Brigade:

    1/5th Lancashire Fusiliers   1/7th Lancashire Fusiliers
    1/6th Lancashire Fusiliers   1/8th Lancashire Fusiliers

126th Brigade:

    1/4th East Lancs. Regt   1/9th East Lancs. Regt
    1/5th East Lancs. Regt   1/10th East Lancs. Regt

127th Brigade:

    1/5th Manchester Regt   1/7th Manchester Regt
    1/6th Manchester Regt   1/8th Manchester Regt

XV Bde RHA (B, L & Y Btys)
1/1st E. Lancs. Bde RFA (4th, 5th & 6th Btys)
1/2nd E. Lancs. Bde RFA (15th, 16th & 17th Btys)
1/3rd E. Lancs. Bde RFA (18th, 19th & 20th Btys)
1/4th E. Lancs. (Howitzer) Bde RFA (1st & 2nd Cumberland Btys)
1/1st E. Lancs., 1/2nd E. Lancs. & 1/2nd W. Lancs. Field Coys RE

52ND (LOWLAND) DIVISION (TF)
Maj.-Gen. G.G.A. Egerton, CB

155th Brigade:

    1/4th R. Scots Fusiliers   1/4th K.O.S.B.
    1/5th R. Scots Fusiliers   1/5th K.O.S.B.

156th Brigade:

    1/4th Royal Scots   1/7th Scottish Rifles
    1/7th Royal Scots   1/8th Scottish Rifles

157th Brigade:

    1/5th Highland L.I.   1/7th Highland L.I.
    1/6th Highland L.I.   1/5th Argyll & Sutherland

Highlanders
1/2nd Lowland Bde RFA
1/4th Lowland (How.) Bde RFA (1/4th & 1/5thCity of Glasgow Btys)
2/1st and 2/2nd Lowland Field Coys RE
Divisional Cyclist Coy

ROYAL NAVAL DIVISION
Maj.-Gen. A. Paris, CB

1st Brigade:
Drake Bn   Hawk Bn RMLI
Nelson Bn   Hood Bn
2nd Brigade:
No. 1 Bn RMLI   Howe Bn
No. 2 Bn RMLI   Anson Bn
3rd (RM) Brigade:
1st, 2nd & 3rd Field Coys Engineers
Divisional Cyclist Coy

IX CORPS

G.O.C. Lieut.-Gen. Hon. Sir F.W. Stopford, KCMG
Br.-Gen., Gen. Staff Br.-Gen. H.L. Reed, VC

10TH (IRISH) DIVISION
Maj.-Gen. Sir B.T. Mahon, KCVO

29th Brigade:
10/Hampshire Regt   5/Connaught Rangers
6/R. Irish Rifles   6/Leinster Regt
30th Brigade:
6/R. Munster Fusiliers   6/R. Dublin Fusiliers
7/R. Munster Fusiliers   7/R. Dublin Fusiliers
31st Brigade:
5/R. Inniskilling Fusiliers   5/R. Irish Fusiliers
6/R. Inniskilling Fusiliers   6/R. Irish Fusiliers
5/R. Irish Regt (Pioneers)
LIV Bde RFA (A, B, C & D Btys)
LV Bde RFA (A, B, C & D Btys)
LVI Bde RFA (A, B, C & D Btys)
LVII (Howitzer) Bde (HQ with A & D Btys only)
65th, 66th and 85th Field Coys RE
Divisional Cyclist Coy

11TH (NORTHERN) DIVISION
Maj.-Gen. F. Hammersley, CB

32nd Brigade:

6/West Yorkshire Regt	8/West Riding Regt
6/Yorkshire Regt	6/Yorks. & Lancs. Regt

33rd Brigade:

6/Lincolnshire Regt	7/S. Staffordshire Regt
6/The Border Regt	9/Sherwood Foresters

34th Brigade:

8/Northumberland Fusiliers	5/Dorsetshire Regt
9/Lancashire Fusiliers	11/Manchester Regt

6/East Yorkshire Regt (Pioneers)
LVIII Bde RFA (A, B, C & D Btys)
LIX Bde RFA (A, B, C & D Btys)
LX Bde RFA (A, B, C & D Btys)
67th, 68th and 86th Field Coys RE
Divisional Cyclist Coy

13TH (WESTERN) DIVISION
Maj.-Gen. F.C. Shaw, CB

38th Brigade:

6/King's Own	6/South Lancs. Regt
6/East Lancs. Regt	6/Loyal North Lancs. Regt

39th Brigade:

9/R. Warwickshire Regt	9/Worcestershire Regt
7/Gloucestershire Regt	7/N. Staffordshire Regt

40th Brigade:

4/S. Wales Borderers	8/Cheshire Regt
8/R. Welch Fusiliers	5/Wiltshire Regt

8/Welch Regt (Pioneers)
LXVI Bde RFA (A, B, C & D Btys)
LXVII Bde RFA (A, B, C & D Btys)
LXVIII Bde RFA (A, B, C & D Btys)
LXIX (Howitzer) Bde (A, B, C & D Btys)
71st, 72nd and 88th Field Coys RE
Divisional Cyclist Coy

CORPS TROOPS

4th (Highland) Mtn Artillery Bde (TF)
    (Argyllshire Bty and Ross & Cromarty Bty)

ATTACHED IX CORPS

53RD (WELSH) DIVISION
Maj.-Gen. Hon. J.E. Lindley

158th Brigade:
    1/5th R. Welch Fusiliers   1/7th R. Welch Fusiliers
    1/6th R. Welch Fusiliers   1/1st Herefordshire Regt
159th Brigade:
    1/4th Cheshire Regt   1/4th Welch Regt
    1/7th Cheshire Regt   1/5th Welch Regt
160th Brigade:
    2/4th Queen's   2/4th R.W. Kent Regt
      (R.W. Surrey Regt)   2/10th Middlesex Regt
    1/4th R. Sussex Regt
8/Welch Regt (Pioneers)
1/1st Welsh & 2/1st Cheshire Field Coys RE
Divisional Cyclist Coy

54TH (EAST ANGLIAN) DIVISION
Maj.-Gen. F.S. Inglefield, CB

161st Brigade:
    1/4th Essex Regt   1/6th Essex Regt
    1/5th Essex Regt   1/7th Essex Regt
162nd Brigade:
    1/5th Bedfordshire Regt   1/10th London Regt
    1/4th Northants. Regt   1/11th London Regt
163rd Brigade:
    1/4th Norfolk Regt   1/5th Suffolk Regt
    1/5th Norfolk Regt   1/8th Hampshire Regt
1/2nd Welsh & 2/1st East Anglian Field Coys RE
Divisional Cyclist Coy

2ND MOUNTED DIVISION
Maj.-Gen. W.E. Peyton, CB

1st (S. Midland) Brigade:
   1/1st Warwickshire Yeo.   1/1st Worcestershire Yeo.
   1/1st R. Glos. Hussars
2nd (S. Midland) Brigade:
   1/1st R. Bucks. Hussars   1/1st Berkshire Yeo.
   1/1st Dorset Yeo.
3rd (Notts. & Derby) Brigade:
   1/1st Sherwood Rangers   1/1st Derbyshire Yeo.
   1/1st S. Notts. Hussars
4th (London) Brigade:
   1/1st County of London Yeo.
   1/3rd County of London Yeo.
   1/1st City of London Yeo.
5th Brigade:
   1/1st Hertfordshire Yeo.
   1/2nd County of London Yeo. (Westminster Dragoons)

AUSTRALIAN & NEW ZEALAND ARMY CORPS
G.O.C. Lieut.-Gen. Sir W. Birdwood, KCSI
Br.-Gen., Gen. Staff Br.-Gen. A. Skeen

1ST AUSTRALIAN DIVISION
Maj.-Gen. H.B. Walker, DSO

1st Australian Brigade:
   1st (N.S.W.) Bn   3rd (N.S.W.) Bn
   2nd (N.S.W.) Bn   4th (N.S.W.) Bn
2nd Australian Brigade:
   5th (Victoria) Bn   7th (Victoria) Bn
   6th (Victoria) Bn   8th (Victoria) Bn
3rd Australian Brigade:
   9th (Queensland) Bn   11th (W. Australia) Bn
   10th (S. Australia) Bn   12th (S. & W. Austr. and Tasm.) Bn

I (N.S.W.) FA Bde (1st, 2nd & 3rd Btys)
II (Victoria) FA Bde (4th, 5th & 6th Btys)
III FA Bde: 7th (Queensland), 8th (W. Austr.) & 9th (Tasm.) Btys
1st, 2nd & 3rd Field Coys Australian Engineers
4th (Victoria) Light Horse Regt

NEW ZEALAND & AUSTRALIAN DIVISION
Maj.-Gen. Sir A.J. Godley, KCMG

New Zealand Brigade:

Auckland Bn	Otago Bn
Canterbury Bn	Wellington Bn

4th Australian Brigade:

13th (N.S.W.)Bn	15th (Queens. and Tas.) Bn
14th (Victoria) Bn	16th (S. & W. Australia) Bn

New Zealand Mounted Rifles Brigade:

Auckland Mounted Rifles	Wellington Mounted Rifles
Canterbury Mounted Rifles	

1st Australian Light Horse Brigade:

1st (N.S.W.) Regt	3rd (S. Austr. & Tas.) Regt
2nd (Queensland) Regt	

Maori Detachment
I New Zealand FA Bde (1st & 3rd Btys & 6th How. Bty)
II New Zealand FA Bde (2nd & 5th Btys & 4th How. Bty)
1st & 2nd Field Coys New Zealand Engineers
New Zealand Field Troop Engineers
Otago Mounted Rifles

2ND AUSTRALIAN DIVISION
Maj.-Gen. J.G. Legge

5th Australian Brigade:
    17th (N.S.W.) Bn   19th (N.S.W.) Bn
    18th (N.S.W.) Bn   20th (N.S.W.) Bn
6th Australian Brigade:
    21st (Victoria)Bn   23rd (Victoria) Bn
    22nd (Victoria) Bn   24th (Victoria) Bn
7th Australian Brigade:
    25th (Queensland) Bn
    27th (S. Australia) Bn
    26th (Queens. & Tas.) Bn
    28th (W. Australia) Bn
4th & 5th Field Coys Australian Engineers
13th (Victoria) Light Horse Regt

CORPS TROOPS

2nd Australian Light Horse Brigade:
    5th (Queensland) Regt   7th (N.S.W.) Regt
    6th (N.S.W.) Regt
3rd Australian Light Horse Brigade:
    8th (Victoria) Regt   10th (W. Aust.) Regt
    9th (Vict. & S. Austr.) Regt
7th Indian Mountain Artillery Bde
    (21st (Kohat) Battery and 26th (Jacob's) Battery)

ATTACHED NEW ZEALAND & AUSTRALIAN DIVISION
Maj.-Gen. H.V. Cox

29th Indian Infantry Brigade:
    14th Sikhs   1/6th Gurkha Rifles
    1/5th Gurkha Rifles   2/10th Gurkha Rifles

CORPS EXPÉDITIONNAIRE D'ORIENT
Commander Gen. Bailloud

1ST DIVISION
Gen. Brulard

1st Metropolitan Brigade:
175th Regiment
1st Régt de marche d'Afrique (2 Bns Zouaves, 1 Bn For. Legion)
2nd Colonial Brigade:
4th Colonial Regt
6th Colonial Regt
6 Batteries of artillery (75-mm)
2 Batteries of artillery (65-mm)

2ND DIVISION
Gen. Brulard

3rd Metropolitan Brigade:
176th Regiment
2nd Régt de marche d'Afrique (3 Bns Zouaves)
4th Colonial Brigade:
7th Colonial Regt
8th Colonial Regt
9 Batteries of artillery (75-mm)

CORPS ARTILLERY

1 Heavy Battery, 120mm
3 Heavy Batteries, 155mm
2 Siege Guns, 240mm
Battery of naval guns

APPENDIX IV

Maps

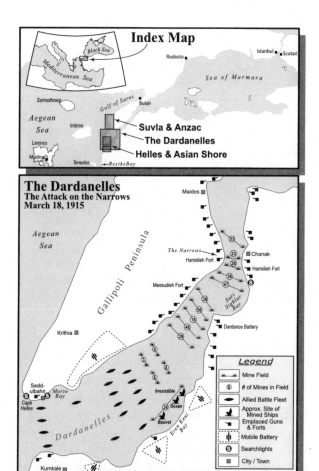

Index Map

Black Sea

Istanbul · Scutari

Rodosto ·

Mediterranean Sea

Sea of Marmara

Sarmothrace

Gulf of Saros

Bulair ·

Aegean Sea

Imbros

Suvla & Anzac

Lemnos

The Dardanelles

Mudros

Tenedos

← BesikeBay

Helles & Asian Shore

The Dardanelles
The Attack on the Narrows
March 18, 1915

Maidos ▣

Aegean Sea

Gallipoli Peninsula

(53)

The Narrows

(23)

Chanak ▣

Hamidieh Fort

(28)

Hamidieh Fort

(39)

S

(47)

Messudieh Fort

(38)

Sari Sighlar Bay

(50)

(18)

(48)

Krithia ▣

(29)

Dardanos Battery

(4)

(3)

(4)

Sedd-
ulbahir

S

Morto
Bay

S

Irresistible

Cape
Helles

(26) Ocean

Bouvet

Eren Keui Bay

Dardanelles

Kumkale ▣

Legend

⋆⋯⋆	Mine Field
(6)	# of Mines in Field
⬮	Allied Battle Fleet
⚓	Approx. Site of Mined Ships
⌐	Emplaced Guns & Forts
⫯	Mobile Battery
S	Searchlights
▣	City / Town

387

Gallipoli 1915

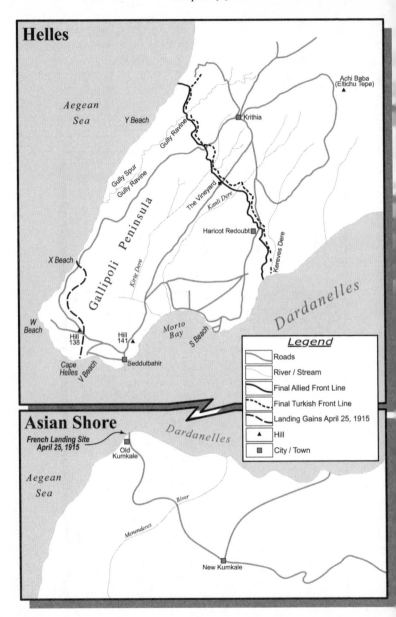

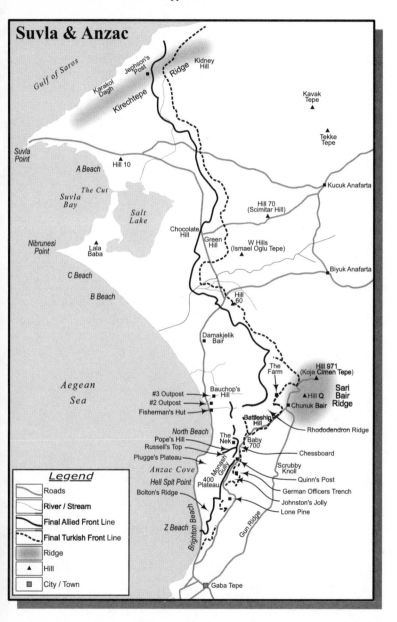

Suvla & Anzac

Gulf of Saros

Karakol Dagh

Jephson's Post

Kirechtepe Ridge

Kidney Hill

Kavak Tepe ▲

Tekke Tepe ▲

Suvla Point

A Beach

Hill 10 ■

Suvla Bay

The Cut

Salt Lake

Kucuk Anafarta ■

Hill 70 (Scimitar Hill) ■

Nibrunesi Point

Lala Baba ▲

Chocolate Hill

Green Hill

W Hills (Ismael Oglu Tepe) ▲

Biyuk Anafarta ■

C Beach

B Beach

Hill 60 ▲

Damakjelik Bair ■

Aegean Sea

The Farm

Hill 971 (Koja Cimen Tepe) ▲

Sari Bair Ridge

Bauchop's Hill ■

#3 Outpost →

#2 Outpost →

Fisherman's Hut →

▲ Hill Q

Chunuk Bair ■

Battleship Hill ■

Rhododendron Ridge

North Beach

Pope's Hill ■

Russell's Top →

Plugge's Plateau →

The Nek ■

Baby 700 ■

Chessboard

Anzac Cove

Hell Spit Point

Monash Gully

Scrubby Knoll ■

Quinn's Post

400 Plateau

German Officers Trench

Bolton's Ridge

Johnston's Jolly

Lone Pine

Z Beach

Brighton Beach

Gun Ridge

Legend

〰	Roads
∿	**River / Stream**
▬	**Final Allied Front Line**
▬ ▬	**Final Turkish Front Line**
▨	Ridge
▲	Hill
■	City / Town

■ Gaba Tepe

ILLUSTRATIONS

26. Turkish heavy machine-gunners in action.
27. Maj.-Gen. H.B. Walker, Gen. Birdwood and Maj. C.M. Wagstaff. LFC
28. Esat Pasa, commander of Turkish III Corps, surrounded by his serious-looking staff. GSA
29. Turkish troops in a well-sandbagged trench at Anzac. GSA
30. A view of Suvla Bay in the far distance and the Salt lake inland on the right.
31. Suvla Point, at the end of Suvla bay.
32. A Turkish ox train.
33. Capt. Lehmann commanding a Turkish artillery unit.
34. Corporal Musticep, who destroyed a French submarine with his artillery piece. GSA
35. An Australian soldier using a periscope rifle.
36. Men bathing off Cape Helles. KCL
37. A typical Anzac trench, with Australian soldiers taking the chance to sleep. LFC
38. Inside a narrow and heavily sandbagged Anzac trench. LFC
39. Another view of the beach at Anzac. LFC
40. Mustafa Kemal explains the situation to a group of parliamentary deputies. GSA
41. A group of unidentified Turkish officers. GSA
42. German and Turkish officers. AWM

SOURCES

AWM – courtesy of the Australian War Memorial collection, Canberra;
GSA – courtesy of the General Staff Archives, Ankara;
KCL – courtesy of King's College, London;
LFC – photographs provided by the Lacey family
of Calgary from a private collection.

All other material is from the author's collection

ACKNOWLEDGEMENTS

I am grateful to the following for granting me permission to quote from mate-rial to which they hold copyright, or which are held in their archives: the Auckland War Memorial Museum Library for the Maj. Curry, Lt-Col. Fenwick, Tpr Frank Hobson, Tpr Law, Nurse Le Gallais, Pte F.E. Mckenzie, and R.J. Speight papers, and the copyright holder of the Tpr Clutha McKenzie papers (Mrs Bridges and Mr Peter Bridges); the Australian War Memorial, Canberra, for the C.E.W. Bean, Col. J.J.T Hobbs (Mr John Hum) and Lt-Gen. Sir William Birdwood (Lady Birdwood) papers; Mr Peter Blackie for the Lt Robert Blackie papers; the British Library for the Maj.-Gen. Aylmer Hunter-Weston and Commodore Roger Keyes papers; the Bundesarchchiv-Militararchiv, Freiburg, for the Carl Muhlmann letter; the University of Calgary Rare Books Archive for the Cpl. William Guy papers; the Master, Fellows and Scholars of Churchill College, Cambridge, and the staff of the Churchill Archives Centre, for the Churchill, Vice Admiral de Robeck and Lt-Col. Hankey papers; the Imperial War Museum, and the copyright holders of the Sir Gerard Clauson (Mr Oliver Clauson), Maj.-Gen. G.P. Dawnay, Rear Admiral I.W. Gibson (Col. D.T.W. Gibson MBE), Admiral J.H. Godfrey, Capt. H.C. Lockyer, Dr Orlo Williams papers, and the unkown copyright holders of the Col. Mahmut and Kemal Atatürk papers; the Kippenberger Military Archive and Research Library, Army Museum, Waiouru, New Zealand, for the Lt Colvin Algie, Lt John Masterman, Sgt Rhind, Col. A.C. Temperley, Sgt Roland Chadwick, Percy George Doherty, Lt Francis Levenson-Gower West, Lt-Col. William Malone and Anonymous Hauraki Battalion papers; the Trustees of the Liddell Hart Centre for Military Archives for the Gen. Sir Ian Hamilton papers; the Mitchell Library, State Library of New South Wales, for the diaries of Col., later Sir, Charles Rosenthal; the National Archives of New Zealand for the Maj.-Gen. Alexander Godley papers; the National Army Museum, London, and the copyright holders, for the Gen. Savory, Capt. Drury, Capt. Milward and Lt Elliott papers; Mrs Oglander and the Oglander family for the Aspinall-Oglander papers held in the Isle of Wight County Record Office; the Strong Oak Press for quotes from John Gillam, *Gallipoli Diary*, 1989; the Alexander Turnbull Library for the Lt Colvin Algie, Lt-

Col. Bishop, Harry Ernest Browne, Robert Hughes, Pte Humphreys, Leonard Leary, Lt-Col. John Luxford, Clyde McGilp, Capt. Tahu Rhodes, Benoni Sandilands, George Tuck, Francis Twistleton and Frederick Varnham papers. To anyone else whose copyright I have unwittingly infringed I offer my sincere apologies.

I am also grateful to the archive and copyright holders of the following photographs for the use of their images: Australian War Memorial, Canberra – photo 42; General Staff Archives, Ankara – photos 6, 8, 16, 18, 23, 24, 25, 28, 29, 34, 40, 41; King's College, London University – photos 3, 5, 10, 36; John and Naomi Lacey, Calgary, private collection – photos 17, 19, 20, 27, 37, 38, 39.

INDEX

Bold references refer to pictures in the plate section

Battles & Campaigns

A series of illustrated battlefield accounts covering the classical period through to the end of the twentieth century, drawing on the latest research and integrating the experience of combat with intelligence, logistics and strategy.

Series Editor

Hew Strachan, Chichele Professor of the History of War
at the University of Oxford

Published

Ross Anderson, *The Battle of Tanga 1914*
William Buckingham, *Arnhem 1944*
David M. Glantz, *Before Stalingrad*
Michael K. Jones, *Bosworth 1485*
Martin Kitchen, *The German Offensives of 1918*
M.K. Lawson, *The Battle of Hastings 1066*
Marc Milner, *Battle of the Atlantic*
A.J. Smithers, *The Tangier Campaign*
Tim Travers, *Gallipoli 1915*
Ross Anderson, *The Forgotten Front: The East African Campaign 1914–1918*

Commissioned

Stephen Conway, *The Battle of Bunker Hill 1775*
Brian Farrell, *The Defence & Fall of Singapore 1941–1942*
Martin Kitchen, *El Alamein 1942–1943*
John Andreas Olsen, *Operation Desert Storm*
Michael Penman, *Bannockburn 1314*
Matthew C. Ward, *Quebec 1759*

If you are interested in purchasing other books published by Tempus,
or in case you have difficulty finding any Tempus books in your local bookshop,
you can also place orders directly through our website

www.tempus-publishing.com

or from

BOOKPOST, Freepost, PO Box 29, Douglas, Isle of Man IM99 1BQ
Tel 01624 836000   email bookshop@enterprise.net